THE MANAGEMENT OF INFORMATION SYSTEMS

McGraw-Hill Series in Management Information Systems

Gordon B. Davis

Consulting Editor

Davis and Olson: *Management Information Systems: Conceptual Foundations, Structure, and Development*

Davis and Everest: *Readings in Management Information Systems*

Dickson and Wetherbe: *The Management of Information Systems*

Dickson and Wetherbe: *The Management of Information Systems Casebook*

Everest: *Database Management: Objectives, Organization, and System Function*

Lucas: *The Analysis, Design, and Implementation of Information Systems*

Lucas: *Information Systems Concepts for Management*

Lucas and Gibson: *A Casebook for Management Information Systems*

Weber: *EDP Auditing: Conceptual Foundations and Practice*

THE MANAGEMENT OF INFORMATION SYSTEMS

GARY W. DICKSON

University of Minnesota

JAMES C. WETHERBE

University of Minnesota

McGraw-Hill Book Company

New York   St. Louis   San Francisco   Auckland   Bogota   Hamburg
Johannesburg   London   Madrid   Mexico   Montreal   New Delhi
Panama   Paris   São Paulo   Singapore   Sydney   Tokyo   Toronto

The editors were Eric M. Munson and Christina Mediate;
the production supervisor was Marietta Breitwieser.
R. R. Donnelley & Sons Company was printer and binder.

THE MANAGEMENT OF INFORMATION SYSTEMS

34567890DOCDOC89876

ISBN 0-07-016825-3

Library of Congress Cataloging in Publication Data
Dickson, Gary W.
  The management of information systems.
  (McGraw-Hill series in management information systems)
  Includes index.
  1. Management information systems—Management.
I. Wetherbe, James C. II. Title. III. Series.
T58.6.D45 1984   658.4'0388   84-767
ISBN 0-07-016825-3

CONTENTS

List of Figures   ix
List of Tables   xiii
Preface   xv

PART 1   INTRODUCTION

1   THE MIS EXECUTIVE   3

PART 2   MIS ORGANIZATION

2   THE ORGANIZATIONAL USE OF COMPUTERS   19
3   ORGANIZING AND STAFFING THE MIS   41
    FUNCTION

PART 3   MANAGING MIS PERSONNEL

4   CONTINGENCY MANAGEMENT AND THE MIS   75
    FUNCTION

5 ACHIEVING JOB PRODUCTIVITY AND   86
   SATISFACTION

PART 4 MIS PLANNING AND CONTROL

6 STRATEGIC PLANNING FOR MIS   119
7 MANAGEMENT ASSESSMENT AND   162
   EVALUATION OF MIS

PART 5 KEY TECHNOLOGY TRENDS AND IMPLICATIONS

8   DATABASE MANAGEMENT SYSTEMS   189
9   DECISION SUPPORT SYSTEMS   220
10 DATA COMMUNICATIONS SYSTEMS   237
11 DISTRIBUTED DATA PROCESSING   274
12 ADVANCED OFFICE SYSTEMS   290
13 ROBOTICS AND MIS   303

PART 6 MANAGING MIS DEVELOPMENT

14 SYSTEMS ANALYSIS AND DESIGN: 321
    STRATEGIES AND PROCEDURES
15 SOFTWARE DEVELOPMENT   355
16 IMPLEMENTATION   380

PART 7 MANAGEMENT OF PRODUCTION AND COMPUTER OPERATIONS

17 COMPUTER CAPACITY PLANNING   413
18 HARDWARE AND SOFTWARE ACQUISITION   440
19 COMPUTER OPERATIONS MANAGEMENT   457
    Index   483

LIST OF FIGURES

1-1.	Evolution of an MIS Executive	8
1-2.	Proportion of Time Spent on Different Activities by MIS Executives	8
1-3.	Proportion of Time Spent with Other Organizational Participants by MIS Executives	9
1-4.	Proportion of Time Spent on Different Subject Matter by MIS Executives	9
2-1.	Nolan's Six Stages of Data Processing Growth	29
3-1.	Alternative Locations for the Information Systems Function	48
3-2.	Basic Structure of an Information Systems Organization	55
3-3.	Information Systems Organization Structured for Managerial Flexibility	55
3-4.	Information Systems Organization Structured with Links to User Organization	56
3-5.	Information Systems Organization in Matrix Form	57
3-6.	Information Systems Organization Structured by User Functions	57
3-7.	Proliferation of MIS Positions Due to Increased Specialization	63
3-8.	Attributes and Weights for the Position of Manager of Programming for Financial Institutions	69
3-9.	Scoring Grid for Applicants for a Manager of Programming for a Financial Institution	71

4-1. A Conceptual Model of Contingency View of Organization and Management   81

5-1. Hierarchy of Needs   88

5-2. Reinforcement Model of Behavior   90

5-3. Classification of Success Factors   93

6-1. Basic Four-Stage Model of MIS Planning   121

6-2. Description of MIS Planning Stages   124

6-3. Major Activities and Outputs in Four Stages of MIS Planning   126

6-4. Model of Ends/Means Analysis   134

6-5. A PERT Chart and Accompanying Project Table   138

6-6. Illustration of a Gantt Chart   139

6-7. Alternative MIS Planning Methodologies Classified by Stage of MIS Planning of Most Significant Impact   140

6-8. Organizational Information Requirements Analysis Planning Model   145

6-9. Manager by Subsystem Matrix   147

6-10. Subsystem Mapping for Maintenance   148

6-11. Framework for Information Requirements Interview   149

6-12. Interviews Mapped to Information Categories   150

6-13. Information Categories by Organizational Subsystems Matrix   151

6-14. Affect of Properties of Project on Selection of Project Planning Technique   156

6-15. Relationship of Adding Personnel to Time Required for Completion of a Project with Complex Interrelationships   156

7-1. A Framework for MIS Evaluation   169

8-1. Contents of a DDA File   190

8-2. Contents of a Savings Accounting File   191

8-3. Contents of an Installment Loan File   191

8-4. Contents of a Mortgage Loan File   192

8-5. Contents of the Payroll File   192

8-6. The Relationships of Data in a Bank's File   195

8-7. Use of Suffixes to Achieve Centralized Account Numbers at a Bank   195

8-8. A Customer Record from a Consolidated File of a Bank   196

8-9. Linking Data Between a Student File and a Class Schedule File   197

8-10. Using Record Keys to Generate Random Addresses on   201
       Disk Storage

8-11. A Hierarchical Indexed-Sequential Structure   202

8-12. Job Classification Indexes for Accessing Employee Data   203
       Records in a Randomly Organized File

8-13. Simplified View of an Integrated Database Using Batch   204
       and Online Processing

8-14. The Relationship Among Application Programs, File-Access 205
       Software, and Computer Files

8-15. The Role of a DBMS   206

8-16. File Contents for an Order Processing System   210

8-17. Symbols Used to Define File Relationships   211

8-18. Initial File Relationship Assumption for Order Processing 211

8-19. Access Paths for Order Processing System   212

8-20. Normalized Files for Order Processing System   215

10-1. A Typical Data Communications System   243

10-2. Types of Communications Services (Some Examples)   244

10-3. Star   261

10-4. Hierarchy   262

10-5. Ring   262

10-6. Linear   262

10-7. Fully Connected   263

10-8. Network   263

10-9. Protocol Summary   269

11-1. Areas of Expertise for Support of Systems Implementation 282
       Activities for DDP

13-1. Illustration of Turret Robot   305

13-2. Illustration of Horizontal Arm Robot   305

13-3. Illustration of Jointed Arm Robot   306

14-1. Components of the Systems Development Life Cycle   322

14-2. Flowchart Symbols   334

14-3. Flowchart for Order Processing   335

14-4. Problem Solving Square   337

14-5. Data Flow Diagrams   339

14-6. Decision Table for Airline Reservation   340

14-7. An Example of a Decision Tree   340

14-8. Components of and Example of Data Dictionary Entry   341

14-9. Linking Design Specification Using Unique Data Names   343

14-10. Systems Development with Heuristic Development   346

14-11. Systems Development with Prototyping   347

15-1. Basic Control Structures of Structured Programming   357

15-2. Logic Flow with Single Entry/Exit and Multiple Control Structures   358

15-3. Top-Down Approach of Software Development   360

15-4. HIPO Hierarchy Chart   361

15-5. HIPO Input, Process, Output   362

15-6. SADT Diagram   363

15-7. W/O Diagram   364

15-8. SDD Truncation of SADT   366

15-9. SDD Modified W/O Diagram   366

15-10. SDD Data/Function Matrix   367

15-11. Standard Checkpoints for Debugging an Information System   374

16-1. The Lucas Model of Factors Influencing Implementation Success   387

16-2. Process Views of Implementing Organizational Change   399

17-1. Computer Capacity Planning Hierarchy   415

17-2. CPU Activity   431

17-3. Meantime Between Hardware Failures   431

17-4. TSO Terminal Usage   432

17-5. Printer Usage   432

17-6. Batch Test Turnaround Regular First Shift   433

17-7. TSO Response (Sample Only -- Not Real Data)   433

18-1. An RFQ for CRT Terminals   445

18-2. Mandatory and Desirable RFP Specifications   447

18-3. An Outline for an RFP   448

19-1. Examples of Allocation of System Availability Responsibility   461

19-2. Administration Hierarchy   462

19-3. Content of a Guidelines and Policies Manual   463

19-4. Problem Management Flowchart   471

19-5. Example of a Problem Report (Courtesy of Norwest Information Services)   472

19-6. Problem Priority Criteria   473

19-7. Coordination Considerations for Change Management   474

19-8. Procedure for Priority 1 Changes   475

19-9. Example of a Change Request (Courtesy of Norwest Information Services)   477

19-10. Procedure for Priority 2 and 3 Changes   478

LIST OF TABLES

1-1.	MIS Executives Interviewed	11
2-1.	Computer Budgets and Their Trends in U.S. Organizations	23
3-1.	MIS Jobs with Brief Descriptions and Average Salary Levels	65
5-1.	Motivational Factors and Q-Sort Statements	96
5-2.	Reinforcement Schedules	104
7-1.	DP Budget as a Percentage of Revenue by Industry	165
7-2.	Allocation of DP Budgets	166
7-3.	Measures of MIS Performance	175
7-4.	Areas and Factors in an MIS Assessment	178
10-1.	Classes of Data Communications Carriers	243
11-1.	Organizational Interaction for Managing DDP	286
12-1.	Taxonomy of Advanced Office Systems	295
14-1.	Analysis Activities	330
14-2.	Decision Centers Involved in Order Processing	333
14-3.	Traditional Life Cycle and Phases of PRIDE, SDM/70, CARA, Spectrum, and Heuristic Design Activities	350
16-1.	Factors Shown to be Associated with MIS Project Success	395
17-1.	Phases and Activities in CCP	416
17-2.	Tools and Methodologies for CCP	423
17-3.	Advantages and Disadvantages of CCP Tools and Methodologies	424
17-4.	Personnel Responsibilities for CCP	434

PREFACE

The rapid emergence of management information systems (MIS) in organizations during the past two decades has created an intense demand for well-trained, capable MIS managers to plan, organize, direct, and control the powerful technology of computer-based information systems. This demand has resulted in a multitude of young, unprepared MIS technicians being catapulted into MIS management positions. The consequences have been predictable and unfavorable. The turnover rate for MIS managers commonly ranges from 25 to 33 percent per year, which compares most unfavorably with non-MIS manager turnover rates of 10 percent per year. Involuntary termination, normally considered a last resort tactic for most management positions, has become too common for MIS management positions.

Many MIS managers have confided to the authors that they had to get a failure or two under their belts before they learned how to be an MIS manager. This partially explains the gypsy nature of many MIS manager careers. It is not uncommon to see an MIS manager resume with three to five MIS management positions listed within a five year period. Not that each job change represents a termination, but things get uncomfortable in one organization and an opportunity to move comes along and...

MIS management is a tough job. And it is not getting any easier. MIS managers must cope with more diverse and complex technology, and MIS has become more interwoven into the complex fabric of modern organizations. MIS managers must be respectable technically in MIS and be above average managers to measure up. Not too surprisingly, employment demand forecasts by leading business journals state that the MBA with expertise in information systems is guaranteed a ticket to future career success.

Fortunately, more and more university MBA programs are offering specialties in MIS. These programs typically provide courses in MIS, system analysis and design, database, decision support systems, and, occasionally, MIS management. There are excellent texts for each subject except for MIS management. With the most recent curriculum recommendations of the Association for Computing Machinery (ACM) and the Data Processing Management Association (DPMA) strongly recommending that a graduate course in MIS management be provided for MIS majors, the need for an MIS management book is greater than ever. A recent survey of MIS executives conducted by the Society for Information Management (SIM) revealed that MIS management is the single most important curriculum area for MBAs in MIS. Yet there is little codified knowledge on managing MIS. The few universities that offer courses in MIS management are forced to use journal articles as a surrogate to a comprehensive text.

The objective of this book is to provide a systematic and comprehensive treatment of MIS management. The topics presented provide a managerial, organizational, behavioral, and technical treatment of MIS management. The book is designed to provide a practical guide and reference for the practicing MIS executive and to provide a course of study for a capstone course for MIS majors.

During the past ten years the authors have conducted courses in MIS in graduate schools of business at the University of Houston and, primarily, at the University of Minnesota. To conduct these courses, the authors have extensively drawn from the business community for distinguished lectures on MIS management issues and have developed extensive reading materials from professional and scholarly journals.

Based upon this material and the research, consulting, and direct management experience of the authors, this book represents a first attempt at coalescing the available knowledge into book form.

The book is divided into seven major sections as follows:
The MIS Executive
MIS Organization
Managing MIS Personnel
MIS Planning and Control
Key Technology Trends and Implications
Managing MIS Development
Management of Production and Computer Operations

The first section consists of an introductory chapter, "The MIS Executive," that provides a historical perspective on MIS executives and defines the characteristics of the successful MIS executive.

The second section, "MIS Organization," consists of two chapters. The first chapter discusses organizational use of MIS. The second chapter discusses strategies for the internal organization of the MIS function and approaches for staffing the MIS organization.

The third section, "Managing MIS Personnel," consists of two chapters. The first chapter discusses general management theory and how it applies to managing the MIS function. Particular emphasis is placed on contingency management theory. The second chapter discusses the behavioral research findings about MIS personnel and its implication for MIS management and strategies for achieving job productivity and job satisfaction.

The fourth section, "MIS Planning and Control," consists of two chapters. The first chapter analyzes strategic and project planning and the various planning methodologies that have been advocated. The second chapter pertains to management assessment and evaluation of the MIS function.

"Key Technology Trends and Implications," the fifth section, provides a review of the most pressing technology issues facing the MIS manager. This section reviews existing technology that is not yet totally absorbed by organizations and forecast future technology developments. There are chapters on database management systems, decision support systems, data communications, distributed data processing, advanced office systems, and robotics.

The sixth section, "Managing MIS Development," is concerned with managing the systems development cycle. The first of three chapters focuses on systems analysis and design strategies and procedures. Emphasis is placed on evaluating different methodologies and selecting an appropriate approach. The second chapter provides practical guides for managing software development via programming standards and controls. The third chapter is concerned with managing the implementation of systems. Special treatment is given to behavioral resistance to systems and minimizing it.

"Management of Production and Computer Operations," the seventh and last section, is directed towards the production side of MIS. There are chapters on computer capacity planning, hardware and software acquisition, and computer operations management.

As discussed earlier, the book is designed for both the practitioner and the student of MIS management. For classroom use, the authors have developed a case book -- *Management of Information Systems Casebook* -- that is most instructive for applying the concepts presented in the book.

It goes without saying that developing a book of this magnitude requires contributions far beyond those of the authors. We are able to recognize literary contributions in the bibliography by referencing outstanding authors who have contributed to the professional and scholarly journals that were so important to our efforts. It is more difficult to recognize the many outstanding MIS practitioners who have shared their wealth of insight and experience with us. As a small effort of gratitude we would like to recognize the Associate Firms of the MIS

Research Center at the University of Minnesota. These organizations have shared their expertise, provided financial support, and allowed access to their organizations for research. The organizations are listed below:

Burlington Northern, Inc.
B. Dalton Bookseller
Cargill, Inc.
Control Data Corporation
Dayton's
Dayton Hudson Corporation
Donaldson Company, Inc.
Economics Laboratory, Inc.
Federal Reserve Bank of Minneapolis
First Computer Corporation
General Mills, Inc.
Honeywell Inc.
International Multifoods
Investors Diversified Services, Inc.
3M
Medtronic, Inc.
Minneapolis Star & Tribune
Modern Merchandizing
National Car Rental System, Inc.
Northern States Power Company
Northwest Computer Services
The Pillsbury Company
The St. Paul Companies, Inc.
State of Minnesota
Super Valu Stores, Inc.
Target Stores

We also acknowledge David M. Lilly, Dean of the School of Management at the University of Minnesota, for providing a supportive environment for this undertaking. A special acknowledgment goes to Ms. Freshteh Azad for her contribution to the chapter on data communications. We also give special thanks to the MBA students who laboriously read through our books and initial drafts while this book was developed.

As we acknowledge the efforts of all who have contributed, we also assume full responsibility for any inadequacies or discrepancies in the book.

Gary W. Dickson
James C. Wetherbe

PART ONE

INTRODUCTION

THE MIS EXECUTIVE

INTRODUCTION

Management Information Systems (MIS) executives have the greatest management challenges and opportunities in modern organizations. Everything is coming their way. The costs of operating organizations are going up at an alarming rate. Labor, management, physical plants, raw materials, energy, and transportation all cost more. The only exception to these phenomena is computer technology. Computer technology continues to offer performance increases that are often incomprehensible and far exceed implementation in organizations. In an era when productivity and cost control can affect organizations' futures, computer technology and those who know how to manage it hold the key to the future.

With challenge and opportunity there is usually risk. MIS management is no exception. Many a well-intended aspiring MIS executive has encountered the "warm" personal experience of involuntary termination. Turnover rates for MIS executives were as high as 50 percent in 1972 and have run as high as 25 to 35 percent in other years.[1] In interviews of 20 MIS executives conducted in 1973, Nolan discovered 7 had been dismissed, 11 had changed jobs in the past 3 years, and only 2 had held the same job for 5 years.[2] Such a turnover rate compares most unfavorably with that of other management positions.

---

[1] R.L. Nolan, "Business Needs a New Breed of EDP Manager," *Harvard Business Review,* vol. 54, no. 2, March–April 1976, pp. 123-133.
[2] R.L. Nolan, "Plight of the EDP Manager," *Harvard Business Review,* vol. 51, no. 3, May–June 1973, pp. 143-152.

Why such a dismal track record for what should be an excellent stepping-stone into greater management responsibility and position? Perhaps it can best be explained by two factors -- *organizational expectations* and *MIS management inexperience*. Both are discussed below.

ORGANIZATIONAL EXPECTATIONS

"Expectations gap" is a term often associated with the advent of MIS in organizations. Expectations gap is the difference between what is expected and what occurs. The term expectations gap was not coined for MIS; the term was, however, popularized by MIS.

Organizations had high, often unrealistic expectations for what computer-based MIS would do for them. Envisioned were systems that would place massive amounts of information at management's immediate disposal. All organizational information would be integrated into one single integrated database. Managers would have terminals on their desks that would allow them to easily monitor organizational operations and forecast future operations by the mere entering of commands into the terminals.

The application of computer technology to business problems hit full stride in the 1960s. This was an era when technology was almost considered an end in itself: if something could be done, it should be done. This was the decade when a person would be put on the moon. Technical feasibility was the primary consideration. Economic feasibility and operational feasibility were secondary. Computer technology was proliferating in organizations.

At the end of the 1960s, organizations were disappointed. They found that technical feasibility was not enough to warrant multimillion-dollar expenditures. They found that often these systems were not worth the expenditure (economic feasibility) or the systems would not work in the context of their organizations (operational feasibility).

Even as organizations began to impose economic feasibility assessments by requiring justification of systems, they found estimates were often several hundred percent off the target. And operational feasibility continues to elude organizations today. To illustrate how something can be technically and economically feasible but not operationally feasible, consider dieting. It is technically feasible and can be cost-justified. However, operationally there are often problems (to the chagrin of millions of people). Similarly, many computer systems encountered resistance caused by behavioral problems in organizations.

The combined effect of technical, economic, and operational problems set MIS back. A survey conducted by McKinsey & Company in 1968 revealed most organizations considered their MIS efforts less than successful.[3]

In short, organizations had been both naive and oversold when it came to MIS. Two articles captured the spirit of the times: "Business Takes a Second Look at Computers" (a special editorial, *Business Week*, June 1971); and "MIS Is a Mirage" by John Dearden (*Harvard Business Review*, January-February 1972). The *Business Week* editorial reviewed the success and failures of many corporations. The results indicated that computer-based information systems in most organizations had fallen substantially below management's original expectations. Most information system prospects failed to deliver what was promised for the cost or in the time frame expected.

For example, Weyerhauser Co., the far-flung forest products complex, had probably made as effective use of computer technology as any other U.S. corporation of that time. However, they had experienced their disappointments. When they began to develop a new online inventory system, they were led to believe they could develop the system in 1 year with 10 people. Instead, the project took 3 years and 50 people. Such experiences were not uncommon.

The all-time low for MIS came in 1972 and occurred with Dearden's "MIS Is a Mirage" article. He basically argued that MIS was a grandiose, unrealistic concept.

The year of "MIS Is a Mirage" was also the year of the worst turnover of MIS executives.

MIS MANAGEMENT INEXPERIENCE

As evidenced by the turnover rate, the history of MIS executives has not been glorious. The phenomenal demand for implementing computer technology into organizations resulted in an accompanying demand for MIS professionals. A demand that could not be met. Even today, the MIS profession ranks as one of the professions with the greatest shortage of qualified people.

The shortage of MIS professionals often resulted in undertrained and inexperienced people being hired into MIS technical positions. The better of these technicians often progressed in MIS management positions at a pace that exceeded their technical and managerial training and their organizational and political maturity. MIS executives were usually 10 years younger than their counterpart managers in other functional areas

[3]McKinsey & Company, Inc., "Unlocking the Computer's Profit Potential," *The McKinsey Quarterly*, Fall 1968, pp. 17-31.

in their organization. Accelerated promotion leads to a situation where ill-prepared managers are put in charge of a complex technology that will bring about dramatic changes in the organization that many organizational participants resist. And, the organizational expectations for the results of change are unrealistic. Under those circumstances the mortality rate of MIS executives is not so alarming after all.

Articles written about MIS management during the past years capture well both the dilemma and evolution of MIS executives. By reviewing the following titles in the order in which they were published an historical perspective of MIS management is portrayed:

"Plight of the EDP Manager," *Harvard Business Review*, 1973,
    by Richard Nolan

"Where Do DP Managers Go from Here," *Infosystems*, 1974,
    by M. Blee

"Business Needs a New Breed of EDP Manager," *Harvard Business Review*, 1976, by Richard Nolan

"DP Needs Managers Not Technicians," *Infosystems*, 1976,
    by R. J. August

"EDP Managers Put on Business Suits," *Fortune*, 1976,
    by Gene Bylinsky

"DP Management Comes of Age," *Infosystems*, 1976,
    by W. A. Sommerfield

"Power, Politics and DP," *Datamation*, 1976, by J. Rue

"Can Today's MIS Manager Make the Transition?" *Datamation*, 1978, by J. C. Gilbert

"A Balanced Orientation for the Information Systems Manager,"
    MIS Quarterly, 1979, by W. M. Taggart and V. Sibley

"The Changing Role of the MIS Executive," *Datamation*, 1979,
    by J. Ferreira and J. F. Collins, Jr.

"Solving a Mismatch in Computer Management," *Business Week*, 1979

"Manager or Technician? The Nature of the Information Systems Manager's Job," *MIS Quarterly*, 1981, by Blake Ives and Margrethe Olson

"Is There Life after Information Systems Management?"
    Corporate Report, 1982, by James Wetherbe

"MIS: A Starring Role at Last: The Changing Role of the DP Manager," *Datamation*, 1982, by Janet Crane

EVOLUTION OF MIS EXECUTIVES

A review of the preceding articles reveals that MIS executives have had to evolve from technicians to managers with little preparation and few role models. They have had to realize their loyalties and commitment to their organizations rather than to their technology. They have had to focus more on interpersonal and administrative skills and delegate to their staff more and more of the technical activity.

Figure 1-1 portrays this evolution of MIS management starting with the 1950s and progressing through the 1980s.

One of the most revealing studies ever made of MIS executives was conducted by Ives and Olson.[4] They observed six MIS executives with major corporations to see how and on what they spent their time.

Figures 1-2 to 1-4 summarize some of their findings. Figure 1-2 indicates that MIS executives spend the majority of their time interacting with people; 78 percent of their time is spent on communicating with people in scheduled meetings, unscheduled meetings, and phone calls. This figure makes a compelling point: an MIS executive must be good at and enjoy working with people. The same is true for virtually all management positions.

Unfortunately, research into what motivates MIS professionals by Couger, Zawacki, and Oppermann indicates that most MIS professionals significantly prefer developing new technical skills to interacting with people.[5] It has been estimated that 80 percent of the problems that occur in organizations are a result of communication breakdowns. Considering all of the problems that occur with MIS in organizations, communication breakdowns are unquestionably a contributing factor.

MIS executives are change agents. They change people's jobs with the systems they install. When people's jobs are being changed, effective, efficient communication is vital. Explanations, training, and reassurance must all take place. But the majority of MIS professionals prefer to work with the technology. Those selected for MIS executive positions must not be from that majority, rather they must have good interpersonal skills.

Figure 1-3 indicates that MIS executives spend most of their time interacting with their own staff: 61 percent of their time is spent with either immediate subordinates or lower-level subordinates; 39 percent is spent with people external to the MIS function.

---

[4]Blake Ives and Margrethe H. Olson, "Manager or Technician? The Nature of the Information System Manager's Job," *MIS Quarterly*, vol. 5, no. 4, December 1981, pp. 49-62.

[5]J.D. Couger, R.A. Zawacki, and E.B. Oppermann, "Motivation Levels of MIS Managers versus Those of Their Employees," *MIS Quarterly*, vol. 3, no. 3, September 1979, pp. 47-56.

	1950s	1960s	1970s	1980s
1. Kinds of experience	Programming	Programming, systems analysis	Programming, systems analysis, project management	Systems analysis, Project management, Systems development
2. Leadership skills	Small teams	Project management	Large project management	Large project management
3. Education and training	Good high school math	Programmer, technical degree	MBA	MBA
4. Technical ability	Card files, batch	High-volume batch, online	Enough not to be snowed	Enough not to be snowed
5. Business acumen	Accounting rationales	Accounting/ business operations	General management/ business	General management/ business
6. Company business expertise	None	Low	High	High
7. Communication skills	Low	Low	Medium	
8. Systems analysis skills	Independent sequential processing	Integrate department & technology	MIS/database orientation	MIS/database/decision support systems orientation
9. Planning skills	None	Short-term	Strategic and short-term	Strategic and short-term
10. Organizing skills	Minimal	Medium	High	High
11. Reporting hierarchy	Low in accounting area	Middle in accounting area	High in administrative area	CEO
12. Organizational skills	Super-clerk/ bookkeeper	Report generator, accountant, record/keeper	Change agent	Change agent leader
13. Loyalties	To computer	To computer department	To organization as a whole	To organization/society

Figure 1-1 Evolution of an MIS Executive

Figure 1-2 Proportion of Time Spent on Different Activities by MIS Executives

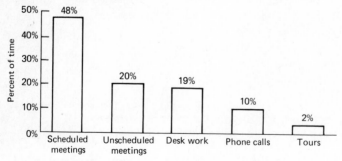

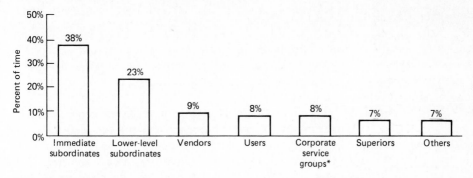

*Personnel, Maintenance, etc.

Figure 1-3 Proportion of Time Spent with Other Organizational Participants by MIS Executives

Figure 1-4 indicates that 43 percent of the subject matter on which MIS executives spend their time focuses on general management issues. The remaining 57 percent concerns technical issues, the majority of them (30 percent) being spent on new computer applications.

The study by Couger et al. revealed that MIS executives tend to use vendor presentations and internal MIS staff for keeping abreast of technical developments.

The MIS executive has evolved from a fairly low level, relatively unimportant service function to an important catalyst for organizational

Figure 1-4 Proportion of Time Spent on Different Subject Matter by MIS Executives

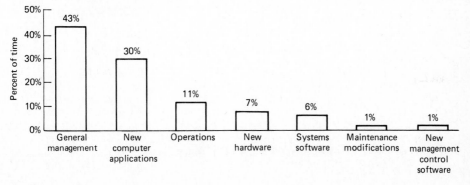

change and profit making. As Ives and Olson conclude from their study:

> Today's information systems manager is clearly more of a manager in the classical sense than a technician. Interpersonal skills and the ability to motivate and guide subordinates are relied on heavily. The manager is surrounded by technical specialists who provide expertise as required. The manager is not preoccupied with the day-to-day operations of the data processing organization, but spends a great deal of time planning the overall strategy for the information system function. A great deal of the manager's planning concerns human resoures.[6]

MIS EXECUTIVES OF THE FUTURE

As stated at the beginning of this chapter, MIS executives hold the key to the future -- everything is coming their way. One indication of this trend is that MIS executives will be in demand more than any other executives over the next several years.

Current MIS Executive's Perspective

To gain perspective on what it takes to be a successful MIS executive, the authors surveyed several successful MIS executives. A list of the executives interviewed is provided in Table 1-1.

The executives were asked to respond to the following four questions:

1. What are the most important skills or capabilities necessary to be a successful MIS executive?
2. What educational and professional background best prepares one to assume responsibility for the MIS function in an organization?
3. What was the career path (no matter how unlikely) that led you to become an MIS executive?
4. What advice would you give someone starting a career in MIS who is interested in progressing into MIS management?

---

[6]Blake Ives and Margrethe H. Olson, "Manager or Technician? The Nature of the Information System Manager's Job," *MIS Quarterly*, vol. 5, No. 4, December 1981, pp. 49-62.

Table 1-1 MIS Executives Interviewed

1. Nancy M. Abraham, Assistant Commissioner
    Department of Administration
    State of Minnesota

2. Sue Eastes, Director
    Project Development
    General Mills, Inc.

3. John C. Field, Vice President
    Information Systems Division
    St. Paul Fire & Marine Insurance Company

4. Ken E. Gelle, Director
    Information Systems
    Northern States Power Company

5. Gene D. Gross, Assistant Vice President
    Data Processing
    Cargill

6. David A. Johnson, Corporate Vice President
    Management Information Services
    National Car Rental Systems, Inc.

7. James D. Nermyr, Vice President and Controller
    B. Dalton Bookseller

8. George M. Perry, Vice President
    Information Systems
    Investors Diversified Services, Inc.

9. James L. Throckmorton, Director
    Systems and Data Processing
    Donaldson Company, Inc.

The following discussion presents a summary of the responses of nine MIS executives to the above questions. The numbers in brackets in this discussion refer to the executives listed in Table 1-1.

Skills and Capabilities

The most common capability of a successful MIS executive, as indicated in the survey results, is the ability to have a broad business viewpoint [1, 2, 3, 5, 6, 9]. Also common was the capability of oral and written communication [1, 4, 6, 8, 9].

Other skills and capabilities cited were as follows:

- Leadership ability [1, 5, 9]
- Enthusiasm [1]
- Sound judgment [1]
- Salesmanship and persuasiveness [1]
- Understanding of technology [1, 5, 6]
- Ability to build and maintain effective relationships within the company [2, 4]
- Breadth of knowledge [2]
- Ability to identify and make progress on the programs that are vital to long-term success of the organization [7]
- Ability to effectively respond to short-range projects [8]
- Ability to effectively handle stressful situations [7]
- Ability to take risks [8]
- Ability to conceptualize [8]

Educational and Professional Background

The educational background that best prepares one to assume responsibility for the MIS function in an organization, in the opinion of the MIS executives surveyed, is an education that combines both business and technical skills [1, 4, 9]. One executive was more specific, indicating that ideally one should have an undergraduate degree in a technical discipline, coupled with an M.B.A. in a non-MIS area [2]; another executive said that one needs an M.B.A. with an MIS concentration [3]. The others had very differing points of view, saying that one needs a B.A. and/or an M.B.A. [5], one needs a liberal arts education [7], and one needs to be an English composition major and a math minor [8].

The professional background needed to successfully head the MIS function in an organization is one in application functions [1, 5, 9] and user environment [1, 9]. A background that is helpful is one that gives you technical experience [3, 6, 7] and managerial experience [3, 6, 7]. One MIS executive indicated that being involved in an entrepreneurial venture with one's own money at stake is very helpful [8]. Finally, whatever background you have, says one executive, a record of success throughout is most important [9].

Career Path

In terms of their professional career paths, all of the executives started out in a technical field. All have had programming experience except one [4]; another started out in operations research before getting into programming [5].

Most MIS executives progressed through the usual positions of programmer, systems analyst, and systems manager, and finally into data processing management [1, 2, 3, 5, 6, 8, 9]. Two of the MIS executives progressed through such scientific positions as engineer, project engineer, project superintendent, project manager, and general manager [4, 7].

Advice

The MIS executives had a lot of advice to give to anyone who is starting a career and is interested in progressing into MIS management:

- Consider a variety of positions [1]
- Build a technical foundation [2, 3, 5, 6, 9]
- Acquire an M.B.A. [2, 9]
- Learn the business [2, 3, 5, 6, 9]
- View things from the boss's perspective [3]
- Accept the fact that the world is not fair and that setbacks will occur [4]
- Be more than an "8 to 5" person [5]
- Be a team player [5]
- Do not move too fast [6]
- Be exposed to a diversity of business situations [7]
- Listen, learn, read, discuss, be available, and be adventurous [8]
- Do 10 hours of work in 8 and then hang around another hour to contemplate and philosophize [8]
- Enjoy yourself [8]
- Work on communication skills [9]
- Develop a record of success [2, 9]

IS THERE LIFE AFTER INFORMATION SYSTEMS MANAGEMENT?

For a final perspective on the role of the MIS executive, the authors interviewed four former MIS executives who not only survived the trials and tribulations of MIS management, but have also been promoted into higher-level management positions -- an unusual achievement for occupants of what is often considered a technical management position.

These rare few have proven that information systems management can be a stepping-stone and not a dead end.

What Does It Take to Be a Successful Information Systems Manager?

Executive 1 has been corporate vice president and general manager of the car rental division of XYZ Car Rental Inc. since 1980. He joined XYZ in 1971 as operations research analyst, was named director of financial analysis in 1975, and was promoted to corporate vice president of management information services in 1977.

"The most important thing," Executive 1 says, "is to have a strong business perspective. The information systems function tends to have too technical of an orientation. A good information systems executive must make every effort to have himself and his staff learn about the business they work in and become committed to making information systems technology improve business operations." One step Executive 1 took was to recruit systems analysts from user departments.

Executive 2, senior vice president of business development for AOK Corp., joined the company in 1973 after holding technical and managerial positions with several other corporations. Executive 2's views echo Executive 1's: "Top management takes technical skills for granted. What they are interested in is what computer technology can do for the business. You have to solve business problems and create business opportunities using the computer in order to be effective."

Executive 3, senior vice president of MNO Insurance Co., was vice president of information systems at MNO from 1977 to 1980. Before that he held positions in information systems management with a computer manufacturer, was director of public relations and placement for a large university, and was a sales representative for another computer manufacturer. Executive 3 agrees with Executives 1 and 2, and adds: "The information systems manager must view the users of information services as customers. In that light, information systems must be customer-driven. The customer may not always be right, but he is always the customer. Also, the information systems manager needs to eliminate the mystique generally associated with computer technology and have information systems become an integral part of the organization."

Executive 4, vice president and controller of PDQ Bookstores, held technical and management positions with several other corporations before becoming vice president of information systems for PDQ. Agreeing with the preceding comments, he adds: "An information systems executive needs to be able to react in high-stress situations positively. He must be able to implement short-term solutions in critical situations while still making progress on long-range information systems requirements."

Advice to New MIS Executives

What advice do these four executives offer to new information systems executives?

Executive 1: "Know the mainstream business, manage expectations, and don't attempt huge, multiyear projects. Break big projects into small projects with short-term deliverables."

Executive 2: "Establish your own credibility, define key support points in the organization to give you feedback on how you are doing, pay close attention to your staffing. That is, good people are the key to success. And never forget that information systems are user systems. Give users credit for good systems. Keep the information systems people quiet; they will get their credit."

Executive 3: "You have to be marketing-oriented. Too often information systems executives say that management doesn't understand them. That is the wrong way to look at it. It is the information systems executive's responsibility to explain information systems technology to management."

Executive 4: "Seek exposure to top management through presentations, outside activities, company programs, and other activities in order to develop strong informal communication with top management. Don't stop learning -- continue to learn about what's happening in the industry, as well as your own company."

SUMMARY

Difficult as the job may be, MIS management is a key opportunity for the future. Organizations more than ever must utilize computers and information systems to remain competitive.

Those in leadership roles in MIS can have a major impact on the success of the organizations in which they participate. To accomplish this, MIS executives must blend management, business, technical, and interpersonal skills.

SUGGESTED READINGS

"Business Takes a Second Look at Computers," *Business Week*, June 5, 1971.

Bylinsky, Gene, "EDP Managers Put on Business Suits," *Fortune*, November 1976, pp. 68-74.

Couger, J. D., R. Zawacki, and E.B. Oppermann, "Motivation Levels of MIS Managers versus Those of Their Employees," *MIS Quarterly*, vol. 3, no. 3, September 1979, pp. 47-56.

Crane, Janet, "MIS: A Starring Role at Last? The Changing of the DP Manager," *Datamation*, January 1982, pp. 96-108.

Ferreira, J., and J. F. Collins, Jr., "The Changing Role of the MIS Executive," *Datamation*, vol. 25, no. 13, Nov. 25, 1979.

"Getting Control of the Systems," *Dun's Review*, vol. 110, no. 7, July 1977, pp. 68-81.

Gilbert, J. C., "Can Today's MIS Manager Make the Transition?" *Datamation*, vol. 24, no. 3, March 1978, pp. 141-151.

Granholm, Jackson W., "The View from the Manager's Office," *Datamation*, August 1976, pp. 52-57.

Hallum, S., and D. D. Scriven, "EDP Objectives and the Evaluation Process," *Data Management*, vol. 14, no. 5, May 1976, pp. 40-42, 50.

Ives, Blake, and Margrethe H. Olson, "Manager or Technician? The Nature of the Information System Manager's Job," *MIS Quarterly*, vol. 5, no. 4, December 1981, pp. 49-62.

McFarlan, F. Warren, "Problems in Planning the Information System," *Harvard Business Review*, March-April 1971, pp. 75-89.

Mintzberg, H., *The Nature of Managerial Work*, Harper & Row, New York, N.Y., 1973.

Nolan, R. L., "Plight of the EDP Manager," *Harvard Business Review*, vol. 51, no. 3, May-June 1973, pp. 143-152.

_____, "Business Needs a New Breed of EDP Manager," *Harvard Business Review*, vol. 54, no. 2, March-April 1976, pp. 123-133.

Rue, J., "Power, Politics and DP," *Datamation*, vol. 22, no. 12, December 1976, pp. 51-52.

"Solving a Mismatch in Computer Management," *Business Week*, April 2, 1979, pp. 73-76.

Taggart, W. M., and V. Sibley, "A 'Balanced' Orientation for the Information Systems Manager," *MIS Quarterly*, vol. 3, no. 2, June 1979, pp. 21-33.

Wetherbe, J. C., and C. J. Whitehead, "A Contingency View of Managing the Data Processing Organization," *MIS Quarterly*, vol. 1, no. 1, March 1977, pp. 19-25.

Wetherbe, James C., "Is There Life After Information Systems Management?" *Corporate Report*, March 1982, p. 42.

PART TWO

MIS ORGANIZATION

THE ORGANIZATIONAL USE OF COMPUTERS

INTRODUCTION

This chapter is intended to provide background information which will provide a perspective on the material which is presented in later chapters. In particular, the magnitude of organizational computer use is stressed, key issues for the MIS manager are identified, some useful conceptual frameworks are provided, and some consideration is given to problems of contemporary computer use.

Recall that when computers first appeared in organizations in the mid-1950s, there were predictions that the total market for such devices might be in the neighborhood of 30 or so machines. These predictions stand in contrast to what we all know really happened. The tremendous proliferation of computers and computing in organizations has presented unique challenges to both senior managers and those managers directly responsible for directing organizational computer use.

One can put forth the proposition that it took about 25 years, from the mid-1950s to the early 1980s, to learn how to use computers in organizations and to effectively manage their use. Now, as will be seen in this chapter, with microcomputer systems and local area networks, the nature of organizational computing is changing dramatically. These changes place new and different requirements on organizations to utilize computers and decision-making technologies.

HISTORY

From the late 1950s, when business uses of computers began to become popular in organizations, until the mid-1960s, batch computer systems were employed. These systems were characterized by card input and output on paper. The computer and all its peripheral devices were physically contiguous and were found in the "computer room." Business applications were typified by simple accounting systems. These systems were written in assembly languages which were unique to one computer. The IBM 1401 computer was typical of what was being employed during this period.

This era was one of organizational learning regarding computer use. In most organizations, a large number of primitive applications were developed. As users became aware of the availability of computing resources, more requests were passed on to the data processing department for computer services. The demand for programming and machine cycles soon outstripped what was available. The result was that more programmers were added to the staff and more (and faster) computers were acquired. Obviously, the budget of the data processing department grew rapidly.

Several technological changes occurred in the mid-1960s which ushered in a new computer era in most organizations. These included the introduction of memories and processors based upon semiconductor technology rather than transistors, the availability of direct-access secondary storage devices, and the widespread use of a telephone-line-based data communication system. Using more simple technologies, researchers at MIT in the late 1950s had shared a central processor among several applications. This research, exemplified by Project MAC (multiple access computing), coupled with the newer technologies mentioned above led to the introduction of a new computing era which lasted until the late 1970s. IBM's System 360 architecture, which has evolved into much of which is being used today, is an example of the "third generation" of computers which characterized an era of organizations centralizing their computing resources.

More complex and integrated applications were developed during this period, often using COBOL or PL/1. Many of these applications were online in the sense that the source of the input and receptor of the output was a terminal instead of being punched card or paper-based. Sharing of the computer resources (based upon the concepts of Project MAC and the new technologies) allowed many applications to "run" concurrently. Computer performance and the economics of computer use resulted in the development of large centralized computer systems. Similarly, programming tended to be done by centralized staffs. The users, when they needed access to data, had to go to the programmer to have a program written in order to get what they needed.

MIS management, at the same time, was under severe pressure from senior management to limit the growth of the data processing budget and to do a better job of managing the MIS function. It was during this period that many of the problems for the MIS executive identified in the previous chapter occurred. By the end of the 1970s it is fair to say that many organizations had stopped, or at least significantly slowed, the growth in computing budgets and felt that the MIS function was being competently managed. On the negative side, users still felt in many cases that it took too long to get access to data (have systems developed) and that the development cost too much.

By 1980, the situation again changed dramatically due to a technological change that issued in a new era. Memory and processor technology, still based upon semiconductors, increased greatly in capacity with large and very large scale integration. Along came the minicomputer and later the microcomputer. Concurrently, the economics of computing changed so that it was no longer true that large centralized systems were the most efficient. Additionally, query and other languages that were very "user-friendly" began to appear. Suddenly, the user no longer had to go to the MIS department to gain access to organizational data.

The MIS manager was threatened with the possibility of a user revolt and a totally new world in which to operate. Now it is possible for users to go down to the local computer store and spend a few thousand dollars to get access to machine cycles, thus bypassing the MIS department. Moreover, word processors (which are computers) are springing up all over the organization. Finally, new technology also makes possible the distribution of data as well as the distribution of equipment and the systems development function.

The MIS manager, having done a pretty good job of learning how to plan and control MIS resources, is suddenly thrust into a very different and more complex world. The future promises even more and rapid change.

THE EIGHTIES AND NINETIES: AN INFORMATION AGE

From very limited beginnings, organizational computer use has grown substantially. Examination of statistics prepared by the International Data Corporation, a firm whose business is to study the computer industry, gives an idea of how widespread computer use is now and how the next 10 years will show remarkable growth:

- About 100,000 computer instructions are executed every second in the United States for each of its citizens.
- Each U.S. citizen "appears" in from 10 to 1000 databases.

● Most homes have 2 to 10 "computers" (microprocessors) in them. By 1990, these processors will outnumber the 20 to 40 electric motors in the home.

● Over the next 5 years, a trillion dollars will be spent in the United States on information processing. Not included in this amount is spending on training, micrographics, electronic mail, and loss from the wrong use of technology or the failure to use it.

● The information processing industry is growing at a yearly rate of 16 percent with many sizeable sectors growing at 25 percent or higher.

● By 1986, there will be over 8 million computers installed in the United States, over 17 million terminals, and over 5 million word processing work stations. This is more than three times the number installed today.

● In 1971, *data processing* (DP) as an industry took in $17 billion. In 1981, the *information processing* industry had grown to $69 billion (a doubling in real dollars). However, with office automation, telecommunication, personal computing, database management, and the like included, the industry total was $130 billion (a fourfold growth in real dollars).

● In 1981, there were about 15 million computers, word processors, telecopiers, and switchboards, compared to 52 million white-collar workers.

● Within 5 years, when the white-collar work force will be 57 million, the number .of these devices will grow to 38 million.

● At these rates, there will be more than one intelligent office "gadget" for every white-collar worker by the end of the decade.

● In 1971, there were about 100,000 keyboard devices (mostly terminals) still controlled by the DP department in end user organizations. By 1981 there were 4 million, and by 1986 there will be 16 million. Three-quarters of these will not be under the control of the DP department.

A trend currently underway is away from total reliance on the large mainframe computer and toward increased use of minicomputers and microcomputers. This trend is supported by figures from International Data Corporation. They show that, in 1971, when the dollar value of computer shipments in the United States was $7.2 billion, mainframe computers accounted for about 95 percent of the total. In 1981, shipments had increased to $17.8 billion, but mainframes accounted for only 60 percent. By 1986, they are estimated to be going to slip to 40 percent of the total. It is interesting to note in passing that IBM and IBM compatible computers account for about 81 percent of the current mainframe market. Honeywell Information Systems, Univac, Burroughs, Control Data Corporation, and National Cash Register make up the remaining 19 percent.

Another set of statistics that tells us something about the organizational use of computers describes how data processing departments spend their funds. Data processing budget allocations are shown in Table 2-1.

In summary, we can see that the world of organizational computing in the 1980s will be different from the one the MIS manager had to deal with in the 1970s. In contrast with most of the computer cycles being expended on large, centralized mainframe computers, in the future a large percentage of the machine cycles will be processed on equipment located throughout the organization. These machines will be minicomputers, personal microcomputers, word processors, and professional work stations. The opportunity exists for the equipment of many manufacturers to be represented in the mix. At the same time, the central mainframe computer will still be present and IBM compatibility at the instruction set level is fast becoming a de facto standard.

In addition to equipment existing throughout the organization, it is likely that large numbers of users are going to develop their own application systems or use powerful new languages to access centralized data. From a world in which the programmer was king, we are moving to a world in which the role of the programmer is likely to be greatly diminished. The user will no longer be completely dependent upon the programmer for access to corporate data resources.

CRITICAL INFORMATION SYSTEMS ISSUES FOR THE EIGHTIES

Clearly, the new world of organizational computing in the next 10 years is quite different from the centralized world in which most current MIS managers are used to operating. New and greater challenges face these managers. One way of finding out what concerns MIS managers is to

Table 2-1 Computer budgets and their trends in U.S. organizations

Category	Percentage Allocation	Trend
Personnel	36	Down
Hardware	31	Down
Media & supplies	11	Up
Software	10	Up
Outside services	5	Up
Communication services	2	Up

ask them. The list of critical information systems issues in the eighties, which is shown below, was generated by a blue-ribbon group of MIS managers responsible for identifying key areas of research to be supported by the Society for Information Management. The seven most highly rated issues, out of a total of thirty-three identified, are listed.

1. Improve accessibility to timely and accurate data by users, possibly without an information systems intermediary.
2. Assure the availability and quality of critical information systems skills.
3. Develop effective planning processes for aligning information systems organization and services to the structure of the enterprise and effectively integrating the functions of administrative information and telecommunication support.
4. Identify information systems skill requirements, determine how to nurture these skills, and find better ways of selecting personnel.
5. Determine the investment to be made in information systems in terms of productivity, growth, or profitability of the enterprise.
6. Anticipate and understand the consequences of new information systems economics and technology.
7. Improve productivity in application development and maintenance.

The list of issues generated by these managers of what would be classified as "leading-edge" MIS organizations reflects the changing nature of the environment in which they must operate. Let us examine further the listed issues in terms of what has been said regarding the current and future trends of computing technology.

The issue rated most critical by the managers supports the fact that these persons are from firms that are quite advanced in their MIS practices and attitudes. The managers recognize the need to provide users with access to data without their having to get a programmer to write a routine to provide it. The managers also realize that the hardware and software technology to accomplish direct user access is here or shortly to arrive. To make accurate data easily available to users has been a long-term goal for MIS, and these managers see the new technology as allowing this goal to be realized during the 1980s.

Issues 3 and 6 simply show a recognition that the world is changing and that the new technology and economics which make equipment easily available throughout the organization require careful planning and control. The managers are concerned that the old planning and control processes are inadequate and that change is needed.

Issues 2 and 4 implicitly state that the managers are concerned that the information systems professional of the 1980s must have different skills from the programmer of past years. Determining what skills are needed and how people with the proper skills are to be acquired, trained, and advanced is the challenge.

Issue 5 is one that has been with MIS managers for many years and is not new, only different. The problem is one of measuring true benefits from the investment made in computing resources. This was difficult enough when we were building rather straightforward systems of a clerical nature, utilizing centralized (identifiable) resources. It is all the more difficult when we must deal with ill-defined, high-level systems which are often user-defined and user-developed. This is even more challenging under the likely condition that the developmental resources are hard to identify and measure using the organization's traditional accounting systems and practices.

Issue 7 raises a very significant concern. The fact is that, at present, a very large part of the time of information systems personnel is spent doing what is classed as maintenance on existing systems. This effort is actually devoted to systems evolution caused by user learning and new requirements caused by changes in the organization's external or internal environment (say, a change in a governmental reporting requirement). Because our systems in place are constructed using a very rigid, inflexible technology (especially software), changing these systems is difficult, time-consuming, and expensive. Furthermore, many large, basic systems have been modified so many times that they are in a patchwork state which is so poor that they need to be redesigned and redone from scratch.

Martin Buss, writing in the *Harvard Business Review*, brings home the same point raised by issue 7 above when he points out that senior management must recognize that a substantial investment may be necessary to redo systems which are large, basic to the company's operation, and hopelessly patched and obsolete.[1] He adds that it is going to be difficult to get senior managers to accept the fact that these investments must be made in systems which they thought were in place and operating satisfactorily. The fact is, however, that to be efficient and flexible these systems must be totally redone to take advantage of new technology.

A brief case example may help illustrate the point. One of us is involved with a project in which a very large firm's worldwide financial and accounting systems are being completely rewritten. To rewrite them and to do so using up-to-date technology is a very large task for a firm the size of the one involved. The project is a 4-year effort in which no tangible results will be seen until the end of the third year. The project team created to do the job has a peak staffing

---

[1] M.D.J. Buss, "Penny-wise Approach to Data Processing," *Harvard Business Review*, vol. 59, no. 4, July-August 1981, pp. 111-117.

level of 225 persons, which does not include outside consultants or contract programming personnel. The 4-year total cost, *exclusive of any computer equipment*, is forecast to be $82 million. The system equipment will include a large mainframe computer, regional mainframe computers, and minicomputers located at remote sites. Both satellite and ground data communication systems will be employed.

Clearly, the management involved in allocating the resources for this level of effort had to be convinced that these levels of expenditure were absolutely necessary. It is also fair to add that these senior managers are at great risk, as their reputations depend on the successful outcome of the project. Their justification for taking both the corporate financial risk and the personal risk was their conviction that the firm could not be competitive beyond the 1980s without the system and its utilization of new technology. They recognized that the system development lead time was such that, to be successful, the system redevelopment would have to begin in the early part of this decade. It is not necessary in this case to elaborate on how much personal risk is at stake on this project for the MIS manager in charge of the project.

In order to understand contemporary organizational use of computers, the statistics, technological projections, and important issues seen by MIS managers are useful. It is also beneficial to examine a few basic conceptual frameworks that have proved useful in the past. These frameworks are useful for two reasons. First, they help explain why and how organizations are using computers as they are. Second, the frameworks assist in providing a common frame of reference for the reader that will be of use in later parts of this book.

BASIC CONCEPTUAL FRAMEWORKS

Although there are a number of conceptual frameworks that stand out in the area of management information systems, two are of particular relevance to the material which is presented in the chapters that follow. One is the "stage hypothesis" developed by Richard Nolan when he was a faculty member at the Harvard Business School.[2] Another framework, the systems hierarchy, was developed by Gary Dickson of the University of Minnesota and is one of the earliest constructs of MIS.[3] This framework's message is still valid and useful today, 15 years after it was proposed.

[2] R.L. Nolan, "Managing the Crises in Data Processing," *Harvard Business Review*, vol. 59, no. 2, March-April 1979, pp. 115-126.
[3] G.W. Dickson, "Management Information-Decision Systems," *Business Horizons*, vol. 11, no. 12, December 1968, pp. 17-26.

Nolan's Stage Hypothesis

Nolan's stage hypothesis first gained popularity when it appeared in an article in the *Harvard Business Review* in 1974.[4] In that article, he suggested that an organization goes through identifiable stages as it computerizes. In 1979, he wrote a second article in the same magazine in which he updated his thinking and added two stages to his original proposal. The discussion below is based upon the second article.

Stage 1: Initiation. In this stage, the computer is introduced within the organization. Users are encouraged to use the system but, due to unfamiliarity, do not yet flock to request applications. The applications that are developed are simple and typically of an accounting orientation. During this stage, the DP organization is often centralized because this organization, like the users, must also learn the new technology.

Stage 2: Contagion. Soon the users become superficially enthusiastic about using the computer and request the development of all sorts of applications. Computer services are often free to them since computing expenses are often carried as an overhead expense during this stage and thus new developments are encouraged. Pressure is exerted by DP to expand computer hardware and the computer staff during this stage to keep up with the demand for services. The budget in the data processing department rises rapidly. The management of the computer department can be characterized as lax, since little planning is done and much control is lacking.

Stage 3: Control. The organization has entered the control stage when senior management becomes very concerned about the level of benefits being received from computer applications versus the cost of the data processing function. When this occurs, a halt is called to budget expansion. The total DP budget is either held constant or the growth rate is sharply reduced. The focus is on giving the department the type of professional management found in other parts of the organization. Planning and control systems are initiated. Emphasis is placed upon documenting existing applications and moving them more toward middle management and away from a focus on strictly operational functions. It is also during this stage that an attempt is made to make the users accountable for their computer use by introducing chargeout systems.

Stage 4: Integration. The integration stage is characterized by an attempt to take advantage of new technology, typically database, by

---

[4]C. Gibson and R.L. Nolan, "Managing the Four Stages of EDP Growth," *Harvard Business Review*, vol. 52, no. 1, January–February 1974, pp. 76-88.

integrating existing systems. The DP function is set up much as a utility to service the users. There is, according to Nolan, a significant transition point in an organization's computer use once this stage is reached.

Stage 5: Data Administration. In the data administration stage, the database technology is in place and a data administration function is created to plan and control the use of an organization's data. By this time, users are effectively accountable for computer resource use and the emphasis is upon common, integrated systems in which data is shared among various functions in the organization.

Stage 6: Maturity. When an organization reaches maturity (and few have), they have truly integrated the computer into their managerial processes. The data resource is, at this time, meshed with the strategic planning process of the organization. Applications mirror the information flows of the organization. Finally, joint user and data processing accountability exists regarding the allocation of computing resources within the organization. The schematic shown in Figure 2-1 depicts a "budget curve" as an organization passes through the stages.

Nolan's stage hypothesis has a number of uses as a conceptual framework. One way of using the framework is to classify organizations in the aggregate into stages. By doing this, one can see how U.S. organizations have passed through the stages. The initiation of business computing, for example, took place in the United States in the late 1950s and the early 1960s. Contagion occurred from the early 1960s up to the late 1960s, say 1968 to 1969. The control stage was entered by U.S. business about the late 1960s and lasted until at least the mid-1970s for many firms. Some organizations are still in this stage. Many firms, however, have integrated applications and have become oriented toward database technology, which marks entry into the next stage. Stage 4 occurred in the mid-1970s and is still under way in most of these firms. Firms entering the data administration stage did so most often in the late 1970s. There are some aspects of a few organizations that currently represent maturity but it would be difficult to point to any organization and say that it is totally mature regarding all aspects of data processing. These time periods for the stages for U.S. organizations overall have been added by the authors to the schematic of Nolan's framework shown in Figure 2-1. The reader must recognize that the time periods are generalizations and that there are still stage 2 firms, stage 3 firms, and so on.

Another use of the Nolan framework is to go into an organization, gather data about its computer use, and identify how the computer use in the organization fits into the framework. This type of exercise is very useful as a precursor to an information systems planning activity.

It is important to understand the current status of the DP organization before embarking on ambitious new plans. Upon leaving the Harvard Business School, Nolan and a colleague established a consulting company whose main business is to make this sort of assessment. To appreciate the richness of this sort of activity, one must understand that the framework is more complex than shown above.

Organizations may be identified as to what stage they are in by several subcategories including: (1) their applications portfolio (how they are using the computing), (2) their type of data processing organization, (3) how they do their DP planning and control, and (4) the way users fit into the applications development process and their responsibility regarding the allocation of computer resources. It is thus possible to say that a firm is in stage 3 on one aspect and stage 4 on another. Few organizations would be at the same level of sophistication on all subparts of the framework.

The chronology below, which was based upon a study by Nolan, Norton, and Company, illustrates the application of the stage hypothesis. The organization, although not actually identified, is a large national agricultural cooperative.

I. Stage 1 at Midwest Co-op.
    A. First DP equipment installed -- 1957.
        1. IBM 402.
        2. Accounting department.
    B. First applications.
        1. Accounts payable and settlements.
        2. Accounts receivable.
        3. General ledger.

Figure 2-1 Nolan's Six Stages of Data Processing Growth

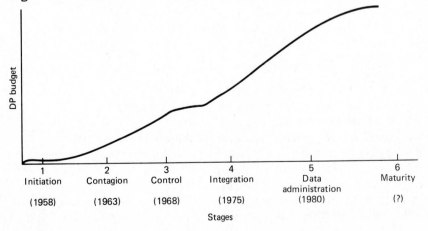

    C. Increased usage in accounting.
       1. IBM 1401 -- 1961.
       2. IBM 360/30 -- 1967.
II. Stage 2 at Midwest Co-op.
    A. Transition to stage 2 -- 1970.
       1. Outside consultant identifies systems opportunities in line functions.
       2. Information systems department established.
    B. Proliferation of systems in line functional areas.
       1. Order processing.
       2. Inventory control.
       3. Sales reporting.
       4. Least-cost feed mix.
    C. Repeated equipment upgrades.
       1. Add memory to 360/30 -- 1971.
       2. Upgrade to 370/135 -- 1972.
       3. Add memory -- 1973.
       4. Upgrade to 370/145 -- 1974.
    D. Cost increase from $1.1 million to $3.5 million.
III. Stage 3 at Midwest Co-op.
    A. Consulting study recommends improved DP management.
       1. Corporate steering committee established.
       2. Working committees organized.
       3. Business systems managers and systems planning function established.
       4. Standards program undertaken.
       5. User participation in systems development and planning increased.
    B. Extension and consolidation of existing applications.
       1. Order processing, inventory, and product cost.
       2. Feed pricing.
       3. General ledger, payroll, and human resources.
       4. Sales, marketing, and distribution information.
    C. Continued equipment upgrades.
       1. Add memory to 370/145 -- 1976.
       2. Upgrade to 370/158 -- 1977.
       3. Convert operating system -- 1978.
    D. Costs continue to increase 20 percent annually.
IV. Stage 4 at Midwest Co-op.
    A. Database management system installation begun -- 1979.
    B. Applications system to database orientation begun -- 1980.
    C. Upgrading of equipment continues.
       1. Add memory to 370/158 -- 1978.
       2. Add attached processor to 370/158 -- 1980.
       3. Install IBM 3033 -- 1982.

Before leaving Nolan's stage hypothesis, we must mention that several academic researchers have attempted to verify the stages by analysis of actual corporate data.[5] These studies have not supported the framework, but it is fair to say that the data used as the basis for analysis is hard to obtain and may be associated with these negative results. In any event, the framework is so intellectually appealing, so useful, and so widely known that it is worthwhile even without empirical support.

Dickson's Systems Hierarchy

In 1968, G. W. Dickson wrote an article that attempted to define the area of MIS. In doing this, he identified several "levels" of systems. The levels he identified and defined are, with slight modification, still valid today. The reason that this framework is useful is that we often speak of MIS as though all systems were management information systems and provided information for management decision making. Clearly, various types or levels of systems exist, the federation of which may be an organization's MIS. The Dickson levels are described below.

Level 1: Clerical Systems. These are systems that replace manual processing or what could be done manually with computer systems. Other names for systems of this type are "transactions processing systems" or "operational systems." About 95 percent of all computer applications today would be classed as being clerical in nature. Accounting applications, online inventory systems, and banking systems are typical. Very up-to-date technology may be employed, but if the nature of the application is such that it could (theoretically) be done manually, then it is a clerical system.

Level 2: Information Systems. In contrast to clerical systems, the purpose of information systems is to provide information to be used in a decision. Control systems that answer questions such as "Do I have a problem?" or "What kind of problem is it?" are of this type. Profit-center financial reports and marketing systems which show what was sold where and to whom are examples of this type of system. Note that the system simply provides information to the decision maker; how that person uses the information is up to him or her.

---

[5]See, for example, D.H. Drury, "An Empirical Assessment of the Stages of DP Growth," *MIS Quarterly*, vol. 7, no. 2, June 1983, pp. 59-70; and H.C. Lucas, Jr. and J.A. Sutton, "The Stage Hypothesis and S-Curve: Some Contradictory Evidence," *Communications of the ACM*, vol. 20, no. 4, April 1977, pp. 254-259.

In passing, it is worth mentioning that originally it was thought that simply summarizing the data in clerical systems would produce information systems. We found, much to our dismay, that this is not the case. Information is decision-oriented, and to support decision making, data must frequently be captured that is not part of the transactions processing system. A short example will illustrate this point. An invoicing and billing system (clerical system) was being designed. Another application, a marketing information system giving product sales by sales agent and sales territory, was also under consideration. The input data for the latter was a part of the billing system. If the billing system had been built without the capability of gathering the marketing data input, it still would have functioned in that customers would be billed. There was no way, however, to get *marketing information* out of the system. The point is that to support information systems, it may be necessary to add data-collecting systems to clerical systems that are already in place.

Level 3: Decision Support Systems. In systems of this type, the emphasis is upon providing aids to the process used to make a decision. Structuring the process with an interactive system that leads the decision maker through the decision is one example of this sort. Using imbedded optimization models, or "what if" capabilities, is another feature characteristic of decision support systems. The decision is still up to the human, but support is provided by the system to explore the problem. This concept is developed more fully in Chapter 9.

Level 4: Programmed Systems. In these systems, the *decision* is turned over to the system. An example would be an inventory reordering system. Here, the system would sense when the inventory had dropped to the reorder level, would select a supplier, generate a purchase order, and communicate it to the selected vendor. This is a simple example. Work going on in the field of artificial intelligence (a branch of computer science) and on "expert systems" will, in the future, result in many decision support systems and programmed systems finding application outside the laboratory. At present, systems of the programmed type are unusual in actual applications, tending to be more of a research topic.

It is important to appreciate that this hierarchy, like Nolan's framework, is impure. Many systems have features of more than one level in the hierarchy, especially when integration is present. The framework is useful, however, in identifying systems or their attributes.

PROBLEMS IN COMPUTER USE

In Chapter 1, a number of statements were made which indicate that there have been problems with the effective use of computers in organizations. It is fair to say that by the end of the 1970s MIS managers had become much more professional than had previously been the case. Many of the serious problems had been overcome. Yet problems still exist and new demands of the distributed era of the 1980s remain to be solved. For these reasons and for the perspective they provide on the material which follows in subsequent chapters, it is worth examining the symptoms of organizational computer problems. We will also discuss some of the basic causes of these symptoms. It is these basic causes with which the successful MIS manager must deal, and many of these, as will be seen, are beyond direct control.

Symptoms

If there are problems with organizational computing, they are reflected in observable outcomes, called "symptoms." The symptoms are various behaviors. The MIS manager should be able to recognize these symptoms when they are present and understand the associated behavior.

Behaviors. Behaviors take three forms: avoidance, projection, and aggression. Avoidance behavior is probably the most common type of behavior associated with systems problems. The failure of users to participate on systems design teams is one form of avoidance behavior. Another is when users do not use the output of systems that is given to them. Still another form of avoidance that is very serious occurs when senior managers fail to get involved with the MIS function and do not give the function the attention it deserves.

The second type of behavior, projection, is also fairly common. It most often takes the form of written and verbal statements blaming the system or systems personnel for something that may or may not be their fault. The statement "It's the system's fault" is a typical accusation. Another example would be the commonly expressed opinion that "The MIS manager is too much of a technician." This may not be true to a large degree, but like the academic who is always an "ivory-tower egghead," the MIS manager suffers somewhat from the curse of the general reputation of MIS managers. Frequently, projection behavior reflects the attitudes of users and senior managers. These attitudes are reflected in everything from formal memoranda to hallway statements. The MIS manager should be careful to monitor these attitudes as much as possible and attempt to determine whether they are caused by actual system problems or whether they are, perhaps, reflecting other, more indirect situations. We will have more to say about the latter situation in the next section.

Behavior of an aggressive nature does occur in the systems domain. We have seen cases of users actually sabotaging systems in overt, physical ways. Honey poured down source recording devices, attacks on disk files with screwdrivers, and hammers applied to terminal keyboards have all been documented. Other, less dramatic sabotage occurs when system input or procedural errors are made on purpose. Finally, senior managers and user personnel can behave in ways that will sink information systems projects. Giving a systems project leader responsibility without authority, key managers damning the system with faint praise, and failing to provide adequate resources to do the system project are all examples of what could be carefully staged system sabotage.

Sometimes behavior of the three types is conscious; sometimes it is not. Frequently, it is a combination of explicit and known behavior with unconscious and unknowing behavior on the part of the person who is involved with the system.

Other Outcomes. Although outcomes represent behavior of a sort, there are several of these in the systems context that deserve special discussion. The first is the condition that was presented in the previous chapter, MIS executive turnover. Certainly, when a high level of MIS executive turnover or staff turnover exists in an organization, it is a symptom of a problem regarding the organization's use of computing resources.

Another common problem symptom is unrealistic budget restrictions placed by senior management on the MIS department. A variant of this symptom that has been observed by the authors occurs when senior management becomes fixated on rate of return for every systems project. To insist on a particular rate of return for many projects is simply inappropriate and causes "game playing." An example would be the case of a very high-level and ill-defined system such as a marketing information system or the case of a request to purchase an expensive but capable financial planning software package. The point is that many ill-defined systems still require judgment and to blindly insist upon total reliance upon quantification is unrealistic. Note that we are not saying that calculation of the rate of return is invalid; we simply wish to apply this tool to appropriate situations. What is being objected to are cases in which resources are withheld from the MIS function under the pretense of applying sound, sophisticated management procedures. When this occurs, it is the symptom of an underlying attitudinal problem.

The problem, in these cases, can best be identified as "lack of support" on the part of key personnel. These people are usually the powerful senior managers. All too often the senior management pays lip service to the idea of supporting the MIS function. This is true even in instances in which resources are provided at the proper level. What is missing, in many cases, are actions which signal the members of the organization that real support for the MIS function is present. A commitment by senior management to spend its valuable time on MIS issues is one form of evidence of this type of support. Another signal is when the organization's reward system is used by those in power to favor those individuals or groups who are "doing the right things" regarding MIS. These overt behaviors along with positive projection toward the MIS function are symptoms of a very healthy situation rather than a problem situation.

Causes

The behaviors which have been discussed are motivated by underlying causes. Many of these causes are overt and easily understood. The most obvious of these are problems with the MIS system, the MIS personnel, and/or the MIS manager. Improper technology, improper use of the technology, "people problems" of all sorts in the MIS function, and a variety of inefficiencies can all cause the problem symptoms that have been discussed. There are, however, some conditions which exist in organizations that are uniquely related to building management information systems and which can result in "problems." These conditions make building and operating systems particularly difficult.

Unrealistic Expectations. In many instances, managerial expectations have been raised too far regarding what can be achieved from an MIS and the level of effort required to build MIS systems. A good current example of this situation is associated with "the office of the future." Management, in many cases, is expecting dramatic improvements in white-collar productivity and innovative new ways of operating the office. If all that is delivered is word processing for the secretarial staff, then there will be problems. Many examples from the past illustrate the expectations problem. Systems delivered late and over cost and systems that do not do what they are supposed to are classic examples.

One message is that managers and users must have realistic expectations about what computing technology can do, how much it costs, and how long it will take to effectively install it. Training and experience are probably the best way to deal with this situation. Another message is that MIS managers and personnel must manage expectations about what technology truly can (and cannot) do and what level of effort will be involved.

The Participants in the Systems Building Process. There are several groups or parties that are involved in the process of building organizational information systems, including senior management, users and user managers, the technical staff, and the MIS management. Each of these groups may have attributes that make the process difficult and result in problems with the organizational information system.

Senior managers, as has been mentioned, tend to avoid information systems issues. In many cases they go into the marketplace to hire an experienced MIS manager (who may have a sufficient technical background but may not be a capable manager) and turn systems matters over to this person. The senior executive, having done this, can now avoid getting involved with systems issues by claiming, "I went out and hired the best, most experienced person available, and we're paying top dollar. I'm putting my faith in X."

Another problem often exhibited by senior management is that they do not fully realize the importance of information systems issues. In such a case the outcome is that rather than "biting the bullet" and making hard decisions, the senior managers make either no decision or the politically expedient one. An example of this situation occurs frequently in the case of distributed systems or in regard to the proliferation of personal computing systems and/or word processing systems. Users and, in particular, profit center managers are allowed to do anything they wish with respect to equipment acquisition and system development. As a result, systems anarchy can occur.

Probably the most common symptom of a problem with executive management in their relation to the computer is that they do a good job of paying lip service to the importance of this function and even provide adequate resources, but they fail when it comes to behaving in ways which indicate support of the function that is observable to others. Spending time on systems issues, properly using the reward system, and treating the MIS manager as a part of the top management team are just a few examples of meaningful behavior that will communicate proper attitudes to others.

Users and user management are often at the heart of information systems problems for a different set of reasons. These groups must play a key role in the determination of what the system is to do. In other words, an active role on the part of users is required in specifying what information the system will provide, and how frequently and in what form it will provide information. Yet, the background, experience, and training of system users is such that they are unfamiliar with the process of requirements determination as well as being unfamiliar with the types of systems under consideration. This is especially true of information systems and decision support systems situations. An experienced marketing manager, for example, may have little idea of what a marketing information system is. Ask several such managers for a description of one, and you will likely receive several different descriptions. The point is that we're asking users to help describe something they've never experienced. A learning situation is present, and yet, in many cases we are building systems with a technology that is so inflexible that the accommodation of learning is almost prohibitively difficult.

The systems builder or technical person also brings characteristics to the systems building process that may inhibit success. In the first place, the systems builder often brings a technical focus to the process. There is little emphasis in the selection or training of systems builders on knowing the business functions with which they are dealing. Even more disturbing is the fact that little emphasis is placed upon enhancing the interpersonal communications skills of the systems builders or giving them training on dealing with organizational change. There is even evidence to suggest that the personal attributes and attitudes of many systems builders are such that they would resist attempts at such training. Thus, we are in the position of having a user who cannot easily provide what is needed and a systems builder who is incapable of working with the user to identify these requirements. This condition, coupled with inflexible technology, is a major contributor to user dissatisfaction with organizational information systems.

Finally, we come to the MIS manager. Although the role of this person was discussed in detail in Chapter 1, it is worth reemphasizing a few key points. First, there has been a tendency to emphasize technical over managerial and organizational skills when selecting personnel for this position. Second, and partly because of the technical emphasis, the MIS managers tend to select and promote those persons in the information systems function having the same orientation as themselves. This condition, of course, exacerbates the technical emphasis in the MIS managerial hierarchy.

Other Background Conditions. There are present in the organizational information systems environment several other conditions which can cause problems. Some of the more important of these conditions are as follows:

Scope. Perhaps in no other organizational function must such a broad amount of knowledge be present in order to operate properly. We have a variety of technologies such as computer hardware, software, and data communications. We also have to keep up on specific managerial tools, e.g., system development methodologies, project management systems, and chargeout mechanisms, and we must also be aware of general managerial tools associated with leadership, organizational change, and implementation procedures. Finally, because of the decision-supporting function, there must be an awareness of quantitative processes and procedures.

Rate of Change. In no other organizational function is the underlying technology changing as much or as fast as in information systems. Thus, we have a broad area to cover, and its component parts are all very dynamic (some more than others).

Rigidity of Technology and Lack of Standards. As has been mentioned, the MIS function must cope with a technology in place that is very rigid and inflexible. The new technology is much better in this regard, but the evolution from the old technology to the new is time-consuming and complex. The lack of standards for hardware and software makes the conversion from the old to the new very difficult. Examples are easy to generate. One has only to consider moving from one database management system to another or the incompatibility between word processing systems to understand these difficulties. These conditions place severe constraints upon the ability of the MIS function to change in an effective and efficient way.

Vendor Push. Purveyors of computer hardware and software are in business to make a profit. If the users of their offerings simply sit tight and use the products they already have, then the vendor revenue will not grow. In order to promote profit growth, vendors are constantly offering new products and, either by economic incentives or through enforced obsolescence, pushing their customer base to move into new products. One example of this type of push on the part of the vendors that may not be obvious concerns new or updated operating systems. As changes in these products occur, the user is almost obligated to move to new systems or suffer inadequate support on the part of the vendor or the inability to utilize other software products offered by the vendor because of incompatibility. The point is that vendors do manipulate their customer base by introducing new products which, for a variety of reasons, are impractical to ignore. The result is continued systems change and frequent short-term degradation of service to the user. Because of the service reduction and because users do not understand conversions and the reasons for them, they can become upset and problem behavior can result.

Inability to Account for Significant Factors. There are a number of factors associated with the systems building process which, although they are subtle, can create problems. The following are a few of them:

Organizational change: Every time a system is introduced, we are dealing with an organizational change, sometimes a very major one. In general, we do not understand the process of introducing organizational change very well, and in particular, we do not often train systems personnel to cope with the process of accomplishing organizational change. This is one reason why what are classified as "implementation problems" frequently plague the introduction of new information systems.

The organizational reward system: The U.S. business system most commonly rewards managers or personnel for performance on a specific job during a short time period, often a year. It is no wonder then that these persons do not see the value associated with putting forth their time and effort on a systems project that may not be clearly related -- in the minds of these persons at least -- to short-term job performance. One often hears such statements as "Why should I spend my time on the systems design project when I get paid to run the accounts payable project? Besides, by the time the system is developed and in place, I'll probably be in another job anyway."

Organizational power structure: Associated with organizational change is the fact that new information systems frequently shift the organizational power structure. This happens because new and better information may be available to persons who previously may not have had this information. As a result, some persons may become more "powerful" and others less so. People tend to act so as to maximize their power and therefore may resist shifts in the informational network.

Organizational learning: We have mentioned that persons dealing with information systems, especially those of a higher level, often learn as they use the systems. In other words, the systems need to change as the learning takes place. This condition means that systems need to be evolvable. But, as we know, our systems technology (especially the software) is not very evolvable. As a result, the system cannot adapt to user learning very easily, and in many cases this results in user dissatisfaction with the system.

Individual use and styles of use: There is a substantial amount of evidence building to the effect that different types of individuals need different and unique types of systems support. Thus, in many cases, the systems need to be tailored to the person they are to support. Given the static, inflexible technology with which we must build systems, this type of hand-tailoring is very impractical. Again, as a result of this condition, the user may be less well served than otherwise would be the case, and user dissatisfaction results.

Difficulty of measuring results: Ideally, the MIS function ought to be able to state accurately the organizational effect (often in profitability) that results from an information systems effort. As we have seen, this is very difficult -- or, in many cases, impossible -- to do. As a result of this condition, the MIS manager is often hard-pressed to demonstrate the value of his function to the organization and frequently must request resources from executive management "on faith." All of these conditions surrounding the information systems building process make the job that much more difficult. The MIS manager must appreciate these conditions and act so as to minimize their negative effects. Only by doing so can the organizational effectiveness resulting from the use of computing resources be optimized.

SUMMARY

Organizations have now had approximately 25 years of computer use involving business applications. The technology employed during this time to develop computer applications has tended to be rigid, and for this reason as well as a number of others, the managerial benefit from these systems has been less than senior management has expected.

We are now on the edge of a new technological era which will see explosive growth in the use of computing power throughout the organization. MIS managers must confront and deal with a number of issues in the next decade that are radically different from those they have dealt with in the past. To enable the MIS manager to successfully move into the new era, it is important that the lessons of the past be understood, that contemporary problems of computer use be recognized, and that the critical new issues be noted.

Certainly, basic frameworks such as the information systems hierarchy and the stage framework are useful as a point of departure for understanding past and contemporary use of computers. The successful MIS manager must, however, move beyond an appreciation of the historical and the present state of affairs and begin to deal with the critical information systems issues of the next decade that will emerge from the changed technology of computing and the new economics associated with computer use.

SUGGESTED READINGS

Benjamin, R. I., "Information Technology in the 1980s: A Long-Range Planning Scenario," *MIS Quarterly*, vol. 6, no. 2, June 1982, pp. 11-32.

Buss, M. D. J., "Penny-wise Approach to Data Processing," *Harvard Business Review*, vol. 59, no. 4, July - August 1981, pp. 111-117.

Dickson, G. W., "Management Information-Decision Systems," *Business Horizons*, vol. 11, no. 12, December 1968, pp. 17-26.

Edelman, Franz, "The Management of Information Resources: A Challenge for American Business," *MIS Quarterly*, vol. 4, no. 1, March 1981, pp. 17-27.

Gibson, C., and R. L. Nolan, "Managing the Four Stages of EDP Growth," *Harvard Business Review*, vol. 52, no. 1, January-February 1974, pp. 76-88.

International Data Corporation, "Trends in Computing: Application of the 80s," *Fortune*, May 31, 1982, pp. 21-70.

Kirchner, E., "Making Every Drop Count: 1982 Budget Survey," *Datamation*, vol. 27, no. 5, July 1982, pp. 57-69.

"Moving Away from Mainframes," *Business Week*, Feb. 15, 1982, pp. 78-94.

Naisbitt, J., *Megatrends*, Warner Books, New York, 1982, Ch. 1.

Nolan, R. L., "Managing the Crises in Data Processing," *Harvard Business Review*, vol. 57, no. 2, March-April 1979, pp. 115-126.

Withington, F. T., "Coping with Computer Proliferation," *Harvard Business Review*, vol. 58, no. 3, May-June 1980, pp. 152-164.

THREE

ORGANIZING AND STAFFING
THE MIS FUNCTION

INTRODUCTION

Two of the most important decisions that must be made in association with an organization's use of computing resources concern acquiring information systems personnel and effectively organizing these persons to perform their duties. These two subjects are the topics treated in this chapter.

Organization involves making decisions in two key areas. The first area of decision making concerns the reporting structure of the information systems group within the overall organization. The second area of decision making relates to the structure of the information systems (IS) organization itself. Decisions in each area, of course, must deal with a number of important issues and trade off a number of factors.

To illustrate a number of organizational issues and to provide a frame of reference for subsequent discussion, the chapter will begin with the presentation of four case examples. The experiences of the four organizations described in the cases will be drawn upon as the discussion advances to the subjects of (1) overall IS organizational issues; (2) consideration of the basic internal organizational structure of the IS organization; and (3) issues associated with staffing the IS function.

CASE STUDIES

To illustrate several points which are related to MIS organizational and staffing issues, four short case studies are offered. The organizations that are the subject of these cases are quite diverse and represent a variety of approaches to the problems of managing information systems. The reader will find the systems management approaches of the firms described in case A and case X to be remarkably similar. The practices of the firms described in cases B and Y are quite different from the other two.

Case A

Firm A is a very large, worldwide construction company. In 1978, the firm's computing was largely centralized except for IBM S/3 computers located at jobsites around the world. In that year, the controller's organization became convinced that existing accounting and financial information systems were inadequate. Working with the data processing department and an outside "Big Eight" accounting firm, the controller's personnel determined that the current systems could not be salvaged. A major project was mounted to design a world accounting and financial information system. Both systems development and equipment procurement were to be involved.

A project team was set up within the controller's organization to plan the new system. A bright and upcoming controller was appointed as the head of the project. Several outside data processing consultants were involved along with personnel from the accounting firm. In about a year, a detailed project description was completed. The system development, it was estimated, would take 3 years and would cost $36 million in constant 1979 dollars *without* including any equipment costs. Equipment would consist of jobsite computers, regional computers, and a central host computer. Communications would involve some satellite links.

The project established a management advisory group (MAG) consisting of several of the firm's top executives. The charter of this committee was to oversee the management of the project and to represent the project to the senior management of the firm. A technical advisory group (TAG) was also created. This committee consisted of two internal data processing persons and four experts from outside the firm. The TAG was to meet quarterly and advise the MAG on the technical viability of the project.

In late 1979, the project team presented a complete project description, proposal, and cost analysis for comment by the TAG. This report was modified according to the comments of the TAG and submitted for approval to the MAG and corporate management. The plan consisted of the output of the first two phases of a commercially available system design methodology. Complete costs *and* benefits were projected. These figures showed a substantial rate of return from carrying out the project. The project was approved by the firm's senior management.

One of the early tasks of the project team (30 persons initially and peaking at over 200 in the middle of the project) was to select a supporting computer system, systems software, and, where appropriate, applications software. In every case, the selections were fully documented, commented upon by the TAG, and approved by the MAG.

The equipment selection and procurement decision was a major one. At the time the project was initialized, Univac equipment was used as the central host computer for both engineering and scientific purposes. The project team spent approximately 6 months gathering information about using additional Univac equipment or whether IBM computers would be more suitable for the project. A 100-page document was produced which did a very complete analysis of the two alternatives on a myriad of factors. The long-run (10-year) costs of both systems were projected. Two IBM options (S/38 and 43xx) were investigated as jobsite computers. The team recommended the IBM option, and their recommendation was seconded by the TAG, approved by the MAG, and accepted by the firm's executive council. A similar decision process was used for systems software (database management system, operating systems, etc.) and applications software. The final equipment configuration was a large IBM central computer with two 4000 series regional computers and System 38s as jobsite computers.

The project was staffed originally with persons from the accounting firm's management services staff, and from other outside consultants and with people carefully selected from the central DP staff. In general, the latter were the "pick of the crop" and represented the younger, more innovative staff members. Additionally, many members of the design staff employed on the project team were carefully selected from the controller's organization. It turned out that the person chosen to head the project became very interested in DP and, by the time the first several months had passed, had become very well acquainted with technical matters and with system development processes and procedures.

Note that, in this instance, control was passed from data processing (they were represented) to the user dominated project team. There was a well-developed plan in place, and the systems development function was decentralized to the user organization. Procurement decision making was formally done, included cost-benefit analysis, and was consulted upon by outside parties. Standards for equipment and software were established early in the project.

In summary, this project represents one that is very large, extremely complex, and very well managed. A variety of technical and political issues surfaced, were studied, and were resolved. The project is proceeding according to schedule and corporate management is pleased.

Case B

Firm B is a large regional newspaper organization. For several years they had considered building a computer system to support subscriber management, newspaper delivery, billing, and accounting. They spent money on two consulting studies concerning the system, neither of which was satisfactory to management. Both of these had followed a study approach based upon IBM's Business Systems Planning (BSP), which had identified general information requirements and system priorities. Finally, a third consulting study was commissioned from a well-known national consulting organization. Based upon this organization's report, a management commitment was made to initiate the computer project. The forecast was that this project would last about 2 years and would cost approximately $2 million.

Like firm A, this organization created a project organization headed by a user. In this case, the user was an accountant. This project team also included consultants from a computer vendor as well as from the vendor supplying the database management system used on the project. Also on the project team were staff drawn from the data processing department and from user organizations. As with firm A, these were generally the best people available.

Also like firm A, new computing equipment was involved in this project. In this case, however, instead of the computer involved in the project being a supplement to the firm's existing equipment, the system was a replacement for what the firm already had. As a result, in addition to new systems being built for the project, conversion of old programs was under way for old systems.

In the case of firm B, a commercially available systems development methodology was selected and utilized throughout the project. As matters proceeded, it became apparent that the project leader (the accountant) never fully adapted to the data· processing environment and was not comfortable in his position. He had a great deal of trouble dealing with the large number of vendors involved in the project and began to conflict with the manager of data processing concerning equipment issues. In addition, the DP staff on the project were constantly being interrupted to consider issues involved with the system conversion. They had, of course, been involved with a number of the old systems being converted.

As the project progressed, it began to get badly behind schedule. The scope of the project was reduced in order to meet the schedule. The project leader became totally dependent upon one of the DP staff on the project team in making estimates of time and cost for the revised project. These schedules began to slip as well. Meanwhile, the general business climate in which the newspaper was operating began deteriorating badly with the result that cost control became the paramount consideration. The project was continually pressed to hold to cost and time schedules. When continued slippage occurred, the firm's senior management discontinued the project and disbanded the project team.

Although this situation is remarkably similar to the one described at firm A, we have a case of one being a success and the other being a failure. In both cases, the scope of the project was underestimated and the project was changed as it went along. In the one case, the firm's management continued the project and in the other case they killed the project.

Case X

Firm X is a large agricultural cooperative included among the "Fortune 500" organizations. As such, it is widely distributed geographically and managerially decentralized. Acquisitions have recently increased the size and complexity of this organization.

Computing has been largely centralized at the corporate headquarters, but one or two remote divisions have had their own DP staffs and equipment (e.g., an IBM S/3). After a consulting study in the early 1970s, a management system in the organization was established to make computing more effective. The system was drawn from the work of Nolan.[1]

The firm's computing management system utilizes several procedures for ensuring user involvement in system design and development. User liaison is accomplished through having business systems managers in each organizational unit and by insisting that a user act as project manager for each major project. A full system of chargeout is employed, and a very detailed systems development life cycle is in place.

The central information systems organization was created in 1970 and has evolved through a series of products (IBM 360 to 370). User organizations have complained that the chargeout system has penalized them for the inefficiency of the central DP organization. Although the firm's DP organization has been totally responsible for procurement decisions regarding the central hardware, it has had little success controlling proliferation of other types and kinds of equipment throughout the organization. Acquisitions have resulted in several incompatible systems but do not account for all of the diversity.

The remote users have argued that the central DP organization has not been providing efficient and effective service. These users have proposed that they be able to acquire their own minicomputers. Over the objections of the central DP organization, they have been allowed to obtain equipment and to begin hiring programming staffs. At present,

---

[1]Richard L. Nolan, "Managing the Computer Resource: A Stage Hypothesis," *Communications of the ACM*, vol. 16, no. 7, 1973, pp. 399–405.

the firm has several types of remote IBM computers as well as equipment manufactured by Honeywell, Burroughs, Datapoint, and Digital Equipment Corporation. A variety of microcomputers are being acquired by the users. The central DP group is unhappy about this situation and is trying to find out what microcomputers are in the organization by taking an equipment inventory.

All this proliferation has occurred despite the presence of a detailed information systems plan which has substantial user input from the user organizations through the business systems managers. The vice president of information systems, after 11 years in the position, has just left to take a job with another firm.

Despite a very formal planning and management system, this firm is not managing its computing resources at all well. The turnover, the high levels of user dissatisfaction, and the attitude of senior management all reflect problems with firm X's use of computing resources.

Case Y

Firm Y is a nationwide leasing company that is a fully owned subsidiary of a financial organization. After several years of severe trouble with their electronic data processing (EDP) organization, an incoming chief executive officer (CEO) appointed a new vice president (VP) for information systems. A dramatic turnaround occurred in the 3 years after these changes.

During the turnaround period, this firm's centralized DP organization went onto a formalized planning system built upon zero-based budgeting. They also went through a conversion of their computing systems from two IBM 370-158s to an Amdahl V/7. Each of these experiences was very positive for both the DP organization and the users.

The new VP of information systems appointed by the CEO had formerly been head of the company's small operations research organization, which was located in the MIS department. This person had a very good reputation with the users for being responsive to their needs and being able to give them quick solutions to their problems. The CEO installed the new VP in the office next to his. Very shortly, the MIS VP contracted with outside consultants to do a study of the MIS organization which would identify its strengths and weaknesses. A large part of this study involved the attitudes of both user and MIS personnel.

Very soon after the completion of the study, a user training program was conducted for the firm's senior management, again using outside resources. The CEO attended all the sessions and was not interrupted by telephone calls or other disruptions, which showed his interest in information systems. After the conclusion of this session, several others were held for the firm's middle managers.

In 1978, it became apparent that, to meet the competition, the firm's automobile rental organization would have to have computerized counter support at its 1000 nationwide rental offices. The decision to develop the system was made primarily because the competition had (or was developing) such a system and because cost savings and "better management information" could be demonstrated.

As with firms A and B, a project team was set up, but in this instance the team was located organizationally within DP. Heavy user involvement was obtained in the system design as a formal strategy. A part of this strategy involved bringing in key user representatives to a week-long meeting held in the firm's headquarters city. The decision regarding the type of terminal equipment to be acquired was made exclusively by DP personnel after the system needs had been established.

Also, like firm A, this firm had a formal project and information systems plan. They decided to centralize applications on the host computer with "smart" terminals distributed in a network. The development staff was centralized but organized into groups attached to specific user organizations. The "counter support systems" project was extremely successful and is operational today.

About a year after the MIS organization had been under the management of the new VP, an incident occurred which sent a message to this organization about the CEO's attitude toward MIS. He had become aware that one division and its management were very resistant to computerization. After several discussions, the CEO removed the division manager and replaced him with the executive to whom the MIS function had been reporting, the controller. This manager immediately began to work with MIS on computer projects within the division. At the time of this personnel change, the CEO established that the VP of MIS would report directly to him.

In 1981, the company president was elevated to the position of executive vice president for the parent organization. The VP of information systems has been promoted into a line organization as VP in charge of the firm's leasing division, making him the number two person in the firm. Overall, this firm changed a very troublesome computer situation into one that was a very positive experience, all in the period of 3 years.

ORGANIZATIONAL ISSUES

The four case studies provide us with a rich environment in which to examine issues associated with MIS management. Clearly issues of MIS planning and control, equipment selection, and project control are involved in the cases that are given. In this chapter, however, we will focus on two major issues with which MIS managers must deal, those of organization and staffing. These issues are also important features of the situations described in the cases. First, let us consider organizational issues associated with MIS. Two considerations are paramount: (1) how the MIS function is fitted into the overall organization, and (2) how a central MIS function is internally structured. Decisions in each of these areas are related to specific issues or problem areas.

Fitting MIS into the Organization

A major decision that must be made by senior management is where a central MIS organization is to report. Partly for historical reasons, the most common place to find the MIS function is in the accounting and finance organization. In this case, MIS normally reports to the controller or the vice president of finance. One may alternatively find the MIS department reporting to: (1) a vice president of administration, (2) the senior executive of an operating division, (3) an executive vice president, (4) the CEO. In the latter case, the chief information officer (CIO) usually carries the title of vice president. The actual title may be vice president of MIS, vice president of administrative services, or vice president of information resources. The various possibilities are shown in Figure 3-1.

The title of the CIO and the position to whom this person reports reflect, in many cases, the support being shown by executive management for the MIS function. This issue is covered in more detail below.

Figure 3-1 Alternative Locations for the Information Systems Function

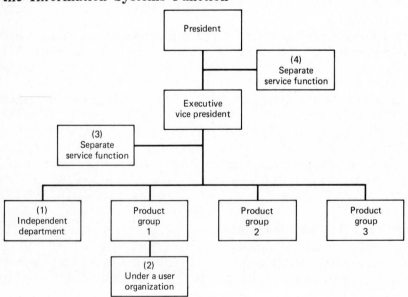

Note here, however, that firm Y, in one of the successful situations described in the case studies, used the reporting relationship to signify to the overall organization the CEO's strong support for MIS.

The reporting relationship of the MIS function is also important in that it reflects the focus of the function. If MIS reports in the accounting-finance line, there is often a tendency to emphasize accounting and finance applications at the expense of those in the marketing, production, and logistical areas. The MIS function needs to take as broad a view as possible to be most effective.

In cases in which the information function is given the title of information resource management or administrative services, it is common that the organization has the charter to do much more than just provide data processing services. In these instances the function usually involves itself in planning and providing total information services for the entire organization. Given the movement of automated information processing activities into the office, the blending of data processing and data communications, and the emergence of other advanced technologies, this type of reporting relationship is very desirable.

Guidelines. There are two important guidelines associated with slotting MIS into the overall organization. The first of these follows from the fact that there appears to be a relationship between the reporting level of the MIS function and the success of the function, especially if the function reports to the CEO. It has been the authors' experience that the level of MIS success is greatly enhanced in cases in which the CEO considers the MIS function an integral part of the business and chooses to emphasize this fact by having the function report directly to the top of the organization.

The second guideline is that it is far better to have a position of VP of administration or director of information resource management than to have the information systems function report to a specific function such as accounting. There are two reasons for this. The first reason is the one mentioned above, that the function needs to have as broad a perspective as possible regarding systems priorities. A second reason is that, with technology moving so fast and in so many areas, it is important to take more than just a data processing or computer perspective. New and related technologies such as data communications, micrographics, reprographics, and word processing illustrate this situation.

Centralization-Decentralization

In the modern computing environment, it is often desirable to distribute equipment and data throughout the organization. We frequently mean this type of distribution when thinking about distributed data processing (see Chapter 11). It is also possible to distribute the development function and the management control of the development process throughout the organization. The latter functions are sometimes not thought of when considering distributed data processing.

All the case studies except case B involved the distribution of computing hardware, and case A depicted a situation in which organizational data was distributed. Cases A and B described instances of the development process being distributed to the user organization. In both cases, a project development team was created and reported to the user organization in the function addressed by the project. In case Y, a project team was created but was housed within the data processing organization. None of the case studies involved the situation in which a permanent development staff is housed within a user organization. Although rare, this approach is becoming more common.

The fact that the case studies describe one instance of the successful distribution of the development function (case A), one instance of an unsuccessful distribution of the development process (case B), and one case of the successful use of a project team within the central DP organization (case Y) shows that there is nothing about distributing or not distributing that will guarantee success or failure. The important thing to note about the distribution of the development process is that the option exists and, if properly performed, may offer advantages in the building of very large systems.

Case X involved a situation in which many systems (which were relatively unsuccessful in terms of user acceptance) were developed centrally. This case also involved the development of systems by programming staffs located in geographically decentralized organizational components. In this case, there was a profusion of computer equipment involved as well as the use of a variety of developmental practices. Whereas the development of systems by the central DP staff was "highly managed," there was little central control of the decentralized computing activity. Senior management basically said that the decentralized units could do anything they pleased with regard to systems that were particular to only one unit.

Case X describes a situation in which an attempt was made to provide centralized computing in a very geographically decentralized and managerially decentralized organization. The company tried to do this with a central development staff and centralized equipment for some systems, using a highly managed approach. At the same time, they gave decentralized units complete autonomy to do as they pleased regarding purely local applications. The case study certainly shows that the central systems were less than successful. We also know of at least one situation in which a desirable integration of two local systems was impractical because of incompatible equipment and software. Firm X was faced with a difficult organizational problem from a computing standpoint. Although they tried hard, they generally failed to slot computing effectively into the organization with which they had to work.

There are several summary comments that can be made regarding the centralization-decentralization of computing personnel and the management control of the systems development process. One is that the overall decisions as to whether development will be distributed are not made by the MIS manager. In most cases, these decisions are made by senior management and provide the environment within which the MIS manager must operate. Certainly, in firms A and B, this was the case. Similarly, the centralization-decentralization pattern of development encountered in case X was the result of a decision made by executive management.

In addition, it is our opinion that to completely give up on central planning and control of the information systems function is folly. To simply say that subunits, which in many cases represent large-scale profit centers, can do as they please regarding equipment and development practices is to shirk a senior management responsibility.

Finally, distribution of resources (especially systems personnel) is not always doomed to failure, nor is it a prescription for success. Depending upon the situation, this action can be very effective, but the personnel involved must be carefully selected and a managerial system must be in place to coordinate with the central DP function and with overall corporate activities.

Advantages and Disadvantages. Centralizing development has certain advantages and disadvantages and so does the decentralization of this function. It is worthwhile reviewing some of the arguments for each of the approaches. As these are being read, keep in mind that the strengths of one tend to be the weaknesses of the other.' Arguments for centralization:

1. It is much easier to consolidate financial and operating data for reporting and evaluation purposes. Without centralization, consolidation is usually obstructed by incompatibilities of different systems, system designs, and data formats.

2. It is easier to attract and manage computer professionals in a centralized system. Centralization, moreover, reduces the impact of both shortages and turnover of development personnel by permitting a staff of larger size. In addition, the larger staff provides a greater opportunity to provide specialists such as capacity planners or data communications experts.

3. Top management can more easily control operating divisions which use uniform information reporting systems. When units individually develop their own reporting systems, there are usually discrepancies in data used, data definitions, and reporting formats. Through centralized systems development, uniformity can be maintained.

4. There is frequently an economy of scale to be gained by centralizing the development staff. Efficiencies are afforded by the

reduction in duplication of effort and better control of the allocation of systems analysis and programming activities.

Arguments for decentralization:

1. A major reason for decentralizing the development function is that the development staff is closer to local problems and gets to know the business of the user better than if the staff were located elsewhere. In general, the argument is that the users are more satisfied with these systems than they are with those developed centrally because their needs are met better.

2. Computer equipment and local staff can be more responsive to both production and development requirements when they are decentralized to user departments. User departments have more discretion in scheduling their resources than centralized groups do. They do not have to compete with other departments for resources.

3. When computer equipment and development groups are decentralized to user departments, it is much easier to allocate their costs. This condition tends to make the user departments more sensitive to cost-benefit considerations because the computing costs directly affect the profitability of their department.

Overall Recommendations. The following guidelines are helpful in making a decision on whether to centralize or decentralize.

Centralized equipment and/or staff tend to be best suited for the following situations:

   I. Information systems for top-level management
  II. Organizationwide, homogeneous functions such as payroll, personnel, and common accounting functions
 III. Work that does not require rapid response time and that can be done more economically on a centralized basis
 IV. Organizational functions that are too small to justify their own computing equipment and/or staff
  V. Situations where integration of information technically requires centralized processing (e.g., airline reservations)

Decentralized equipment and/or staff tend to be best suited for the following situations:

   I. Situations where rapid and flexible response time for development and/or production is required
  II. Situations where the systems are unique and heterogeneous to a decentralized operation (e.g., a conglomerate may own several companies that are in different businesses)
 III. Information systems for which there is no compelling reason to centralize (e.g., a stand-alone inventory system)

The four companies described in the case studies had different approaches to the centralization-decentralization situation. Company Y was very successful using a centralized format. Company A was successful taking a partially decentralized approach in that they used a project team. Company B, taking a similar approach, failed. Company X totally failed to match their computing organization to their overall organizational structure. Their lack of success can be partially attributed to the fact that they tried to employ a centralized MIS organization under conditions of extreme organizational decentralization. A large retail organization, facing similar organizational circumstances, has taken a decentralized approach and has been highly successful. This organization has separate divisions in the department store business, the discount business, and the specialty business (e.g., bookstores). The firm argues that because the divisions are different in design, merchandise offerings, and market orientation, they need total autonomy. These conditions and philosophy have resulted in separate, freestanding computing organizations which have been highly successful. Company X would have been a more successful computer user had it adhered to a similar approach to the relationship between the MIS function and the overall organization.

Management Support and Image Enhancement

The authors have noted that two factors seem to stand out in those organizations that tend to be successful computer users: the support shown for the MIS function by the organization's senior management and the consequent image the function has in the organization. In the case studies, company Y is a classic example of this situation. Recall that the new CEO took a number of actions to show support for the MIS function and enhance the image of the function.

Some of these actions are obvious and others are more subtle. Among the more obvious are (1) putting the MIS VP's office next to the CEO's, (2) supporting an executive training series in MIS and attending the sessions in an uninterrupted manner, (3) elevating the head of MIS to vice president reporting to the CEO instead of having a "staff vice president" reporting to the controller. Less obvious is that the CEO used the organizational reward system to show support for MIS. The fact that a division head who was not supportive of MIS was replaced received considerable notice in the organization. Budget commitment to the MIS function plus the undertaking of a major MIS project affecting the entire rental organization are other signs of support for MIS in the case of firm Y. Overall, the management support and image enhancement provided in the organization are among the very best ever observed by the authors. It is our belief that this situation, coupled with good management on the part of the MIS vice president, was greatly responsible for one of the most dramatic turnarounds we have ever seen in an organization's MIS effectiveness.

Guidelines. The attitudes and actions of senior management regarding the MIS function are extremely important to the function's success. Unfortunately, it is simple to preach the sorts of things that management "ought to do." It is quite another thing to bring about the proper actions. At this point perhaps the best we can do is to identify some of the sorts of actions on the part of senior management that would be beneficial:

1. Place the MIS function in the organization in such a way that it is visible, has access to senior management's attention, and is slotted so as to have a broad perspective regarding supply of the organization's information.

2. Provide adequate resources for the MIS function.

3. Give time and effort to MIS issues facing the organization. In other words, become involved with MIS planning, policy, and control issues.

4. Use the organizational reward system to support those individuals and subunits that are doing the right things regarding MIS and its use.

5. Select an MIS manager who is a *manager*, one who can be a part of the senior management team, and treat this person as part of this team.

The three "external" issues regarding the MIS organization -- the reporting relationship, the degree of centralization-decentralization, and the amount of support shown for the function by top management -- all can be asserted to be associated with MIS success. The decisions involved in these areas are, in general, made by senior management, not by MIS managers. It is important that senior management appreciate the importance of these decisions and be made aware of the guidelines that have been offered.

BASIC ORGANIZATIONAL STRUCTURE

One of the most important managerial issues regarding MIS is that of structuring the MIS organization itself. This must be done keeping in mind issues of managerial efficiency and the overall effectiveness of the unit (especially in serving the needs of the users). Whereas the issues of the MIS function's relationship with the overall organization are often beyond the MIS manager's purview, decisions involving the internal structure of the organization are usually made by the MIS manager. The most common basic structure of an information systems organization is shown in Figure 3-2. Note that the computer operations function and the systems development function report to the chief information officer (CIO).

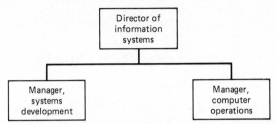

Figure 3-2 Basic Structure of an Information Systems Organization

There have recently been instances in which development and computer operations have been separated into different parts of the organization but this is relatively uncommon at present. The argument favoring such a departure is that the data processing operation is much like a factory and should be run as such. Thus, being such a departure from systems development, the operations function needs a completely different type of management and should report to a different superior manager. The discussion which follows will assume that the more normal basic structure shown in Figure 3-2 is employed.

The internal structure of the information systems organization must cope with a number of situations. One involves the trade-off between managerial flexibility and efficiency versus service to the user. Another is the issue of maintaining existing systems and providing for evolution of these systems as user needs change and/or new external requirements become apparent. A third concerns the monitoring of the information systems function by the overall organization, setting the priorities for the organization, and aligning the information systems planning with overall organizational directions. In addition, there are several other organizational issues that do not fit in any one category.

Managerial Efficiency versus User Service

From an efficiency standpoint, the MIS manager would prefer to structure the development function as shown in Figure 3-3. (We are

Figure 3-3 Information Systems Organization Structured for Managerial Flexibility

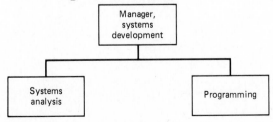

assuming here that one group of persons acts as analysts and another group does the programming.) The beauty of this organization is that it is very flexible. If new systems development requirements come along, it is easy to assign persons from the analysis and programming pool to do the job. The difficulty, especially from a user perspective, is that the analysts and programmers assigned to their project may have no experience with the problem or familiarity with the problem area. In addition, they are often an unknown quantity since they may not have worked before with this user.

An attempt to ease these problems has resulted in another structure which is shown in Figure 3-4. Note that another subunit, user liaison, has been added. The persons in this unit, typically experienced senior analysts, are responsible for working with the user organizations to determine their information needs and with the analysts and programmers to meet these needs. Typically, one person from the user liaison group works with one user organization. In this way the user liaison gets to know the user's business and becomes well known to persons in the user organization. In addition, the user liaison can translate business problems into a more technical language when communicating with the systems developers. One problem of this organization is that there is often confusion about the responsibilities and the authority of the user liaison and the responsibilities and the authority of the users or systems personnel. Another problem is that this system is very dependent on the skills of each user liaison.

Another organizational form which has been tried to balance managerial needs and user requirements is a matrix organization, as shown in Figure 3-5. In a matrix organization, there is a pool of programmers and there is a pool of analysts. The people in these pools report to positions with titles such as manager of programming, and manager of analysis, respectively. In addition, however, there is a subunit composed of project leaders. These persons report to a manager, perhaps having the title of manager of project development. When a new project comes along, it is assigned to a project leader who negotiates with the manager of analysis and with the manager of programming to

Figure 3-4 Information Systems Organization Structured with Links to User Organization

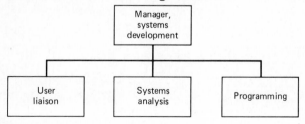

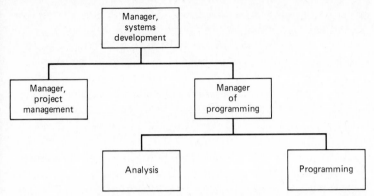

Figure 3-5 Information Systems Organization in Matrix Form

form a project team. A programmer or analyst is typically involved with one project at a time, but a project leader may be involved with as many as three projects at the same time. The project leaders tend to work with particular user organizations but the analysts and programmers do not. This organizational form is very efficient, but it has the disadvantage of each analyst and each programmer having two bosses, because each of these persons reports to a project leader for project-related matters and to the manager of their function for overall matters. Performance is evaluated by the functional manager with input from project leaders with whom an individual has worked. This system has great potential for difficulties when conflicts arise.

Figure 3-6 shows what the authors believe is the best compromise structure. This is a functional organization in which analysts and programmers are grouped to service a particular user group. This is difficult to manage in the sense that the structure is not very flexible. Slack resources may exist in one subunit while another is overloaded. This shortcoming is balanced by the fact that, over time, the systems development personnel become very familiar with the function they are serving. Furthermore, by working together over many projects, many

Figure 3-6 Information Systems Organization Structured by User Functions

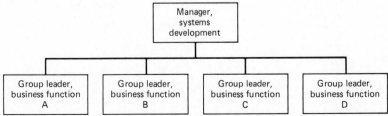

strong interpersonal relationships are formed which usually work well to ease problems of communication and systems implementation.

Before leaving this topic, it should be noted that for very large projects it is often the case that special project teams are formed. In the case studies, companies A, B, and Y all used this approach. Another organizational form not specifically discussed because of an assumption of a centralized information systems function is to place the analysis and programming function in the user organization. This is really a variant of the functional structure. This has been a recent trend, but in the authors' opinion should be approached with caution. Unless good plans and standards are in place and the user organization is very familiar with managing data processing, many difficulties, not the least of which is cost escalation, can occur when systems development is distributed.

Analysis and Programming

In the discussion above, it was assumed that one set of persons did systems analysis and another group did programming. This is only one way of dividing the systems development task. Another, obviously, is to have a person perform both analysis and programming. Some data processing organizations do it one way and others do it the other. Research has shown that this issue involves a trade-off between efficiency and effectiveness. Powers and Dickson found that when the functions were separated, projects tended to be performed more efficiently, as they came in closer to cost and time estimates.[2] On the other hand, using the separate functions also tended to produce projects with less satisfied users.

Another issue to keep in mind involves career paths. Frequently it is the practice to start persons out in programming and, over time, move them into analysis. Vitalari's research questions this practice.[3] He found that successful systems analysts tended to solve problems differently from their less successful counterparts. Furthermore, the kind of problem solving that was associated with successful performance had little to do with programming skills. Thus, we may question whether persons who are good programmers will be good analysts. Evidence is building which suggests that the keys to successful systems analysis involve problem solving, interpersonal communication skills, and organizational skills. It may be that analysts should be specially recruited and have different training from those persons who have had a career writing computer programs.

[2]R. Powers and G. Dickson, "MIS Project Management: Myths, Opinions, and Reality," *California Management Review,* vol. 15, no. 3, Spring 1973, pp. 147-156.

[3]N. Vitalari and G.W. Dickson, "An Investigation of the Problem Solving Behavior of Systems Analysts," *Communications of the ACM,* vol. 26, no. 10, November, 1983.

Maintenance

Another issue, whose resolution will affect the MIS internal organization chart, is maintaining existing systems. Two major alternatives exist for performing this function. The first is to have the person or persons who developed the system be responsible for correcting any errors that show up after the system is put into operation. These persons also modify the system as changes come up as a result of new user needs or business requirements. The second approach to dealing with system change is to create a separate maintenance function which handles all system modifications of a modest nature. Sometimes such a function is placed in the systems development subunit, and sometimes the function is found in the systems operations subunit.

Each of the two approaches to performing systems maintenance has advantages and disadvantages. Having the systems developers do their own maintenance is efficient. The developers know the system well and can more easily make modifications. The difficulty is that if these persons know they will be doing their own maintenance, they tend to keep some of the documentation in their heads rather than writing everything down in the system documentation. Further, if this is the practice and someone leaves, it is very difficult for a new person to figure out what needs to be done to modify the system. Another difficulty with this approach is that developers can spend an excessive amount of their time performing maintenance. In many cases, this allocation of time is difficult to track, and therefore, the organization does not recognize the amount of its resources being allocated to maintenance.

Having a separate maintenance function has the disadvantage that the maintenance programmers have a lot of learning to do each time a new task is encountered. Further, doing nothing but systems maintenance can get boring to many persons if they are in this function for a long period of time. On the other hand, some people like to do maintenance programming and are very good at it. Some organizations use maintenance programming as a first year training assignment for new programmers. Other advantages of a separate maintenance group are that it tends to force good system documentation on the part of developers, it makes for easy accounting of maintenance activity, and it buffers the organization against losing key development personnel.

On balance, the advantages of a separate maintenance function outweigh the disadvantages in the opinion of the authors. We recommend the creation of a maintenance function and even see some advantage in placing this subfunction in the operations unit.

The Information Center Concept

The concept of an "information center" as an addition to the MIS organization has recently appeared. This subunit would be set up to help users get certain systems built quickly and would provide tools which could be employed by users to build their own systems. Tools such as database management systems (see Chapter 8), report generators and query languages, time-sharing, and fourth-generation software packages (see Chapter 9) would be provided.

The concept, furthermore, would suggest that the few persons working in the center should be especially user-oriented in their outlook. This attitude should be shown in the training provided by the staff at the center and in the way they help the users with any problems that they might have. One medium-sized high-technology company has even used its reward system to encourage the use of new tools. This company employs an information center within its MIS function. Users who take classes in the tools provided by the center and become "certified" in their use receive a $250 bonus. Another large firm provides a fourth-generation language through its information center to its users. The particular package made available is a heavy consumer of computing resources if it is not used efficiently in an application. If the use is "one shot," the MIS function does not care how inefficient the user may be. But, if the use becomes repetitive, then the personnel of the information center will work with the user to streamline the application to make the use of the software more efficient.

The information center is also an ideal way to encourage the use of microcomputers   and to manage their proliferation. Certain micro- computers can be designated for suppport, training classes can be held in their use, software for them can be made available, and an agreement can be made to help users who have trouble with the supported microcomputers. This approach can be one key in effectively controlling the distribution of microcomputers throughout the organization.

Finally, the information center can be used as a place to house a few "commandos," or "guerrilla warriors," who can be available to build important user systems very quickly. These systems, frequently stand-alone decision support systems (see Chapter 9), can be constructed by the staff of the information center much more quickly than can systems using traditional software and systems development methods. Because of the impact of such systems and the rapidity with which they can be made available, the information systems function often gets a very good reputation in the user community when this approach is taken.

The Steering Committee

The company described in case X was an example of a very "highly managed" information systems organization. Yet, the situation described was not a very successful one. One of the management tools used by firm X was a corporate steering committee. A group of several senior managers representing various organizational units was set up to establish information systems priorities and to ensure that the information systems function was meeting the needs of the enterprise. This group was not successful in achieving these objectives. The problem with the steering committee set up by firm X, like many such committees, was that its members only paid lip service to their responsibilities. In this case, the committee met quarterly and simply "blessed" the actions and recommendations made by the vice president of information systems. In effect, they never made the mental commitment to perform the tasks they should have performed as a high-level steering committee.

Despite the fact that the situation described here is typical of what many companies have experienced when they have attempted to set up a corporate steering committee to oversee the information systems function, others have used such a committee very positively. What is the difference? Perhaps there are two key reasons why some committees are successful and others are not. The first reason is associated with the support-and-image issue discussed above. It is vitally important that the most senior member of the steering committee be committed to the organization's successful use of computing resources and show this commitment by words and deeds. If the senior member of the committee, frequently the CEO or a senior vice president, has taken the time to understand the responsibilities regarding MIS and to exercise this knowledge on the steering committee, then a major step toward a successful MIS experience has been taken. The proper signals by this corporate sponsor or mentor to the others in the organization will enhance the importance of the information systems function. One very simple way to do this is by proper participation in the steering committee.

The second reason that some steering committees are successful is that they do the proper things and do them well. Nolan describes the duties of the steering committee as follows:[4]

1. Direction setting: This means to work on linking the corporate strategy with the computer strategy. Planning is the key activity.

2. Rationing: The committee approves the allocation of resources within the information systems organization.

3. Structuring: The committee deals with how the MIS function is slotted in the overall organization. The issue of centralization-decentralization of MIS resources must be resolved.

4. Staffing: Key MIS personnel decisions involve a consultation-and-approval process. The selection of the CIO is of paramount importance.

5. Evaluating: The committee should establish performance measures for the function and see that they are met.

---

[4]R. Nolan, "Managing Information Systems by Committee," *Harvard Business Review*, vol. 60, no. 4, July-August 1982, pp. 72-79.

The most successful MIS steering committees typically are well supported with a staff. These committees react well to the plans and actions of others but do not work especially well in developing plans and actions. Thus their activities are frequently iterative in nature. Material is presented to the committee, modifications are requested and made, and the committee reacts again. Often several cycles are involved.

The firm described in case A effectively used both an MIS corporate steering committee and a major project steering committee (referred to as the management action group). One source of input to the latter group in their deliberations was the evaluation and recommendations made by the technical advisory group (a small group of systems experts composed of persons from outside the company).

Outside Advisors

One tactic that has been successfully used by a few firms and can be expected to become more popular in the future is to use outside experts in an advisory capacity that differs from the typical consultant's role. The technical advisory group used to advise the management action group in case A is an example of this sort of arrangement. These advisory groups are small, typically three or four persons. Each person is a recognized expert, and all usually come from different outside sources. Some may be consultants, some may be professors, and some may be experts from a noncompeting firm. These groups most often give advice and counsel to the head of MIS, to a corporate steering committee, or to the head of a large project team.

The outside advisory group typically meets only periodically, usually for 2 or 3 days, and reviews an entire project or the MIS function itself. In some cases, they spend a good deal of time getting reports from project personnel or MIS managers on the state of affairs. At the conclusion of their meeting, they draft a formal report on both the strengths and the weaknesses of the project or function they are evaluating. These outside experts can provide great comfort to nontechnical managers regarding the health and/or risks of a project. Look to see more use of these small groups in MIS organizations in the future.

STAFFING

Although MIS staffing does not show up as an explicit problem in any of the four cases at the beginning of this chapter, staffing issues were major considerations in the two instances involving project teams. In each case, the project leader had the problem of selecting good personnel for the project team. In firm A, for instance, there were felt to be too many team members from outside consulting firms on the project after about a year, and these persons had to be replaced with professionals hired from outside the firm. Firm B, on the other hand, put so many of its good people from the centralized MIS group on the project team that it had to replace them with newly hired persons from outside the firm. Staffing the MIS function has traditionally been a problem due to three factors: demand and supply, evaluating qualifications, and compliance with affirmative action guidelines.

Difficulties in Staffing

The lack of qualified MIS professionals to fill the immense demand is well known. MIS professionals rank third behind physicians and veterinarians for the career area with the greatest shortage of professionals during the next decade. This shortage has resulted in "pirating" among organizations as they attempt to hire staff away from each other. It also results in ambitious MIS professionals job-hopping to get higher salaries. And, of course, the shortage results in less-than-qualified people being placed in positions that they are not prepared for.

Evaluating the qualifications of applicants for MIS positions was difficult in the early years of MIS and has gotten worse with the proliferation of specialization in MIS positions, as shown in Figure 3-7.

Figure 3-7 Proliferation of MIS Positions Due to Increased Specialization

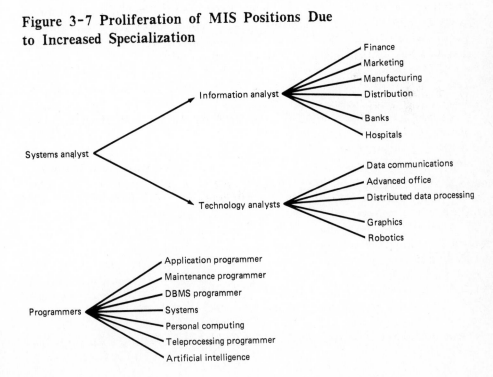

For example, a few years ago, selecting a computer programmer would typically consist of finding someone with COBOL programming experience (usually with accounting applications). Today, technological innovations such as database management systems, teleprocessing, distributed data processing, advanced office systems, decision support systems, and computer-assisted design greatly differentiate skills of programmers and systems designers. Also, the types of applications undertaken have changed substantially. Today, instead of primarily being used in accounting applications, information systems are used in virtually all aspects of organizational operations and decision making.

Title VII of the Civil Rights Act of 1964 and the advent of affirmative action programs have further complicated the problem of personnel selection from a procedural perspective. The number of complaints of discrimination, especially those involving race and sex, has grown steadily during the years since this civil rights law has been operational.

Therefore, management's problem is threefold. First, there are not enough qualified MIS professionals to go around; second, it is increasingly difficult to evaluate what have become more specialized and diversified qualifications; and third, personnel selections must be justifiable if they are audited by an affirmative action officer of the Equal Employment Opportunity Commission (EEOC). Justifying personnel selections can be difficult on those occasions when, as a result of national advertising, several hundred applicants apply for a position. Only one has to file a complaint because he or she feels discriminated against because of age, sex, race, or religion to require the reexamination of the entire selection process.

MIS Positions

Over the more than two decades organizations have had business computers, the types of jobs available in the computing function have expanded dramatically. At first only a few job titles were to be recognized. Now, a vast array of types of jobs exist in computing. Table 3-1 lists only a few job titles and a brief explanation of what each job entails. Also shown in the table is the 1982 average salary for each job as reported by the magazine *Datamation*.[5]

Many of the jobs shown in Table 3-1 have several levels depending upon educational level and experience. The average salaries shown are based upon the senior level and are reported by firms having a data processing budget in excess of $1 million per year. The senior level is based upon a bachelor's degree and a minimum of 4 years DP

[5]Stephen B. Gray, "DP Salary Survey," *Datamation*, vol. 28, no. 11, October 1982, pp. 114-131.

Table 3-1 MIS jobs with brief descriptions and average salary levels

1. *Vice President of MIS:* The senior executive responsible for all corporate information systems. Responsible for long-range planning, budgeting, and operations ($52,400).

2. *Director of Data Processing:* In charge of all DP at the divisional or department level. Responsibilities parallel those of corporate officers, but may be at least partially guided by decisions made at corporate level ($50,700).

3. *Systems Analyst:* Confers with users to define and formulate logical statements of business problems and devise procedures for solutions through use of DP systems ($28,000).

4. *Applications Programmer:* Develops, designs, and prepares computer programs ($28,200).

5. *Systems Analyst/Programmer:* Performs the functions of both the systems analyst and applications programming positions ($28,600).

6. *Systems Programmer:* Programs, maintains, and introduces modifications to systems software ($35,300).

7. *Database Administrator:* Analyzes an application's computerized information requirements and coordinates data collection and storage needs ($33,600).

8. *Data Communications Analyst:* Specializes in network design, traffic analysis, and data communications software ($28,100).

experience. Persons with lesser qualifications may fit either the intermediate or junior levels. The average pay of these levels is approximately 10 to 15 percent lower for each reduction in level. Several other factors also influence the average salary: location in the country, the type of industry, and the size of the data processing organization.

Job Descriptions

The common approach to conveying to prospective employees the availability and merits of a job opening is a job description. The very brief job descriptions shown in Table 3-1 are examples, but actual job descriptions are much richer. Job descriptions, particularly detailed job descriptions, are frequently used as a framework to evaluate candidates' qualifications and to justify selection of one candidate over others. To be used in this manner, it is imperative that job descriptions are detailed and current.

Well-defined position requirements can provide assistance in and substantiation for selecting job applicants. They have been successful for well-defined and relatively stable positions such as data entry operators, control clerks, and computer operators. However, in the more technologically diversified positions of programming, systems analysis, technical services, and management, job descriptions usually lack the precision and the flexibility to satisfactorily serve as the basis for a personnel selection exercise.

For example, in filling a programmer slot in one situation, management might be looking for an individual with extensive payroll experience, familiarity with a certain database language, and experience with a particular teleprocessing monitor on a certain hardware configuration using a specific operating system. In filling another programmer position in the same organization, management might be interested in an individual with order entry experience, the ability to utilize distributed data processing with a specific minicomputer, and the ability to program microprocessor-based intelligent terminals. In still another situation, management might need a programmer proficient at computer-aided design programming to work with the engineering department.

For the three positions discussed above, no single job description is going to adequately define or provide for selection criteria of one candidate over another. Also, a single programming manager is not likely to have the requisite expertise to properly evaluate all three candidates with or without detailed job descriptions.

Personnel Selection

There are two basic ways in which the data processing department can obtain personnel. The first, and most common, is to go out on the open job market and obtain experienced personnel. This method, although the most expensive, is frequently employed since the organization probably needs personnel who are productive as soon as possible. In these days of shortages in computing personnel, it is usually quite expensive to take this approach, but it may be necessary. In addition to being expensive directly, outside hiring can have some hidden costs. This can occur when the outside person is brought in at a salary so high that it is above others in the organization having equal or superior qualifications. In these cases, the internal personnel may have to have salary increases to keep them happy.

A second method of acquiring DP personnel is to provide training to people without DP skills. These persons can come from within the organization or be newly hired from outside. The firm described in case Y was very successful in training about 15 persons in data processing that had previously been secretaries, clerks, and the like. They put these persons through a training program that took almost a year. The results were very satisfactory, especially since there was the feeling that the employees, having spent a number of years with the firm, would be more loyal than would otherwise be the case.

Training persons in data processing can also be expensive because of the training costs, even though the salary levels of the personnel are often much less than would be the case if experienced personnel were hired from outside. There is also the cost of having inexperienced personnel for a period of time. However, there are advantages in terms of firm loyalty and having a continuous supply of trained persons. Many of these junior persons can be groomed for eventual managerial positions. When only outside technical persons are added to the DP organization, it is often the case that embryo managers are missing when they are needed.

Our recommendation is that, if possible, a mixed strategy be employed regarding personnel. First, have a good training program for entry-level DP personnel. This approach is necessary to ensure a continuing flow of good DP personnel, especially potential team leaders and junior managers. Second, where key skills are necessary and are needed in a short time frame, go to the marketplace to acquire these talents quickly.

No matter what the source of the personnel, one of the most difficult tasks is selecting among potential job candidates. In addition to normal interviewing, there are a few formal techniques available that have proved to be of use in selecting data processing personnel.

Testing. Tests have been employed for a number of years to determine which people will make successful computer programmers and analysts. These aptitude tests can be administered to potential candidates and can be used to select those who will be given training. Three well-known tests are the Wolfe test from Wolfe Computer Aptitude Testing, Ltd., the Berger test from Psychometrics, Inc., and the Computer Programmer Aptitude Battery distributed by Science Research Associates, a subsidiary of IBM. Many DP managers report that persons who score very high on these tests do very well as programmers. High or moderate scores appear, on the basis of experience, to be difficult to interpret.

There are several cautions to consider regarding testing. The first is that, according to the Equal Opportunity Employment Act, the aptitude tests must be "valid." Unless they pass rigid validity standards, the user may be faced with a class action suit. This means that it is much better to use popular (and, hopefully, validated) tests than to develop a "homegrown" test. A second caution is that most of these tests aim at measuring programming aptitude and one should not assume that they are at all valid for evaluating systems analyst skills. The Berger test supplies a good deal of information regarding its validity. The Wolfe test is reported to take about 5 1/2 hours whereas the Berger test can be completed in approximately half this time.

A final word of caution is that the tests are only indicators and to follow their results without any deviation is very limiting. In other words, their results (although especially useful in choosing entry-level persons for DP training) should be used only as guidelines.

For more senior positions, the interview by a personnel specialist and a manager or two is often used in selection. There is a relatively new approach which supplements these sorts of interviews and has been shown to lead to good selection decisions: the use of persons in the selection process that will be peers of the prospective employee.

Group Analysis. To resolve the deficiencies inherent in having a manager and/or a personnel specialist attempt to recruit, evaluate, select, and, if necessary, justify a personnel selection, staffing based upon group analysis techniques has proved effective.[6] By using a group of people to conduct a staffing exercise, the diverse expertise necessary to define and evaluate various qualification requirements can be accomplished. The type of procedure used to conduct a staffing decision by group analysis is outlined below.

Formulate Selection Group. The group designated to perform a personnel selection should be composed of individuals collectively competent to define and evaluate all key attributes necessary to fill a vacant position. Preferably, the members of the selection group should have a vested interest in the successful filling of the position. An essential group member (and the likely chairperson) is the immediate supervisor of the position to be filled. Other potential members of the committee include members of the candidates' peer group, technical specialists, consultants, and members of the user community. Peers, technical specialists, and, if necessary, consultants can help considerably in defining and evaluating technical skills. Users can assist in defining and evaluating the user-relevant expertise of candidates.

By having a diversified selection group of three to six members, a rigorous evaluation process can be undertaken. Also, a new employee is likely to gain more acceptance from the organization when it is known that a select group of people collectively evaluated the new employee instead of only the immediate supervisor making the evaluation.

Determine and Rate Attributes. The selection group should define the various attributes or qualifications a candidate should have to properly perform the duties of the position being filled. Attributes are typically categorized under such subjects as education, work experience, test scores (if applicable), and, when relevant, management experience. A sample profile of attributes for a management position is illustrated in Figure 3-8.

Once attributes are defined, the next step is to weight the value of each attribute as it relates to the position under consideration using, for example, a 10-point scale for each attribute. This is a critical step in the process because it prevents the group or members of the group from

[6]H. Albert Napier, "Peer Evaluaton Selects Professionals." *Journal of Systems Management,* January 1980, pp. 6-9; and James C. Wetherbe, and V. Thomas Dock, "Breaking the Description Dilemma: Personnel Selection by Group Analysis," *Datamation,* December 1978, pp. 16-42.

Attribute	Weight
Education	
EDP Training	8
Bachelors	10
Masters	3
	21
Work Experience	
Financial Applications	8
COBOL	8
Assembler	5
Online	6
General EDP	8
	35
Management Experience	
Supervisory Responsibilities	8
Professional Training	4
Communication	8
	20

Figure 3-8 Attributes and Weights for the Position of Manager of Programming for Financial Institutions

overemphasizing an attribute when evaluating a specific candidate for a position. For example, it may prevent a manager who is unable to evaluate technical skills from placing too much emphasis on the only attributes he or she is qualified to evaluate, such as education or interpersonal skills. Sample weights for attributes are also illustrated in Figure 3-8.

Score Applicants. Applicants are scored by having each member of the group review applications or resumes and score each candidate on a scale, say from 1 to 5, on each attribute. In those cases where a group member is unqualified to score a specific attribute, he or she should defer to those group members who are qualified. Scoring can be done individually and the results combined for discussion, or the scoring can be done collectively as a group effort. Whatever method is used, attribute scores should be averaged and then totaled to compute a composite score for each applicant.

The scoring of applicants provides the means for determining which applicants should be considered for interviews. It also provides documentation to justify reasons for selecting specific applicants for interviews over the other applicants. Since this is a group decision based upon a well documented and rigorous process, excellent justification is available should affirmative action issues be raised by any applicants who complain of unfair treatment.

It is, of course, important that the scoring criteria be fair and justifiable. For example, for most MIS positions it is appropriate to score an applicant with a degree in MIS over an applicant with a degree in general business, whereas the applicant with a degree in general business could justifiably be scored higher than an applicant with a degree in history. Figure 3-9 illustrates what an applicant score sheet might look like.

Interview Top Applicants. Ideally, each of the top two or three candidates should be interviewed. The interview should consist of a 1- or 2-day visit to the MIS department depending upon the importance and the level of the position being filled. The total time interval between candidates' visits should be as short as possible to ensure a continuity of evaluation of all candidates. Each candidate should meet with the various members of the selection group on a one-on-one basis and then meet with the entire group. The one-on-one meetings appear to be best used to establish rapport with the candidate and to let him or her ask most of the questions. The group interview is an excellent forum for the group members to ask challenging questions of the candidate where the entire group can observe the candidate's responses.

After the meeting with the candidate, the group should meet to discuss their perceptions of the candidate and reevaluate the impact of those perceptions on the scores of the applicant. That is, the group may want to adjust the original scores that were based upon application or resume evaluations after they have the advantage of the greater insight that is possible from a personal interview.

Select a Candidate. The final decision on a candidate should be based upon the group analysis, but it should ultimately reside with the immediate supervisor. It would of course be unwise for a supervisor to significantly deviate from the recommendation of the group, just as it would be unwise of the group to force one of two comparably qualified applicants on the immediate supervisor.

Use of Group Analysis. Intuitively it would seem that using group analysis for staffing decisions, as described above, would result in better evaluation of candidates, better conveyance to applicants that they have been thoroughly evaluated, and a stronger signal to applicants that they are qualified to handle the job if it is offered to them and that they will have widespread support if they will accept it. The consequences of using group analysis for staffing decisions, it would appear, should be a better acceptance rate, less turnover, and minimum problems with affirmative action complaints, all of which help the demand and supply dilemma due to the shortage of MIS professionals.

A study conducted at the University of Houston indicated that an organization could experience almost twice the acceptance rate and half the turnover rate by employing group analysis techniques.[7] Also, group analysis documentation has proved quite effective in the event of affirmative action questions and hearings.

[7] H. Albert Napier, op.cit., pp. 6-9.

Attributes	Education							Work Experience											Management Experience							Composite Score	Ranking
	EDP training	W.S.*	Bachelors	W.S.	Masters	W.S.	T.W.S.†	Financial Apps.	W.S.	Cobol	W.S.	Assembler	W.S.	Online	W.S.	General EDP	W.S.	T.W.S.	Supervisory Resp.	W.S.	Professional Trng.	W.S.	Communication	W.S.	T.W.S.		
Weight	8		10		3			8		8		5		6		8			8		4		8				
Applicant A	4	32	4	40	5	15	87	2	16	4	32	3	15	0	0	3	24	87	3	24	2	8	3	24	56	230	5
Applicant B	5	40	5	50	0	0	90	4	32	5	40	5	25	3	18	5	40	155	0	0	0	0	2	16	16	261	4
Applicant C	5	40	5	50	0	0	90	5	40	5	40	2	10	4	24	5	40	154	4	32	3	12	5	40	84	328	2
Applicant D	3	24	3	30	0	0	54	3	24	3	24	2	10	0	0	3	24	82	2	16	1	4	1	8	28	164	6
Applicant E	4	32	4	40	1	3	75	4	32	5	40	3	15	2	12	4	32	131	4	32	4	16	3	24	72	278	3
Applicant F	5	40	5	50	5	15	105	4	32	5	40	3	15	4	24	5	40	151	5	40	3	12	5	40	92	348	1

*W.S.: weighted score

†T.W.S.: total weighted score

Figure 3-9 Scoring Grid for Applicants for a Manager of Programming for a Financial Institution

SUMMARY

The four case studies presented in the early part of this chapter demonstrated a wide variety of issues associated with organizing the information systems resources of an enterprise. We have attempted to show how critical it is to deal appropriately with these issues in order to successfully employ computing resources within an organization. It is the authors' feeling that the success of an organization's information systems function is directly related to how well it deals with these issues.

There is strong evidence, related to the case examples, to suggest that the success of firms A and Y as compared with firms B and X was connected to effectively dealing with the issues identified and discussed in this chapter. Knowing the issues to consider and having an appreciation of the guidelines offered to deal with them should be of considerable assistance in achieving the results of firms A and Y rather than those of firms B and X.

SUGGESTED READINGS

Galbraith, J., *Organizational Design*, Addison-Wesley, Reading, Mass., 1977.

Gray, Stuart, "1982 Salary Survey," *Datamation*, vol. 28, no. 11, October 1982, pp. 114-131.

Longenecker, Justin G., *Principles of Management and Organizational Behavior*, Merrill, Columbus, Ohio, 1973.

Miner, John B., and Mary G. Miner, *Personnel and Industrial Relations, A Managerial Approach*, Collier-MacMillan, London, 1973.

Mintzberg, H., *The Structuring of Organizations: A Synthesis of the Research*, Prentice-Hall, Englewood Cliffs, N.J., 1979.

Napier, H. Albert, "Peer Evaluation Selects Professionals," *Journal of Systems Management*, January 1980, pp. 6-9.

Norman, A. K., *Industrial and Organization Psychology*, Prentice-Hall, Englewood Cliffs, N.J., 1971.

Paul, L., "Programmer Aptitude Tests Worth the Risk," *Computerworld*, November 29, 1982, p. 1.

_____,"Bank Coins Program to Identify, Retain Best DP Trainees," *Computerworld*, Feb. 7, 1983.

Wetherbe, James C., and V. Thomas Dock, "Breaking the Description Dilemma: Personnel Selection by Group Analysis," *Datamation*, December 1978, pp. 16-42.

Zmud, Robert W., *Information Systems in Organizations*, Scott, Foresman, Glenview, Ill., 1983.

PART THREE

MANAGING MIS PERSONNEL

FOUR

CONTINGENCY MANAGEMENT AND THE MIS FUNCTION

INTRODUCTION

This chapter relates contingency management theory to the MIS function of the organization. The technology and environment of an organization or an organizational function establish the organization's position on a continuum ranging from closed/stable/mechanistic to open/adaptive/organic. The application of this concept to the MIS function provides practical guidelines for the MIS manager. Production, development, and technical service are three components of the MIS function related to contingency management theory. The overall MIS manager will generally ascend to his or her position from a management position in one of the three fundamental MIS areas -- development, production, or technical services. A manager from the development area will most commonly possess expertise in managing systems analysis and programming activities. A production type manager will generally have been associated with managing such activities as computer operations, data entry, data control, and production processing. A technical services manager will generally have expertise in system programming and perhaps data communications or database management.

Some organizations fill MIS management positions from a functional area other than MIS. This is usually done when the organization wants to ensure that the MIS manager has solid organizational expertise and when MIS candidates are viewed more as technicians than managers. In these situations the manager generally has expertise in one or more functional areas and has varying degrees of expertise in MIS.

As a successful lower-level manager from the development, the production, or the technical services functional area, or from another functional area, advances to an MIS managerial position, he or she is often bewildered to discover that a previously successful managerial style is not effective in managing this new domain. For example, when a development manager is promoted to a position with overall MIS responsibility, he or she usually discovers significant differences pertaining to the management of the production function vis-a-vis the management of the development function. It is not an uncommon scenario for a new MIS manager, though systematically applying the managerial techniques that elevated him or her to MIS manager, to encounter problems in coping with a new set of managerial contingencies. The following comments made by an individual recently promoted to an MIS managerial position say it well:

> I thought I really understood management. In my previous position my staff and I got along very well and we had good productivity. But, in this new job, I have really had problems. I am not doing anything different yet I have really alienated a lot of my staff.

In this chapter the cause of this phenomenon is investigated. More importantly, specific management techniques will be presented to address this issue.

MANAGEMENT THEORY: A CURRENT PERSPECTIVE

Two basic conceptual models of organization and related management structures have emerged from management theory and research. The two models are referred to as closed/stable/mechanistic and open/ adaptive/organic.[1]

The closed/stable/mechanistic organization model emerged from traditional and bureaucratic management theory. This approach emphasizes the rational nature of organizations and advocates a management structure to run organizations. The closed/stable/ mechanistic model is most clearly expressed in the principles of classical management literature.

The open/adaptive/organic model emerged from systems theory. It emphasizes the environmental openness and problem-solving nature of organizations and advocates a more loose-knit, decentralized, participative management structure. The open/adaptive/organic model is most clearly represented by the principles of behavioral management literature.

[1]Fremont E. Kast and James D. Rosenzweig, *Contingency Views of Organization and Management*, Science Research Associates, Chicago, Ill., 1973.

These two basic management approaches are quite opposite in perspective. In fact, it is confusing to find such a dichotomy in managerial approaches coexisting in management theory. Even more confusing is the fact that supporters of either management approach can present convincing illustrations of the success of their respective approaches. Although this might imply that a manager can successfully utilize either approach, this is certainly not the case. The closed/stable/mechanistic and the open/adaptive/organic approaches have each been successful in some environments and less than successful in others. This indicates that the success of a managerial orientation is a function of the situation in which it is being applied. If this is the case, then a manager must determine what orientation is appropriate for his or her environment.

Contingency Theory

A particularly enlightening development in management theory is the contingency approach to management and organization.[2] The basic foundation of the contingency theory is the fact that the effectiveness of a management approach is contingent upon the organizational environment in which it is applied. This, of course, abandons the concept that there is a "best way" to manage. Instead, the best way is the way which fits the organizational constraints and contingencies. This realization considerably resolves the contradictions which have manifested themselves between existing management theories and explains why the advocates of the various theories are convinced of the effectiveness of their respective theories. The theories that worked did so because they were appropriate for what was being managed. In fact, many of the existing theories were developed by trial and error in the environment for which a specific management theory was appropriate.

It is important to realize that because a management approach's working in one, or even several, environments fails to establish it as a universal solution. As a rather extreme example, the closed/stable/mechanistic approach of autocratic leadership with its high degree of structure and well-defined procedures has proved most successful in the management of assembly-line workers. The same management approach applied to an organization of innovative research scientists would likely be ineffective. In this latter environment the personnel in the organization would likely be more effectively managed with a flexible, autonomous, and participative orientation.

The realization that the effectiveness of a management approach is contingent upon the environment in which it is applied has led to

---

[2]Fremont E. Kast and James E. Rosenzeig, *Contingency Views of Organization and Management*, Science Research Associates, Chicago, Ill., 1973.

attempts to isolate key variables that differentiate organizational environments. In an impressive series of joint research ventures involving practicing managers and academicians, a substantial database has been established that provides a reasonable, well-defined framework of managerial contingencies and appropriate management approaches. The experimental design of the majority of these research projects is quite similar. Generally, the investigators study the managerial approach utilized by successful and less successful organizations having similar environments. The investigator then attempts to determine the characteristics of the managerial approach that tends to "best fit" a certain set of variables.

Though it is impossible to adequately review even the major research findings in the context of this chapter, the next section will highlight the main concept. However, the references provided with each concept will provide interested readers with sources for further investigation.

Technology and Environment

A careful review of contingency-oriented research indicates that the technology and environment of the organization have consistently dominated as the key variables that characterize an organization. In the context of these studies, technology is generally defined as the human and mechanical process by which an organization produces its goods and/or services. For example, the processes by which an organization produces bicycles, bricks, computers, or health services constitute an organization's technologies. The environment is generally defined as those entities or factors external to the particular organization or organizational subunit. An organization's environment includes such things as customers, competitors, and government regulation. The environment of an organizational subunit includes such things as other organizational subunits and top management as well as certain dimensions of the overall organizational environment. For example, the marketing department would interface with the manufacturing department (another subunit) and with customers (a dimension of the overall organizational environment).

The technology and environment of an organization establish the organization's position on a continuum ranging from closed/ stable/mechanistic to open/adaptive/organic. A closed/stable/mechanistic organization has a predominantly routine and predictable situation where productivity is a major objective. Technological and environmental forces are relatively stable and certain. Consequently, decision-making tends to be straightforward and programmable. An example of a closed/stable/mechanistic organization would be the banking industry which until recently had used virtually the same technology and encountered the same environment for over 20 years.

Alternatively, an organization that is characterized as being open/adaptive/organic would be involved with nonroutine activities where extensive creativity and innovation are required. Technology and the environment tend to be volatile, presenting considerable uncertainty. Conflict results from complex problems, and unclear courses are characterized as risky and uncertain. Few optimum decisions are possible. An example of an open/adaptive/organic organization would be the electronic calculator industry, which has had both extremely dynamic technology and environment.

An issue of technology that often causes confusion is organizational complexity. The technology of an organization can be complex but still be closed/stable/mechanistic within the context of the organization. For example, a computerized process control system for a chemical processing plant can be quite complex from a technological perspective. However, if the chemical firm has contracted the development and maintenance of this computerized system to an engineering firm, the chemical firm's interaction with the computerized system becomes one of monitoring and responding to problems with specific and programmable procedures. Even if the system fails, the decision-making process of the chemical firm's personnel is routine: they call the engineering firm to fix the system. The technology, though complex, is still closed/stable/mechanistic in operation. What determines the degree to which a technology creates an open/adaptive/organic situation, then, is a function of the number of problems it presents and the complexity of the problematic search to resolve these problems.

Few organizations or organizational subsystems can be categorized as being completely closed/stable/mechanistic or open/adaptive/organic. Rather, organizations generally tend, in varying degrees, toward one or the other orientation. Also, an organization's position on the continuum between these orientations will occasionally vary, perhaps radically, with time. Variation would occur in the case of an organization's encountering changing technologies and/or environments. For example, the energy crisis considerably impacted the marketplace for automobile manufacturers and resulted in a less stable and less predictable environment. The transition from electromechanical to electronic cash registers for electronic retail terminals significantly altered the technology used in the retail industry, resulting in increased uncertainty and also a need for more flexibility in production and marketing. As the banking industry moves into advanced technologies to replace the traditional check, banking is moving into a more open/adaptive/organic situation.

The realization that organizations vary in form from closed/stable/mechanistic to open/adaptive/organic to accommodate their technology and environment provides the basic framework for applying contingency management approaches. Empirical evidence indicates that a management style more aligned with the closed/stable/mechanistic approach tends to be more effective in relatively routine and predictable situations. Management can operate in a more structured, centralized, and process-oriented mode. Conversely, the open/adaptive/organic management approach tends to be more effective in situations where employees have to cope with greater uncertainty and complexity. Management must provide a more autonomous and participative setting for what will generally be a more sophisticated level of staff. In fact, in most open/adaptive/organic settings, staff members will generally have more expertise in special areas than their managers.

Contingency Management

In summary, current management thinking emphasizes the fit between management structures and styles and the situation confronting the organization in producing a desired set of goods and/or services. It recognizes the open-systems nature of organizations with all of the implications thereof, and at the same time the rational requirement that an organization produce results. The focus is on the analytical, decisional, conflict-resolving, coordinative, and coalignment role of management as it pertains to the organization's technology and environment. Appropriate action is determined by analysis of the situation in which the manager is responsible for creating a set of causes that will produce the desired results.

Contingency analysis can be applied to subsystems within organizations or functional areas within subsystems. To the extent subsystems (or functional areas) are similar, they should be designed in a similar way. If subsystems are trying to produce different outputs with different technologies and have different organizational interactions, they should be designed and managed differently. Figure 4-1, which is based on work done by Kast and Rosenzweig, provides a comprehensive view of organizational characteristics and their relationship to the contingency view.

IMPLICATIONS FOR MIS MANAGEMENT

The application of contingency theory to managing the MIS organization provides interesting and useful implications.[3] As mentioned earlier, the MIS data processing organizations are broadly organized into production, development, and technical services activities. The organizational forms of each activity can now be analyzed from a contingency perspective.

---

[3]James C. Wetherbe and C. J. Whitehead, "A Contingency View of Managing the Data Processing Organization," *MIS Quarterly*, vol. 1, no. 1, March 1977, pp. 19-25.

Systems and Their Key Dimensions	Charateristics of Organizational Systems	
	Closed/Stable/Mechanistic	*Open/Adaptive/Organic*
Environmental Suprasystem:		
General nature	Placid	Turbulent
Predictability	Certain, determinate	Uncertain, indeterminate
Boundary relationships	Relatively closed, limited to few participants (sales, purchasing, etc.) Fixed and well defined.	Relatively open. Many participants have external relationships. Varied and not clearly defined.
Overall Organizational System:		
Goal structure	Organizations as a single-goal maximizer	Organization as a searching, adapting, learning system which continually adjusts its multiple goals and aspirations.
Decision-making processes	Programmable, computational	Nonprogrammable, judgmental on
Organizational emphasis	on performance	problem solving
Goals and Values:		
Organizational goals in general	Efficient performance, stability, maintenance	Effective problem solving innovation, growth
Pervasive values	Efficiency, predictability, security, risk aversion	Effectiveness, adaptability, responsiveness, risk taking
Goal set	Single, clear-cut	Multiple, determined by necessity to satisfy a variety of constraints
Involvement in goal-setting process	Managerial hierarchy primarily (top down)	Widespread participation (bottom up as well as top down)
Technical System:		
General nature of tasks	Repetitive, routine	Varied, nonroutine
Input to transformation process	Homogeneous	Heterogeneous
Output of transformation process	Standardized, fixed	Nonstandardized, variable
Methods	Programmed, algorithmic	Nonprogrammed, heuristic
Structural System:		
Organizational formalization	High	Low
Procedures and rules	Many and specific, usually formal and written	Few and general. Usually informal and unwritten
Authority structure	Concentrated, hierarchic	Dispersed, network
Psychosocial System:		
Status structure	Clearly delineated by formal hierarchy	More diffusive. Based upon expertise and professional norms
Role definitions	Specific and fixed	General and dynamic. Change with tasks
Motivational factors	Emphasis on extrinsic rewards, security, and lower-level need satisfaction (Theory X view)	Emphasis on intrinsic rewards, esteem, and self-actualization (Theory Y view)
Leadership style	Autocratic, task-oriented, desire for certainty	Democratic, relationship-oriented Tolerance for ambiguity
Power system	Power concentration	Power equalization
Managerial System:		
General nature	Hierarchical structure of control, authority, and communications, combination of independent status components	A network structure of control, authority, and communications. Co-alignment of interdependent, dynamic components
Decision-making techniques	Autocratic, programmed, computational	Participative, non-programmed Judgmental
Planning process	Repetitive, fixed, and specific	Changing, flexible, and general
Control structure	Hierarchic, specific, short-term, external control of participants	Reciprocal, general, long-term. Self-control of participants
Means of conflict resolution	Resolved by superior (refer to "book")	Resolved by group ("situational ethics")
	Compromise and smoothing	Confrontation
	Keep below the surface	Bring out in open

Figure 4-1 A Conceptual Model of Contingency View of Organization and Management

PRODUCTION

The production activities of computer operations, data entry, data control, and production processing involve, if properly managed, relatively stable and predictable technology. The capacity of production resources lends itself to reasonably accurate estimation. For example, keypunch capacity can be estimated in keystrokes per hour, and computer time for production computer runs is reasonably stable. Consequently, the work flows of production activities lend themselves to relatively accurate and stable scheduling and routine procedures.

The computer, auxiliary hardware, and application system, though certainly complex, are usually maintained outside of production. That is, computer and auxiliary hardware problems are usually addressed by the vendor. If the production personnel encounter a problem with a complex application system (e.g., a computer program or a documentation error) the normal procedure is to call in the appropriate development personnel for problem resolution.

The environment of the production activity can also be viewed as relatively stable. Users' production requirements are usually established by the development group. If a user requests something that transcends existing production system capabilities, the request is referred to the appropriate staff in the development organization.

With a relatively stable technology and environment in the production area, a management style leaning toward the closed/stable/mechanistic approach appears appropriate. Fairly formalized policies and procedures can be established. Emphasis can be placed on measurable productivity, and control and management decisions can generally be centralized.

Certainly there would be cases when a production organization would move to a less stable and less certain mode. For example, during a computer conversion or in changing from keypunch to terminals for data entry, the production function will shift away from stability and certainty. However, once the "dust" clears, the production organization will tend to stabilize in a more closed/stable/mechanistic form again.

Development

The development activities of systems analysis, design, programming, maintenance, etc., use a technology that is less stable and offer a multiplicity of alternatives for decision making. Cost-benefit considerations can become quite elusive though generally not as elusive as discovering real user needs. Development staff is involved with evaluating and deciding how much, in what way, and when to automate critical organizational activities. The developer has the problem of the prototype's ultimately becoming the production system. Consequently, few systems optimize computer resource utilization, completion dates are seldom estimated accurately, and few systems completely satisfy user requirements.

Since the users are the primary factor of the development organization's environment, the environment can certainly be viewed as relatively unstable and uncertain. This situation, combined with the development organization's unstable technology, establishes a setting which can best be managed in an open/adaptive/organic mode.

The development organization can also move toward a more closed/stable/mechanistic form. This would generally occur when the development group is not engaged in new systems development and is only involved in addressing the maintenance of existing stable production systems.

Technical Services

As discussed in Chapter 3, the internal organizational structure for MIS departments varies. In particular, the functions of systems programming, data communications, and database administration have diverse reporting relationships within an MIS department. These three functions may individually or collectively report to the manager of systems development, production, or MIS, or perhaps a technical services management position might exist.

For the purposes of this contingency management discussion, all three areas are considered collectively, irrespective of where they report.

All three areas are most closely aligned with an open/adaptive/organic environment. They all deal with complex technology that requires sophisticated expertise and decision making. These areas, perhaps more than any others in the MIS function, involve expertise that is least likely to be possessed by the MIS manager.

The environment of these technical areas includes other staff in the MIS function, vendor representatives (particularly programmers and analysts), and, in some organizations, users. Overall, this is a rather unstable and unpredictable environment to have to face.

As with development, the technical services area calls for a relation-oriented management style. This can be difficult to initialize if one or more technical services functions report to the production manager. Unless the production manager recognizes the difference between production personnel and tasks, problems concerning technical services personnel and tasks are likely. Also, a production manager in this situation must be able to deal with conflicting perspectives and attitudes. Production personnel often resent the autonomy granted technical services personnel, and technical services personnel often consider production personnel as inferior and treat them accordingly.

For example, systems programmers may try to come into the machine room and literally take the computer away from the computer operators whenever they need to make an operating system change. A production manager must watch the relationship between technical services and production closely.

Like all organizational activities, technical services can vary in its position on the continuum between the closed/stable/mechanistic orientation and the open/adaptive/organic orientation. For example, an organization that uses only standard vendor software for its operating system, data communications, and database management system is going to have a more stable and predictable technical services environment than an organization that extensively modifies such software or even develops their own. Also, advances in development technology can cause a shift toward a more closed/stable/mechanistic situation. For example, structured programming techniques have made software engineering a more stable activity.

SUMMARY

A contingency view of managing the data processing organization provides a useful and operational framework for the MIS manager. It provides a strong case for managing the production activity with a more closed/stable/mechanistic approach and managing the development and technical services activities with a more open/adaptive/organic approach.

A contingency view provides further explanation of why a previously successful lower-level manager may encounter difficulty managing a new position in an old way and provides a more appropriate course of action for effective MIS management. An open/adaptive/organic approach in a production environment will likely result in a decrease in productivity. When the work to be done is already relatively structured and defined, there is little reason for participative management and autonomous decision making. It is more important that each individual follow previously established instructions and procedures. Emphasis must be placed on what, when, and how things are to be done. Conversely, applying rigid control practices in a development organization will likely stifle creativity, and generate resentment and a high rate of turnover. Emphasis must be placed on what and when things are to be done, and personnel must be given latitude to determine how things should be done. The EDP manager must balance structure orientation and relations orientation for the production, development, and technical services functions of the data processing organization.

SUGGESTED READINGS

Ackoff, Russell L., "Management Misinformation Systems," *Management Science,* vol. 14, no. 4, December 1967, pp. 147-156.

Anderson, William S., "Bridging the Systems Expectation Gap," *Data Management,* vol. 12, no. 11, November 1974, pp. 29-32.

Bowers, David G., and Stanley E. Seashore, "Predicting Organizational Effectiveness with a Four Factor Theory of Leadership," *Administrative Science Quarterly,* vol. 11, no. 2, 1966, pp. 238-263.

Burns, Tom, and George M. Stalker, *Management of Innovation*, Tavistock Publications, London, 1969.

Fiedler, Fred E., "Validation and Extension of the Contingency Model of Leadership: A Review of Empirical Findings," *Psychology Bulletin*, vol. 76, no. 2, 1971, pp. 128-148.

Hellriegel, Don, and John W. Solcum, Jr., *Management: A Contingency Approach*, Addison-Wesley, Reading, Mass., 1974.

House, Robert J., "A Path Goal Theory of Leader Effectiveness," *Administrative Science Quarterly*, vol. 16, no. 3, September 1971.

Hunt, Raymond G., "Technology and Organization," *Academy of Management*, September 1970, pp. 235-252.

Kast, Fremont E., and James E. Rosenzweig, *Contingency Views of Organization and Management*, Science Research Associates, Chicago, Ill., 1973.

_____ and _____, *Organization and Environment: A Systems Approach*, 2d Ed., McGraw-Hill, New York, 1974, pp. 510-511.

Lawrence, Paul R., and Jay W. Lorsch, *Organization and Environment*, Irwin, Homewood, Ill., 1967.

_____ and _____, *Organizational Structure and Design*, Irwin, Homewood, Ill., 1970.

Management Science Publishing Company, "Where Next for the DP Manager?" *Automatic Data Processing Newsletter*, vol. 20, no. 8, Apr. 12, 1976.

McKinsey & Company, Inc., "Unlocking the Computer's Profit Potential," *The McKinsey Quarterly*, Fall 1968, pp. 17-31.

Morse, John J., "Organizational Characteristics and Individual Motivation," in P. Lawrence and J. Lorsch (eds.), *Studies in Organization Design*, Irwin, Homewood, Ill., 1970, pp. 84-100.

Newman, William H., "Strategy and Management Structure," *Journal of Business Policy*, Winter 1971-1972, pp. 15-156.

Perrow, Charles, "A Framework for the Comparative Analysis of Organizations," *American Sociological Review*, April 1967, pp. 194-208.

Terreberry, Shirley, "The Evolution of Organizational Environments," *Administrative Science Quarterly*, March 1968, pp. 490-613.

Thompson, James D., *Organizations in Action*, McGraw-Hill, New York, 1967.

Wetherbe, J. C., and C. J. Whitehead, "A Contingency View of Managing the Data Processing Organization," *MIS Quarterly*, vol. 1, no. 1, March 1977, pp. 19-25.

Woodward, Joan, *Management and Technology*, Oxford University Press, London, 1965.

Yuki, Gary, "Toward a Behavioral Theory of Leadership," *Organizational Behavior and Human Performance*, vol. 6, no. 4, July 1971, pp. 414-440.

FIVE

ACHIEVING JOB PRODUCTIVITY AND SATISFACTION

INTRODUCTION

This chapter reviews leading motivational theories and extracts from them practical motivational guidelines for the MIS manager. An effective and efficient method of determining motivational factors for individual MIS personnel is proposed. Strategies for administering and scheduling these factors as consequences of employee performance are presented.

The question "How do I motivate my people?" remains one of the most challenging questions faced by managers. There are many approaches to answering this question -- some more valid and practical than others. Since MIS managers often are promoted into management from technical positions, they are often not prepared to deal with perplexing, ill-defined issues such as motivating staff.

This chapter is organized as follows:

1. Review literature on motivational theory.

2. Extract from these theories the most practical strategies for MIS management.

3. Develop practical, operational approaches to implementing motivational strategies.

DRAWING FROM THE BEST OF MOTIVATIONAL THEORIES

The most highly regarded of motivational theories are as follows:

● Maslow's need hierarchy	A. G. Maslow	1943
● Reinforcement	B. F. Skinner	1953
● Attribution theory	F. Heider	1958
● Herzberg's dual factory theory	F. Herzberg	1959
● Expectancy theory	V. Vroom	1964
● Goal setting	E. A. Locke	1976

A brief review of each of these theories is provided below.

Need Hierarchy

Maslow[1] contended that individuals are motivated to satisfy the following set of needs:
1. Basic physiological needs
2. Safety, security
3. Social activity
4. Esteem, status
5. Self-actualization

According to Maslow, fulfillment of these needs tends to be hierarchical, as depicted in Figure 5-1. That is, individuals fulfill these needs sequentially, starting with physiological needs and ascending up the hierarchy to self-actualization. For example, an individual's physiological needs have to be largely fulfilled before safety (the next level of needs) will motivate behavior. As a need becomes satisfied, it loses its potential as a motivator.

Maslow's theory is straightforward and intuitively appealing. However, there is little empirical evidence to support the concept of sequential dependency in the satisfaction of needs. Factor-analytic studies have been unable to reproduce Maslow's specific factors of motivational needs.

The major contribution of Maslow's theory comes from the notion of appealing to individual needs to motivate employees. Motivation of employees is achieved by identifying the needs of an employee and

---

[1]A. H. Maslow, "A Theory of Human Motivation," *Psychological Review*, July 1943, pp. 370-396.

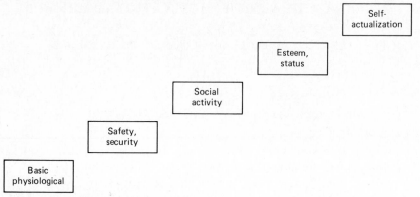

Figure 5-1 Hierarchy of Needs

linking the satisfaction of those needs (as much as possible) to the performance desired by the manager. For example, if an employee has a need for esteem, a manager could communicate that satisfactory performance on a project will result in significant recognition and visibility within the organization, thereby enhancing the employee's opinion of his or her self-worth.

Dual-Factor Theory

Herzberg[2,3] proposed a motivational theory based upon dual factors that concern employees -- hygiene and motivational factors. Hygiene (or maintenance) factors are important in preventing employees from becoming dissatisfied. They are associated with company policy and administration, working conditions, salary, interpersonal relations, personal life, job security, and status. According to Herzberg, the absence of hygiene factors results in dissatisfaction, while their presence results in no dissatisfaction. In either case, he argues that they are not useful motivators.

Motivational factors are associated with the work itself, achievement, growth, responsibility, and recognition. The presence of motivational factors, Herzberg argues, will provide motivation.

Herzberg's theory has caused considerable controversy. Primary criticism of the theory focuses on the notion that hygiene factors cannot motivate workers. Other research does not generally support Herzberg's contention.

[2]F. Herzberg, "One More Time: How Do You Motivate Employees?" *Harvard Business Review*, vol. 46, no. 1, 1968, pp. 53-62.

[3]F. Herzberg, B. Mausner, and B. Snyderman, *The Motivation to Work*, Wiley, New York, 1959.

Though Herzberg's theory has its weaknesses, aspects of it are useful. Like Maslow, Herzberg's theory is a need-satisfaction-based theory. In particular, job enrichment, advancement, achievement, recognition, growth on the job, and responsibility are useful concepts for positively motivating employees. However, the nature and needs of different employees and jobs must be considered. Depending on the situation, strategies such as job enrichment may be ineffective.

Goal Setting

Locke has proposed a model of task motivation based upon the premise that an employee's conscious attention to goals is the primary determinant of motivation.[4] His theory, called "goal setting," also asserts that difficult goals result in greater effort than easy goals. Furthermore, specific goals, he contends, result in greater effort than generalized or no goals.

In general, research is supportive of Locke's proposition with one qualification. For difficult goals to be effective motivators, they must be accepted by the employees as being realistic and worthwhile. Employee participation in goal setting is a way to facilitate acceptance of goals; however, research results for improving performance through participatory versus assigned goal setting are mixed and inconclusive.

Reinforcement

One of the better-known and more controversial theories of motivation centers on the work of Skinner and others[5,6] in the area of reinforcement (or behavior modification). The notion behind reinforcement theory is that behavior is a result of consequences. Consequences that reinforce behavior tend to cause that behavior to be repeated and vice versa.

A model of the reinforcement theory is depicted in Figure 5-2. Behavior is postulated to be stimulated by antecedents that set the stage for behavior to occur. Typically the employee has behavioral alternatives with which to respond. The behavior selected by the employee is influenced by the consequences or perceived consequences of the behavior.

According to this view, an employee learns through experience what behavior results in what consequences and tends to proceed accordingly.

---

[4]E. A. Locke, "The Nature and Cases of Job Satisfaction," in M. Dunnette (ed.), *Handbook of Industrial and Organizational Psychology,* Rand McNally, Chicago, 1976.

[5]B. F. Skinner, *Operant Behavior: Areas of Research and Application,* Appleton-Century-Crofts, New York, 1966.

[6]____, *Contingencies of Reinforcment,* Appleton-Century-Crofts, New York, 1969.

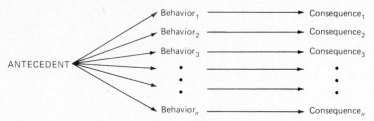

Figure 5-2 Reinforcement Model of Behavior

Therefore the manager must administer consequences in a manner which elicits the desired behavior from employees. For example, a systems analyst realizes he or she is behind schedule on a project (antecedent). There are several behavioral alternatives, among which are allowing the project to be late or working overtime to complete the project on schedule. If completing a project on schedule is reinforced, then that behavior is motivated and more likely to recur. If meeting or not meeting a project deadline goes unnoticed (i.e., either behavior results in the same consequences), there is little organization-based motivation to complete the project on schedule. However, the employee may be internally motivated (e.g., from pride or a sense of responsibility) to complete the project on schedule anyway.

Reinforcement theory's message to the manager is that attention must be given to what consequences are provided for different behavior for the organization to properly influence employee behavior.

There are four basic reinforcement strategies, as defined below:

- Positive reinforcement involves *presenting* employees with a *desirable* consequence following particular behavior, causing an *increase* in the frequency of that behavior.

- Negative reinforcement involves *withdrawing* an *undesirable* consequence from an employee following particular behavior, causing an *increase* in the frequency of that behavior.

- Punishment involves *presenting* an employee with an *undesirable* consequence following particular behavior, causing a *decrease* in the frequency of that behavior.

- Extinction involves *withholding* a *desirable* consequence from an employee following particular behavior, causing a *decrease* in the frequency of that behavior.

Positive reinforcement is referred to as a positive strategy; the other three strategies are categorized as negative control strategies. Positive reinforcement strategies are generally preferred because they contribute to good rapport between a manager and a subordinate. The negative control strategies of negative reinforcement, punishment, and, to a lesser extent, extinction can cause a subordinate to resent or even fear the manager responsible for administering consequences. Though positive reinforcement is preferred, it is often not practical or appropriate. The primary problem is that before positive reinforcement can be used, an employee must perform as required. If an employee is not doing this, a positive strategy is ineffective.

The controversy about reinforcement theory centers on ethical concerns of manipulating people. However, regardless of one's views, reinforcement theory is potentially useful to managers attempting to motivate employees.

An operational problem with reinforcement theory is the difficulty in determining exactly what reinforces behavior in different employees. Often managers make incorrect assumptions in this area and can actually punish an employee when attempting to provide positive reinforcement. Promoting someone into management who really prefers technical tasks is an example of incorrect application of this strategy.

For reinforcement strategies to work, a manager must assess what reinforces behavior in different employees and administer consequences accordingly.

Expectancy

Vroom[7] is the originator of the expectancy theory of motivation. The model is based upon the following concepts:

Valence: the effective orientation toward particular outcomes. Valence may be positive (outcome is desirable), negative (outcome is undesirable), or zero (outcome makes no difference).

Expectancy: the employee's view of the risk or probability that he or she can perform a particular task and that performance of that task will be followed by a particular outcome.

[7]V. Vroom, *Work and Motivation*, McGraw-Hill, New York, 1970.

Force: the combined effect of valence and expectancy on an employee, directing him or her to engage in certain behavior. The higher the valence and the greater the expectancy, the greater is the force to perform a particular act.

Vroom suggests that valence and expectancy are independent variables affecting the dependent variable, force. Consequently, for employees to be motivated by the organization, the organization must first have a consequence that is positively valent or desired by the individual. Next, the individual must also believe the consequence will be forthcoming if requirements are met. The individual must also believe he or she is capable, or has a reasonable chance, of doing what is required.

Expectancy theory provides one of the better frameworks for analyzing and understanding motivation. To address valence the manager needs to identify outcomes that are valued by the employee. To address expectancy the manager needs to focus on two issues. First the manager must ensure that the employee is able to perform as required. To accomplish this, the employee may need training, assistance, more self-confidence, etc. Second, the employee must believe that if he or she performs as required, the desired outcome will be forthcoming. To accomplish this, the manager needs to closely link performance to outcome (e.g., through incentive plans, merit raises, promotion, praise, or better communication).

Attribution Theory

A topic of current interest in physiological research is attribution theory. This theory involves what Heider[8] originally termed a "naive psychology" and describes how the average individual explains (attributes) causes of events. This cognitive approach is less stimulus-response-oriented than reinforcement theory and therefore has more of a human orientation.

An understanding of the basic idea provides enough insight to appreciate the fundamental contribution of the theory. An individual may believe that events were caused by factors under control of the environment or under the control of a person.

Figure 5-3 describes how four important factors for success may be classified into two dimensions.[9] Ability, effort, task difficulty, and luck are common attributions which can be related to internality and stability.

---

[8]F. Heider, *The Psychology of Interpersonal Relations*, Wiley, New York, 1958.

[9]B. Weiner, D. Russell, and D. Lerman, "Affective Consequences of Causal Ascriptions," in J.H. Harvey, et al. (eds.), *New Directions in Attribution Research*, vol. 2, Erlbaum, Hillsdale, N.J., 1978.

	Internal	External
Stable	Ability	Task difficulty
Unstable	Effort	Luck

Figure 5-3 Classification of Success Factors

For example, a successful system implementation may be described by the developer as a good job (implying internal attributions), but users may attribute the success to other factors. If past performance has been very stable, the developer could perceive his or her own ability to be the reason for success. The users may believe that the task is just not very difficult. If there was previously wide variation in success, the developer may feel that effort explains current success, while the users may attribute success to luck.

Currently, attribution theory is an active area of research. While the basic concepts of causation and control have remained as important issues, many different studies have made this a complex area. For example, intentionality,[10] achievement motivation,[11] and role perspective[12] are a few of the major variables which can be related to attributions.

For MIS, causal inferences may have impacts on motivation. If an individual considers luck or task difficulty to be a major success factor, levels of effort or cooperation with training programs may be undesirably low. Experiments which specifically address MIS issues are needed for proper applications of the theory.

Practical Guidelines

Though each of the preceding theories takes a somewhat different view of motivation, some similar guidelines can be extracted for practical use. Specifically, the following guidelines emerge.

1. Efforts to increase motivation must first focus on the employee's needs (Maslow, Herzberg).

2. Work assignments and goals should be realistic and clearly defined; rewards for performance should be practical and fulfill the motivational needs of the employee. The employee must be competent to

---

[10] B. Weiner, "An Attributional Interpretation of Expectancy Value Theory," in B. Weiner (ed.), *Cognitive Views of Human Motivation*, Academic Press, New York, 1974.

[11] and A. Kukla, "An Attributional Analysis of Achievement Motivation," *Journal of Personality and Social Psychology*, vol. 15, 1970, pp. 1-20.

[12] E. E. Jones, and R. E. Nisbett, "The Actor and the Observers: Divergent Perceptions of the Causes of Behavior," in E. E. Jones, et al. (eds.), *Attributions: Perceiving the Causes of Behavior*, General Learning Press, Morristown, N.J., 1972.

do the work required and must believe that his or her needs will be reasonably fulfilled by the work and the rewards of doing the work well (Locke, Vroom).

3. Consequences or outcomes of good performance must approximate the expectations of the employee (Skinner, Heider).

These guidelines are simple enough to understand but extremely difficult to effectively and efficiently apply. Why? First, needs of employees are difficult to define because they vary among employees and they change over time. Frequently employees are not even sure themselves what they want from their work experience. Second, management is often negligent in clearly defining to employees what is expected of them, and/or they are not responsive to employee needs when employees are responsive to organizational demands.

The issues of identifying employee needs and effectively using them as motivators are addressed in the following two sections. First, a method for identifying employee needs is presented, and second, strategies for effectively administering consequences or outcomes are discussed.

IDENTIFYING EMPLOYEE NEEDS

Couger and Zawacki's[13] research into what motivates MIS professionals has shed considerable light on the unique needs of MIS professionals. They have found that MIS professionals in general have an extremely high need for growth and personal development relative to professionals in other occupations. Conversely, MIS professionals have an extremely low social need (need to interact with others) relative to professionals in other occupations. This profile indicates that the needs of MIS professionals are going to be a moving target due to the high-growth need. It also indicates that many rewards valued by other employees may not be valued by MIS professionals (e.g., more visibility through user contact or a management position).

In assessing the needs of a particular employee a manager must be very careful and very specific. Statistics on what in general motivates a category of employees (e.g., programmers) may be irrelevant to particular employees. For example, on the average most programmers would be motivated by an opportunity to work with new technology. (Such motivation would be consistent with high-growth need.) However, a programmer who is lacking confidence may see such an opportunity as a threat to his or her job security. Or, a programmer who has just

---

[13]Daniel Couger and Robert Zawacki, "What Motivates DP Professionals?" *Datamation*, September 1978, pp. 116-123.

found out she is pregnant may not want to get into a demanding project during the forthcoming year and have to leave the project before it is completed.

Q-Sort

The authors have successfully experimented with Q-sort as a method of addressing the issue of identifying employee needs for both professional and nonprofessional MIS staff. The Q-sort approach is designed to provide a good indication of MIS personnel needs both at the present and in the future. Incorporating Q-sort into the motivational strategy for MIS professionals shows considerable promise.

Q-sort is a method of assessing the preferences of individuals. Techniques of this sort became popular in the fields of social and clinical psychology in the 1950s.[14] Q-sort has since been used successfully in a wide range of applications, including personnel analysis in high-technology professions. Q-sort is a comparative rating method in which individuals are required to rank available alternatives. This ranking is typically conducted within categories ranging from extremely desirable to extremely undesirable. The number of categories and the number of alternatives that are allowed to be included in a category are Q-sort design decisions.

Q-Sort Design

The version of Q-sort used by the authors is based upon a design and instrument originally developed by Gray[15] for use in administering incentives to engineers and scientists. The design and instrument were modified for use in an MIS environment.

Fifty statements representing available alternatives are included in the Q-sort, 5 within each of 10 categories (see Table 5-1). Each category represents a potential motivating factor as defined in earlier research. The specific statements within each category are based upon a pilot study conducted by the authors.

The Q-sort instrument, including instruction for use and date sheets (but not the Q-sort card deck), is in the appendix at the end of this chapter. For each of the 10 motivational factors there are 3 positive statements and 2 negative statements. For example, under the factor

---

[14]Daniel Couger and Robert A. Zawacki, "What Motivates DP Professionals?" *Datamation*, September 1978, pp. 116-123.

[15]Richard C. Gray, "Development of an Efficiency Criterion for Administering Incentives to Engineers and Scientists," Ph.D. dissertation, Oklahoma State University, 1972.

Table 5-1 Motivational factors and Q-sort statements

Code*	Achievement
12	Successful completion of a major project
89	Mastery of a new, difficult skill
54	Completion of project made possible by your contribution
97	Inability to complete work assignment
74	Marginal performance record

Code	Responsibility
37	Freedom to plan own work
94	Responsibility for critical project
51	Autonomous work environment
17	Little latitude allowed to make own decisions
10	Subordinate role in work assignment

Code	Advancement
69	Promotion within administrative ranks
42	Lateral move for opportunity for promotion
71	Promotion within technical ranks
66	Present position maintained
34	Demotion accepted to remain employed

Code	Recognition
04	Assignment to a project that has high visibility
85	Considered very capable by organization
19	Considered an expert in your specialty
53	Contributions to project unnoticed by management
63	Lack of recognition by co-workers

Code	Work itself
80	Interesting work assignment
67	Self-satisfying work
22	State-of-the-art work activity
92	Boring work
16	Work that is not difficult

Code	Wage level
52	Increase in salary (15% of base wage)
44	Higher wage maintained than members of peer group
77	Pay scale upgraded for your current position
27	Reduction in pay to remain employed
93	Across-the-board wage freeze

Table 5-1 (continued)

Code	Leisure
60	Four ten-hour days per week (same day)
78	Time off after completing a major project on schedule
70	Provision for time off without pay
33	Overtime required to complete project
15	Vacation time decreased (one week less)

Code	Working conditions
91	Clean working conditions
14	Comfortable room temperature
59	Modern office furnishings
25	Unavailability of office supplies
20	Noisy work environment

Code	Supervisory relationships
47	Friendly supervision
75	Technically competent supervision
64	Adminstratively competent supervision
72	Lack of communications with supervision
95	Partiality exhibited by supervision

Code	Organization policy
50	Well-defined personnel policies
45	Consistent organizational policies
08	Input allowed to organizational policy formulation
55	Inflexible organization policy
79	Policies not appropriate for your position

*Code numbers are used for recording statements on Q-sort Data Sheet. They were selected from a random number generator. These numbers appear with the proper statement on each card in the Q-sort deck.

achievement, positive statements are: (1) successful completion of a major project, (2) master a new, difficult skill, and (3) your contribution makes it possible to complete a project. Negative statements, as related to achievement, are (1) unable to complete work assignments and (2) marginal performance record. The use of both positive and negative statements is consistent with Goodling's[16]

[16]R.A. Goodling and G.M. Guthrie, "Some Practical Considerations in Q-Sort Item Selection," *Journal of Counseling Psychology*, vol. 3, no. 3, 1956, pp. 70-72.

suggestion to maintain a balanced Q-sort. The use of one more positive than negative statement provides a slightly positive bias which is proposed for this type of sort since many respondents will be indifferent about some positive statements.

Individuals' comparative evaluations of alternatives change over time. For example, an employee might view a promotion into management as undesirable today but may view it as desirable 5 years from now. In designing a motivational strategy for an employee it is important to know current as well as forecasted needs and aspirations of an employee. To compensate for the time factor, respondents conduct three sorts. The first sort represents current attitudes. The second and third sorts reflect attitudes as projected into the future 3 and 5 years respectively.

Q-Sort Procedure

The procedure for conducting a Q-sort is straightforward. The materials required to conduct a Q-sort consist of the instructions and work sheets provided in the appendix and a Q-sort deck. A Q-sort deck is a deck of small (e.g., 2 by 4 inch) cards, each with a different statement from the 50 statements listed in Table 5-1 printed on it.

In accordance with the instructions provided in the appendix, individuals are asked to conduct three sorts, one for the present and one each for 3 and 5 years in the future. The fifty statements (cards) are sorted into nine categories which range from extremely undesirable to extremely desirable, as shown on the work sheets. The ordering of statements resulting from the sort for each of the three time frames is recorded on the appropriate work sheets. The individual sorting the cards must rank and record two statements as extremely desirable and two statements as extremely undesirable, three statements as highly desirable, and three as highly undesirable, etc., according to the number of spaces provided on the work sheets under each category for recording statements. Statements are recorded on the work sheets by filling in the blank lines with the random numbers printed on the cards. (Numbers are used to save space and time.)

The final result of the Q-sort procedure is a comparative ranking by an employee of each statement for the three time frames.

Interpretation of Q-Sort Results

The process of conducting a Q-sort is instructive to both the employee and the manager. The comparative ranking feature puts the incentives that might be available to an employee into perspective. For example, few employees would not like a 15 percent increase in salary. But a 15 percent salary increase might be a second choice to an interesting work assignment. This information can be valuable to the employee's manager. For example, a 15 percent salary increase may not be possible, but an interesting work assignment might be. Accordingly, the manager has at least one incentive to offer that is valued by the employee.

To systematically interpret and evaluate an employee's Q-sort the following guidelines are recommended:

1. Review the ranking of statements, particularly focusing on the statements ranked in the desirable and undesirable ends of the work sheets. These are the items that are most important to the employee.

2. Look for situations where the three positive statements for a particular factor (e.g., achievement) are rated moderately to extremely desirable and the two negative statements are ranked moderately to extremely undesirable. This situation indicates that this factor is extremely important to the employee.

3. Discuss the rankings with the employee. During the discussion, determine how the employee relates the statements to his or her situation. For example, say an employee has ranked "freedom to plan own work" as extremely desirable. The manager needs to know (1) what specifically that statement means to the employee, (2) whether or not that need is currently fulfilled, and (3) if it is not fulfilled, under what conditions the employee would consider the need fulfilled. Accordingly the manager might ask, "What does freedom to plan your own work mean to you?" The answer to this question can be followed with, "How close does your current work situation approximate freedom to plan your own work as you define it?" If the work situation does not fulfill this need the employee can be asked, "What changes are required in your work situation that would allow you adequate freedom to plan your own work?"

For negative statements the question would be modified to see if the employee was dissatisfied about a statement and under what conditions that dissatisfaction could be resolved.

4. After the evaluation of the sort for the present time period is complete, steps 1 through 3 are repeated for the sorts that represent employee attitudes for 3 and 5 years into the future. Questions asked in step 3 are modified to a future time frame. For example, "What type of advancement into administrative ranks are you looking for in 5 years?" Such information is particularly helpful for career path planning. For example, if an employee with a technical degree wants to move into management in 5 years, he or she might be advised to pursue an M.B.A. on a part-time basis during the interim.

This type of discussion provides a great deal of insight for the manager as to what an employee wants from his or her job and provides the framework for developing a relevant incentive system and career path planning strategy for the employee. Once the manager understands the needs of the employee, the manager can begin to communicate what is required of the employee to maintain fulfillment (if the need is currently fulfilled) or achieve fulfillment (if the need is currently not fulfilled). The manager can also discuss how to avoid the outcomes the employee considers to be undesirable. The result is better understanding and communication, more realistic expectations, and a good indication of incentives that motivate an employee.

Scoring Q-Sorts

In addition to the interpretation of individual employee ranking of statements, Q-sorts can be scored to develop a composite score for each of the 10 motivational factors. The composite scores provide individual profiles of the major motivational factors for each employee. And, individual profiles can be combined to develop cluster profiles for departments, job classifications, etc. These clusters can be used to analyze groups of employees in order to compare a specific employee's factors with the overall factors for one or more groups.

Scoring of Q-sort is conducted as follows:

1. Each positive statement is scored according to its categorical ranking (i.e., a positive statement ranked under category one is given the score of 1; a positive statement ranked under category 2 is given the score of 2, etc.).

2. Each negative statement is scored so that it has the impact of its equivalent positive statement. Negative statements ranked in categories 5 to 9 are scored negatively according to categorical ranking (i.e., a ranking of 5 is scored minus 5). Negative statements ranked in categories 1 to 4 are scored by inverting their rank (i.e., a ranking of 1 is scored as a 9; a ranking of 2 is scored as an 8; etc.).

A measure of composite desirability for any of the 10 motivational factors is simply the algebraic sum of the statement desirability measures for that factor. The scoring convention allows a maximum score of 44 for any one factor and a minimum score of minus 14. A neutral ranking of all five statements for a factor results in a score of 5, which corresponds to the midpoint, or the "zone of indifference." Accordingly, composite motivational scores for a factor greater than or equal to 5 denote desirable attitudes toward that factor; scores less than 5 denote undesirable attitudes toward that factor.

ADMINISTERING CONSEQUENCES

The use of Q-sort can facilitate the difficult task of assessing the relevant motivational factors for an employee. Once these factors are defined, the next step is to properly convey to the employee the organizational requirements that must be fulfilled in order to have his or her motivational factors fulfilled. Next, rewards for good performance must be effectively administered. Before discussing either the conveying of requirements or the administering of consequences, a review of positive and negative control strategies is required.

Positive Versus Negative Control

The motivational factors as defined by the employee's Q-sort can be used as the basic reinforcers of behavior through positive and negative control strategies. As discussed earlier, positive control consists of providing desirable outcomes. The statements ranked as desirable in an employee's Q-sort provide a repertoire of positive reinforcers for a manager to administrate to an employee. Negative control uses (1) negative reinforcement (withdrawing undesirable consequences when there is desirable performance), (2) punishment (providing undesirable consequences when there is undesirable behavior), and (3) extinction (withholding a desirable consequence when there is undesirable performance). The statements ranked as undesirable by an employee in a Q-sort offer alternatives for negative reinforcement and punishment. Extinction involves withholding outcomes that are based upon statements ranked as desirable.

Negative control, though generally an effective means of influencing employee behavior, has a serious drawback: it often has undesirable side effects. Perhaps the most common one is that an employee develops fear or resentment toward a manager who frequently presents undesirable consequences. Employees tend to avoid that manager. Negative control also tends to elicit dysfunctional emotional behavior such as anger and a desire for revenge.

Positive control is virtually without undesirable side effects. Since positive control provides employees with desirable consequences, the manager will usually be regarded cordially. Employees tend to do what is requested of them, and dysfunctional emotional behavior is not provoked.

However, to administer positive control, an employee must first exhibit desirable behavior. This can be a problem with positive control tactics. A manager must wait for desirable behavior to occur before it can be reinforced. Therefore, time and patience are often required.

Though positive reinforcement is generally considered more effective and desirable, negative control enjoys considerable popularity. This popularity is attributed to several factors.

First, negative control is closely aligned with traditional values such as the "eye for an eye" philosophy. Second, negative control tends to be satisfying to the manager applying it (i.e., a manager's frustrations are often relieved by taking them out on a subordinate who has performed poorly). Third, negative control tactics require less effort and creativity (i.e., it's far easier to punish an employee for undesirable behavior than to develop a positive control strategy). Finally, negative control can be applied more quickly than positive control. For example, when employees make mistakes, they can be punished immediately rather than when they do what is right. In certain situations, a manager may not be able to wait to apply positive control (e.g., in the case of security violations or of reckless behavior which endangers the safety of other employees).

When positive control strategies either require too much time or are not achieving desired results, negative control must be used. Negative control can be combined with positive control to minimize undesirable side effects. Thus, if a programmer is punished for not completing a project on time, he or she is quickly given another project to rectify himself or herself. If the programmer completes this next project on schedule, positive reinforcement is provided. The information provided from the Q-sort provides several alternatives for selecting an appropriate reinforcement for the situation. When an employee is subjected to punishment, negative reinforcement, or extinction, he or she should be immediately provided with an opportunity to obtain positive reinforcement.

Conveying Organizational Requirements

Properly informing employees of what is expected of them in order to obtain desired outcomes is critical. Failure to do so can result in frustration, confusion, and poor performance from employees. There are three straightforward strategies for conveying performance requirements -- communication, imitation, and shaping.[17] Each strategy can be used with positive control or negative control as discussed below.

Communication.
Communication is the most straightforward positive control strategy. It consists of clearly articulating to an employee, preferably at the beginning of a work relationship, what the expectations are for the employee's performance. If the employee adopts the desired behavior, he or she should be provided with positive reinforcement.

In spite of the simplicity of this approach, managers frequently fail to capitalize on it. Managers are often too busy or are simply negligent about providing necessary reinforcement, and this is unfortunate. Employees can be very impressionable, particularly when a new work relationship is being developed. If a manager fails to systematically reinforce an employee for desired behavior, the frequency of that behavior will decrease unless it is reinforced by some other means.

Consider a programmer who meets several demanding programming deadlines that were requested by his or her supervisor. If the supervisor fails to recognize, or otherwise reinforce, the programmer's efforts, the

---

[17]James C. Wetherbe and Robert Justis, "Employee Behavior — Reinforcement Is the Trigger," *Data Management*, November 1979, pp. 20-21, 28.

programmer may consequently assume that the supervisor is not really sincere about the importance of meeting deadlines. Therefore, the programmer may decide not to be as concerned or as punctual about future deadlines. The supervisor would then have to use negative control strategies to change the programmer's behavior.

In short, the supervisor would have missed the opportunity to use a more effective and efficient positive control strategy. The programmer would have been disappointed for not getting credit for doing a good job and would have been humiliated at having his or her subsequent performance criticized.

Proper use of positive control can prevent a work relationship from deteriorating to the point where negative control is required.

Imitation. Imitation can be used in situations where a manager's expectations have been communicated, but an employee is still not exhibiting the desired behavior. The manager can tactfully, but publicly, reward another employee who is performing effectively (e.g., with a promotion, or an increase in salary).

This approach allows the manager to avoid criticizing the employee who is not yet performing up to standards, and it thereby allows the relationship between the manager and the underachiever to remain positive. The objective is to provide a behavior model for the underachiever to emulate. If the underachiever takes the cue and properly imitates good behavior, the manager administers positive reinforcement.

An effective means for establishing an environment for imitation is to either hire or transfer an outstanding employee into a group of underachievers. The new employee can then set a new standard for the underachievers to imitate. However, care must be taken to provide the new employee with reinforcement and ensure that he or she is not pressured by the underachievers to lower performance standards.

Shaping. Shaping, the third strategy, can be applied in combination with communication or imitation. In many situations, employees attempting to perform in a manner consistent with management expectations may not perform totally as desired; that is, they will approximate what has been requested. In these cases, a manager can shape (or mold) substandard behavior into the desired behavior. Initially, the manager reinforces any behavior that approximates the desired behavior. As reinforcement is administered, the manager indicates how the performance can be improved even more.

Over a period of time, the manager becomes more discriminating in what is reinforced, thereby establishing a higher standard that more closely aligns with the desired behavior. If the shaping process is systematically applied, the employee will eventually achieve the desired behavior.

Table 5-2 Reinforcement schedules

Schedule	Description	Examples	Effects	Illustration
Continuous	Reinforcement presented each time behavior occurs	Piecework—paid for every task completed	1. High rate of behavior acquisition 2. Continuous high rate of performance 3. Rapid extinction when reinforcers are withdrawn 4. May result in early satiation	P — Withdrawal E — Continuous R L
Intermittent (reinforcer does not follow every response)				
Fixed Ratio (FR)	Reinforcement presented after behavior occurs a fixed number of times	Production piecework; incentive ratio, i.e., units/hr.	1. Often a performance pause after reinforcer is presented 2. Maximum reinforcement by performing behavior as quickly as possible	F E — E O V — Fixed Ratio

Schedule	Description	Examples	Effects		
Fixed Interval (FI)	Reinforcement presented after a fixed time period	Monthly wage; scheduled evaluations	1. Pronounced performance pause following 2. Leads to less consistent rates of behavior	R E	Fixed Interval
Variable Ratio (VR)	Reinforcement presented after behavior occurs a certain number of times—the number varies around an average	Slot machines fishing; some sales bonuses or commissions	1. Performance consistently high 2. Extinction slower than FR schedule 3. Considered the best schedule	M L S A N	Variable Ratio
Variable Interval (VI)	Reinforcement presented after a certain time interval—the length of time varies around an average	"Pop" quizzes or evaluations; praise; recognition	1. Tends to produce sustained performance 2. High frequency does not speed up reinforcement like VR or FR	C E	Variable Interval

Scheduling Reinforcement

Scheduling reinforcement is often as important as is the consequence administered.[18] It is usually not practical to reinforce an employee each time he or she exhibits desirable behavior. Often, reinforcement has to be administered periodically. In such cases, proper scheduling of reinforcement can become a problem.

How can a manager effectively schedule reinforcement? This question requires an explanation of reinforcement schedules and their effect on behavior.

There are two basic types of scheduling: continuous and intermittent. Intermittent scheduling consists of four subtypes: fixed ratio, variable ratio, fixed interval, and variable interval. A description of each is provided in Table 5-2.

If a computer operator is complimented every time he or she tidies up the computer room at the end of his or her shift, behavior is being continuously reinforced. As depicted in Table 5-2, this behavior will probably stop if the manager (consciously or unconsciously) stops commending the employee. When continuous reinforcement is withdrawn, the change in consequences is noticed by the employee. Therefore, if continuous reinforcement is not practical, a manager is wise not to start it.

The fixed ratio and fixed interval schedules tend to create cyclical behavior patterns. The employee tends to increase the frequency of desired behavior as he or she approaches the next scheduled reinforcement. Behavior frequency declines after reinforcement.

The cyclical nature of fixed ratio and fixed interval reinforcement scheduling indicates that total reliance on annual or monthly performance reviews for reinforcement will have disappointing results.

The variable ratio and variable interval schedules provide the most sustained performance level. An employee appears to be more reinforced by a schedule that introduces an element of surprise (i.e., by rewarding an employee when he or she is not expecting it). Consider the effect on a programmer if a high-level manager drops by the office to commend him or her for exceptional performance on a particular project. Receiving unscheduled rewards such as promotions, salary increases, or recognition tells an employee that good performance is noticed and appreciated all the time -- not just when reviews are scheduled. However, in many organizations certain rewards can only be provided on a fixed ratio or fixed interval basis. For example, salary increases or promotions can only be awarded during an annual review. The Q-sort reveals a number of possible reinforcers, many of which are independent of fixed schedules.

---

[18]James C. Wetherbe and Robert Justis, "Employee Behavior — Scheduling Is the Trigger," *Data Management*, January 1980, pp. 30-33.

Nevertheless, particular care is required to effectively administer variable reinforcement. It is easy for a manager to overlook reinforcing an employee when reinforcement is done on a variable basis. Since most organizations have fixed schedules of reinforcement (e.g., annual reviews), a manager often defaults to the fixed schedule.

However, a manager who adds systematic scheduling of variable reinforcement to the fixed schedules can usually achieve a higher level of personnel productivity.

SUMMARY

By effectively administering consequences, the MIS manager can exert considerable influence over the behavior and productivity of personnel. Though there are different points of view on motivation, certain practical guidelines can be drawn from existing motivational theory. First, motivation must focus on identification of employee needs. Second, work assignments and objectives should be realistic and clearly defined, and rewards for performance should reasonably fulfill the needs of the employee. Third, consequences for good performance must approximate the needs of the employee.

Q-sort offers a methodology for identifying employee needs. Proper identification of needs combined with proper administration of consequences provides a practical motivational framework. Administration of consequences preferably is accomplished by using positive control strategies, though negative control strategies are often necessary. Positive control can be effected through communication, imitation, and shaping. Scheduling of reinforcement is most effective when using a variable ratio and variable interval scheduling rather than totally depending on traditional fixed interval or fixed ratio scheduling.

SUGGESTED READINGS

Block, J., *The Q-Sort Method in Personality Assessment and Psychiatric Research*, Charles C. Thomas, Springfield, Ill., 1961.

Campbell, J. P., M. D. Dunnette, E. E. Lawler, and L. E. Weick, *Managerial Behavior Performance and Effectiveness*, McGraw-Hill, New York, 1970.

Couger, D., and R. A. Zawacki, "What Motivates DP Professionals?" *Datamation*, September 1978, pp. 116-123.

Dickson, G. W., and J. C. Wetherbe, "Increasing the Productivity of MIS Personnel: The Motivation Issue," MIS Research Center Working Paper 81-08, March 1981.

Goodling, R. A., and G. M. Guthrie, "Some Practical Considerations In Q-Sort Item Selection," *Journal of Counseling Psychology*, vol. 3, no. 3, 1956.

Gray, R. C., "Development of an Efficiency Criterion for Administering Incentives to Engineers and Scientists," Ph.D. dissertation, Oklahoma State University, 1972.

Hay, J. E., "Self-Ideal Congruence Among Engineering Managers," *Personnel and Guidance Journal*, June 1966, pp. 1084-1088.

Heider, F., *The Psychology of Interpersonal Relations*, Wiley, New York, 1958.

Hersey, P., B. Hersey, and H. Kenneth, *Management of Organizational Behavior Utilizing Human Resources*, Prentice-Hall, Englewood Cliffs, N.J., 1972.

Herzberg, F., "One More Time: How Do You Motivate Employees?" *Harvard Business Review*, vol. 46, no. 1, 1968, pp. 53-62.

_____, B. Mausner, and B. Snyderman, *The Motivation to Work*, Wiley, New York, 1959.

House, R. J., and L. A. Wigdor, "Herzberg's Dual-Factor Theory of Job Satisfaction and Motivation: A Preview of the Evidence and a Criticism," *Personnel Psychology*, vol. 20, 1967, pp. 369-389.

Hulin, C. L., and M. R. Blood, "Job Enlargement, Individual Differences, and Worker Responses," *Psychological Bulletin*, vol. 69, 1968, pp. 41-55.

Jones, E. E., and R. E. Nisbett, "The Actor and the Observer: Divergent Perception of the Causes of Behavior," in E.E. Jones, et al., (eds.), *Attribution: Perceiving the Causes of Behavior*, General Learning Press, Morristown, N.J., 1972.

Latham, G. P., and G. A. Yukl, "A Review of Research on the Application of Goal-Setting in Organizations," *Academy of Management Journal*, vol. 18, 1975, pp. 299-302.

_____, "Assigned Versus Participative Goal Setting With Educated and Uneducated Wood Workers," *Journal of Applied Psychology*, vol. 60, 1975, pp. 299-302.

Locke, E. A., "Toward a Theory of Task Motivation and Incentives," *Organizational Behavior and Human Performance*, vol. 3, 1968, pp. 157-189.

_____, "The Nature and Causes of Job Satisfaction" in M. Dunnette (ed.), *Handbook of Industrial and Organizational Psychology*, Rand McNally, Chicago, 1976.

Luthans, Fred, and Robert Kreiter, *Organizational Behavior Modification*, Scott Foresman, Glenview, Ill., 1975.

March, J. G., and H. A. Simon, *Organizations*, Wiley, New York, 1958.

Maslow, A. H., "A Theory of Human Motivation," *Psychological Review*, July 1943, pp. 370-396.

McGinnies, E., *Social Behavior: A Fundamental Analysis*, Houghton Mifflin, Boston, 1970.

Michael, J., and L. Myerson, "A Behavioral Approach to Counseling and Guidance," *Harvard Educational Review*, vol. 32, no. 4, Fall 1962, pp. 382-402.

Millenson, J. R., *Principles of Behavioral Analysis*, Macmillan, New York, 1967.

Mingo, K., "Applications of the Q-Sort Method to Manpower Analysis," paper presented at XVIII International Congress of the Institute of Management Science, Imperial College, London, June 1970.

Myers, M. A., "Who Are Your Motivated Workers?" *Harvard Business Review*, January-February 1964, pp. 73-88.

Nunnally, J. D., *Psychometric Theory*, McGraw-Hill, New York, 1967.

Pavlov, I. P., *Conditioned Reflexes: An Investigation of the Psychological Activity of the Cerebral Cortex*, G.V. Aroup (trans., ed.), Oxford University Press, London, 1972.

Skinner, B. F., *The Behavior of Organisms*, Appleton-Century-Crofts, New York, 1938.

_____, *Science and Human Behavior*, The Free Press, New York, 1953.

_____, *Operant Behavior: Areas of Research and Application*, Appleton-Century-Crofts, New York, 1966.

_____, *Beyond Freedom and Dignity*, Bantam, New York, 1971.

Steers, R. M., "Task-Goal Attitudes, Need for Achievement, and Supervisory Performance," *Organizational Behavior and Human Performance*, vol. 13, 1975, pp. 392-403.

Terpstra, D. E., "Theories of Motivation -- Borrowing the Best," *Personnel Journal*, June 1979, pp. 376-379.

Thorndike, E. L., *Emotional Psychology: The Psychology of Learning*, vol. II, Columbia University, Teachers College, New York, 1913.

Vroom, V., *Work and Motivation*, McGraw-Hill, New York, 1970.

Wabba, M., and L.G. Bridwell, "Maslow Reconsidered: A Review of Research on the Need Hierarchy Theory," *Organizational Behavior and Human Performance*, vol. 15, 1976, pp. 217-240.

Watson, J. B., "Psychology as the Behaviorists View It," *Psychology Review*, 1913, pp. 158-177.

_____, *Behaviorism*, Norton, New York, 1924.

Weiner, B., "An Attributional Interpretation of Expectancy-Value Theory," in B. Weiner (ed.), *Cognitive Views of Human Motivation*, Academic Press, New York, 1974.

_____, and A. Kukla, "An Attributional Analysis of Achievement Motivation," *Journal of Personality and Social Psychology*, vol. 15, 1970, pp. 1-20.

_____, D. Russell, and D. Lerman, "Affective Consequences of Causal Ascriptions," in J. H. Harvey, et al. (eds.), *New Directions in Attribution Research*, vol. 2, Erlbaun, Hillsdale, N.J., 1978.

Wenrich, W. W., *A Primer of Behavior Modification*, Brooks/Cole, Belmont, Calif., 1970.

Wetherbe, J. C., and R. Justis, "Employee Behavior -- Reinforcement Is the Trigger," *Data Management*, November 1979, pp. 20-21, 28.

_____ and _____, "Employee Behavior -- Scheduling Is the Trigger," *Data Management*, January 1980, pp. 30-33.

NATURE AND PURPOSE OF QUESTIONNAIRE

The attitude that an individual has toward his or her work results from many conditions occurring both on and off the job. In general, this attitude or feeling toward a job varies between individuals and varies with time for each individual.

This instrument has been designed to measure the extent of satisfaction that individuals derive from their jobs when confronted with specified job-related conditions that are time-dependent. The extent of satisfaction is expressed in terms of varying degrees of desirability associated with each condition.

A great many of the conditions associated with the work environment can be controlled or significantly influenced by management. This influence is realized through the controlled distribution of incentives to employees. The results of this study will tend to indicate the nature and magnitude of those incentives which promote conditions on the job perceived by employees to offer the greatest amount of satisfaction for the longest period of time.

PROCEDURE

The information that you will need in order to complete this procedure is provided on a deck of 50 small cards. A brief statement of a job-related condition or situation is printed on each card. The two-digit number appearing in the upper right-hand corner of each card is a randomized code which has no relation to the printed statement. Three Q-sort work sheets are provided to conduct three sorts -- one for the present and one each for 3 and 5 years in the future. On each work sheet, the numbers 1 to 9, together with descriptive phrases ranging from "extremely undesirable" to "extremely desirable" are printed across the top of the page. These numbers and descriptive phrases constitute nine categories of desirability. Each category has a fixed number of lines in which statements can be recorded (e.g., extremely desirable has two and highly desirable has three).

The general procedure to follow is to sort the 50 statements (cards) into the 9 categories in a manner which reflects your interpretation of the relative desirability of the statements. You are asked to complete this sorting procedure three separate times according to the instructions provided below for sort 1, sort 2, and sort 3.

You will need a large, empty flat surface on which to sort the cards. Begin by placing the category cards in a row with card number 1 at the left and card number 9 on the right. These nine cards constitute the headings for the nine categories of desirability.

The procedure for actually sorting the 50 cards is optional; however, it is suggested that you begin by reading all statements and separating the corresponding cards into a "desirable" group and an "undesirable" group. (It is best not to stack the cards when you are sorting them; instead spread them out so that you can see all of them at once.) From the desirable group select two cards to place in category 9, and from the undesirable group select two cards to place in category 1. Arrange them in a row below the category cards representing these categories. Then select three cards from the desirable group to place in category 8 and three cards from the undesirable group to place in category 2. Proceed in this manner, working from the ends of the distribution toward the center, selecting the number of cards needed to fill the spaces provided on the work sheet under each category. The ten cards needed to fill the spaces under category 5, a "neutral zone," may come from either category or from both. When you have chosen cards for each category, you may make any changes you desire as long as you maintain the required number of cards in each category.

When you are satisfied that the cards have been sorted to best represent your interpretation of the desirability of the statements on them, record the number on each card in the appropriate space on the work sheet. The relative sequence in which statements are recorded under each category heading is not important; however, you must be careful to ensure that the number is recorded under its proper category and on the proper work sheet. When you have completed one sort and have recorded the results on the work sheet, pick up the cards, shuffle them, and complete another sort in accordance with the appropriate directions.

Sort 1

Complete the first sort for your current work environment. That is, the first sort should reflect the situation in which you are presently working.

If you are a newly hired employee, assume that you are already working on your first job. Assume that the total work environment is satisfactory; that is, assume that you are reasonably happy with your job.

Sort 2

Assume that the conditions which you selected as extremely desirable on sort 1 have been realized. *Three years* have passed since sort 1 was completed. Assume that you are still reasonably happy with your job and have no immediate plans to seek work elsewhere. Complete sort 2 with the assumption that these conditions are those under which you are working.

Sort 3

Assume that the conditions which you selected as extremely desirable on Sort 2 have been realized. *Two years* have passed since sort 2 was completed; thus, *five years* have passed since sort 1 was completed. As before, assume that you are reasonably happy with your job and have no immediate desire to seek work elsewhere. Complete sort 3 with the assumption that these conditions are those under which you are working.

SORT 1
(Time frame 0 years)

| 1 Extremely | 2 Highly | 3 Moderately | 4 Fairly | 5 Neutral | 6 Fairly | 7 Moderately | 8 Highly | 9 Extremely |

─────── Undesirable ───────   ─────── Desirable ───────

(2)   (3)   (6)   (9)   (10)   (9)   (6)   (3)   (2)

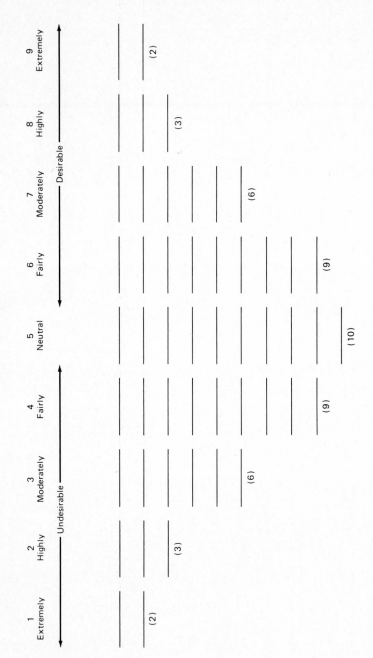

SORT 2
(Time frame 3 years)

	1 Extremely	2 Highly	3 Moderately	4 Fairly	5 Neutral	6 Fairly	7 Moderately	8 Highly	9 Extremely
		Undesirable				Desirable			
	(2)	(3)	(6)	(9)	(10)	(9)	(6)	(3)	(2)

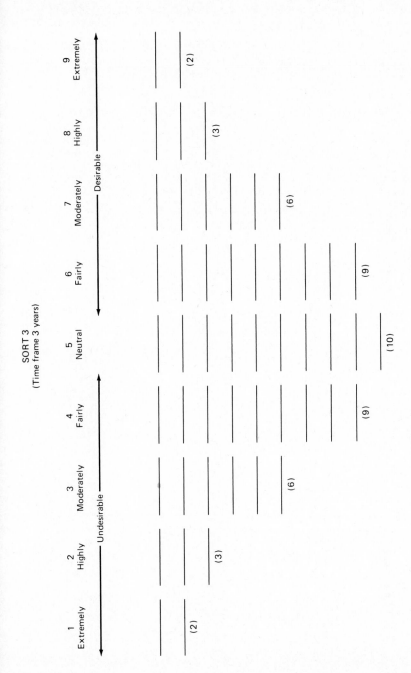

SORT 3
(Time frame 3 years)

PART FOUR

MIS PLANNING AND CONTROL

STRATEGIC PLANNING FOR MIS

INTRODUCTION

This chapter reviews MIS planning and planning problems. A four-stage model of MIS planning consisting of strategic planning, organization information requirements analysis, resource allocation, and project planning is discussed. Methodologies that have been proposed for use in MIS planning are discussed and classified according to their use in one of the four stages of the MIS planning model.

EVOLUTION OF MIS PLANNING

The forces necessitating effective MIS planning are well-documented and accepted. The need to plan seems clear. How to plan is less obvious. The stages of the EDP growth model developed by Nolan and discussed in Chapter 2 provide valuable insights into the evolution of MIS planning.[1] During the first stage -- initiation -- the organization is oriented to its new computer resource through accounting transaction applications. As the potential benefits of the computer begin to become apparent, heavy demand for services results in stage 2, during which there is a proliferation of applications throughout the organization. In these two first stages there is little or no formal planning or control of information systems activities. This deficiency, complicated by ever-

---

[1]R. L. Nolan, "Managing the Computer Resource: A Stage Hypothesis," *Communications of the ACM,* vol. 16, July 1973, pp. 399–405.

increasing demands for information service systems, results in a skyrocketing MIS budget. In response, upper management charges the MIS manager with designing and implementing adequate planning and control systems. This marks emergence into stage 3. Most organizations that have been involved in MIS for several years are in stages 4 and 5. According to Nolan, few organizations have achieved MIS maturity.

It is instructive to consider the nature of these initial efforts to establish planning and control systems. Analysis of MIS activities discloses that the logical entities consuming MIS resources are application development projects and their completed manifestations -- operational application systems. These become the focus of initial planning and control systems. Systems development methodologies are adopted, and project management systems are installed. These include the use of well-defined project phases, specified deliverables, formal user reviews, and sign-off points. Techniques such as structured design, HIPO (Hierarchy plus Input-Process-Output), structured programming, and walk-through are used to better manage the systems development process. Additionally, attention is focused on processing completed systems efficiently. High availability and reliability is emphasized, and computer operations planning and scheduling is initiated.

In terms of Anthony's three levels of organizational planning and control -- operational, managerial, and strategic -- these initial mechanisms address operational MIS planning.[2] As the organization becomes more sophisticated in its use of MIS, emphasis shifts to management (or resource allocation control). A manifestation of this shift is the organization of the MIS function into a corporate computing utility. Some form of chargeout is implemented in an attempt to shift accountability for MIS expenditures to the users. There is some question concerning the effectiveness of chargeout as a cost control tool, but in theory, chargeout fosters greater user attention to benefits and costs and results in more effective planning.

Collectively, these measures have an effect on planning, and a process identifying demands for MIS services is developed. Typically, annual planning cycles are established to identify potentially beneficial MIS services, to perform some aspect of cost/benefit analysis, and to subject the portfolio of potential projects to some resource allocation mechanism. An MIS steering committee composed of key managers representing major functional units within the organization often performs these functions. The steering committee is created to oversee the MIS

[2]R. N. Anthony, *Planning and Control Systems: A Framework for Analysis*, Division of Research, Graduate School of Business, Harvard University, Boston, Mass., 1965.

function, to ensure that adequate planning and control processes are present, and to direct MIS activities in support of long-range organizational objectives and goals. The steering committee reviews the project portfolio, approves those projects thought to be beneficial, and assigns relative priorities. The approved projects can then be mapped into a development schedule, usually encompassing a 1- to 5-year time period. This schedule becomes the basis for determining MIS support requirements: long-range financial requirements for hardware and software, personnel, and facilities.

The planning process described above is typical of the traditional approach to MIS planning currently practiced by many organizations. Figure 6-1 is a conceptual model of this process.

The specifics of MIS planning processes will, of course, vary among organizations. For example, not all organizations have a high-level steering committee. Project priorities may be determined by the MIS manager, his or her superior, or company politics or even on a first-come-first-served basis. Organizations with decentralized MIS functions often employ integrative mechanisms such as formal review and consolidation meetings to determine their overall MIS plan. In cases of strong divisional autonomy, no centralized planning may be attempted, in which case a process similar to that depicted in Figure 6-1 may be utilized by each divisional MIS group. Acknowledging variations, the model reasonably represents traditional MIS planning.

THE PROBLEMS OF MIS PLANNING

The most common difficulties experienced in MIS planning are

1. Alignment of the MIS plan with the overall strategies and objectives of the organization
2. Design of an information system structure or architecture for the organization as a framework within which applications are to be designed and developed
3. Allocation of information system development and operations resources among competing applications
4. Completing information system projects on time and on schedule
5. Selection and use of methodologies for performing the first three processes

Figure 6-1 Basic Four-Stage Model of MIS Planning

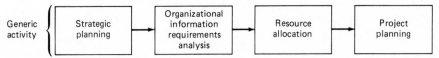

Alignment of the MIS Plan with the Organizational Plan

The first problem is making sure the MIS planning process identifies and selects information systems applications that fit the priorities established by needs and priorities of the organization. However, the organizational strategies and plans may not be written, or they may be formulated in terms that are not useful for information system planning. It is therefore often difficult to ascertain the strategies and goals to which the information system plan should be aligned; but without this alignment, the information system plan will not obtain long-term organizational support. If the selection and scheduling of information system projects is based only on proposals submitted by users, the projects will reflect existing computer-use biases in the organization, aggressiveness of some managers in submitting proposals, and various aspects of organizational power rather than the overall needs and priorities of the organization.

Design of an Information System Architecture

The term "information system architecture" refers to the overall structure of the information system. This structure consists of the applications for the various levels of the organization (operations, management control, and strategic planning) and applications oriented to various management activities (planning, control, and decision making). The system structure or architecture also includes databases, model bases, and supporting software. An information system architecture for an organization should guide long-range development but also allow response to diverse short-range information system demands.

Selecting an information system architecture is difficult. The difficulty stems from two processes: the architecture selection (assuming a complete and correct understanding of requirements) and the eliciting of requirements. If organization information requirements are well specified, the number of alternative architectures can be fairly large. If requirements are fuzzy and poorly specified, the alternatives for information system architecture expand further. Even after introducing constraints such as a limited vendor list and stable software, the analysis of alternatives can yield recommendations that are subject to question.

The process of obtaining information requirements can, at best, result in a tentative set of fairly complete, reasonably correct requirements. At worst, the information requirements can be incomplete and incorrect. In the absence of well-defined processes for information requirements determination, it is difficult for an organizational unit or functional area to define completely its information requirements. The managers of the units are constrained in defining information needs by their bounded rationality. Many useful computer-based solutions are not considered. Also, perceived information needs are biased by human processing limitations that cause users to "fix" on recent problems as the most important and to draw unwarranted conclusions from a small number of occurrences of some event.   These and other human limitations in defining information requirements mean that when managers are required to define their information needs without the aid of systematic information requirements determination processes, the result is a set of requirements that are probably not complete or arranged in "real" priority order by the submitters.

Allocation of Development Resources

The rational, organization-optimal allocation of development resources among competing units is difficult, especially if the portfolio of potential applications does not fit into an overall organizational plan and functional-organizational unit requirements do not fit into some orderly framework that establishes completeness and priority.   Organizational dynamics such as relative power and aggressive advocacy may be used in place of some rational allocation.

Completing Projects on Time and on Schedule

Few information system projects are completed on time or on schedule. Consequently, MIS management's credibility suffers.   Project plans are seldom accurate, as time and resource requirements are generally underestimated.

Selection of Methodologies

The last major problem is the selection of one or more planning methodologies from the set of competing methodologies (especially methodologies for developing the application portfolio and allocating resources).   In the literature, each of the methodologies tends to be presented as "the solution."   Enthusiastic developers (and even some users) provide testimonials of the power of the methodologies in MIS planning processes.   But, even though the techniques are similar, they are not directly equivalent.   Presumably each methodology has a set of circumstances under which it is superior.   There is very little guidance in the literature to make such a selection, taking into account the contingencies an organization is facing.   In fact, there is no overall framework for classifying methodologies.

The discussion of problems in MIS planning suggests a need for a comprehensive model of MIS planning so that the process can be researched, explained, and applied.

Major MIS Planning Activity	Description
Strategic MIS planning	Establishing the relationship between the overall organizational plan and the MIS plan
Organizational information requirements analysis	Identifying broad, organizational information requirements to establish a strategic information architecture that can be used to direct specific application system development projects
Resource allocation	Allocation of both MIS application development resources and operational resources
Project planning	Developing a plan that expresses schedules and resource requirements for specific information system projects

Figure 6-2 Description of MIS Planning Stages

FOUR-STAGE MIS PLANNING MODEL

A basic, generic MIS planning model has been formulated based on observation of planning efforts, the literature, and an analysis of methodologies being used in the planning process. The basic MIS planning model depicted in Figure 6-2 consists of four major generic activities: strategic MIS planning, information requirements analysis, resource allocation, and project planning.

Most organizations engage in each of these four stages, but involvement tends to be evolutionary and governed by problems as they occur rather than by a plan for engaging in each stage as appropriate. Planning methodologies often are chosen during these stages on the basis of persuasive power of methodology developers rather than on the basis of a reasoned choice of a methodology for a given stage of MIS planning. The basic MIS planning model presented here provides a framework for study and evaluation of the MIS planning process and for mapping methodologies to the basic activities.

The four-stage basic MIS planning model can be illustrated by a case study in which an organization followed the steps described by the model. A Fortune 100 company, on the basis of recommendations from its external auditors, was upgrading its computing capabilities from predominantly batch-oriented, second-generation systems. Major problems were being encountered in the accounting area in terms of processing speed and ability to integrate data. For example, processing was so slow in accounts payable that the company's credit rating was being affected. Therefore, the company made a . *strategic* decision to upgrade its computing capabilities to an online database environment with initial emphasis on improving accounting processing. Other applications were also to be reviewed. Although it did not use a formal approach, the organization had, at this point, gone through the strategic stage. The top management of the organization was strategically determining MIS objectives.

During the next 6 months, the organization hired a new MIS management team and had it analyze the new system and look at overall information requirements. The MIS group used IBM'S BSP (business system planning) methodology to conduct a comprehensive study. This period can be characterized as an organizational *information requirements analysis* stage.

During the following 18 months, several systems were implemented in both the accounting and the operational areas. User management began to complain about two issues: they wanted more systems and they wanted faster responses for new systems. But MIS costs had proliferated during the preceding 2 years. Top management and consequently MIS management had become concerned about allocating limited resources to increasing demand. This put the organization in the *resource allocation* stage. They decided to install a chargeout system to allocate resources.

The case illustrates how, on the basis of organizational requirements, MIS planning moves from one stage to another. It also illustrates how specific formal models may be selected for use in each of the three stages. In the case situation, the formal models were BSP in the organizational information requirements analysis stage and chargeout in the resource allocation stage. There was no use of a formal model in the strategic planning stage, but strategic MIS decisions were a function of overall company strategy. The organization used Gantt charts for *project planning*.

The very general four-stage model presented in Figure 6-2 can be expanded to include major activities and outputs of the three stages, as shown in Figure 6-3. By adding this detail, the model moves from a high level of abstraction to a more concrete formulation of MIS planning activities.

Strategic MIS Planning

During the strategic planning stage, it is critical to align MIS strategic planning with overall organizational planning. To accomplish this the organization must

- Assess organizational objectives and strategies
- Set MIS mission
- Assess the organizational environment
- Set MIS policies, objectives, and strategies

The output from this process should be an accurate perception of the strategic aspirations and directions of the organization, a new or revised

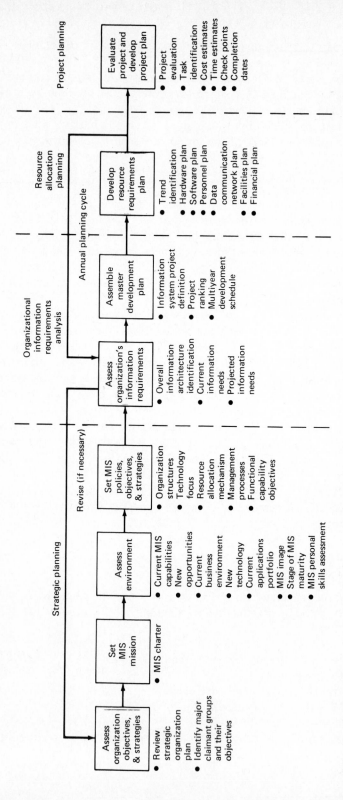

Figure 6-3 Major Activities and Outputs in Four Stages of MIS Planning

MIS charter, an assessment of the state of the MIS function, and a statement of policies, objectives, and strategies for the MIS effort.

Organizational Information Requirements Analysis

The first phase of the organizational information requirements analysis (OIRA) stage consists of assessing current and projected information needs to support decision making and operations of the organizations. This effort is not to be confused with or replace the detailed information requirements analysis associated with application system specifications (as detailed in a report and in terminal display layouts). Rather, this is a higher level of information requirements analysis aimed at developing an overall information architecture for the organization or a major sector of the organization.

The second phase of the OIRA stage consists of assembling a master development plan. This plan is derived from the information architecture and defines specific information system projects, ranking of projects, and a development schedule.

Resource Allocation

Resource allocation consists of developing hardware, software, data communications, facilities, personnel, and financial plans needed to execute the master development plan defined in the OIRA stage. This stage provides the framework for technology procurement, personnel planning, and budgeting to provide appropriate service levels to users.

Project Planning

Project planning consists of evaluating the project in terms of requirements and difficulty. Providing definitions of tasks that need to be performed is the next step. Finally, time, cost, and completion estimates must be developed and checkpoints to be used for evaluating project progress must be defined.

Staging of the Model

As depicted in Figure 6-3, the activities within stages and the stages themselves have a sequential flow starting with "Assess organizational objectives and strategies" and ending with "Evaluate project and develop project plan." A complete execution of the model is not necessary in each planning cycle. As Figure 6-3 portrays, the annual planning cycle may consist only of assessing organizational information requirements, assembling a master plan, and developing a resource allocation and project plan. The time interval between executions of an entire model is a function of how rapidly the organization's overall objectives and strategies are changing in ways that impact MIS requirements. The interval between comprehensive planning cycles may vary from 1 to 5 years.

METHODOLOGIES FOR USE IN MIS PLANNING

The next issue is the relationship of the various planning methodologies to the four-stage planning model. Several of the most publicized planning methodologies are listed below:

- Strategy set transformation
- Business systems planning (BSP)
- Critical success factors (CSFs)
- Business information analysis and integration technique (BIAIT)
- Ends/means analysis
- Return on investment
- Chargeout
- Zero-based budgeting
- Program evaluation review technique (PERT)
- Gantt charts
- Milestones

A brief description of each approach is presented together with a discussion of its relationship to the three major planning activities.

Strategy Set Transformation

King[3] proposes an approach to the strategic phase of MIS planning that he calls "strategy set transformation." The overall organizational strategy is viewed as an "information set" consisting of the mission, objectives, strategies, and other strategic variables (e.g., managerial sophistication, proclivity to accept change, and important environment constraints). Strategic MIS planning is the process of transforming the organizational strategy set into an "MIS strategy set" consisting of MIS system objectives, constraints, and design strategies.

The first step of this methodology is the identification and explication of the organizational strategy set. The obvious starting point in this activity is a review of the organization's written strategic or long-range plan. If such a document does not exist or if it is deficient in providing purposeful guidelines for managerial decisions, a strategy set

---

[3] W. R. King, "Strategic Planning for Management Information Systems," *MIS Quarterly*, vol. 2, no. 1, March 1978, pp. 27-37.

may be constructed. King describes the strategy set construction process as

1. Delineating the claimant structure of the organization (i.e., owner, managers, employees, suppliers, customers, creditors, governmental agencies, local communities, competitors, etc.)
2. Identifying goals for each claimant group
3. Identifying organizational purposes and strategy relative to each claimant group

Once the tentative statement of the organizational strategy set has been developed, it should be presented to top managers for review and comments.

The next major step involves transforming the organizational strategy set into an MIS strategy set consisting of system objectives, constraints, and design principles. The transformation process involves identification of the MIS strategic elements for each element within the organizational strategy set. Information analysts then construct alternative structures for the overall MIS architecture subject to the MIS objectives, strategies, and constraints enumerated as the MIS strategy set. The general alternatives are then presented to management.

As an example, a claimant group may be creditors. They have goals of protecting their assets and their relative priority for repayment plus making sound decisions on extending additional credit or enforcing repayment of existing debt. The organizational purposes and strategy of this claimant group include timely analysis of financial statements of the company to which they have extended credit to determine ability to repay the loans and to identify any impairment of security for the debt. One system objective of the company MIS is therefore to provide prompt information to all major creditors. The information should allow a creditor to reevaluate the decision to extend additional credit or to continue with existing credit. The alternative structures for achieving these MIS system objectives are to provide regular financial statements in the traditional format and to make these available to the creditors or to provide a special report for creditors that will present data in a form that is especially useful to creditors. This latter option might even include comparative industry data to show the relative credit worthiness of the company within its industry.

This methodology focuses exclusively on strategic MIS planning. To be successful, this approach requires accurate and concise articulation of organizational objectives and strategies. Identification of the organization's claimant structure offers a useful framework to define this information, but the activity is still somewhat unstructured and subjective. Assuming the organizational strategy set can be adequately defined, this technique can result in a strategic MIS plan with an appropriate long-range time frame and a high level of integration with overall business strategy. Information analysts may be used to interpret or elicit the organizational strategy set and then to enumerate the MIS strategy set elements and develop alternative general designs for the overall MIS architecture. Because of the subjective nature of the process, there should be significant management and user input and review.

Business Systems Planning

Business systems planning (BSP) is a comprehensive planning methodology developed by IBM. BSP was initially developed for IBM's internal use, but as IBM customers expressed interest in learning how they might better manage their MIS resources, BSP was released as a generalized methodology to assist in this task. It is supported by IBM manuals and training courses.

BSP basically involves a two-phase approach. It is conducted by a BSP planning team composed of both user and MIS personnel. Phase I focuses on developing a broad overall understanding of the organization, identifying how MIS currently supports the business, specifying the gross network of information systems required to support the business, and identifying the highest priority subsystems to be implemented within the network. Data is primarily gathered through interviews with numerous managers to determine their environment, objectives, key decisions and problems, and perceived information needs. The analysis concentrates on business processes without regard for organization structure.

The objective of phase II is to develop a long-range plan for the design, development, and implementation of a network of information systems to support the business process identified in phase I. The current information systems are assessed, and weaknesses and deficiencies are noted. Processes and users that share data are identified, and the potential for common information systems across organizational boundaries is determined. The output of phase II is the information systems plan. This plan describes the overall information systems architecture and defines the scheduling implementation of individual systems within the overall network. It serves as the blueprint for development of an integrated MIS.

BSP can also be described as a process which elicits, analyzes, and synthesizes information to result in a plan:

1. In the eliciting and discovery activity, the questions center on organizational functions performed, decisions made, and problems requiring information.

2. In the analysis activity, organizational processes are summarized and associated with information needs and requirements data.

3. The synthesis activity specifies applications to meet needs, database requirements for applications support, and priority for development.

The fundamental thrust of the BSP approach is toward identifying the information necessary to run the organization. It is suggested that the master development plan include resource requirements, but the principles and guidelines of the methodology are directed at information requirements analysis.

BSP utilizes a top-down approach to identification and definition of information requirements. Information concerning the organizational processes and associated information needs is obtained by the BSP study team via observation and interviews. This approach can be effective in identifying current requirements, but without explicit consideration of overall strategic plans and objectives the resulting plan could lack the proper long-range perspective. Another drawback of the interview approach is the significant personnel time required to collect and analyze information. A sizable number of managers must be interviewed in order to develop a broad understanding of the organization's processes and of the associated information requirements. Although IBM proposes a variety of useful matrices and other graphical techniques to assist the BSP team in collecting the data, analysis of the rather large volume of data and synthesis of the data into a viable information system plan can be somewhat difficult.

Critical Success Factors

A framework advocated by Rockart[4] argues that the information needs for top managers can be derived from critical success factors, i.e., the key areas for any organization in which performance must be satisfactory if the business is to survive and flourish. Critical success factors (CSFs) differ among industries and for individual firms within a particular industry.

As an example, Rockart cites the four industry-based CSFs of supermarkets as having the right product mix available at each store, keeping it on the shelves, effectively advertising to attract shoppers to the store, and correct pricing. Since these areas of activity are major determinants of a supermarket chain's success, the status of performance in these areas should be continually measured and reported. The Rockart

---

[4]J. F. Rockart, "Chief Executives Define Their Own Data Needs," *Harvard Business Review*, March–April 1979, pp. 81–93.

research team at MIT has identified the four primary sources of CSFs as

1. Industry-based factors
2. Competitive strategy, industry position, and geographic location
3. Environmental factors
4. Temporal factors

The CSF approach involves a series of interviews (though not nearly so many as with BSP) conducted in two or three sessions. In the first session the manager is queried as to his or her goals and the CSFs that underlie those goals. Considerable discussion may be required to ensure that the analyst thoroughly understands the interrelationships between the goals and CSFs. Every effort is made to combine or eliminate similar CSFs, and an initial set of performance measures is developed. The second session is a review of the first and primarily focuses on identification of specific performance measures and possible reports. Additional sessions are held as necessary to obtain agreement on the CSF measures and reports for tracking them. The reports and related information systems required to provide them are designed by the MIS group.

Business Information Analysis and Integration Techniques

An interesting and innovative approach to information analysis and planning has been developed by Burnstine.[5] Called business information analysis and integration technique (BIAIT), it is distinctly different from other approaches. Most planning approaches tend to use open-ended questions that elicit information from managers about their information requirements and the properties of those requirements. Open-ended questions such as "What information do you need to support your decision making?" allow managers complete freedom to articulate their requirements.

Burnstine, through extensive experimentation with over 400 items, has factored out seven close-ended questions that can be used to determine a normative set of information requirements. These questions require only a binary (yes or no) response from a manager. From the responses to these questions, by those managers affected by a system, overall information requirements can theoretically be defined. This capability is independent of organizational or departmental size and is independent of the products or services provided.

[5]D. C. Burnstine, *BIAIT: An Emerging Management Discipline,* BIAIT International, New York, 1980.

The key focus of the seven classification questions is on orders and suppliers. Suppliers are persons, departments, or organizations that respond to orders. Orders are anything that requires a response from a supplier. The entity ordered is either a thing, a place, or a skill. The key point is that if a supplier, be it an organization, department, or an individual, receives no orders, it has no reason for existing.

The seven questions of BIAIT are as follows:

1. Do you bill customers or accept cash?
2. Do you deliver products or services in the future or immediately?
3. Do you create and maintain profiles of customers' buying behaviors or not?
4. Do you negotiate prices or operate on a fixed price basis?
5. Do you rent or sell your products or services?
6. Do you recall and update the products you offer or update your services?
7. Do you make to order or provide from stock the product or service that you supply?

These seven questions allow an analyst to classify an organization in terms of its systems and establish a generic model of the information-handling activities necessary for it to operate.

The generic model is customized by the unique characteristics of the organization. A helpful by-product of this process is that it defines who the data owners and data users should be. BIAIT is still in an experimental state but initial applications show promise.

Ends/Means Analysis

Ends/means (E/M) analysis is a new planning technique developed by Wetherbe and Davis[6] at the MIS Research Center at the University of Minnesota. The technique can be used to determine information requirements at the organizational, departmental, or individual manager level.

Based upon general systems theory, the technique focuses first on the ends, or outputs (goods, services, and information), generated by an organizational process. Next, the technique is used to define the means, or inputs (processes), used to accomplish the ends.

The ends or output from one process, whether the process be viewed as an organizational, departmental, or individual process, is the input to some other process. For example, the inventory process provides input

---

[6]J. C. Wetherbe and G. B. Davis, "Strategic MIS Planning Through Ends/Means Analysis," MIS Research Center Working Paper, University of Minnesota, 1982.

for the production process, the accounting process provides budget information for other organizational processes, and the marketing process provides products to customer processes.

End/means analysis is concerned with both the effectiveness and the efficiency of generating outputs from processes. "Effectiveness" pertains to how well the outputs of a process fill the input requirements of another process. "Efficiency" pertains to resources required and the use of those resources to transform an input into an output.

A model of ends/means analysis is provided in Figure 6-4. The model provides two types of information: effectiveness and efficiency. Effectiveness information is based upon what constitutes effectiveness for outputs and what information or feedback is needed to evaluate effectiveness. Efficiency information is based upon what constitutes efficiency in an input and transformation process and what information or feedback is needed to evaluate efficiency.

As an example of the flow of questions in ends/means analysis, an inventory manager might specify the following:

1. Ends specification: The outputs or end result of the inventory management function is an inventory that is as low as possible but maintained at an acceptable level of availability.

2. Means specification: The inputs and processes to accomplish the ends are

    a. Forecasts of future needs
    b. Amounts on hand and on order
    c. Items that are obsolete or in unuseable condition
    d. Safety stock policy
    e. Demand variations
    f. Cost of ordering and holding inventory
    g. Cost of items
    h. "Stock-outs"

3. Efficiency measures for inventory management are number of orders placed, cost of holding inventory, and loss on disposal of obsolete or unuseable inventory.

Figure 6-4 Model of Ends/Means Analysis

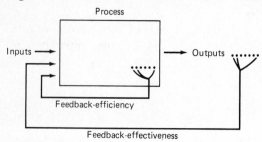

Process

Inputs →

Outputs ......

Feedback-efficiency

Feedback-effectiveness

4. Effectiveness measures are the level of inventory and the number and seriousness of stock-outs.

Ends/means analysis has been used in diverse industrial settings with positive results. Information requirements are determined that are usually more extensive than those generated by using other techniques. The problem with most information planning tools is that they usually result in information systems that provide efficiency-oriented information. However, managers agree it is more important to be effective than to be efficient. Ends/means analysis brings out effectiveness information requirements. Such requirements typically transcend departmental boundaries, and therefore ends/means analysis is especially useful for a database planning effort.

Return on Investment

Return on investment (ROI) is a cost-benefit analysis technique widely used in a variety of planning applications. Typically, projects are ranked in descending order by ROI and the highest ranked projects providing an acceptable rate of return are selected. Considerations other than ROI, such as resource constraints, organizational priorities, or politics, may alter the selection process.

Many organizations apply ROI analysis to MIS projects in an attempt to make them pass the same criteria as other organizational undertakings. To the extent cost and benefits are quantifiable, ROI is a useful planning tool. Unfortunately, MIS projects often do not lend themselves to easy quantification and estimation of costs and benefits. The costs and benefits of MIS projects are viable, complex, interrelated, and difficult to estimate. This often negates a meaningful ROI analysis.

Chargeout

Some form of chargeout system is frequently used as a basis for planning and controlling MIS. In large organizations, the MIS function is often organized as a service bureau charged with providing MIS services to all organizational subunits. Fee schedules are developed for each unit of service (e.g., CPU seconds, DASD (direct access device) I/Os, lines printed, or programming time) with the objective of recovering (or partially recovering) MIS expenditures. (See Hootman for detailed discussion of chargeout system design.) Users are charged for those MIS services consumed. In theory, holding users responsible for the cost of their information systems fosters greater planning and control of those systems.

Chargeout-based planning systems are typical of the traditional approach to MIS planning discussed earlier. In addition to the chargeout system, this approach usually includes guidelines, procedures, and schedules to specifically direct planning efforts, but the focus is frequently toward justifying the costs of proposed new information systems relative to the benefits. Planning decision making is decentralized to user departments. This can tend to limit the search for potentially beneficial new information systems, especially with respect to integrated systems affecting multiple departments and to applications areas with intangible benefits. Wetherbe and Dickson[7] identify a number of problems associated with chargeout-based planning, including high expense (in terms of both administrative and computer processing overhead), complexity, market imperfections, and difficulties with the development of integrated multidepartmental systems.

The nature of chargeout-based planning systems varies throughout organizations. However, without specific procedures to the contrary, there are no systematic mechanisms linking chargeout-based information system planning to broader organizational strategy and objectives. This may result in strictly bottom-up development of information systems with short-range time frames.

Zero-Based Budgeting

Zero-based budgeting (ZBB) is a highly structured planning technique developed by Peter Pyhrr as an alternative to incremental budgeting.[8] Its use has been fairly widespread in various governmental and private organizations.

Wetherbe and Dickson[9] suggest the use of ZBB as an MIS planning and control tool and as an alternative to chargeout-based systems. The first step in this process involves conceptually reducing all MIS activities to zero base, i.e., no development or maintenance of information systems. Next, all potential information systems applications are identified and structured into sequentially dependent incremental service levels. Expected benefits and MIS resource support requirements are listed for each service level. The projects are combined into an applications portfolio and submitted to a steering committee (or some other resource allocation mechanism) for priorities to be established. The projects are listed in ranked order of priority, and cumulative resource requirements are calculated. Wetherbe and Dickson advocate the use of the Delphi technique to conduct the ranking of projects.

---

[7]J. C. Wetherbe and G. W. Dickson, "Zero-Based Budgeting: An Alternative to Chargeout," *Information and Management,* vol. 2, no. 5, November 1979, pp. 203-213.

[8]P. A. Pyhrr, "Zero-Based Budgeting," *Harvard Business Review,* vol. 48, November-December 1970, pp. 111-121.

[9]J. C. Wetherbe and G. W. Dickson, op. cit.

Selection of projects to be implemented becomes a function of the MIS funding level.

This technique is particularly useful in identifying applications that have outlived their usefulness. It has a strong bottom-up orientation, and the service level concept could conceivably result in a logical evolutionary design of the MIS. This methodology has a strong focus on resource allocation, but again, there is no explicit strategic planning cycle or direct link to the host organization's overall planning process. Compared with ROI, ZBB allows a more subjective analysis that does not require quantification of all costs and benefits. Compared with chargeout, using an MIS steering committee to establish priorities adds a centralized, high-level perspective to planning decision making, but the lack of explicit consideration of strategic MIS planning may result in a planning process with a short-range time frame.

The amount of personnel time required to utilize the ZBB approach can be significant. Information analysts must devote a considerable amount of time interacting with users in identifying information system projects and structuring proposed systems into incremental service levels. Also, preoccupation with service level definition may narrow the search for alternatives.

Milestones

Milestone planning techniques allow projects to evolve as they are developed. Rather than try to fully predict all project requirements and problems in advance, management allows the project to progress at its own pace. Milestones, or checkpoints, are established to allow periodic review of progress. These periodic evaluations allow management to determine whether a project appears to merit further commitment of resources, whether project adjustments are necessary, or whether the project should be discontinued.

PERT

PERT (program evaluation and review technique) is a commonly used planning tchnique. A PERT plan diagrammatically represents the tasks required to complete a project. It explicitly establishes sequential dependencies and relationships among the tasks. A PERT diagram consists of both activities and events. Activities are defined as time- and resource-consuming efforts required to complete a segment of the total project. Events represent the completion of segments or parts of segments of the project. Activities. are represented by solid lines with directional arrows; events are represented by circles. Dotted lines are used to represent sequential dependencies where there is another, but no task has to be performed to progress from the first event to the second one. Activities and events are coded or described to designate their functions in the overall project.

Figure 6-5 shows a PERT chart and an accompanying project table that defines the responsible personnel and estimated and actual times and costs for each task in the project. By comparing the actual times and costs with the planned times and costs in the PERT chart, mangagement can monitor and control project performance.

A final advantage to PERT is that the total time required to complete the project can be determined by locating the longest path (in terms of time) in the chart. This path is referred to as the "critical path." For scheduling purposes, any delay of tasks in the critical path is an equivalent delay on the overall project.

Figure 6-5 A PERT Chart and Accompanying Project Table

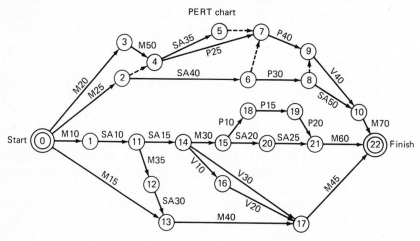

PERT chart

Project Table

Task	Responsibility	Planned start	Planned completion	Actual start	Actual completion	Planned costs	Actual costs
M10	JCW	1/10	1/15	1/10	1/15	N/A	N/A
M15	SCM	1/10	1/30	1/10	1/15	N/A	N/A
M20	JCW	1/15	1/30	1/15	1/30	N/A	N/A
M25	JCW	1/15	1/30	1/15	2/02	N/A	N/A
SA10	NJW	1/15	1/30	1/15	1/30	$ 800	$ 670
M50	SCM	1/30	2/05	1/30	2/04	N/A	N/A
SA15	NJW	1/30	2/07	1/30	2/06	$1200	$1250
SA40	BWB	1/30	2/25	2/02	2/26	$3600	$3200
SA35	RER	2/05	2/20	2/08	2/20	$ 500	$ 750
P20	JLP	10/01	10/25	10/05	10/25	$1100	$1400
SA50	NJW	10/25	11/10	10/20	11/10	$1500	$1500
V40	IBM	10/25	11/10			$5000	
M60	JCW	10/25	11/20			$2000	
M45	SCM	10/25	11/20			$1000	
M70	JCW	11/10	11/20			$2500	

Legend:
M = managerial, SA = systems analysis, P = programming, V = vendor

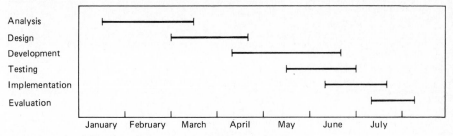

Figure 6-6 Illustration of a Gantt Chart

Gantt

Gantt charts are a planning technique that, like PERT, define what tasks are to be performed, when they are to start, and when they are to be completed. Figure 6-6 illustrates a Gantt chart.

A Gantt chart does not show sequential dependencies as are shown by a PERT chart. For example, in Figure 6-6, the chart does not state that analysis must be done prior to starting of design. Therefore, a Gantt chart does not have as much information as a PERT chart, but it is much easier to prepare.

A particularly nice feature of Gantt charts is the ability to factor a macro Gantt chart into one or more levels of micro Gantt charts. For example, in Figure 6-6 the line labeled analysis could be made up as a separate Gantt chart consisting of the subtasks that constitute analysis (e.g., feasibility study, interview, flowcharting). Such a subchart provides more detail, allows for specific assignment of responsibility, and facilitates better estimation of time requirements.

RELATIONSHIP OF METHODOLOGIES TO MIS PLANNING MODEL

The methodologies that have been reviewed fit into the framework of the basic MIS planning model. Each may be classified as applying primarily to one of the four generic activities (see Figure 6-7):

1. Strategic planning
2. Organizational information requirements analysis
3. Resource allocation
4. Project planning

Strategy set transformation is the only methodology described in this chapter that falls into the strategic planning category. In fact, it is the only methodology we are aware of that is designed to provide a direct link to overall organizational strategic planning.

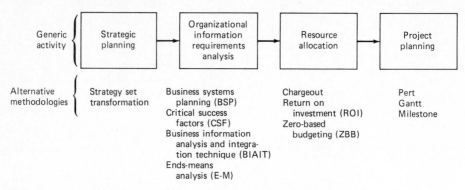

Figure 6-7 Alternative MIS Planning Methodologies Classified by Stage of MIS Planning of Most Significant Impact

BSP, CSF, BIAIT, and E/M analysis fall into the organizational information requirements analysis category. The four approaches differ in their methods and comprehensiveness. BSP is the most comprehensive and labor-intensive approach and generates a more extensive definition of total information requirements. CSF and E/M analysis are less labor intensive and direct information requirements analysis at higher-level management requirements. BIAIT is a highly structured engineering approach that appears to be efficient in arriving at a set of normative requirements. A concern is whether it is applicable to high-level decision making information requirements.

Chargeout, ROI, and ZBB fall into the resource allocation category. All three approaches are concerned with allocating resources; however, their orientations are quite different. Chargeout advocates decentralized "marketplace" decision making with cost recovery. ZBB advocates centralized planning committee decision making with MIS expenses carried as overhead. ROI can be used in either centralized or decentralized decision making.

PERT, Gantt, and milestone planning techniques fall into the realm of project planning and management. PERT is the most formal and structured of the three techniques, Gantt is less structured and formal than PERT, and the milestone technique is the least.

The ability to classify the various planning methodologies within the four-stage model adds clarity to their use and purpose. Since each of the planning methodologies has been implemented in a number of organizations, this indicates that under certain circumstances, each of the planning methodologies performs a useful and needed function.

GUIDELINES FOR MIS PLANNING

At the beginning of the chapter, the major problems of MIS planning were identified as

1. Alignment of MIS strategy with organizational strategy
2. Developing an information architecture
3. Resource allocation
4. Completing information systems projects on time and on schedule
5. Selecting a methodology for the above steps

These problems are addressed directly by the four-stage MIS planning model. The first four problems correspond to the four stages of the model. Given the framework of the model, the set of appropriate methodologies is specified for each stage. This aids in selecting a methodology for each stage.

Practical guidance for MIS planning can be gained from the model. It can aid in recognizing the nature of the MIS planning problems and in selecting the appropriate stage of planning. Too often, this recognition does not occur. For example, some organizations may view their MIS functions as making minimal contributions to organizational objectives. In seeking to resolve this problem, some organizations have installed a chargeout system (resource allocation planning) to make MIS pay its own way. Other organizations have conducted a BSP (OIRA planning) exercise to resolve the same problem. While these activities may result in improved MIS services, the MIS planning model suggests they are probably not the appropriate methodologies in this situation. If the MIS effort is not responsive to the organization, the four-stage MIS planning model indicates a strategy-oriented planning effort should precede OIRA and resource allocation planning exercises.

To establish MIS planning, an organization should conduct a stage assessment to determine the extent to which each stage of MIS planning has been accomplished. This can be performed by analyzing the major activities and outputs of the four-stage planning model depicted in Figure 6-4. After the MIS planning needs at each stage have been established, appropriate methodologies can be selected.

Stage Assessments

A stage assessment is performed for each of the four stages of the MIS planning model. To conduct a strategic stage assessment an organization should ask the following questions:

I. Is there a clear definition of organizational objectives and strategies?
    A. Has the strategic organizational plan been reviewed?
    B. Are the major claimant groups and their objectives identified?

   II. Is there an MIS mission expressed in an MIS charter?

III. Is there an assessment of the MIS environment?

     A. Are MIS capabilities adequately assessed?

     B. Are new opportunities identified?

     C. Is the current business environment understood?

     D. Is the current applications portfolio defined and documented?

     E. Is the MIS image healthy?

     F. Is the stage of EDP growth understood?

     G. Are MIS personnel skills accurately inventoried?

IV. Are MIS policies, objectives, and strategies established?

     A. Is the MIS organization appropriate to the overall organization?

     B. Is the MIS technology focus appropriate to the technology focus of the organization?

     C. Are the objectives for allocating MIS resources appropriate?

     D. Are the MIS management processes appropriate?

     E. Are the functional capability objectives appropriate?

If answers to these questions indicate a strategic stage weakness, a strategic planning exercise is in order. Strategy set transformation offers a formal methodology for conducting such an exercise. However, a formal methodology may not be necessary.

Before conducting an OIRA stage assessment an organization should ask the following questions:

   I. Is there an adequate assessment of organizational information requirements?

     A. Is the overall organizational information architecture identified?

     B. Is there a good understanding of current information needs of the organizations?

     C. Is there a good understanding of projected information needs of the organization?

     D. Are the major databases and their relationships defined?

  II. Is there a master MIS development plan?

     A. Are MIS projects defined?

     B. Are projects ranked by priority?

     C. Is there a multiyear development schedule?

If an organization does not have acceptable answers to the OIRA stage questions, an OIRA planning exercise is in order. Examples of formal planning methodologies available to conduct such an exercise are BSP, CSF, E/M analysis, and BIAIT.

To evaluate the current status prior to conducting a resource allocation stage assessment, an organization should ask the following questions:

I. Does the organization have a resource requirements plan?
    A. Are trends identified?
    B. Is there a hardware plan?
    C. Is there a software plan?
    D. Is there a personnel plan?
    E. Is there a data communications plan?
    F. Is there a facilities plan?
    G. Is there a financial plan?
II. Does the organization have an adequate procedure for resource allocation?

If an organization does not have acceptable answers to the resource allocation stage questions, a resource allocation planning exercise is in order. Formal planning methodologies available to conduct such an exercise are chargeout, ROI, and ZBB.

To evaluate the status of project planning an organization should ask the following questions:

- Is there a procedure for evaluating projects in terms of difficulty or risk?
- Are project tasks usually identified adequately?
- Are project cost estimates generally accurate?
- Are project time estimates generally accurate?
- Are checkpoints defined to monitor progress of projects?
- Are projects generally completed on schedule?

If an organization does not get satisfactory answers to the project planning questions, a review of project planning techniques is in order. Techniques available to improve project planning include PERT, Gantt, and milestone.

Selecting a Methodology

The four-stage planning model provides considerable insight into the MIS planning issues. This should reduce confusion among competing planning methodologies. For example, it can prevent an organization from using a resource allocation methodology when an OIRA or strategic methodology is appropriate. However, the planning model does not indicate which of several methodologies categorized within a planning stage should be used for that planning stage.

Only limited research is available to evaluate the comparative advantages of one technique or combination of techniques over another for the first three stages of the model. Organizations must evaluate the methodologies available in the context of the specific issues they are facing. There is, however, some valuable insight for selecting techniques for the OIRA and project planning stages. These issues are discussed below.

ORGANIZATIONAL INFORMATION REQUIREMENTS ANALYSIS

Some interesting work in the OIRA planning stage has resulted in the development of a hybrid technique for conducting an `OIRA.[10] This methodology, which is presented below, is based upon comparative research involving three methods of enterprise requirements analysis: BSP, CSF, and ends/means analysis.

Figure 6-8 portrays the model for conducting an OIRA. To provide concreteness to the methodology, the results of a case study are used to illustrate documents generated during the study. The company agreeing to share the results of an OIRA study is EPIC Realty Services Inc., leasors of single-family dwellings. Headquartered in Washington, D.C., with offices in major cities throughout the United States, the company manages over 6000 homes.

Define Underlying Organizational Subsystems

The first phase of the OIRA is to define underlying organizational subsystems. An organizational subsystem is a fundamental organizational activity that is necessary for the operation of the organization. For EPIC Realty Services Inc., the major subsystems are as follows:

1. Credit
2. Leasing
3. Maintenance
4. Delinquency and evictions
5. Marketing
6. Advertising
7. Accounts receivable and collections
8. Corporate accounting
9. Market and product analysis
10. Client reporting
11. Appraisal

---

[10]J. C. Wetherbe and G. B. Davis, "Developing a Long-Range Information Architecture," *Proceedings of the National Computer Conference,* Anaheim, Calif., 1983.

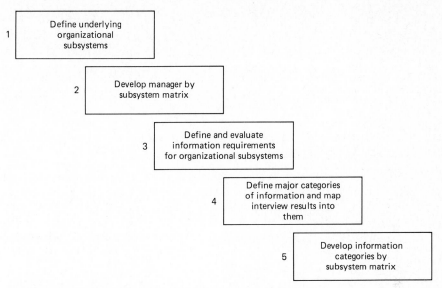

Figure 6-8 Organizational Information Requirements Analysis Planning Model

12. Insurance
13. Sales
14. Personnel and administration
15. Inspections
16. Audit
17. Inventory
18. Legal

These subsystems are obtained by an iterative process of discussing all organizational activities and defining them as belonging to broad categories of subsystems. As new activities are considered, they should be placed in categories previously defined or a new category should be created.

Develop Subsystem-Manager Matrix

Once the underlying organizational subsystems are defined, the next phase of the OIRA planning exercise is to relate specific managers to organizational subsystems. The resulting document, called a "manager-subsystem matrix," is illustrated in Figure 6-9. Note that the subsystems across the top of the matrix are the same as those identified in phase I.

The matrix is developed by reviewing the major decision responsibilities of each middle to top manager and relating the decision making to specific subsystems. The matrix documents the managers having major decision making responsibility for each specific subsystem. Note that personnel changes or organizational changes can easily be reflected in an adjusted matrix.

Define and Evaluate Information Requirements for Organizational Subsystems

This phase of the planning model obtains the information requirements of each organizational subsystem by group interviews of those managers having major decision-making responsibility for each subsystem. Merely asking managers to define their information requirements is frequently not satisfactory. The reasons for this are the limitations of humans as information processors. Because of these limitations, it is necessary to provide some structure to aid the managers in thinking about information requirements. Various methodologies for eliciting information requirements are basically different structures for aiding managers in the cognitive process of formulating requirements.

Research has been conducted to evaluate three approaches to structuring the set of questions for information requirements interviews. Questions based upon three methods were tested (BSP, CSF, and E/M analysis). The conclusions were interesting:

● Different managers liked different methods. No one method was dominant.

● The methods were additive, using more than one approach (in any order). The first method obtains the most requirements, but each additional method brings out additional requirements.

● Since it is not possible (at this time) to know the method that a manager will favor, the most efficient procedure is to use all three methods.

● The order of use of the three techniques is in order of cognitive difficulty (the strain it puts on the managers' thought processes) and comprehensiveness.

The interview method is therefore a structured interview using questions based upon BSP, CSF, and E/M analysis. Interviews typically take 1 to 4 hours per subsystem. The maintenance subsystem at EPIC illustrates the steps of the structured interview.

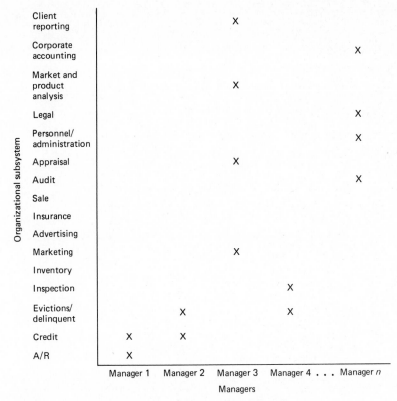

Figure 6-9 Manager by Subsystem Matrix

Statement of Purpose. The first step of the interview is to get the managers to agree upon a statement of purpose for the subsystem under consideration. For example, the purpose of maintenance was defined as keeping the rental property at a satisfactory availability level with minimal cost and processing vendor payments.

Subsystem Mapping. The second step of the group interview is to define the relationship of the subsystem with all other subsystems internal to the organization or with entities external to the organization. A map of these relationships is constructed by drawing the subsystem under consideration in the center of a chalkboard or flip chart pad and around it drawing the subsystems and entities with which it interacts. Next, directional arrows are labeled and used to define the types of transactions or information flow that occurs (Figure 6-10).

The subsystem mapping serves as an excellent tool for making the managers aware of the full scope of the subsystem under consideration.

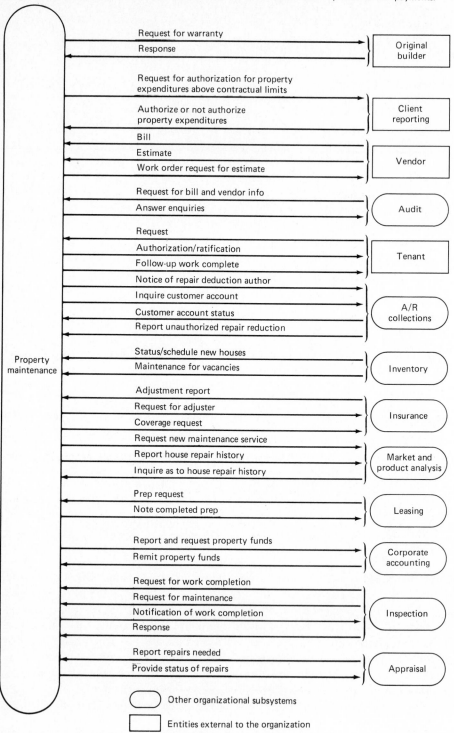

Figure 6-10 Subsystem Mapping for Maintenance

Most interviews of this nature provide considerable enlightenment to the managers involved, as they are usually not aware of the array of activities that occur with subsystems they are familiar with.

BSP, CSF, Ends/Means Questionnaires. After the subsystem mapping is complete, information requirements are elicited using questions that are based upon BSP, CSF, and E/M analysis. The specific questions and the way in which they are asked are a key issue.

After interviewing several hundred managers in different organizations, we have found that the obvious question -- What information do you need? -- is the wrong question. It is the less obvious but properly asked *indirect* questions that do the job. For example, the following is a good series of questions to ask:

1. What are the major problems that this subsystem has in accomplishing its purpose?
2. How could they best be solved?
3. Can better information help?

The third question reveals information requirements, but the preceding questions set the stage for the third question.

Figure 6-11 portrays the framework for the information requirements interview using the three techniques -- BSP, CSF, and E/M analysis. Note that all questioning leads to information required. The following are the specific questions asked during the group interview:

Business Systems Planning (Problems and Decisions)
1. What are the major problems encountered in accomplishing the purposes of this subsystem?
    a. What are good solutions to those problems?
    b. How can information play a role in any of those solutions?
2. What are the major decisions in managing this subsystem?
    a. What improvements in information could result in better decisions?

Figure 6-11 Framework for Information Requirements Interview

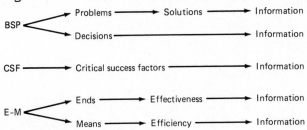

Critical Success Factors (CSFs)

1. What are the CSFs of this subsystem? (Note most executives have four to eight of these.)

2. What information is needed to ensure critical success factors are under control?

Ends/Means Analysis

1. What makes goods or services provided by this subsystem effective to users?

    a.   What information is needed to · ensure that the subsystem is effective at providing those goods or services?

2. How do you define efficiency in providing goods or services by this subsystem?

    a.   What information is needed to evaluate the efficiency of this subsystem?

The interview will result in a variety of information requirements being defined as needed by the subsystem. A separate interview is conducted for each organizational subsystem.

Define Major Information Categories and Map Interviews into Them

The process of categorizing information is an iterative one, similar to that used for defining organizational subsystems. By placing the information categories defined from the organizational subsystem interviews into broad generic categories of information, an overall profile of information categories needed by the organization can be developed. Figure 6-12 illustrates this process.

Figure 6-12 Interviews Mapped to Information Categories

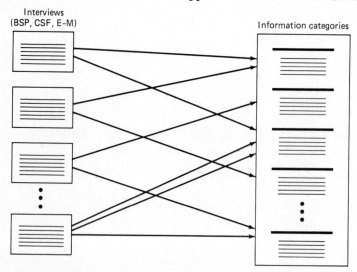

Interviews
(BSP, CSF, E-M)

Information categories

Organizational subsystems

Information categories	Leasing	Maintenance	A/R	Credit	Evictions/ delinquent	Inspection	Inventory	Marketing	Advertising	Insurance	Sale	Audit	Appraisal	Personnel/ administration	Legal	Market and product analysis	Corporate accounting	Client reporting
Contract	B/3	U/3	U/3	B/2	U/2	U/2	B/3	B/3	U/1	U/3	B/3	U/3	B/3		B/3	B/3	U/3	U/3
Policy/training	U/3	U/3	U/2	B/3	B/3	U/3		U/3		U/3	U/3	U/3	U/3	B/3	B/2	U/2	U/2	U/2
Customer financial	B/3		B/3	B/3	B/3		B/3		U/3		B/3	U/2				B/3		
Customer demographics	B/3		U/2	U/2	U/2		B/3		U/3		B/3					B/3		
Complaint	S/2	B/3	B/2	S/3	U/2	B/3	B/3			U/2	B/3	U/3	S/2	B/2	U/2	B/3	B/2	U/3
Leasing/transactions	B/2		U/3									U/2			U/2		U/3	
Vendor		B/3	B/2		B/3	B/3	B/3		B/3	B/2	B/3	U/2	B/3		B/3		B/3	B/3
A/P		U/2	B/1		B/2				B/3		U/2	U/3	U/3	S/3	B/2		B/3	B/3
A/R		U/1	B/3	S/3	B/3		B/3			S/3	S/3	U/3			U/3		B/3	B/2
Maintenance	S/3	S/3	B/3			B/3	B/3			B/3	S/3	U/3	S/2		U/1	S/2	U/2	B/2
Warranty		B/2				B/2	B/3			B/3	U/2	U/2					U/2	
Inventory	B/3	U/2	B/2		B/3	B/3	B/3	B/3	B/2		B/3				U/1	U/3	B/3	B/2

Legend:
S = supply   1 = low
U = use   2 = medium
B = both   3 = high

Figure 6–13 Information Categories by Organizational Subsystems Matrix

Develop Information-Subsystem Matrix

By mapping information categories against the organizational subsystems, an information-category organizational-subsystem matrix can be developed. Figure 6-13 illustrates such a matrix for EPIC.

Note that at the intersections of information categories and subsystems there are coded values defined as follows:

Utilization or Source	*Priority*
S = source	1 = low priority
U = use	2 = medium priority
B = both	3 = high priority

Managers are asked during the interview what the value is of different types of information and where it might be acquired. Their responses can be coded into the table and the scores can be totaled and used as a rough indicator of composite value of a category of information to all subsystems with which it intersects. The utilization or source also indicates whether a subsystem can generate the information needed within its own boundaries or whether it needs to obtain the information from another subsystem.

As shown in Figure 6-13, the source and the use of information involve different subsystems. This difference stresses the importance of an organizationwide planning effort for information requirements analysis to avoid redundant internal generation of information among subsystems.

USE OF THE OIRA PLANNING RESULTS

The results of the OIRA exercise are twofold: (1) It identifies high-payoff information categories and (2) it provides an architecture for information projects.

Identifying High Payoffs

By evaluating composite scores for information categories, the categories with the highest scores can be given first consideration for feasibility studies. Note that the information-category-subsystem matrix does not tell you whether it is technically, economically, or operationally feasible to improve an information category. The matrix only indicates relative value of information. Feasibility studies and project definitions must still be done as usual.

Provide Architecture

By clearly defining the intersection of information and subsystems, an organization can avoid the problem of building separate, redundant information systems for different organizational subsystems. When an organization decides to improve information for one organizational subsystem, other subsystems that need such information can be taken into consideration. This avoids building separate information systems for each subsystem, which often requires reworking or duplicating what has already been done. By doing the conceptual work first, an organization can identify information system projects that will do the most good and lead to cohesive integrated systems. This is far better than randomly selecting projects that result in fragmented, piecemeal systems that are continually being reworked or abandoned because they do not mesh with the organization's overall requirements. This means planning from the top down rather than from the bottom up.

Executive's Perspective

Perhaps the best way to illustrate the value of an organization's having an organizational information architecture for MIS is by quoting the president of EPIC a year after he personally led the development of their architecture.

> I had worked in top management in one of our other subsidiaries and experienced the disappointment that comes from developing systems in the traditional FIFO, piecemeal way with the consequences of redundant, non-integrated and inaccessible information.
>
> When I took over a new subsidiary, I decided there must be a better way. There was. By developing an information architecture before developing systems we have been able to pull all our systems together. Our short-run system decisions are dovetailing into our long-range systems. We know where we are going and getting there.
>
> Beyond that, just the process of going through an organizational information requirements analysis gave me and my management invaluable insight into our business.

PROJECT PLANNING

Perhaps the biggest mistake made in project planning is that a budget and schedule get set first. For example, management decides to put in a new budget system in 9 months and is willing to spend $250,000. This leaves one important issue undefined -- what exactly the new system will do. Setting budget and time frames prior to defining the system constrains design. By default management has defined the limits of the new system.

The proper sequence for managing a project is to first get a good functional definition of the system and then have people with experience and expertise in information system project management develop a budget and schedule. If management cannot live with the schedule or the budget, they can then ask what reductions in capability of the new system can be made to improve the schedule and/or budget.

In developing a budget, a schedule, and specifications for a system, several properties of projects and of project management should be understood and considered. The project properties that most significantly influence the overall nature of a project are the following:

1. *Predefined structure:* The more predefined structure a project has, the more easily it can be planned and controlled. For example, transaction-processing applications inherently have a great deal of predefined structure. Their structure reduces the difficulty of designing computer applications to process them. Conversely, decision support systems (e.g., a market forecast system) are not usually well structured. They require considerable definition and structuring before they can be computerized.

2. *Stability of technology:* The greater the experience with a given technology to be used for a new system, the more predictable the systems development process. On the other hand, when a new information system is to use new and unproven hardware and/or software, many unforeseen problems that impede the development process may arise.

3. *Size:* There is an inverse relationship between project size, in terms of person years and costs, and the ability to accurately plan the number of person years and the costs that will be required to complete the project. That is, the larger the project, the more difficult it is to estimate the resources required to complete it.

4. *User proficiency:* The more knowledgeable and experienced user-managers are with the area in which they work and the more knowledge and experience they have in developing systems, the higher their "user proficiency" and the easier it is to develop a system for them. Less knowledge and experience among users result in greater difficulty in developing systems.

5. *Developer proficiency:* The more knowledgeable and experienced the systems analyst assigned to a project is, the easier the project will go. Again, lack of knowledge and experience can cause greater difficulty with a project.

Any given project can possess any variation of each of the preceding properties. For example, a project can have a predefined structure, but use unstable technology, be a massive undertaking, and have low user and developer proficiencies. (Most initial online airline reservation systems can be described in this fashion.)

The more defined a project's structure is, the more stable the technology to be used is; the smaller the size of the project, and the higher the user and the developer proficiency, the more straightforward the project is. The more one or more of these properties deviates in the opposite direction, the less straightforward the project.

Techniques for Project Management

The techniques for managing information systems can be categorized as informal (milestone), formal (PERT), and in between (Gantt). Selection of the appropriate orientation for a given project is contingent upon the properties of the project. Informal techniques are appropriate for projects that are not straightforward and predictable. Formal techniques are better-suited for projects that are relatively straightforward and predictable.

Guidelines

The inappropriate application of formal or informal project management techniques can have unfortunate consequences. The use of informal techniques for a straightforward project needlessly forgoes planning definition and control. For example, PERT and Gantt planning techniques provide structure for time and cost estimates. To forgo such planning is unfair to the organization and to the systems developers whose performance cannot be evaluated as accurately as it could be if more formal techniques were used.

The use of formal techniques for projects that are not straightforward or predictable generally results in dysfunctional constraints on what needs to be a relatively innovative and creative process. Systems developers are often forced to cut corners and stifle innovative processes in order to keep the project on schedule and within budget. There must be sufficient slack to nurture innovation when approching new areas of systems development.

The techniques used for projects can be combinations of formal and informal techniques. For example, if the specific project tasks and their sequential dependencies are known, but the length of time they will take and the cost are not known, a PERT chart can be constructed without time and cost estimates. Such an approach provides more definition than a milestone approach without unduly constraining the project with time and cost estimates that may be unrealistic.

Figure 6-14 illustrates the relationship between project characteristics and the selection of project-planning techniques. There are a number of products marketed that provide software support for PERT, Gantt, or milestone approaches. Each product can be evaluated on its own merit, given that the organization buying the product understands its project-planning requirements.

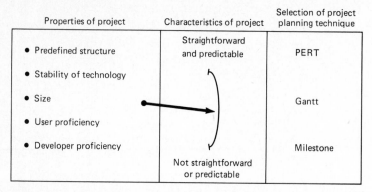

Properties of project	Characteristics of project	Selection of project planning technique
• Predefined structure	Straightforward and predictable	PERT
• Stability of technology		
• Size		Gantt
• User proficiency		
• Developer proficiency		Milestone
	Not straightforward or predictable	

Figure 6-14 Affect of Properties of Project on Selection of Project Planning Technique

A key concept of project management is the commitment of human resources to projects. These resource commitments are generally expressed in terms of time periods such as person-months (or person-hours, -weeks, or -years).

A common management error is to assume that persons and person-months (or whatever time unit is used) are directly interchangeable. For example, a project requiring 4 people 8 person-months (i.e., 2 months elapsed time) to complete usually cannot be completed in 1 month by adding 4 more people to the project. The complex interrelationships of most projects result in diminishing returns when more than a workable number of personnel are assigned to a project. If too many workers

Figure 6-15 Relationship of Adding Personnel to Time Required for Completion of a Project with Complex Interrelationships

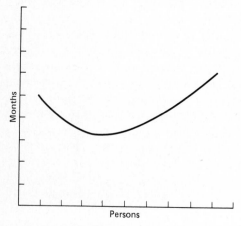

are assigned to a project, they can literally get in one another's way to such an extent that the additional personnel are more of a hindrance than an asset to project completion.

The relationship between adding personnel to a project and the time required to complete the project is shown in Figure 6-15. Note that adding personnel expedites project completion up to a point, but then it begins to delay the project. A saying that illustrates the mythical person-month well is "A woman can have a baby in nine months but you can't put nine women on the effort and get a baby in one month."

Who Should Manage the Information Systems Project?

No one disputes the idea that the membership of a project team organized to develop a new information system should include both information systems staffers and prospective users of the system. But the logical next question still produces debate: "Who should take charge of the project?"

The manager of an information system project should, in the authors' view, be the highest-level manager whose responsibility transcends all business functions affected by the new system. This person should be a user-manager who is so talented and crucial to the operation of the user area that he "absolutely, positively, under no circumstances" can be spared to head up the project. This manager should be given adequate time away from his or her primary responsibilities to run the project.

That is asking a lot, of course, but consider the purpose of information systems. Information systems support managers' decision making, and decision making is the most important thing managers do. Those who will be using the system to make decisions should, it seems clear, be in command of making decisions about the information system they will use.

Fearful of the complexities of computer technology, users have generally been quite willing -- even eager -- to turn over both team leadership and membership to technically oriented information systems personnel. The systems developed by a technical team usually work, but they just as often fail to provide all of the information users need. After repeated systems failures, it has become axiomatic in the industry that user involvement is imperative during systems development. User personnel are routinely assigned at present to project teams. However, users have often assigned newly hired employees or others they could easily afford to spare. The thinking has been, "Whoever is assigned to the project will disappear into the 'black hole' of corporate information systems, and we may never see that person again. So, give them someone we can afford to lose." Such team members obviously lack the intimate knowledge with critical decision making that the most valuable managers have, and are thus ill-equipped for their assignment.

3M's Approach

3M's Harold Klenk is a financial user-manager who knows the importance of users leading information-systems projects. Klenk has held both information and user-management positions for 3M during the past 30 years, and is now controller for staff operations at corporate headquarters. He says, "I can't overemphasize the importance of users managing information-systems projects. It is so fundamental. I can give you example after example of systems that have failed because of lack of user involvement in the process. Technical people tend to focus on a technical solution, and often lose sight of the business problems. Users have the best understanding of the business problem and needed solution. They *must* manage the project."

In addition to the managerial and operational advantages of having users run projects, there are perceptual and political advantages. Klenk continues, "A company's data processing department does not wave a magic wand and give users new systems. Users are the ones that know what they need and have the requisite expertise to bring it about. If a user is not in charge of the project it makes it too easy for users to blame problems on the information systems function. And there will be problems without user leadership. Blaming [the] information systems [department] for these problems saves face for the user, but is little consolation to the corporation."

Although systems development projects managed by information systems personnel can be successful, the odds for success are much better with user leadership and user responsibility. User participation is not enough; what's needed is commitment -- a distinction well illustrated by a plate of ham and eggs: The chicken is involved but the pig is committed.

SUMMARY

The four-stage model of MIS planning provides a framework for addressing critical issues and problem areas of MIS planning. The first stage of the model -- strategic planning -- addresses the problem of alignment of the MIS effort with the overall strategic objectives of the organization. The second stage -- organizational information requirements analysis -- addresses the problem of development of a long-range information architecture for the organization. The third stage -- resource allocation -- addresses the allocation of information system development and operational resources among competing applications. The fourth stage addresses project planning and management.

The four-stage model provides a framework in which competing and diverse planning methodologies can be categorized. The model can thus lead to better MIS planning and aid MIS planning research.

SUGGESTED READINGS

Ansoff, H. I., "State of Practice in Planning Systems," *Sloan Management Review*, vol. 18, Winter 1977, pp. 1-24.

Anthony, R. N., *Planning and Control Systems: A Framework for Analysis*, Division of Research, Graduate School of Business, Harvard University, Boston, Mass., 1965.

Beard, L., "Planning a MIS: Some Caveats and Contemplations," *Financial Executive*, vol. 45, May 1977, pp. 34-39.

Bowman, B., G. B. Davis, and J. C. Wetherbe, "Modeling for MIS," *Datamation*, July 1980, pp. 155-162.

Burnstine, D. C., *BIAIT: An Emerging Management Discipline*, BIAIT International, New York, 1980.

Bush, R. L., and I. E. Knutsen, "Integration of Corporate and MIS Planning: Its Impact of Productivity," *Proceedings of Ninth Annual Conference of the Society for Management Information Systems*, Chicago, Ill., 1977.

Business Systems Planning -- Information Systems Planning Guide, IBM Corporation, Publication GE20-0527.

Carlson, W. M., "Business Information Analysis and Integration Technique (BIAIT) -- The New Horizon," *Data Base*, vol. 10, no. 4, Spring 1979, pp. 3-9.

Davis, G. B., *Management Information Systems: Conceptual Foundations, Structure, and Development*, McGraw-Hill, New York, 1974.

_____, "Strategies for Information Requirements Determination," *IBM Systems Journal*, vol. 22, no. 1, 1982, pp. 4-30.

Diamond, S., "Contents of a Meaningful Plan," *Proceedings of the Tenth Annual Conference of the Society for Management Information Systems*, Chicago, Ill., 1979.

Drucker, P. F., *Management: Tasks, Responsibilities, Practices*, Harper & Row, New York, 1974.

Ein-Dor, P., and E. Segev, "Strategic Planning for Management Information Systems," *Management Science*, vol. 15, November 1978, pp. 1631-1641.

Forster, A. J., "Effective Strategies and Techniques for the Development of MIS Master-Plans for Top Management Approval," *Proceedings of the Tenth Annual Conference of the Society for Management Information Systems*, Chicago, Ill., 1978.

Gibson, D. G., and R. L. Nolan, "Managing the Four Stages of EDP Growth," *Harvard Business Review*, January-February 1974, pp. 76-88.

Gurry, E., and R. Bove, "Effective Data Processing Planning," *CPA Journal*, vol. 47, August 1977, pp. 46-47.

Head, R. V., "Strategic Planning for Information Systems," *Information Systems*, vol. 25, October 1978, pp. 46-47.

Holloway, C., and W. R. King, "Evaluating Alternative Approaches to Strategic Planning," *Long-Range Planning*, vol. 12, no. 4, August 1979, pp. 74-78.

Hootman, J. T., "Basic Considerations in Developing Computer Charging Mechanisms," *Data Base*, vol. 8, no. 4, Spring 1977, pp. 1-13.

Kerner, D. V., "Business Information Characterization Study," *Data Base*, vol. 10, no. 4, Spring 1979, pp. 10-17.

King, W. R., "Strategic Planning for Management Information Systems," *MIS Quarterly*, vol. 2, no. 1, March 1978, pp. 27-37.

Lyles, M. A., "Making Operational Long-Range Planning for Information Systems," *MIS Quarterly*, vol. 3, no. 1, January 1979, pp. 16-21.

McFarlan, F. W., "Problems in Planning the Information Systems," *Harvard Business Review*, vol. 49, March-April 1971, pp. 74-89.

McLean, E.R., and J.V. Soden (eds.), *Strategic Planning for MIS*, Wiley-Interscience, New York, 1977.

Mulvihill, D.E., and B.J. Cohen, "Strategy Formulation and Information Systems: Setting Objectives," in F.W. McFarlan and R.L. Nolan (eds.), *The Information Systems Handbook*, Dow Jones-Irwin, Chicago, Ill., 1975, pp. 19-31.

Munro, M.C., and B.R. Wheeler, "Planning, Critical Success Factors, and Management Information Requirements," *MIS Quarterly*, vol. 4, no. 4, December 1980, pp. 27-38.

Nolan, R. L., "Managing the Computer Resource: A Stage Hypothesis," *Communications of the ACM*, vol. 16, July 1973, pp. 399-405.

_____, "Managing the Crises in Data Processing," *Harvard Business Review*, March-April 1979, pp. 115-126.

Pyhrr, P. A., "Zero-Based Budgeting," *Harvard Business Review*, vol. 48, November-December 1970, pp. 111-121.

Rockart, J. F., "Chief Executives Define Their Own Data Needs," *Harvard Business Review*, March-April 1979, pp. 81-93.

Rush, R. L., "MIS Planning in Distributed Data Processing Systems," *Journal of Systems Management*, vol, 30, no. 8, August 1979, pp. 17-26.

Schwartz, M. H., "MIS Planning," *Datamation*, vol, 16, no. 10, September 1970, pp. 28-31.

Shidal, J. G., "Long-Range DP Planning," *Journal of Systems Management*, vol. 29, April 1978, pp. 40-45.

Soden, J., "Pragmatic Guidelines for EDP Long Range Planning," *Data Management*, vol. 13, September 1975, pp. 8-13.

_____and C. Tucker, "Long-Range MIS Planning," *Journal of Systems Management*, vol. 27, July 1976, pp. 28-33.

Steiner, G. A., and J. B. Miner, *Management Policy and Strategy*, Macmillan, New York, 1977.

Wedley, W., "New Uses of Delphi in Strategy Formulation," *Long-Range Planning*, vol. 10, December 1977, pp. 70-78.

Wetherbe, J. C., and G. W. Dickson, "Zero-Based Budgeting: An Alternative to Chargeout," *Information and Management*, vol. 2, no. 5, November 1979, pp. 203-213.

_____, and G. B. Davis, "Strategic MIS Planning Through Ends/Means Analysis," MIS Research Center Working Paper, University of Minnesota, 1982.

_____and _____, "Developing a Long-Range Architecture," *Proceedings of the National Computer Conference*, AFIPS Press, Anaheim, Calif., May 1983, pp. 261-269.

Zachman, J. A., "Control and Planning of Information Systems," *Journal of Systems Management*, vol. 28, July 1977, pp. 34-41.

_____, "The Information Systems Management System: A Framework for Information Systems Planning," *Proceedings for the Ninth Annual Conference of the Society for Management Information Systems*, Chicago, Ill., 1977.

Zani, W. M., "Blueprint for MIS," *Harvard Business Review*, November-December 1970, pp. 95-100.

MANAGEMENT ASSESSMENT AND EVALUATION OF MIS

INTRODUCTION

Probably the most frequent statements coming out of corporate executive suites regarding management information systems are these: "How much money should we be spending on MIS?" and "What is the bottom-line impact of the money we are spending now on MIS?" These statements both reflect concern with evaluating the MIS function. The reader may recall that in Chapter 2 we listed what MIS executives from leading-edge companies thought were the critical information systems issues for the 1980s. Reexamination of that list indicates that determining how much to spend on MIS is listed fifth.

In 1977 and 1978, the *Management Information Systems Quarterly* published a number of interviews with senior executives from leading U.S. organizations. Each executive indicated that evaluating the contribution of the MIS function to the organization was a very critical issue for them. Careful reading of the interviews shows that no two executives had the same views on how the value of the function ought to be determined, and, in fact, none offered any operative ways of learning how good a job MIS was doing for the organization.

Sometimes, to make a point, we have said that the most common way to evaluate the MIS function is to listen to "screams in the hallways." The notion is that when user-managers get dissatisfied enough with the MIS function, they will complain so loudly that senior management will take action. Although we express this statement facetiously, it is often close to the truth in many organizations. The problem is that evaluation of the MIS function and specific information systems is so difficult that hard-nosed executives simply throw up their hands in desperation when confronted with this problem.

We know what we want to do: we want to determine the cost-benefit ratio or the rate of return on MIS investment. What we do not know are practical and accurate ways to achieve this objective. To substantiate this point, all the reader has to do is to examine the MIS literature. Standard texts and journal articles either do not address this issue at all or they provide only "approaches" to solving the problem. Many of these are very theoretical in nature. We wish we could provide the ultimate answer to the evaluation question. Unfortunately, we cannot. What we can do is to explore the nature of the problem and make sure its facets are fully presented. Secondly, we can summarize a number of the evaluative frameworks and provide some normative guidelines.

THE NATURE OF THE MIS EVALUATION PROBLEM

The first thing that must be recognized about the problem of MIS evaluation is that we must be careful to define the type of evaluation we are talking about. One type of evaluation, the most difficult, is to measure the net contribution of the MIS function to the overall organization. In other words, how good a job is the MIS function doing? A second type of evaluation is determining the contribution of a specific MIS system, say, a marketing information system. These types of evaluations are related in that the sum of the latter types of evaluations, in essence, constitute the total evaluation.

A second point to be made is that the viewpoint reflected in the previous paragraph is essentially an economic one. Another view is to take a more managerial approach. In this view, one would acknowledge that an economic evaluation of the overall MIS function might be impractical but the function can still be evaluated in an almost clinical sense. Here we would take all the normative things we know about MIS and conduct an examination to determine the extent to which "good" practice was being followed. This view is associated with a concept called a "management assessment" of the MIS function. In the opinion of the authors, given our present state of knowledge, this is the most viable current approach to evaluation of the overall MIS function. A third view of the evaluation of the problem might have an accounting orientation. From this viewpoint the MIS function would be examined with the objective of minimizing the "risk" or "exposure" of the overall organization to inadequacies in MIS performance. As will be seen, competent MIS evaluation will have aspects of all these approaches, but the management assessment philosophy should predominate. Before moving on to a consideration of specific evaluative approaches, the discussion of a few points is in order.

Why Evaluate the MIS Function?

The primary reason that senior executives want to evaluate the MIS function is that the organization devotes a large amount of organizational resources to this activity. The second reason is that, in many enterprises, there is the vague feeling that the benefits being received from MIS are not as great as would be expected given the level of expenditure. Since American business executives are brought up on the credo of measuring a return on an investment, it is natural that they would like to evaluate MIS from an ROI perspective.

A third reason for the formal evaluation of the firm's MIS is that for years this function has not been subjected to the same standards that have been applied to other organizational units, e.g., product groups or functions such as production or marketing. Those responsible feel that the time has come to formally measure the MIS function even if the common rate-of-return analysis is impractical. A fourth reason for evaluation is that senior management may feel that the corporation is at great risk should the computing function fail. Merten and Severance[1] found that, in a survey of senior executives, their number one concern regarding risk to the corporation was the exposure of the data processing function to risk from computer failure, computer crime, and misuse of computer resources.

All four of these reasons for evaluating the MIS function are associated with measurement in an absolute sense. In other words, they are related to the question, "How well are we doing?" A fifth reason for evaluation is to have a basis for comparison over time. By assessing the function's strengths and weaknesses, management can also get an answer to the question, "Are we making improvement over time?" This type of analysis is especially important as corrective actions are applied to correct weaknesses. It is very useful to have a formal measure to determine whether the action achieved its purpose. A final reason for evaluation is also related to the concept of the dynamics of the MIS function. Before embarking on new systems or a major systems planning activity, it is very useful to know the current state of affairs or the starting point. In other words, in order to get to a new point, it is absolutely critical that one know from where one is starting. To make this point using another context, consider that to get efficiently to Chicago it is very useful to know whether one is going from Minneapolis or St. Louis.

---

[1]Alan Merten and Dennis Severance, "Data Processing: A State-of-the-Art Survey of Attitudes and Concerns of DP Managers," *MIS Quarterly*, vol. 5, no. 2, June 1981, pp. 11-32.

In view of all these reasons, there is an attitude on the part of most senior executives -- one that is very strong in many -- that the corporate MIS function should be formally evaluated in one way or another. MIS managers need to be able to respond to the request for formal evaluation and to have answers ready to the questions, "How much we are getting for our expenditure for computing?" and "How good a job is our computing function doing as compared to that of our competitors?"

Expenditure Standards

One very straightforward way to address the basic question of how much an organization should be spending on computer resources is to compare the organization's expenditures with those of the competition or with industry standards. Table 7-1 shows these standards for the year 1981.

Unfortunately, the standards are not a very good way to determine how much should be spent on organizational computing, principally because if the expenditures are generating a good rate of return, more should be spent. If less than a desirable rate of return is being generated by computing expenditures, then the organization should spend less. The problem, as will be seen in the section to follow, is that the calculation of rate of return from computing is a worthwhile objective but often an impractical one. Therefore one is often left with only industry standards for comparison.

Another type of comparative data involves the distribution of computing expenditures rather than absolute levels of spending. Table

Table 7-1 DP budget as a percentage of revenue by industry

Industry	Budget %
Banking	1.62
Engineering/construction	0.62
Govt. agencies (fed, state, city)	1.09
Hospital/health care	1.56
Insurance	1.49
Utilities	1.44
Retailing	0.87
Transportation	0.95
Manufacturing	
Electrical/electronic	1.44
Food/drugs	0.38
Machinery	1.00
Apparel/textiles	1.21
Chemicals/petroleum	0.63

Source: John M. Lusa and Raymond S. Winkler, "The Real Truth about DP Salaries," *Infosystems*, vol. 29, no. 6, 1982, p. 35.

Table 7-2 Allocation of DP budgets

DP budget expense	Infosystems %	Datamation %
Personnel	44.3	36.0
Hardware and maintenance	29.8	31.0
Supplies	8.0	11.0
Outside services	7.4	5.0
Outside software purchases	6.7	10.0
Other	3.8	5.0
Communication services	—	2.0

7-2 presents data from two popular sources on patterns of spending in data processing organizations.

Comparing the percentage of computing expenditures for one's own organization to the standard percentages given in the tables is one very easy way to determine what ought to be spent and how the expenses ought to be allocated. The shortcomings of this approach are that in most cases there are compelling reasons to spend more or less than the average. As has been emphasized, the ideal is to spend on data processing up to the point at which the rate of return on the expenditure is maximized. Determining when this point has been reached, however, is fraught with difficulty.

Economic Evaluation: Cause and Effect

As will be seen in the more detailed discussion to follow, determining the costs of or the investment in MIS (especially the costs within the data processing function) is relatively straightforward. The problem is in measuring the benefit stream. First, for some MIS investments, determination of the specific benefits is virtually impossible. A good example is measurement of the benefits accruing from the acquisition of a fourth-generation software package to support financial modeling (see Chapter 9). Approaches to the benefit measurement problem will be given subsequently, but here we want to raise the issue of measuring cause and effect as related to (1) specific systems built by the MIS organization and (2) tools provided to the MIS function or to end-users (e.g., fourth-generation software packages aimed at increasing programmer productivity).

When turning to the evaluation of the entire MIS function, the problem of cause and effect becomes even more difficult. Who is to say that the new materials requirements planning system contributed $6 million to total firm profits in the first 6 months of the year? Maybe a substantial proportion of this increased profit came from the fact that the enterprise changed its marketing territories. The point is that, in any organization, a multitude of things are taking place at the same time, and it is very difficult to separate those effects produced by the MIS from those produced by other factors. Finally, there is the issue of time lag. Even supposing that the profit impact of each information system can be separated out, the timing of the benefits of all of them acting together is difficult to measure accurately and reliably.

The net result of these arguments is that although it would be extremely desirable to measure the overall economic benefit to an organization from its information systems function, it is unlikely that this can be done in a practical way. For these reasons, the overall economic evaluation of the MIS function is normally not performed, and we treat the economics of information systems only with regard to specific systems. We usually do the latter only when considering whether to make an investment in the system and not after the fact in an evaluative sense.

Since we cannot practically evaluate the MIS function in an overall economic sense and since we do not wish to suggest the fallback position of senior executives keeping attuned for "screams in the hallways," then a periodic management assessment of the MIS function is appropriate as the best compromise. As will be seen, the economic issues will not be completely ignored in this process.

Effectiveness and Efficiency

In any evaluation of the MIS function, the evaluator must concentrate on both the effectiveness and the efficiency of the function. Too often, the focus is only on the latter due to the fact that better measures are available. How do we differentiate between effectiveness and efficiency?

Effectiveness, in this context, is associated with the degree to which the management information systems help the organization achieve its objectives. The ideal of measuring the overall economic contribution of the MIS function to the organization is one example of an attempt to assess effectiveness. Efficiency, on the other hand, is often related to the cost, accuracy, and timeliness of information. Our goal is usually to achieve a given level of effectiveness at maximum efficiency. Unfortunately, in many cases, a given level of efficiency is achieved with little formal concern for effectiveness. When the evaluation of the MIS function considers only cost, utilization of hardware resources, and/or budget performance, then it is fair to say that an efficiency orientation exists.

Hamilton and Chervany[2] describe two views of system effectiveness.

[2]Scott Hamilton and Norman L. Chervany, "Evaluating Information Systems Effectiveness — Part 1: Comparing Evaluation Approaches," *MIS Quarterly,* vol. 5, no. 3, September 1981, pp. 55–69.

One they call a "goal-centered view" and the other they call a "systems resources view."

Goal-Centered View. This view first identifies the task objectives of the MIS function and then identifies measures of task attainment. Effectiveness is evaluated by comparing performance to objectives. The economic evaluation of which we have been speaking is a good example of this view.

Systems Resources View. By using this view, actual performance is compared to some goal or normative performance level. An example of this approach would be to survey user attitudes toward MIS and compare them to some desired level.

In conducting an evaluation of the MIS function, both effectiveness and efficiency should be considered. Further, both views of effectiveness have their place in the evaluative process, but it is fair to say that the systems resources view is most heavily relied upon because of the problems associated with implementing goal-centered procedures.

The conceptual framework provided by Hamilton and Chervany is a useful overview of the evaluation process. They assert:[3]

> The MIS function is to develop and operate/maintain information systems that will enhance the organization's ability to accomplish its objectives. Accomplishment of this objective can be evaluated from two perspectives:
>
> I. The efficiency with which the MIS development and operations processes utilize assigned resources (staff, machines, materials, money) to provide the information system to the user.
>
> II. The effectiveness to the users, or the users' organizational unit, using the information system in accomplishing their organizational mission.

Figure 7-1 shows the framework following from these perspectives. For the *efficiency-oriented* perspective shown on the left-hand side of the figure, the levels are defined as follows: level 0, the requirement of the information system; level 1, the resource consumption necessary to provide the information system; level 2, the production capability or capacity of the resources; and level 3, the level of investment in resources. For the *effectiveness-oriented* perspective on the right-hand side of the figure, the levels are defined as follows: level 1, the information provided by the information system, and the support provided by the MIS function to the users of the system; level 2, the use of the system and the effect on user organizational processes and performance; and level 3, the effect of the information system on organizational performance.

[3]Ibid., p. 56.

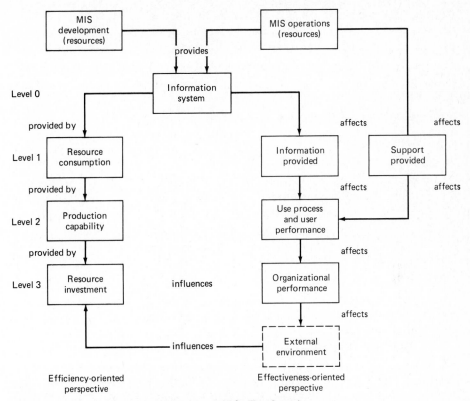

Figure 7-1 A Framework for MIS Evaluation

Source: Scott Hamilton, and Norman L. Chervany, "Evaluating Information Systems Effectiveness -- Part I: Comparing Evaluation Approaches," *MIS Quarterly,* vol. 5, no. 3, September 1981, p. 57.

With the above discussion in mind, we are now ready to turn to the subject of conducting a formal assessment of the MIS organization. The questions to be answered are "How well is the MIS function contributing to the organization?" and "Is the function performing efficiently?"

FORMAL EVALUATION OF MIS

We have noted that there are several views which can be taken in evaluating MIS. In this section, we will discuss some of the major ones. Our discussion will begin by considering the formal economic evaluation of one specific information system. Next, our discussion will move on to the evaluation of the overall MIS function. First, we will present the view of this activity from the perspective of the chief information executive; second we will examine a more global view, that of the EDP auditor; and finally we will consider the most global view, that of the senior management of the organization. It is the last view that is commonly referred to as a management assessment.

Measuring the Value of an Information System

This discussion applies to the evaluation of one specific data processing or information system. It is based upon the purely economic evaluation that was discussed above. Under normal circumstances, the procedures to be described are applied prior to the development of the system, usually as part of the project proposal that is used as input to the project selection process.

The approach taken to economically evaluate a system is the same as that applied to any capital investment. The argument is that an organization can make investments in many things, which can be one or more information systems. The task is to decide upon the set of investments to make, given constraints on the organization's financial resources in any given time period, which will maximize the overall rate of return.

To develop an information system requires a fixed investment. The components of this investment include development salaries (both systems personnel and users), expenditures for computing resources, supplies, and other expenses (such as consulting fees, purchased software, and travel). On a large project, these expenses may be spread over several years, but for analytical purposes, they are considered to be made in time period 0.

Once the system is installed, financial benefits accrue to the organization in each time period (for our purposes consider a time period to be a year). These benefits, of course, must be expressed in economic terms, and this, as was noted in the discussion in the previous section, is frequently difficult. Some help on this activity will be addressed later in the text. In each operating period there are also costs. Usually, these costs are primarily associated with the use of computing resources, but they may involve salaries for maintenance (system evolution), training, or other types of expenses. For each period, the difference between the economic measure of the benefits and the expenditures is called the "cash flow." It is the cash flow which provides the return on the investment involved in building and implementing the system.

Our goal is eventually to evaluate the overall investment from an economic viewpoint. Let us examine in more detail the inputs to the evaluative process. The costs, as were mentioned, are of two types: costs associated with systems development and implementation, and period costs associated with the operation of the system. The costs included in each type of cost were mentioned above and in specific cases are usually not too difficult to identify and estimate. The benefits are frequently harder to quantify, but a framework may facilitate this process.

First, for any period it may be possible to quantify "clerical cost reduction" or "clerical cost avoidance." The former obviously is derived from a reduction in staff which can be attributed to the new system. Elimination of clerks or operating personnel is usually associated with this type of saving. The latter benefit comes about because, with the new system, additional personnel need not be added as business volume grows. To estimate these savings, of course, one must have an estimate of the growth in business activity and the relationship between the business activity and personnel requirements in the area affected by the new system. Thus, the first area of potential benefit is clerical cost reduction and/or clerical cost avoidance.

The second area from which benefits may accrue is "operational savings." Benefits of this type occur because the new system reduces the cost of operation (in ways other than reducing or avoiding clerical cost). Probably the best example of an operational saving would be a new inventory system that would reduce raw material and work-in-process inventory by some percentage. The operational savings in any period would be the reduction in the dollar value of the inventory multiplied by the interest rate associated with the cost of carrying inventory for the period. Other examples of operational savings are reduced travel expenses, reduced supply costs, and/or reduced levels of machinery required because of improved utilization.

A third category of benefit is what is called "increased operational revenues." This type of benefit is the most difficult to quantify of those thus far discussed. An example of operational revenue could be a case in which greater sales are forecast to be generated because of a new information system having as its purpose the allocation of advertising expenditures. All benefits under the classification operational revenue are associated with greater revenue coming into the organization as a result of the new system. This type of benefit, for use as part of a cash flow, must be measured in terms of its profit contribution. In other words, if, because of a new marketing information system, corporate revenues are increased by $10,000 monthly, the monthly cash flow from the system would be the $10,000 multiplied by the firm's profit margin. Note that operational savings have a direct effect on profit whereas an increase in operational revenue has an indirect effect. For example, in a firm having a 10 percent profit margin, operational revenues must be increased by $100,000 to equal operational savings or a clerical cost reduction of $10,000. The latter figure is what is called "net operational revenue."

These categories of benefits represent "hard" cash inflows. If management wishes to do so, they may add a period cash inflow from "intangible" or "unquantifiable" benefits. It is also possible to conduct the economic evaluation in such a way as to discover what these amounts would have to be in order to make the expenditure in the information system attractive. We will return to this type of analysis later.

Having identified the system costs and quantified the system benefits period by period, we now can write an equation for the cash inflows:

Cash flow (period t) =
sum of system benefits (period t)
   - sum of system operating costs (period t)   (1)

We are now ready to perform the economic analysis. There are two ways of doing this, the first of which is to compute the present value of the investment in the new system and the second of which is to compute the rate of return from developing the new system. Under normal circumstances the two methods will yield equivalent results. There are some assumptions associated with each approach, however. In addition, for cases in which a cash flow in a period turns negative (suppose that it was forecast that in the fourth year of a system a major enhancement would be required) the rate-of-return approach can yield results that are difficult to evaluate. It is beyond the scope of this book to fully discuss these theoretical issues associated with the two methods, but, if in doubt, the user is usually better off to apply the present value approach.

Present Value Method

Using the "present value method" we compute an amount for the new system which takes the time value of money into consideration. We then compare the amount computed with the investment required to build and implement the new system. If the computed amount (PV) is greater than the investment (I), then it is favorable (in an economic sense) to make the investment in the new system. The equation to make the present value calculation is

$$PV = \sum_{t=1}^{n} \frac{CF_t}{(1+i)^t} \qquad (2)$$

where CF = cash flow from the system in time period t
  i = interest rate at which
    the firm borrows money
  n = number of years the system is expected
    to operate before being replaced

Rate-of-Return Method

Using the "rate-of-return method," we compute the rate of return that will result from making an investment in the new system. To make a decision about whether to build and implement the new system, one compares the calculated rate of return with that which is desirable (as set by senior management) or that which is returned from alternative investments. To calculate the rate of return, one writes an equation such as equation 3 and solves the equation for r. The equation is

$$\sum_{t=1}^{n} \frac{CF_t}{(1+r)^t} - I = 0 \tag{3}$$

where CF = cash flow from the system in time period t

r = rate of return on the investment

n = number of years the system is expected to operate before being replaced

I = investment required to build and implement the new system

By using either method, any expenditures for system maintenance or enhancement should be included in the period operating costs. If, in any year, the operating costs exceed the cash flow, then the rate-of-return method can yield results that are difficult to interpret. Otherwise, the two methods should give similar results. If a major system enhancement or rewrite is known to be planned for the future, it is usually preferable to do the analysis for the number of years the system will run without the change and treat the enhancement as a new system.

Note that if the present value method or the rate-of-return method shows that the new system is extremely desirable when just clerical savings, operational savings, and operational revenues are forecast, then from the economic perspective, one would expect the system to be approved. If, on the other hand, either method yields a result that is not satisfactory to management, one can solve for the "intangible benefits" which would be required in order to make the new system economically attractive. These values can be presented to management, and they can decide whether these benefits will actually result from use of the system planned, or whether they should take the risk that these benefits will not occur and develop the system anyway. At least, the degree of risk is quantified using this approach.

As we said at the beginning of this subsection, this type of economic analysis is usually applied when deciding whether or not to make an investment in a new system. Unfortunately, after the favorable systems are built and installed, most organizations do not go back and recompute the costs and benefits and reconstruct the analysis. This sort of postimplementation evaluation ought to be done on all systems. First, this activity would improve the accuracy of the estimating process through learning. Second, if carefully done, it would provide some sort of economic measure of the value of the organization's entire portfolio of applications.

Two Perspectives for Assessing the MIS Function

Matlin[4] proposed a method for answering the question, "What is the value of our investment in management information systems?" To a large extent, his proposal is similar in philosophy to summing up the individual economic evaluations of systems to arrive at an overall value for the total investment in information systems. As we explained in the introduction to this chapter, there are many practical difficulties associated with a purely economic view of the MIS evaluation. For these reasons, other, more comprehensive and managerially-based approaches to the evaluation have been suggested. Each of these approaches can be classified according to a particular point of view or perspective.

The authors have already mentioned that the view of senior management (or management assessment) is the preferred form of MIS evaluation. It will be seen that management assessment encompasses the features of economic evaluation, the MIS managerial view, and the financial control view. We believe, however, that it is appropriate to present the traditional views separately since these are often what one encounters in practice (if, indeed, any formal evaluative system at all is in place). As the next two subsections are considered, the reader should keep in mind that neither perspective or view is broad enough and, at least in our opinion, should be subsumed in a more global assessment.

The Perspective of the MIS Manager. One very important task of the MIS manager is to evaluate how good a job the MIS function is doing. The sorts of measures of MIS performance that the MIS manager might employ are shown in Table 7-3. This table also identifies certain measures that might relate to areas absolutely critical to the performance of the MIS function. In other words, if performance in the areas related to these measures is poor, the MIS manager must take corrective action.

It is important for the MIS manager to identify the critical success factors for the MIS function, to set measurable objectives for these factors, and to compare actual performance on the factors with the

---

[4]Gerald L. Matlin, "What Is the Value of Investment in Information Systems?" *MIS Quarterly*, vol. 3, no. 3, September 1979, pp. 5-34.

Table 7-3 Measures of MIS performance

Financial performance

Budget compliance (for the overall organization)—CSF

Cost recovery (if on cost recovery chargeout)—CSF

Distribution of costs by industry standards

Organizational efficiency

Developmental performance

   Meeting project time and cost goals—CSF
   Staff turnover—CSF
   Size of system request backlog
   System maintenance cost (as % of total cost)

Operational performance

   System availability/downtime—CSF
   Late jobs—CSF
   Online response time—CSF
   System utilization
   Throughput (job steps performed per standard time period)
   Job reruns (%)

Managerial performance

Attitudes of senior management—CSF

Attitudes of user managers—CSF

Performance on evaluation by external assessors (consultants,
  external auditors et al.)—CSF

Other

Availability of capacity in systems resources (hardware and personnel)
  to meet future operational and developmental requirements—CSF

goals.   This approach is highly related to the critical success factor method suggested for use in information requirements analysis and discussed in relation to MIS planning[5] in Chapter 6.

Clearly there are many measures in Table 7-3 that are related to one another; there are probably other measures that could be added, and there is plenty of room for argument as to which measures are related to critical factors.   Additionally, note should be taken of the fact that the first two categories of measures (financial and organizational efficiency) are subject to formal measurement, whereas the attitude measures associated with managerial performance are frequently only subjectively measured.

[5]John F. Rockart, "Managers Define Their Own Data Needs," *Harvard Business Review*, vol. 57, no. 2, March–April 1979, pp. 81–93.

If one were to examine a well-run MIS organization, statistics would be kept on many of the formally measurable items listed in Table 7-3 and the MIS manager would have a good indication for the more unquantifiable items. But this view of the MIS "world" is only one of several. Table 7-3 makes reference to at least one of the other views, that of the external auditor, or what we will call the perspective of the financial controller.

The Perspective of the Financial Controller. If the MIS function is evaluated by internal or external auditors, the perspective likely to be taken is that of financial control. As will be evident, this perspective is founded upon the premise of minimizing risk, especially financial risk, to the organization from suboptimal performance on the part of the MIS function.

It is fairly common to have the MIS function assessed or evaluated by auditors of one type or another. Their findings are usually presented to the chief financial officer of the organization. These findings are often communicated to other senior managers and, most certainly, to the MIS manager. Most of the evaluation is based upon comparing MIS practice with normative guidelines available to the auditors. Because of this approach, the evaluation is much less quantitative than the one based upon the measures normally employed by the MIS manager. The auditors will typically make judgments in the following areas:

I. Reliability and integrity of information:
  A. Financial and operating systems and their reports should contain accurate, reliable, timely, complete, and useful information.
  B. Controls over the system record keeping and reporting should be adequate and effective.
II. Compliance with policies, plans, procedures, laws, and regulations:
  A. Management systems should be in place to set policies and procedures regarding the use of information and information systems development. Planning systems should also be in place. These policies, procedures, and planning systems should be complied with. Finally, systems should not violate local, state, or federal laws or regulations.
III. Safeguarding of assets:
  A. Systems should be evaluated to ensure that they are safe from various types of losses, such as those resulting from theft, fire, and improper or illegal activities.
IV. Economical and efficient use of resources:
  A. Standards should exist for economical and efficient use of the system's resources (equipment and personnel). An evaluation should establish that standards have been developed; that they are understood by systems personnel; that deviations from

operating standards are identified, analyzed, and communicated to those responsible for corrective action; and that corrective action is taken when standards are not complied with.

V. Accomplishment of established objectives and goals for operations or programs:

  A. Management should have established operating or program goals and objectives, developed and implemented control procedures, and accomplished desired results. A determination should be made to ascertain whether such goals and objectives conform with those of the organization and whether they are being met.

One can see that an assessment based upon these areas of evaluation will check objectives, policies and/or procedures, and planning plus the accuracy, timeliness, and security of systems. Much of the assessment procedure will consist of interviews and examination of standards and documents. Clearly, the financial control perspective is different from that of the MIS manager. One of its attributes is that it is more global in its perspective. The two approaches together would be superior to either one by itself.

Note that the MIS manager is uniquely qualified to conduct an MIS evaluation of the first type and that personnel with an auditing orientation are best qualified to conduct and report on the second type of evaluation. Still, in the opinion of the authors, a great deal is missing if only one or even both of the above types of evaluations are available to senior management concerning the performance of the MIS function. What is needed is an even more global assessment which encompasses economic factors, MIS internal performance factors, and factors associated with financial control together with other factors related to MIS performance which have evolved from our 25-year experience with the organizational use of computing technology.

CONDUCTING AN OVERALL ASSESSMENT OF THE MIS FUNCTION

We have examined three limited perspectives on evaluating an MIS function and the contribution it makes to its parent organization. The results from each perspective are valuable, but in our opinion they fall short of what is required. We are suggesting that a more comprehensive evaluative framework should be applied. This framework, as will be seen, draws upon those that have already been presented but adds areas and factors not included in any of the approaches discussed thus far.

A complete check on the "health" of an MIS organization should include a host of factors. At the outset of this discussion, the authors want to be forthright and point out that no organization of which they are aware has conducted an assessment which includes all the factors which will·be identified. Management should examine the complete set of factors that can be assessed and pick and choose those to be included in a particular assessment. The choice should be based upon the desired completeness of the assessment, the cost of assessing a particular factor or set of factors, and the perceived benefit that assessing a factor will have.

The results of the assessment, moreover, should be used for both a static and a dynamic evaluation. The former involves identification of problem areas to which corrective action can be applied. Dynamic assessment means that assessments are repeated over time to ensure that the problems have been corrected and that overall performance of the function is improving. To reduce cost and effort, assessments after the first one may deal with only a subset of areas rather than the more comprehensive set evaluated the first time that the process is employed.

Areas for MIS Assessment

If one were to search the MIS literature for material on MIS evaluation, one would discover that there is little material on this subject and what there is addresses only parts of the overall problem. Several areas are mentioned by most of the limited sources, none of the areas are included by all, and each source seems to include one or two areas not addressed by any of the others. We have attempted to be as comprehensive as possible in the inclusion of areas and factors which should be associated with an assessment of an MIS organization and its contribution to the overall enterprise. Table 7-4 lists the areas and factors which could be included in an overall MIS assessment.

Note that in Table 7-4 some factors from the economic assessment are repeated as well as some from the perspective of the MIS manager

Table 7-4 Areas and factors in an MIS assessment

Process by which projects are selected for inclusion in MIS plan
   (including resource allocation mechanisms such as cost/benefit analysis
   and/or zero-based budgeting)

User management role in MIS planning and priority setting

System development practice and project control

Availability, quality, and use of formal system development methodology

Availability, quality, and use of structured design methods

Availability, quality, and use of project control system

System development productivity aids (hardware/software,
   prototyping/heuristic design, information center concept and
   technologies)

Role of user in design and implementation process

Table 7-4 Areas and factors in an MIS assessment (continued)

Responsiveness to user requests, especially in the case of
systems problems or the need for quick but minor systems evolution

Quality of user documentation

System development chargeout system

Quality of systems documentation

Applications portfolio

How computing resources are being employed (including systems currently
operational, under development, and planned)

Transactions-oriented systems
Monitor systems
Exception systems
Inquiry systems
Analysis (DSS) systems

Quality of the applications (including the appropriateness of the content
of the systems, their timeliness, and their accuracy)

Operational efficiency

Appropriateness of hardware and software (including systems software)

Evolvability of hardware and software

Efficiency of hardware utilization

Chargeout system for system operation

Hardware and systems downtime

Systems for data security and privacy

Backup, recovery, and disaster systems

Personnel evaluation

Technical quality of DP analysts and programmers

Staff professionalism

Business knowledge of DP personnel

User MIS knowledge

Appropriateness of training—user and systems

MIS job satisfaction

Compensation and career planning system

MIS measurement systems

Meeting project time and cost goals

Staff turnover

Maintenance cost

Systems responsiveness

EDP audit reports

Industry standard comparison

MIS organization

Reporting relationship and fit with overall organization

Internal organization structure and functions

and from the perspective of the auditor. A complete assessment, to be reported to senior management (including the financial controller) and to MIS management, as suggested in Table 7-4, would include many more factors than would be included in any assessment based upon a limited perspective. We have identified a fairly comprehensive list of factors. The question now is "How do we perform the assessment?"

Procedures for MIS Assessment

The party conducting the MIS assessment would usually utilize several methods of data collection. The first would be interviews with senior management, users and user management, and with MIS personnel. Some interviews would involve attitudinal questions, whereas other interviews would deal with factual matters. A second evaluative tool would be the use of formal questionnaires. More than one might be involved depending upon the completeness of the assessment. Formal questionnaires for measuring the job satisfaction of MIS personnel is one example of a special-purpose questionnaire. A third procedure involves examination of procedure documents, documentation, and reports. The evaluation resulting from this process would be highly judgmental.

To do a complete MIS assessment would usually take at least a month. Another period would be required to write a report and to prepare an oral presentation for management. The report ought to be presented to senior management as well as to MIS management. A formal response ought to be prepared to state how to address problems that have been identified in the assessment.

As we have said, what is included in each assessment will differ according to circumstances. The following case study will show how one organization went about an MIS assessment and what was included.

A CASE STUDY

Company A had, in the opinion of the local data processing community, an awful reputation regarding their computer organization. They had a history of user complaints, they had gone through three MIS managers in 5 years, and they had an unmotivated data processing staff which had experienced high levels of turnover. All this was common knowledge throughout the data processing community. In 1978, the firm brought in a new chief executive officer. This man was in his position about 3 months when he decided that the organization simply could not function as he wanted it to with the situation existing in data processing. His first step was to move the current head of MIS to another position within the company and replace him with a person that had been with the firm for 25 years and had the reputation of being a superior manager. This man had no formal data processing experience other than that of a user. In the latter role, he had been one of the loudest complainers about the data processing organization. The CEO said, in effect, "You've been complaining about DP for all these years. Now I'm going to give you a chance to make it right." The CEO also made the point that, in his opinion, the effective performance of the data processing function was vital to the organization. His actions supported these words.

The new head of MIS recognized that although he knew that there were problems in data processing, he did not know exactly what they were or what was causing them. In addition, he knew little about what to do to effectively manage the function. He decided to call in an outside firm to conduct an assessment of the organization's information systems. He selected consultants well known for assessing an organization's use of the computing resource. The procedure employed by the consulting firm was as follows:

I. Interviews were conducted with:
   A. All MIS systems managers to identify perceived strengths and weaknesses
   B. User-MIS personnel pairs involved in all major systems to check the match in perceptions and attitudes
   C. A sample of systems personnel to gain opinions on problems and strengths of MIS
II. Questionnaires were employed to:
   A. Measure MIS personnel job attitudes
   B. Measure self-reported and superior-reported skills of MIS personnel
   C. Measure "professionalism" of MIS personnel
III. Observations were made and data was gathered concerning:
   A. MIS planning, priority setting, and resource allocation
   B. Systems development life cycle performance and procedures
   C. Project planning and control
   D. Efficiency of computer operations
   E. Availability of and compliance to documentation standards
   F. Security
   G. Applications portfolio
   H. Information system managerial policies

The assessment process took about a month. About 2 weeks after the completion of the assessment, a written report was presented by the consultants to senior management and the head of MIS. A meeting was held with the consulting firm to present the results and to discuss the situation. The report emphasized the good factors about MIS in the organization and identified problem areas and possible causes of the problems. In order to illustrate the results of the management assessment, we have excerpted some of the findings from the summary of the report. These provide a flavor of the process and its results. The entire report, of course, provided all the detail necessary to support the summary conclusions given below.

I. Strengths of the User Support Function and MIS Personnel
    A. Functional organization structure definitely increases the quality of user support
    B. There are many good application systems
    C. There are some very satisfied user groups
    D. There are many well-qualified (especially technically) MIS personnel
II. Problems of the User Support Function and MIS Personnel
    A. As perceived by the users:
        1. Many analysts do not understand business needs
        2. There are inadequate MIS people resources
            a. There is not enough quality among personnel
            b. Response time to requests is poor
        3. The communication between users and systems is only fair
            a. In many cases it is difficult for the user to determine whom to talk to
            b. Users cannot get computer capacity and systems personnel shifted easily among projects
    B. As perceived by systems personnel:
        1. Systems personnel, in general, do not know enough about the business function they are serving
        2. There are inadequate MIS personnel resources
            a. The shortage causes unsatisfied requests
            b. A one-person-one-system situation results
            c. People end up serving several user groups
            d. There is inadequate space
        3. Communication with users is only fair
            a. A user liaison is not specified on some systems
            b. There is a lack of interest in MIS direction
        4. There is a lack of systems planning on the part of users
III. Personnel Skills Analysis
    A. The personal skills needing the most work or training are:
        1. Leadership
        2. Delegation
        3. Communication
        4. Training of subordinates
    B. Technical skills exist in small subsets of people
    C. Most systems personnel feel "adequate but in need of improvement" in frequently required job skills

IV. Professional Activity Analysis
  A. Only 20 percent of MIS staff belong to a professional organization
  B. The majority do not keep up on the field by reading data processing periodicals or other relevant literature
 V. Hardware and Software Evaluation
  A. The *strengths* are:
    1. A good ability to forecast the capacity of or load on the system
    2. Technical expertise of personnel
    3. Performance measurement system
    4. The capability and expandability of the hardware itself
  B. The *problems* are:
    1. The physical security
    2. The software status:
      a. Of the operating system
      b. Of the "homegrown" file manager
    3. The availability of space
    4. Documentation for system "pass off" from development to operations
VI. Management System Evaluation
  A. The *strengths* of MIS and its management system are:
    1. The functional organization structure
    2. The user review meetings
    3. A concerned top management
    4. The beginnings of the use of the zero-based budgeting system
  B. The *problems* of MIS and its management system are:
    1. Shortcomings in the planning process, including:
      a. Lack of a link to the corporate plan
      b. Lack of an MIS master plan developed with user involvement
    2. Shortcomings in the manner in which MIS is evaluated:
      a. By top management
      b. By MIS management
    3. Inadequacies in the system design and project control processes
      a. Design is too ad hoc and varies by group
      b. Project control is inappropriate and cost-ineffective
    4. Documentation is weak and inconsistent
VII. Job Diagnostic Survey Results
  A. The overall job attitudes of people working in the information services division are about average when compared to national benchmarks available for similar jobs

1. Systems analysis, in particular, is at or slightly below the average scores recently reported in a national survey
2. Systems operations scores are slightly higher than systems analysis, a surprising result. No benchmarks are available to which systems analysis can be compared.

B. There are substantial differences in worker attitudes when analyzed by the manager to whom they report

At the meeting there was considerable discussion of the results of the assessment and of corrective action to be applied to remedy the problems. Over a period of time, many procedures were changed and improved, training for both users and technical personnel was undertaken, and an emphasis on "MIS professionalism" was adopted. Each year, an update of the assessment is conducted and continuous corrective action is applied.

In this instance the MIS organization, over a period of about 4 years, erased their poor reputation and replaced it with an extremely positive one. The company's CEO and the head of MIS were heard to say that the MIS assessment was critical in the improvement. It gave them targets for improvement and allowed a measurement of change over time. They continued to repeat the assessment on an annual basis but in a shorter form than the one used for the initial assessment. The MIS steering committee (formed as the result of a recommendation in the original assessment) considers review of the annual MIS assessment one of its most important and worthwhile tasks.

SUMMARY

The question frequently arises as to who should conduct the management assessment of the information systems organization. The issue is whether an outside party ought to be engaged to conduct the assessment. It is the opinion of the authors that it is usually preferable if the assessors come from outside the enterprise.

The best system is as follows. First, the head of the MIS function should have formal measures of the efficiency of the MIS organization. Senior management ought to receive periodic performance reports from the head of MIS which include these performance measures. The form of the report ought to be such that senior management can quickly examine current performance and see how performance has changed over time.

In addition, senior management ought also to receive on an annual basis a summary of an MIS audit. This assessment can be performed by either the internal audit staff or external auditors, or both can make studies. In the case of an information systems assessment by external auditors, their report ought to contain statements concerning the adequacy of internal review of the MIS function.

Finally, senior management ought to receive a report based upon an overall management assessment of the MIS organization. Naturally, this assessment would comment upon the MIS efficiency measures as developed by the head of MIS and upon the assessments conducted under the perspective of financial control. This assessment, of course, would add to both of the more limited assessments and address most or all of the areas identified as part of the MIS assessment.

Obviously, conducting several assessments of the MIS function, each with a slightly different orientation, can be time-consuming and expensive. There are two reasons why, in our opinion, the cost and the effort are worthwhile. First, the quality and the reliability of the MIS function are of extreme importance to the effective performance of the organization and deserve to be subject to careful scrutiny. Second, the overall assessment of the MIS function, if done properly the first time, need not be very expensive or time-consuming to conduct on a periodic basis. The process can be routinized and, in most cases, easily updated. Detailed analysis need be devoted only to problem areas once a baseline is established.

It is important to reiterate that the overall management assessment of the MIS function ought to stress areas of strength as well as areas of weakness. Senior management needs to know what is good about the MIS function as well as what could be improved. Many of the firms which perform MIS assessments employ processes that feature the reporting of both good and bad attributes, and especially after the first assessment, they are efficient in terms of effort, time, and cost.

SUGGESTED READINGS

Abrams, Robert J., John J. Foley, and Laurence G. Robbins, "The Stage Assessment," in Richard L. Nolan (ed.), *Managing the Data Resource Function*, West, St. Paul, Minn., 1982, Chap. 10.

Alloway, Robert M., and Judith A. Quillard, "Top Priorities for the Information Systems Function," CISR Working Paper No. 79, Center for Information Systems Research, MIT, September 1981.

Gibson, C., and R. L. Nolan, "Managing the Four Stages of EDP Growth," *Harvard Business Review*, vol. 52, no. 1, January–February 1974, pp. 76-88.

Hamilton, Scott, and Norman L. Chervany, "Evaluating Information System Effectiveness -- Part I: Comparing Evaluation Approaches," *MIS Quarterly*, vol. 5, no. 3, September 1981, pp. 55-70.

Kleijnen, Jack P. C., *Computers and Profits*, Addison-Wesley, Reading, Mass., 1980, pp. 69-73.

Matlin, G. L., "How to Survive a Management Assessment," *MIS Quarterly*, vol. 1, no. 1, March 1977, pp. 11-18.

McFarlan, F. Warren, "Management Audit of the EDP Department," *Harvard Business Review*, vol. 51, no. 3, May-June 1973, pp. 131-142.

_____, James L. McKenney, and Philip Pyburn, "The Information Archipelago -- Plotting a Course," *Harvard Business Review*, vol. 61, no. 1, January-February 1983, pp. 145-156.

Nolan, Richard L., "Managing the Computer Resource: A Stage Hypothesis," *Communications of the ACM*, vol. 16, no. 7, July 1973.

_____, "Managing the Crises in Data Processing," *Harvard Business Review*, vol. 57, no. 2, March-April 1979, pp. 115-126.

Standards for the Professional Practice of Internal Auditing, Institute of Internal Auditors, Altamonte Springs, Fla., 1978.

Zmud, Robert W., *Information Systems in Organizations*, Scott, Foresman, Glenview, Ill., 1983, Chap. 12.

PART FIVE

KEY TECHNOLOGY TRENDS
AND IMPLICATIONS

EIGHT

DATABASE MANAGEMENT SYSTEMS

INTRODUCTION

The use of database management systems represents one of the most significant trends in the field of computer-based information systems. A database management system (DBMS) is a collection of software for processing a collection of interrelated data, known as a "database." In this chapter, both the need for and the characteristics of database technology are discussed. The effects of database management systems on the systems development process are also pointed out.

INTEGRATION OF ORGANIZATIONAL INFORMATION

A particularly perplexing problem with information systems has been the inability to integrate organization information. The need for integrated information for higher levels of management is best illustrated by the pyramidal structure of most organizations: there exists an ever-widening succession of levels from the top to the bottom of such organizations.

If an organization is to remain viable and operational, the activities of lower-level functional units must be coordinated and conflicts resolved by the integrative activities of higher levels of management. Ultimately, the chief executive office must ensure the integration of the activities of the overall organization. For example, production activities must be coordinated with marketing activities in order to maintain a balance between products produced and products sold. Coordination of these different organizational activities requires the integration of information about the activities so that they can be properly managed and controlled.

The speed and capabilities of computer systems appear to offer great promise in overcoming the information integration constraint inherent with manual information systems. But managers of many organizations that have invested in computer technology have been quite disappointed; much of the information stored in their computer systems cannot be integrated easily.

A Banking Example

The reasons for the lack of integration of organizational information are illustrated by the following example. Consider a bank that installs its first computer system. The largest and most cost-effective application to computerize is demand deposit accounting (DDA), or checking accounts. A systems analyst is assigned to work with users to automate this system. DDA is a highly structured process that lends itself to computer processing. Account numbers can be used as keys, and the data to be stored in computer files is primarily the data used in the manual system, with some enhancements. Figure 8-1 depicts the data contained in a DDA file. Once stored in the computer system, the DDA file can be used to generate a variety of reports and/or terminal displays associated with the management and control of DDA.

During the development and implementation of the DDA systems, the bank decides to begin implementation of a computer-based savings

Figure 8-1 Contents of a DDA File

1. Account Number	17. Officer Code
2. Name	18. Date DDA opened
3. Spouse's Name	19. Current Balance
4. Address	20. Last Statement Date
5. Telephone Number	21. Balance Forward — Last Statement
6. Date of Birth	22. Amount of Credits — Current Period
7. Sex	23. Number of Credits — Current Period
8. Marital Status	24. Amounts of Debits — Current Period
9. Number of Children	25. Number of Debits — Current Period
10. Number of Dependents	26. Number of Returned Checks Year-to-Date
11. Rent or Own	27. Date of Last Deposit
12. Occupation Code	28. Service Charge
13. Years Employed	29. Date of Last Overdraft
14. Income Range	30. Amount of Last Overdrafts
15. Credit Rating	31. Number of Overdrafts
16. Line of Credit	

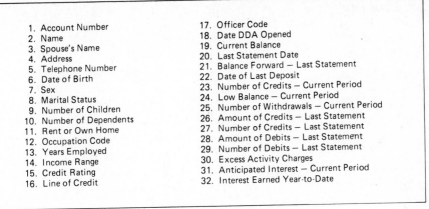

Figure 8-2 Contents of a Savings Accounting File

account system. Another systems analyst is assigned to work with users to automate this system. Input transactions, reports, and files are designed, based upon the manual savings accounting system as shown in Figure 8-2.

The bank continues its development of computer-based information systems by automating its installment loan system and its mortgage loan system. Existing account numbers are used for each system, and existing data-capture methods are expanded to obtain all of the data shown in Figures 8-3 and 8-4.

The bank also automates its payroll system. The file for this system includes the data shown in Figure 8-5.

Figure 8-3 Contents of an Installment Loan File

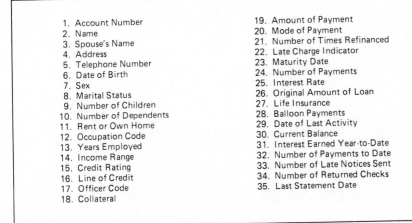

1. Account Number	21. Late Charge Code
2. Name	22. Amount of Payment
3. Spouse's Name	23. Mode of Payment
4. Address	24. Escrow Payment
5. Telephone Number	25. Original Amount of Loan
6. Date of Birth	26. Maturity Date
7. Sex	27. Interest Rate
8. Marital Status	28. Terms In Months
9. Number of Children	29. Date of Last Appraisal
10. Number of Dependents	30. Amount of Appraisal
11. Rent or Own Home	31. Purchase Price
12. Occupation Code	32. Percent of Loan Guaranteed
13. Years Employed	33. Late Charge Rate
14. Income Range	34. Date of Last Activity
15. Credit Rating	35. Escrow Balance
16. Line of Credit	36. Number of Late Notices
17. Officer Code	37. Number of Months to Go
18. Original Date of Loan	38. Interest Paid Year-to-Date
19. Property Identification	39. Principal Remaining
20. FHA or VA Number	

Figure 8-4 Contents of a Mortgage Loan File

The development of these five information systems has spanned 4 years and cost several hundred thousand dollars. Bank employees and managers responsible for DDA have their own information systems; bank employees and managers responsible for savings accounts have their own information systems; and so forth. However, there are some serious problems. Each system was developed as an independent subsystem; no thought was given to interfacing the subsystems to provide integrated processing or reporting.

Redundancy

The first problem with the bank's information systems is that there is a great deal of redundancy in the data collected, stored, and processed. Consider a bank customer who has a checking account, a savings account, an installment loan, and a mortgage loan. Though the bank is dealing with one customer, its information systems treat this customer as

Figure 8-5 Contents of the Payroll File

1. Social Security Number	11. Vacation Leave
2. Name	12. Federal Withholding
3. Address	13. FICA
4. Department Code	14. State Taxes
5. Job Title	15. Insurance
6. Date of Hire	16. Regular Earnings Year-to-Date
7. Marital Status	17. Federal Withholding Year-to-Date
8. Number of Dependents	18. FICA Year-to-Date
9. Pay Rate	19. State Taxes Year-to-Date
10. Sick Leave	20. Net Earnings Year-to-Date

four customers. The customer has four account numbers (one in each information system).

Certain data are redundantly collected, stored, and processed in each system. Specifically, data elements 1 through 16 are identical in each of four files (see Figures 8-1 to 8-4). If a customer has more than one checking account, savings account, or loan, the redundancy becomes even greater. This redundancy creates the following problems:

1. Customers are required to supply much duplicate data for each account they open, even when some or all of the data needed has been collected previously.

2. Storage space is wasted because the same data is stored in different places in the same file and/or in different files.

3. Processing time is wasted. For example, a customer's address may be stored in eight different places in the bank's computer files because of redundancy.

4. Inconsistencies and/or other errors develop in data files. The majority of information systems fail to update all redundant data. For example, a customer's address may be updated in the DDA file but not in the savings account or loan files. Consequently, there are inconsistencies as to the address of that customer.

Integration

Besides creating inefficient redundancies, the independent-subsystem structure causes difficulties in integrating information. The systems and file have been developed along departmental or functional boundaries. The account numbers are not logically related and cannot be used for cross-referencing customers' accounts. This seriously limits reporting capabilities. For example, a loan officer may want to check information pertaining to a loan applicant's checking and savings accounts. However, there is no linkage to this data from the loan system. Indeed, the loan officer may have to ask the loan applicant if he or she has checking and/or savings accounts with the bank and what his or her account numbers are.

Consider a case where the management of the bank wants to increase mortgage loans to offset several large savings deposits. Management decides to send letters encouraging specific customers to consider buying homes, using convenient financing available through the bank. Management also decides that the best customers to send such letters to are customers meeting the following criteria:

1. Customers who do not own homes
2. Customers who have good checking account records (i.e., few or no overdrafts)
3. Customers with sufficient funds in their savings accounts to make down payments on homes

4. Customers who have good payment records on any installment loans with the bank

Though the data necessary to identify such customers is available in the different files on the different information systems (see Figures 8-1 to 8-4), there is no convenient way to integrate it. Extensive programming and clerical work are required to satisfy such an information request. Management is understandably disappointed.

The problem is that the bank's information systems are not designed to integrate information to serve management's needs. Integration of information is more readily achievable when considered prior to developing and implementing systems. After the fact, integration can be unwieldy; it may even require new systems development.

It is important to point out that not all organizational information needs to be integrated. For example, the contents of the payroll file in Figure 8-5 are independent of the contents of other files. Though bank employees may have checking accounts, savings accounts, and/or loans with the bank, there is little incentive to endure the expense of structurally relating this data in the computer system (i.e., because a bank usually has several thousand accounts but only a few hundred employees). Any requirements to relate employee data to data in the other information systems can usually be handled more cost-effectively on a manual basis.

Thus, organizational information may not be integrated because of oversight or because the data cannot be integrated practically. The former situation is caused by poor systems analysis and design. The latter is caused by the nature of the data being processed. Figure 8-6 shows the relationships of the data contained in the bank's five files.

The scenario of the bank can be translated into other organizational settings. For example, in a university, student data, course data, faculty data, and classroom facilities data should all be integrated. In a manufacturing plant, sales data, inventory data, production resources data, and purchasing data should be integrated.

In retrospect, it is not difficult to see that, when appropriate, information systems should be integrated. However, few organizations have attempted such integration in their initial attempts to develop computer-based information systems. Many information systems are developed as high-speed automated versions of existing manual systems. Since manual systems do not lend themselves to integration with other manual systems, the computer versions of these systems retain this nonintegration orientation. The opportunity to integrate the manual systems as they are computerized is not exploited. Rather, the personnel developing the systems react to management's demands for integrated information after it becomes apparent that there is a structural deficiency within their initial development efforts.

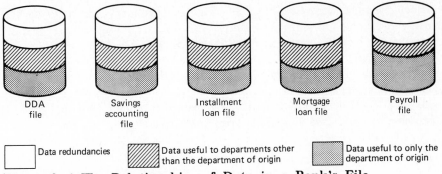

| DDA file | Savings accounting file | Installment loan file | Mortgage loan file | Payroll file |

☐ Data redundancies   ▨ Data useful to departments other than the department of origin   ▨ Data useful to only the department of origin

Figure 8-6 The Relationships of Data in a Bank's File

Difficulties in Integrating Data

A number of organizations have attempted to integrate their information systems either initially or during early revisions of their initial systems. Though their insight and efforts have enabled them to more readily integrate data and, therefore, reduce redundancies, they have still encountered problems. The programming of data relationships that transcend departmental or functional boundaries is extremely complex. To achieve integration requires consolidation of files and/or linking of data stored in separate files.

In our example above, four systems of the bank (DDA, savings, accounting, installment loans) can be integrated into a single centralized file. One way this can be accomplished is by assigning to each customer a single account number and using suffixes to designate the accounts the customer has with the bank. Figure 8-7 illustrates such a

Figure 8-7 Use of Suffixes to Achieve Centralized Account Numbers at a Bank

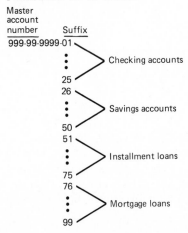

customer account structure. Note that a customer can have several checking accounts, savings accounts, and loans. The unique identity provided for each customer account allows the accounts to be consolidated into one file as shown in Figure 8-8.

This bank is unlike most organizations in that, generally, an organization's separate files cannot practically be consolidated into a single file. If consolidation is not possible, integration of data is sometimes accomplished by linking the data from separate files.

A University Example

Consider a student file and a class schedule file used in a registration system at a university. Integration of the data in the files is required to determine what classes each student is scheduled for and what students are scheduled for each class.

In a poorly designed registration system, integration of data can be accomplished by redundantly storing pertinent class data (class number, name, instructor, room, days, time, etc.) for each student in the student file. Also, all pertinent data about schedules (student number, name, major, classification, etc.) for each course must be redundantly stored in the class schedule file. These redundancies create problems. If 200 students are enrolled for a class, the data pertinent to that class is stored 200 times in the student file (i.e., once for each student). If the room number in which the class is to be held is changed, updating this data requires updating all 200 copies of it stored in the student file as well as the original version stored in the class schedule file.

Figure 8-8 A Customer Record from a Consolidated File of a Bank

326-47-9867-00 Customer data
326-47-9687-00 Checking account 1 data
326-47-9867-02 Checking account 2 data
326-47-9867-26 Savings account 1 data
326-47-9867-52 Installment loan 2 data
326-47-9867-76 Mortgage loan 1 data

Rather than redundantly storing class data in the student file and student data in the course file, a more efficient approach can be taken. It involves storing only the keys to the class and student file which are the class numbers of each class a student is scheduled for. The class number can then be used as an index to the class schedule file, which can then be accessed to obtain the data describing the class. If 200 students are enrolled in a course, the data for each of the students would include an index to the class data (but no additional class data is actually stored in the student file). Consequently, class data such as time, place, and instructor need only be changed in the course file to properly reflect changes for each student scheduled for the class. A reciprocal arrangement is possible for the class schedule file. Only the index to the students scheduled for a class need be stored in the class schedule file -- not the student data.

The concept of linking data between files is illustrated in Figure 8-9. Note that this linking process appears somewhat complex, even though only a few linkages are depicted. In a real system, the student file will likely contain several hundred classes. If the university decides to integrate a student fee file, faculty file, and facilities file (i.e., buildings and rooms) with the student and class schedule file, the

Figure 8-9 Linking Data Between a Student File and a Class Schedule File

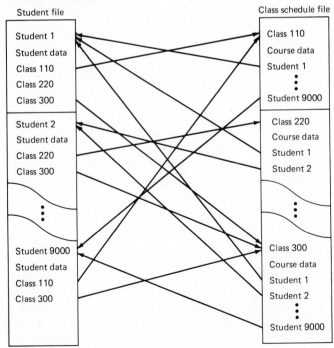

linkages between files will become even more complex. Herein lies the problem with traditional approaches to integrating data from separate files. First, programming such complex relationships is a massive task. Second, since the needs for all relationships and data elements are to a great extent unforeseen and/or continually changing, additional data elements and relationships must be added and programmed into the system. A simple adding of a few data elements to a file can necessitate modification of several dozen programs that access the file. Even when data integration is achieved through file consolidation, system modifications can have serious rippling effects throughout computer programs involved in the system. Consequently, many organizations have found up to 80 percent of their programming staff's efforts are directed toward making modifications to existing systems rather than toward developing new ones.

DATABASE TECHNOLOGY

The first section of this chapter defines and describes the major factors contributing to the difficulties of integrating organizational data for management information. These factors are reviewed below:

1. Some data is not suited for integration or does not need to be integrated
2. Organizations often fail to consider data integration when designing and developing their information systems
3. There is considerable technological complexity in integrating organizational data in separate files

The first factor is one that simply needs to be recognized. Organizations must accept the fact that not all organizational data can be neatly integrated into a single, all-encompassing database. The second factor can be overcome by better planning and more top management involvement in the design and development of organizational information systems. The third factor reflects technological constraints. An organization that has overcome the first two factors generally knows the right way to approach the development of integrated information systems. However, the organization may need help in doing it. A database management system provides the technology to more effectively and efficiently achieve integrated information systems.

Files and Access Techniques

Before proceeding with a discussion of database technology, a review of files and file access techniques may be helpful.

A file is a collection of related records. For example, a payroll file consists of a payroll record for each employee. The records in a data file are composed of data elements. Some data elements commonly included in a payroll file are employee name, social security number, address, salary, and deductions.

Files are generally stored on magnetic tape or magnetic disk. Data is accessed using access techniques provided by the operating software. The three basic techniques for accessing files are

- Sequential access
- Direct access
- Indexed access

The following sections discuss common implementations of these techniques.

Sequential Access. Sequential access pertains to storing and retrieving records in a "one-after-the-other" order. Records are generally stored in ascending or descending order by a record key. A record key is a unique unchanging piece of information such as an account number, a name, or a social security number. Sequential access is the only access technique used with magnetic tape drives, which are, by design, sequential access devices.

The storage and retrieval of records in sequential order is similar to the approach used in manual systems (e.g., of personnel folders stored alphabetically in a filing cabinet). Accordingly, sequential access has traditionally appealed to organizations converting from manual to computer-based systems. This appeal, combined with the early dominance of magnetic tape as a cost-effective storage medium, has led to the use of sequential access files in most initial computing efforts.

Sequential access is used primarily in batch-processing environments. It is particularly effective when transaction activity is evenly distributed among the records in the file. For example, in payroll processing, the information on time cards is recorded for all hourly employees and payroll checks are printed for all employees. When a sequential file is updated, the transactions are sorted into the same sequence as the file and then sequentially matched against the file.

Direct Access. Sequential access is inefficient for batch-processing applications in which only a small proportion of the records in a file are affected by a given batch of transactions. The entire file may have to be passed to update a few records. For online processing, sequential access is inadequate. The time lapse of several minutes generally required to locate a record sequentially is unacceptable.

Sequential access fails to take advantage of two exceptional capabilities of computer technology: speed and direct access. Direct access is an alternative to sequential access that significantly accelerates the process of storing and retrieving records by capitalizing on both the computational speed of the CPU and the access speed of the disk drive. Disk drives are capable of directly accessing a particular record, so the disk location of the record is required. The location is indicated by the address assigned to it, which is saved when the record is stored or recalculated on the basis of the record key when the record is sought.

In sequential access, the location of a record is a function of its proximity to preceding records. Since processing begins at the first record of the file, it is only necessary to know the address of the location of the first record. All subsequent records follow the first record.

Since direct accessing requires the address of the specific location of a record desired, direct access requires an addressing scheme that computes a unique address for each record. Generally, the record key (e.g., social security number, account number, or part number) must be transformed into a disk storage address.

The most common approach to transforming record keys into storage addresses involves an arithmetic procedure that generates "random addresses" from record keys. There are several randomizing algorithms. The most common algorithm involves the generation of addresses by dividing the record key by a positive prime number (usually, the prime number is the largest prime number that is less than the number of available addresses). The remainder of a division operation is used as the address locator. Figure 8-10 shows the generation of random addresses from record keys when 1000 addresses are available.

A randomizing algorithm always generates the same address for a particular key. Therefore, given the key to a record, the computer can calculate the disk address and then access the record in a matter of milliseconds.

Occasionally, a random-address generator generates the same address for two or more keys. The second and succeeding records with duplicate addresses are referred to as "synonyms." When a synonym occurs, the record having the duplicate address can be stored in a location next to other synonyms of the record stored at the computer address, or it can be stored in a general overflow area. In either case, if a desired record is not located at the computed address (this is determined by checking the key stored in the record), a sequential search of synonyms is invoked until the desired record is located. This sequential search slows processing slightly. A good randomizing algorithm generates few synonyms. If a random-address generator produces many synonyms for a particular set of keys, analysis and modification of the randomizing algorithm is needed.

Another drawback of a direct-access technique is that, by design, it usually leaves large gaps between records on a disk. This results in wasted disk space. Some of the gaps may be consumed by synonyms, but considerable wasted space still remains. An offsetting advantage is the incredible speed with which records can be accessed, regardless of the size of the file.

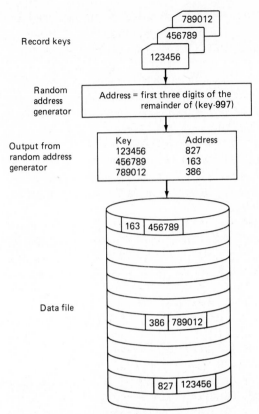

Figure 8-10 Using Record Keys to Generate Random Addresses on Disk Storage

Perhaps the most challenging concept to grasp with respect to direct access is that the physical locations of records bear no relationship to the logical view of the data. The random generation of addresses physically scatters records throughout the disk, so that, without knowledge of the randomizing algorithm used to transform the keys, locating a record requires a sequential search through a nonsequentially ordered file. The use of a randomizing algorithm is an extraordinary deviation from the way that files are maintained manually. However, it is a highly suitable technique for computer-processed files. A file of several thousand or even several million records can be located instantaneously.

Indexed Access. Indexed access pertains to using tables of key fields that provide the disk addresses of records stored in a file. Indexed-access techniques are used with either sequential or direct-access files.

The simplest form of indexed access is referred to as "indexed sequential." This technique involves the use of indexes to segment a sequentially stored file to facilitate quicker access. To access a specific record, a search is made of the index file to determine the address of the first record of the segment in which the record is located.

Since the index file is much smaller than the actual data file, indexed-sequential processing greatly accelerates locating a specific record; substantial sequential processing is eliminated. For large files, multiple levels of indexes (i.e., hierarchical indexes) are used to locate records more quickly. Figure 8-11 shows a hierarchical indexing scheme using three levels. The major-level index points to the intermediate-level index, which points to the minor-level index, which points to the actual data file.

Indexed-access techniques can also be used to access records by means other than record keys. This provides flexibility that is especially useful for querying a data file. For example, the personnel office can request the records of all employees who are accountants. Such access to records is accomplished by setting up indexes based upon one or more fields of the records. In the same way that the index in this book points to each page that contains a particular word, a field index points to each record that contains a certain field value. Figure 8-12 illustrates a job classification index for a personnel file.

Indexes can be set up for several record fields. This allows even more discrimination in making a data-file query. Instead of just requesting the records of all employees who are accountants, the query can also specify that the employees have a college degree and 2 years of

Figure 8-11 A Hierarchical Indexed-Sequential Structure

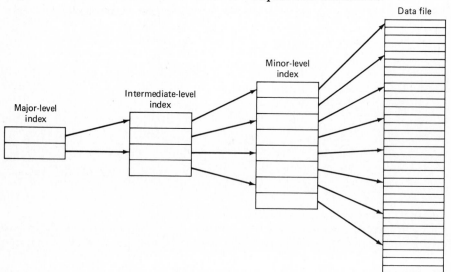

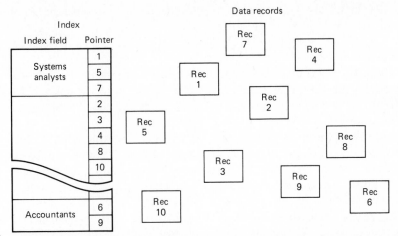

Figure 8-12 Job Classification Indexes for Accessing Employee Data Records in a Randomly Organized File

experience within the organization. One way of responding to this query requires that an index exist for job classification, education, and number of years within the organization. The query is satisfied by identifying all records not pointed to by the first index, and then progressively eliminating records that are not pointed to by the second and then the third index. After this process of elimination, only records that satisfy all the selection criteria remain. These records can then be directly accessed using the addresses provided by the indexes.

The use of indexed access on fields other than the record key is more suitable for higher-level decision-making and planning functions than for routine transaction processing. It allows convenient and less restrictive retrieval of information, but considerable programming time and computer processing are required to set up and maintain the indexes as records are added to and deleted from the data file.

Database

The preceding discussion of file access techniques was oriented toward a single-file environment. An MIS can be envisioned as a federation of information systems, integrated as necessary. Database technology is a step beyond file-access techniques and is a key factor in achieving an MIS. It provides software to facilitate the integration of the various data files of an organization.

Management Information Systems and Database Systems

When organizational data is interrelated and stored together to serve one or more applications, the collection of data is generally referred to as a "database." Data redundancy is seldom totally eliminated, but it is controlled and significantly reduced. Figure 8-13 is a simplified view of files integrated into a database structure.

For example, a university may have a database for a student information system consisting of student, course, and facilities files and a database for a financial information system consisting of general ledger, accounts receivable, accounts payable, and payroll files. When an organization decides to have two or more databases, the databases are disjoint in structure.

As discussed earlier in the chapter, programming data interrelationships to achieve integration and reduce redundancy is a complex task. Computer programs must use one or more of the file-access techniques (i.e., sequential, random, or indexed) to provide explicit instructions as to the physical locations of the data elements required to satisfy a particular online terminal query or to produce a particular batch report. Figure 8-14 shows the relationship among applications programs, file-access software, and computer files.

For example, a program may need to access several interrelated data elements from records located in different files. The program must use indexes to compute physical addresses for each file in which data is contained, retrieve the entire record from each file, and then extract the data elements required from each record. Accordingly, programs must be coded to consider the physical locations and structures of all files, records, and data elements in the database. If a new data element is added to a record, resulting in a new record format, all programs accessing that record must be modified (even those to which the new data element is irrelevant). Ideally, application programs should be able to access the data in a database, independent of the physical structure of

Figure 8-13 Simplified View of an Integrated Database Using Batch and Online Processing

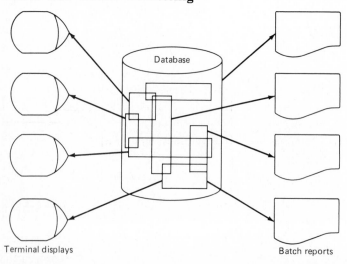

Terminal displays   Batch reports

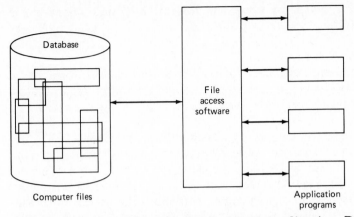

Computer files   Application
                                   programs

Figure 8-14 The Relationship Among Application Programs, File-Access Software, and Computer Files

the data in the database. In other words, a program should be able to ask for and get only the data elements needed without having to get and process the entire set of records in which the data elements are located.

Database Management Systems

During the early 1970s, generalized software packages were developed by various companies to reduce the difficulties of integrating the data contained in a database. These software packages are referred to as "database management systems" (DBMSs). Their developers have made a significant contribution to the design and implementation of integrated computer-based information systems.

A DBMS can be envisioned as an additional layer of software between file-access software and application programs (see Figure 8-15). Ideally, DBMS software provides

Figure 8-15 The Role of a DBMS

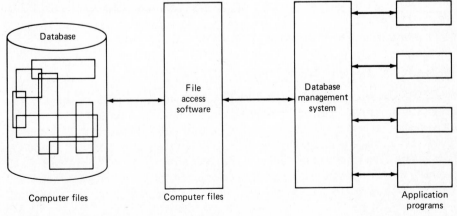

Computer files   Computer files   Application
                                                                programs

Data independence, which provides data for different applications where the applications access the data of different purposes by using different search strategies

Computer program independence, which allows application programs to be coded in different languages and allows for modification of a database without requiring modifications to application programs unless specific data elements or data structures used by the applications program are modified

A DBMS reduces the complexity of application programs. They no longer have to cope with the physical locations and structures of the files and records. With a DBMS, any data element or combination of data elements can be used to index a group of data from a record or records. The DBMS, in conjunction with the file-access software, handles the necessary logistics of retrieving and storing specified data elements in the proper physical locations within the database.

Many vendors and software companies offer sophisticated advancements to their DBMS software packages in the form of query languages. A "query language" is a set of easy-to-use computer instructions. These instructions are designed to allow a person who is not trained in computer programming to retrieve, modify, add, or delete selected data elements on the basis of stated conditions.

The use of query languages or fourth generation languages is becoming increasingly popular because of the proliferation of computer terminals, personal computers, ad hoc retrieval requests from all levels within an organization, and the ever-improving software packages readily available for most user applications. Such advancements place the computer in the hands of the user and help remove the aura of mystery that surrounds computers.

Thus, a DBMS allows the users of a database to view the database in terms of applications necessary to support their departmental or functional area. Their access to the database is not complicated by other data elements in the database. This means that data elements can be added to or deleted from the database without affecting any applications programs other than those that use the data elements being added or deleted. A DBMS greatly reduces the difficulty of both establishing and modifying integrated files.

Physical vs. Logical View

A DBMS allows users of a database to take logical views of data. For example, a design engineer might want to view data in terms of all the components necessary to manufacture a particular product. Someone in inventory management might want to view that same data differently. For example, an inventory manager might want to know all of the final products within which a particular component is used in manufacturing. The difference in logical views is caused by the different uses made of the data. The engineer is concerned with designing products, while the inventory manager is concerned with making sure components are available for production requirements.

The way a particular logical view is supported can vary depending upon the physical data structure. There are three basic techniques for supporting logical views of data:

Location of data. Logical records are located together. For example, sequentially organized records support a sequential, logical view of data.

Imbedded pointer. Records contain imbedded pointers. For example, imbedded points are used in a "chain" of "list" structure, where each record having a similar attribute such as job category have "pointers" imbedded in the records pointing to the next record in the chain or list.

Inverted indexes. Indexes are established totally separate from the physical records. For example, the indexes in the back of this book point to pages which contain certain information. Similarly, indexes can be established which point to records that contain certain attributes such as job class and education.

Hierarchical, Network, and Relational Views

There are three common logical views of data -- hierarchical, network, and relational. A hierarchical view of data views data much like an organizational chart. As an example, this view is useful for a bill-of-material application in manufacturing where an inventory must be kept of all the components and sub-assemblies necessary to manufacture a product.

A network view of data focuses on sets of records and the linkages between them. A network view is illustrated by a hospital application where patients are logically linked to rooms and to doctors.

The relational view of data is at a higher level of abstraction than are the hierarchical and network views. Comparing the relational view to the hierarchical and network views is a little like trying to compare a query or fourth generation language with COBOL, PL/1, or FORTRAN. In a relational view, the user is thinking in terms of a logical set of data elements such as customer data, order data, and inventory data. The elements may be physically located throughout several types of physical records but this is kept transparent to the user. Different data elements are "joined" from different physical records to create a variety of logical "relations," as required by the user.

History and Trends of DBMS Products

Early DBMS products such as IBM's IMS used the physical structure techniques of locating logically related records and imbedded pointers to support hierarchical logical views. Products such as Lincom's TOTAL and Cullinane's IDMS used imbedded pointers to support network structures.

A big debate emerged in the early 1970s about whether the hierarchical or network structure was better. The Conference of Data Systems Languages (CODASYL) established a database task force to develop an industry standard model for database using COBOL as an interface language. The proposed model advocated the network view of data, was objected to by IBM, and has not yet been accepted by the American National Standards Institute (ANSI). Accordingly, there are no accepted industry standards for DBMS.

In the late 1970s the innovation of the relational view of data emerged, revolutionizing logical views of data and further confusing the hierarchical vs. network debate. Software AG's DBMS, called ADABAS, became a popular product approximating the relational view of data.

Today, leading database experts generally agree that a good DBMS should allow users to view data in hierarchical, network, or relational terms depending on their requirements. The trend is to support these three logical views using inverted indexes. Inverted indexes allow the logical view of data to be independent of the physical structure of records and is, therefore, more flexible for design, modification, and use than are the physical techniques of record location and imbedded pointers.

In 1981, IBM announced its first relational DBMS: SQL (Structured Query Language/Data System), which put the industry leader, in terms of market share, in sync with leading database experts' thinking. During the 1970s and 1980s, thirty DBMSs supporting the relational model, primarily using inverted indexes, were introduced from independent vendors. Products include FOCUS, RAMIS, and NOMAD.

Other trends in DBMS include database machines which are computer or computer-like devices that execute DBMS software or firmware relative to a logical data file. The database machine sits logically and physically between a general purpose computer and at least part of a required disk system. The database machine relieves the central processor of data retrieval processing tasks and can increase the central processor's performance by 20 to 30 percent.

DBMS are also common on mini- and microcomputers and in many respects are more powerful and easier to use than DBMS found on large computers. The improvement in these smaller machine DBMSs is primarily a result of the designers of small computer DBMSs being able to learn from the mistakes made in designing large computer DBMSs.

SYSTEMS ANALYSIS IN A DATABASE ENVIRONMENT

A database approach to information systems development does have effects on systems analysis and systems administration. To achieve integration and the control and reduction of data redundancies, much more coordination and control of the systems development process are required.

Systems Administration

Most organizations are in the fourth stage of EDP growth before they attempt to integrate organizational data into one or more databases. During the preceding third stage of EDP growth, most organizations establish an MIS steering committee composed of top-level managers. This management involvement and perspective is crucial to ensuring a systematic view and the coordination of information systems activities in a database environment. Since top management represents the point where the organization is physically integrated, the managers at this level can best direct the proper integration of organizational data.

Database Administration

The integration of data into one or more centralized databases requires centralized coordination and control of data elements and their structure. For example, since data elements are referred to by data names, care must be taken to ensure that each data element within a database is assigned a unique name.

To help ensure proper administration of a database, the position of database administrator has been established in many organizations. The database administrator is primarily involved in planning and controlling the overall structure and contents of an organization's database(s).

The overall structure and contents of a database are referred to as its "schema." A more limited view of the database taken by an individual application is referred to as a "subschema." That is, each application uses only a portion of the overall database. The integrity and proper operation of the overall database and of the multiplicity of computer programs that access subsets of the database are concerns of the database administrator.

Data Element Dictionary

The contents of the database are defined by a data element dictionary, which documents such things as the data element's name, definition, and source, and where it is used, maintained, and stored. Since a database generally serves several application systems, there is a need to restrict access to data elements. The database dictionary is usually expanded to define who is authorized to access what data elements.

Systems Analysis

The use of a DBMS significantly enhances the effectiveness and efficiency of information systems developed by systems analysts. The

DBMS makes it easier to integrate the collection, processing, storing, and reporting of organizational data. Another benefit of a DBMS is that it generally leads to increased involvement by top management.

The process of systems analysis is not significantly affected by the implementation of a DBMS. The systems analyst continues to develop systems specifications -- output definitions, input definitions, decision tables, flowcharts, etc. However, in a database environment, the data element dictionary is controlled by the database administrator. Accordingly, as a systems analyst determines the data elements necessary to support the system, he or she reviews them with the database administrator. Data elements that already exist in the database can be made accessible to the information system. This data sharing is one of the primary means of controlling data redundancies. Any new data elements required for the information system can be assigned unique names and entered into the database under the supervision of the database administrator. After all new data elements have been defined, the database administrator can handle any physical structuring required to incorporate the new data elements into the database.

File Relationships

When using a DBMS it is important that the systems analyst and database administrator properly define the relationship between files in a

Figure 8-16 File Contents for an Order Processing System

INVENTORY MASTER FILE	CUSTOMER MASTER FILE	ORDER FILE
*ITEM-NUMBER	*CUSTOMER-NUMBER	*ORDER-NUMBER
DESCRIPTION	CUSTOMER-NAME	CUSTOMER-NUMBER
CLASS	CUSTOMER-ADDRESS	CUSTOMER-NAME
VENDOR-NUMBER	ZIP-CODE	DATE
ITEM-WEIGHT	PHONE-NUMBER	ITEM-NUMBER
OUT-OF-STOCK-CODE	YEAR-ACCT-OPENED	QUANTITY
TAX-CLASS	CREDIT-LIMIT	
UNIT-OF-MEASURE-CODE	CREDIT-RATING	
UNIT-OF-MEASURE	CREDIT-RATING-DATE	
SALESPERSON-COMMISSION-RATE	SALESPERSON-NUMBER	
SUGGESTED-RETAIL-PRICE	SERVICING-BRANCH-CODE	
PRICE-CODE	DATE-OF-LAST-SALE	
PRICE-A	CURRENT-BALANCE	
QUANTITY-BREAK-A		
PRICE-B		
QUANTITY-BREAK-B		
PRICE-C		
QUANTITY-BREAK-C		

Repeat for each item ordered (ITEM-NUMBER, QUANTITY)

*Record identifier

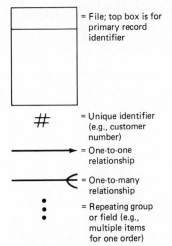

= File; top box is for
primary record
identifier

= Unique identifier
(e.g., customer
number)

⟶ = One-to-one
relationship

= One-to-many
relationship

= Repeating group
or field (e.g.,
multiple items
for one order)

Figure 8-17 Symbols Used to Define File Relationships

system.   Relationships determine the access paths required between files.
Consider the customer, order, and inventory files illustrated in Figure
8-16 and the relationships that exist between them.   For example, one
customer may have multiple orders (called a one-to-many relationship).
Accordingly, that data must be organized and programs written to
support these relationships.

Figure   8-17   provides   structured   symbols   for   defining   file
relationships.   To use the symbols, all files in a system are initially
assumed to have one-to-many relationships with all other files in the
system.   For example, in the order processing system, it is assumed that
one customer can relate to many orders and to many inventory items;
that one order can relate to many customers and many inventory items;
and that one inventory item can relate to many orders and to many
customers (see Figure 8-18).

The next step is to challenge each relationship to see which ones
actually exist.   For example, it is possible that one order could be for

**Figure 8-18 Initial File Relationship Assumption for
Order Processing**

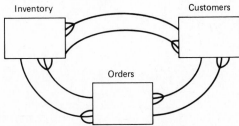

Inventory

Customers

Orders

more than one customer, but in practice is never the case. Under these circumstances the one-to-many relationship should be redefined as a one-to-one relationship.

Once the actual relationships are defined, the next step is to reduce the possible relationship to those relationships that are actually needed to support the information system. As will be demonstrated shortly, supporting relationships increase the complexity and expense of running a system; therefore only these relationships that are needed should be implemented.

Reducing relationships to the minimum required involves analyzing the output requirements to determine what types of file relationships and access paths must be operationalized among the files to efficiently generate the outputs. For example, is there a need to determine which customer an order is for? The answer is yes. Is there a need to determine what orders a customer has? The answer is yes again. Therefore the one-to-one relationship between orders and customers, and the one-to-many access path between customers and orders must exist. These relationships can be achieved by storing customer numbers in the order file and storing order numbers (a repeating group) in the customer file (see Figure 8-19).

Next the relationship between the order file and the customer file can be evaluated. Is there a need to determine information about inventory items on an order? The answer is yes. Is there a need when looking at an inventory item to find out which order a particular inventory item is ordered for? Here the answer is no. Therefore, no access path is required.

Finally, there is no real need to directly access customer information from inventory information or to access inventory information from customer information. Therefore, that relationship requires no access path. Figure 8-19 also shows the access paths for the inventory file. Note that just because an access path does not exist, does not mean that the relationship not supported no longer exists or cannot be operationalized. For example, let's say that management would like a report showing a frequency distribution or count of inventory items purchased by each customer once a month. To support this inquiry

Figure 8-19 Access Paths for Order Processing System

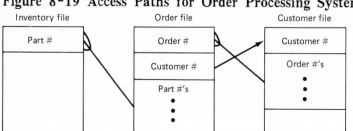

directly would require a one-to-many access path from the customer file to the inventory file. Since that does exist, a less efficient alternative is required. Specifically, the order file would have to be sorted by inventory number within customer number. From this sorted file the management report could easily be generated. This approach requires considerable processing and would not likely be done online. However, since this output is not generated often, this approach would be appropriate. If management wanted this report periodically throughout the day, an access path to support the relationship may be required.

Whether or not an access path is required should be based upon an evaluation of need and frequency of access. The need and frequency should be carefully reviewed with and approved by the user.

Normalization of Data

Once basic records and access paths are defined for files in a database, the systems designer needs to ensure that the record designs do not create data integrity problems. Common integrity problems include:

1. Difficulty in accurately identifying, locating, or updating all records given a specific set of attributes.
2. Needessly repeating fields in records, therefore requiring redundant storage and updates.
3. Inconsistencies among data.
4. No records within which to store certain fields.

To avoid or minimize the likelihood of the preceding problems occurring, a technique called normalization is used.

Normalization of data pertains to guidelines for record design that prevent update errors and data inconsistencies. Though the normalization guidelines are helpful for control purposes, they are usually in conflict with information retrieval performance. Normalization generally results in the creation of additional records which results in more effort to respond to information retrievals.

Accordingly, a systems designer *should not* feel obligated to fully normalize all records, only to consider what level of normalization should be considered after evaluating the tradeoffs between performance and control. Also, the designer should consider how to overcome any potential problems where normalization does not exist.

There are five levels of normalization. Hence designers talk about first, second, third, etc., levels of normalized form. Each level is discussed below.

First Normal Form. First normal form tries to avoid the first type of data integrity problem -- difficulty in accurately identifying, locating, or updating all records of a certain type. First normal form is achieved by having no repeating groups.

The problem with repeating groups is that special care must be taken to locate all records when records are qualified by fields that repeat. For example, consider the following two records from an order file.

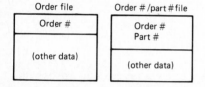

If we wanted to find all orders that require Part #66, there is no exact field on each record to search. Rather, the program has to navigate through the repeating groups checking each field value to make sure all Part #66s are located. Also, if a record needs more repeating groups than have been allocated, the record size cannot handle it.

Normalizing this situation requires that the single record type be decomposed or replaced by two record types as follows:

Order file	Order #/part # file
Order #	Order # Part #
(other data)	(other data)

Thus, there would be a regular order file containing order data but excluding part number. And there would be a new file containing records with only one order number and one part number per record. With this record design, to find all order numbers that require part #66, we simply search through the order #1/part number file.

Is this a better design? It depends. If searches and updates based upon part number within order number are frequent, the answer is yes. If searches are infrequent or nonexistent, the answer is no.

Note in Figure 8-19 that the customer file also had a repeating group called order number. If the entire order processing system were to be put in first normalized form, the new file design would be as illustrated in Figure 8-20. This design eliminates data integrity problems caused by difficulty in accurately identifying, locating or updating records, but does require two additional files.

Second Normal Form. Second normal form is achieved when all fields in the record (other than the record identifier) do not define a fact about a subset of the key. Second normalization is only relevant when

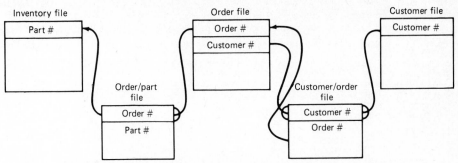

Figure 8-20 Normalized Files for Order Processing System

the record identifier is a composite of two or more fields. For example, consider the following inventory record:

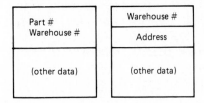

The record identifier consists of both the part number and the warehouse number. Address, however, is a fact about the warehouse number but not a fact about part number. This results in address being redundantly stored and updated in every record that refers to a part stored in that warehouse. To achieve second normal form, the record shown above would be replaced by two records as follows:

<table>
<tr><td>
Part #
Warehouse #

(other data)
</td>
<td>
Warehouse #
Address

(other data)
</td></tr>
</table>

This requires additional records and should only be considered when there is a multiple field record identifier that might cause a problem.

Third Normal Form. Third normal form is achieved when non-record identifier fields are not facts about other non-record identifier fields. For example in the following record, part number is the record identifier. If each bin number is located in one place, then bin location is a fact about bin number. The problems that this creates are the same as those caused by a violation of second normal form -- redundant storage and update as well as the potential for data inconsistencies. Also, if there was no part stored in a bin number there would be no record in which to keep the bin number or its location.

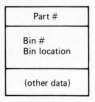

To achieve third normal form, the single record must be replaced with two records.

Part #	Bin #
Bin	Bin location
(other data)	(other data)

Since additional records are required, third normal form should only be considered when non-record identifiers are facts about other non-record identifying fields; and this relationship might cause problems.

In summary, to achieve second and third normal form requires that a non-record identifying field must "provide a fact about the key, the whole key, and nothing but the key."

Fourth Normal Form. Fourth normal form is achieved when a record type does not contain two or more independent, multivalued facts about an entity. For example, in the first level normalization of the order, customer, and inventory files (see Figure 8-20), let's say we tried to get by with one new file instead of two new files. The new file would be as follows:

Further, let's say that one order can be shared among more than one customer (e.g., two customers purchase one large shipment to get a quantity discount). Customer number is dependent on order number and part number is dependent on order number, but customer number and part number are independent of each other. This can cause problems in the integrity of retrieval and maintenance of the file.

The best way to solve the problem is to do what was done in Figure 8-20 -- create two separate record types.

Fifth Normal Form. Fifth normal form is aimed at minimizing data redundancies and record types. It is achieved when record types cannot be reconstructed from several smaller record types. That is, it cannot be reconstructed from record types which have fewer fields than the original. Under such situations the smaller records should be evaluated to determine if some can be combined without violating levels one through four of normalization. For example, in Figure 8-20, the order number/part number file record type could be combined with the order file record types to create a new record type. But this would require repeating groups as was done in Figure 8-19, and would, therefore, violate first normal form.

Review. In review, normalization is a way to check data integrity. It provides a rigorous way to evaluate the logical design of the data. However, physical data design may have to use a few "tricks" such as repeating groups to keep the cost and performance of the system acceptable.

Database management systems greatly facilitate the physical implementation of a logical design. But each database management system has limitations that may require the designer to make physical design adjustments to achieve logical design requirements.

SUMMARY

One of the early expectations of organizations establishing computer-based information systems was that the systems would be able to integrate all organizational data into a single, all-encompassing database to serve management's information requirements. However, the integration of organizational data has been constrained by the failure to plan for integration during systems development, the unsuitability of some organizational data for integration, and the technological difficulties of integrating data. When organizational data is not integrated, redundancy in data collection processing, storage, and reporting occurs.

The integration of data requires that data files be consolidated and/or logically linked together. The programming difficulties of this integration have been greatly reduced by the advent of DBMSs. A DBMS handles the logistics associated with the physical structure of the data. The applications programmer can concentrate on the necessary logical structures.

DBMSs support logical views of data (e.g., hierarchical, network, and relational) through different physical techniques such as physical location of records, imbedded pointers, and inverted indexes.

To help ensure proper planning and control of an organization's databases, a database administration function is often established. The database administrator makes certain that all naming, defining, linking, and accessing of data elements are conducted in a centralized, orderly manner. In a DBMS environment, the systems analyst coordinates his or her need and use of data elements in the context of the overall database. Logical database design and normalization of data become key issues in a database environment.

SUGGESTED READINGS

Amadio, M., "IBM's Software Strategy for Large Systems Users," *Computerworld*, March 15, 1981, pp. 7-14.

Beeler, J., "DBMS Theory Seen Unappealing to End Users," *Computerworld*, June 22, 1981, pp. 18.

Canning, R. G., "Trends in Data Management," Pt. 1, *EDP Analyzer*, vol. 9, no. 5, May 1971; Pt. 2, *EDP Analyzer*, vol. 9, no. 6, June 1971.

CODASYL Systems Committee, "A Survey of Generalized Data Base Management Systems," Technical Report, May 1969.

_____, "Feature Analysis of Generalized Data Base Systems," Technical Report, May 1971.

Codd, E. F., "SQL/DS -- What It Means," *Computerworld*, February 16, 1981.

Date, C. J., *An Introduction to Database Systems*, Addison-Wesley, Reading, Mass., 1975.

"DBMS on Desk-Top Computers," *Computer Decisions*, May 1981, pp. 62-64.

Dearden, John, "MIS Is a Mirage," *Harvard Business Review*, January-February 1972, pp. 90-99.

Dumas, R. L., "Relational Data Base: What Is It, What Can It Do?" *Data Management*, January 1981, pp. 15-17.

Engles, R. W., "A Tutorial on Data Base Organizations," in Halpern and McGee (eds.), *Annual Review in Automatic Programming*, vol. 7, Pt. 1, Pergamon, Elmsford, N.Y., 1972, pp. 1-63.

Everest, G. C., "The Objectives of Database Management," *Proceedings 4th International Symposium on Computers and Information Science*, Plenum, N.Y. (in press).

Good, P. I., "Applying Microsystems," *Computer Decisions*, April 1981, pp. 48-52.

Henkel, T., "Data Base Technology Said Lagging Theory," *Computerworld*, May 11, 1981.

"Independents React to SQL," *Computerworld*, March 23, 1981.

Kroenke, David, *Database Processing*, Science Research Associates, Chicago, Ill., 1977.

Labern, B., "Advances in DBMS Create Gap in Security, Control," *Computerworld*, May 11, 1981.

"Managing Your Database Effectively," *Computer Decisions*, May 1981, pp. 34-52.

Martin, James, *Principles of Data-Base Management*, Prentice-Hall, Englewood Cliffs, N.J., 1976.

_____, "An End-User's Guide to Data Base," *Computerworld*, May 4, 1981.

Meltzer, H. S., "Data Base Concepts and an Architecture for a Data Base System," presentation given to SHARE Information Systems Research Project, SHARE 33, Boston, Mass., August 20, 1969.

Miller, F. W., "Navigating through DBMS Waters," *Infosystems*, March 1981, pp. 70-78.

Nolan, Richard L., "Computer Data Bases: The Future is Now," *Harvard Business Review*, September-October 1973, pp. 98-114.

_____, "Natural Project Control," *Computerworld*, August 3, 1981.

"Opening Up Data File to Laymen," *Business Week*, August 10, 1981, pp. 64-66.

Palmer, I., *Data Base Systems: A Practical Reference*, Q.E.D. Information Sciences, Wellesley, Mass., 1975.

Rauzino, V. C., "The Looming Battle Between Data Base Machines and Software Data Base Management Systems," *Computerworld*, December 9/January 5, 1981, pp. 8-12.

Ross, R. G., *Data Base Systems -- Design, Implementation and Management*, AMACOM, New York, 1978.

_____, "IBM's Distributed Processing Capabilities for Large Scale Data Base Systems," *Computerworld*, July 13, 1981, pp. 1-10.

Schoor, R., "Relational Data Base Management Systems: Fact and Fiction," *Computerworld*, December 29/January 5, 1981, p. 13.

Schulte, R., "DBMS Challenges File Management," *Mini-Micro Systems*, May 1981, pp. 151-156.

Schussel, George, "The Role of the Data Dictionary," *Datamation*, June 1977, pp. 129-148.

Schuster, S. A., "Relational Database Management for Online Transaction Processing," *Data Management*, October 1981, pp. 55-57.

Snyders, J., "Those Belated Distributed DBMSs," *Computer Decisions*, February 1981, pp.76-96.

Wetherbe, James C., *Systems Analysis for Computer-Based Information Systems*, West, St. Paul, Minn., 1979.

Withington, F. G., "Computer Technology: State-of-the-Art," *Journal of the American Society for Information Science*, March 1981, pp. 124-130.

NINE

DECISION SUPPORT SYSTEMS

INTRODUCTION

This chapter defines the concept of decision support systems (DSS), discusses the decision support concept, and illustrates some cases of the use of DSS. For many years educators, consultants, and scholars have expected more from computer technology and decision-aiding technologies than these processes have been able to deliver. In fact, what has been sought is a way of assisting with the management of an organization utilizing the computer as a decision-aiding mechanism. The ability of using the computer to process an organization's payroll falls far short of this goal.

Although the concept has been around for a long time, it is only recently that the technology and its use have evolved to the point at which real decision-aiding computer systems have become a reality. Now, the MIS manager needs to become aware of the concept of DSS and how it relates to data processing and to management information systems.

HISTORY

Way back in 1958 when they were first describing the area they called "information technology," Leavitt and Whisler included as its components (1) the ability to process large amounts of data rapidly, using the large scale computer; (2) the capability to integrate this processing with models and statistical methods; and (3) the advantage of being able to use the computer to simulate human decision making.[1]

It was about 10 years later that the importance of the integration of computer processing with modeling tools such as linear programming and/or simulation as an interactive tool for use by a manager again gained prominence in the literature.[2] The notion of a systems hierarchy was introduced. At the first level were classic data processing systems (called "clerical" or "transactions processing systems") in which the computer does little more than replace human manual processing. The second level (information systems) was associated with those instances where the computer was used to provide information for use in a management decision (frequently control systems). It is the third and fourth levels that relate to DSS. The third level, called "decision systems," represented those instances in which the purpose of the system was to aid the *process* by which the decision was made. Here, modeling, analysis, and simulation were listed as important tools. The fourth and final level dealt with situations in which the system actually "made" the decision and was given the title of a programmed system.

It is worth noting that the idea of a human-machine interactive system in which the decision task was divided between the human and the machine in a synergistic problem-solving system was emphasized. The idea was that each component did those parts of the task for which it was best suited, which resulted in an interactive dialog being employed in the problem-solving (decision-making) process.

The notion of decision support as a formal concept is usually traced back to the work of Michael Scott Morton and Thomas Gerrity in the 1970s.[3] The titles of Gerrity's doctoral thesis and Scott Morton's research report are both very illustrative of the DSS concept as we know it today. DSS work and the popularity of the concept lay dormant for a number of years until a conference on the subject was held in San Jose, California, in 1977.[4] The event which truly popularized DSS was the publication of a book by Peter Keen and Michael Scott Morton, *Decision Support Systems: An Organizational Perspective*, which appeared in 1978.[5]

[1]Harold J. Leavitt and Thomas L. Whisler, "Management in the 1980s," *Harvard Business Review*, vol. 36, no. 6, November-December 1958, pp. 81-97.

[2]Gary W. Dickson, "Management Information-Decision Systems," *Business Horizons*, vol. 11, no. 12, December 1968, pp. 17-26.

[3]J.S. Scott Morton, *Management Decision Systems: Computer-Based Support for Decision Making*, Division of Research, Harvard University, Cambridge, Mass., 1971; T.P. Gerrity, Jr., "The Design of Man-Machine Decision Systems: An Application to Portfolio Management," *Sloan Management Review*, vol. 12, no. 2, pp. 59-75.

[4]Eric D. Carlson (ed.), "Proceedings of a Conference on Decision Support Systems," *Data Base*, vol. 8, no. 3, Winter 1977.

[5]Peter G. W. Keen and Michael S. Scott Morton, *Decision Support Systems: An Organizational Perspective*, Addison-Wesley, Reading, Mass., 1978.

Since that time, the literature has been filled with DSS articles, and MIS managers have been deluged with advertisements for DSS products. In 1981 a professional meeting on the subject of DSS was held in Atlanta, Georgia, and it proved to be so popular that now an annual DSS conference is held.[6] In fact, the DSS movement has even spread to Europe with two conferences on DSS being held at the International Institute for Advanced Systems Analysis near Vienna, Austria.[7]

Since the DSS movement has picked up so much momentum and is a concept plus a set of tools that are likely to come to the attention of the MIS manager, this chapter will now turn to a more complete discussion of what DSS is and how it is likely to affect the MIS manager.

THE DSS CONCEPT

The definition of "decision support system" that is used in common practice is

An interactive computer-based system that helps decision makers utilize data and models to solve unstructured problems.[8]

To appreciate the importance of what is being described, it is necessary to go back and examine the nature of the traditional data processing systems and information systems that organizations have been using since the early 1960s. Data processing systems, recall, simply substitute computer processing for human processing. Payroll, accounts payable, inventory, and airline reservation systems are all examples of applications that would be classified as data processing. An information system would typically take the form of a predefined report, say, a profit center performance report.

Any information coming out of the data processing system would be produced by summarizing the data flowing through the system. The information produced by the information system would be very static and rigid in nature. If a manager or other user wanted to ask a question of either type of system that had not been completely anticipated, the following process would take place.

[6]Donovan Young and Peter G.W. Keen (eds.), *DSS-81 Transactions*, Execucom Systems Corporation, Austin, Tex., 1981; and Gary W. Dickson (ed.), *DSS-82 Transactions*, Execucom Systems Corporation, Austin, Tex., 1982.

[7]G. Fick and R. Sprague, Jr. (eds.), *Decision Support Systems: Issues and Challenges*, Pergamon, London, 1980; and H.G. Sol, "Processes and Tools for Decision Support," *Proceedings of the 1982 IFIP/IIASA Working Conference on Decision Support Systems*, North-Holland, Amsterdam, 1982.

[8]R.H. Sprague and E.D. Carlson, *Building Effective Decision Support Systems*, Prentice-Hall, Englewood Cliffs, N.J., 1982, p. 4.

First, the questioner would have to make a request to the information systems department to have a program written to answer the question. Frequently this process would also require that the requestor have the budget to pay for the services of the information systems department. Once these hurdles had been passed, the next step would be to design the program, write it, test it, and deliver it in an operational form to the requesting party. By this time several months typically have passed (frequently more than were originally estimated and often at a cost higher than originally estimated).

Even more frustrating to the user is the case in which the MIS group comes back to say that the data required to answer the question is "not in the system." In such cases, a system to capture the data or to recode the data into the proper format is so expensive and/or time-consuming that the user decides to retain the manual desk-drawer system presently in use.

The problems with traditional systems and with the traditional way of developing systems include all of the following:

1. The systems are not "user-friendly" -- for the user to get anything out of them, the use of a technical intermediary, the programmer, is required.

2. The technology with which the programmer must work is rigid and hard to change, with the result that a great deal of time and effort is needed to respond even to simple requests.

3. The systems tend to support routine questions but do not service unusual requests or address high-level decisions.

4. Many of the systems do not provide for interactivity between the user and the decision maker in a way in which problem exploration can take place. By returning to the definition of DSS, we can now see how the DSS concept addresses many of these problems.

Directed Toward Unstructured Problems

Decision support systems commonly address problems at the higher levels of an organization, and these problems are not "structured," in the sense that well-known procedures for their solution are not known. Examples of structured problems would be reordering inventory, determining a budget, or deciding whether the rate of return on an investment justifies an expenditure. Unstructured decisions, on the other hand, are represented by examples such as hiring a manager, planning a level of advertising expenditure, or deciding whether to introduce a new product or program. Unstructured or semistructured decisions frequently are best made by "experts," who have a great deal of past experience and a good body of knowledge upon which to draw. In such cases, judgment, training, and experience are prime requisites to doing well.

Decisions of this type often involve multiple criteria for success, with the result that a number of trade-offs must be made. The analysis of trade-offs is many times an iterative procedure in which the decision maker will make a "cut" at the solution to the problem, evaluate the result, and then make some modifications to the solution and try again. This procedure stands in contrast to the one employed to solve structured problems, in which only one pass through a process is required to reach a satisfactory solution.

Interactive

Because of the nature of the problems addressed by decision support systems, an interactive system is required. In other words, the system supports the decision maker by facilitating the problem exploration process. This is done in many cases by providing a system which suggests solutions to the decision maker along with a rich body of data about the consequences of accepting the solution. In this way, the decision maker can evaluate the outcome of taking a particular course of action and, if a shortcoming exists, can modify the solution and try again. In this way, the solution to one trial may suggest to the decision maker what ought to be changed before another try is made. A scenario of this approach would be as follows.

Suppose the decision maker, supported by a DSS, first explores the data associated with a particular problem. From this analysis phase, a first solution is postulated. The decision maker inputs this solution to the DSS, and performance results are generated. Evaluation of these results shows that shortcomings exist and perhaps even suggests why these have occurred. The decision maker then would go back to the analysis module and would modify the solution and try again. This interactive process would be repeated until a satisfactory solution had been generated.

Helps Decision Making

Decision support systems do not make the decisions; they aid the decision maker. Even in cases in which expert knowledge is built into the DSS, the concept of decision assisting in contrast to decision making is a key to the concept of DSS. The human decision maker still retains decision autonomy and frequently exercises a great deal of judgment in the DSS process.

Uses Data and Models

In order to accomplish its task, a DSS must have access to data and must contain algorithms or processes to assist the decision maker. In some cases, these DSS subsystems act independently, and in others they are integrated.

The data subsystem of a DSS must maintain the data and provide easy access to it. Consider the use of a DSS in which the user simply wants to retrieve a single data item, say, an inventory level of some raw material. This type of request is the simplest form of an access to data. A more complex case would be the generation of an ad hoc report. As an example, suppose a manager wanted a report of all the firm's customers living in the state of Iowa who, in the last six months, had purchased more than $10,000 of a particular class of product. These two examples, one simple and one complex, illustrate data functions that ought to be available in a DSS.

The modeling subsystem of the DSS would support analytical functions. Take the case of a manager wishing to project the company's financial picture under several economic conditions and with several product-pricing strategies. Another example would be a case in which a bank wanted to correlate the activity in checking accounts in terms of transactions per month with the number of years the account holder had been doing business with the bank. This case would require formal statistical analysis. The use of a sophisticated mathematical programming algorithm to assist in a bank's asset allocation planning would be a third example of modeling.

In a final example, the use of modeling may not be obvious but it is involved. The difference is that in this case the model is built around capturing expert knowledge in contrast to utilizing a mathematical process as in the previous cases. Suppose in this case that a commercial loan officer at a bank is faced with making a rather substantial loan to a manufacturing company. This officer might have built into a DSS the "decision advice" of a predecessor, a person with 40 years experience with the bank in making commercial loans. An "expert" DSS system could have been created in which the experienced loan officer's decision-making procedures could be replicated by the system. In this way, the present decision maker would have the "advice" available from the expert.

In the discussion above, the examples are such that the data and modeling subsystems are independent. In actual operation, these frequently must be integrated. A common example would be one in which a highly complex, logical selection of data was performed using the data subsystem and then this data was used as input to the modeling subsystem.

Easy to Use

Although this feature was not mentioned in the definition presented above, user-friendliness is a cornerstone of the DSS approach. Whereas traditional data processing systems require a programmer to obtain information from the system for the user, the same is not the intent regarding decision support systems. A user or user representative acquires information from a DSS by using English-like statements or by using what is called a "query language" or a "report generator."

In contrast to procedure-oriented languages like COBOL, PL/1, or Fortran, decision support systems are based upon fourth-generation languages that are very high level in nature. In fact, one statement in these languages may be the equivalent of from several to over a hundred statements in one of the procedural languages. Additionally, these systems are set up with system prompts and "help" commands to make system use easy for a technical novice.

Such languages contain commands with substantial power. An example would be the command FIND, which can be enhanced with logical statements. Using this command, a user might input a statement such as

```
FIND ALL CUSTOMERS WITH PURCHASES >
    10000 IN MARCH AND WITH
    ORDERS < 10 OR WITH ZIPCODE =
    5XXXXX TO 63XXX
```

The result would appear in a preformatted report or in a report defined by the user on the spot using a powerful DISPLAY command. Data-oriented commands, modeling commands involving statistical analysis and/or projection of data, and commands for display (including graphics) are designed under the DSS philosophy to be easy enough to use that managers and professionals will be able to develop their own systems. Moreover, using these languages, the end-user has access to data and information without resorting to a programmer and without the delays involved in developing traditional data processing systems.

TECHNOLOGY FOR DSS

In order to understand how the DSS concept is implemented, a discussion of the various technologies and tools employed is useful. As will be seen in the discussion below, some of the building blocks of decision support systems are computer hardware and software, while other building blocks are more conceptual in nature.

Before beginning the discussion of DSS technology, it is important to reemphasize that DSS differs sharply from traditional data processing systems. The programs of traditional data processing systems are written in languages such as COBOL or PL/1 and are typically run on large centralized systems. If they produce reports at all, the results are often of a standard format, available only at routine intervals.

Database

One key technology for the development of decision support systems is database management. The user/manager of decision support systems is frequently required to abstract a single item of data from a database, produce ad hoc reports from a database, and/or perform complex logic on data in a database to abstract subsets of data having certain properties. These data can either be output in a predefined format or in one designed by the user "on the fly." The abstracted data may also be available for analysis or manipulation by models or algorithms.

At present, these data management functions are in software, although in the future, database management is projected to be moved to hardware or firmware. Most frequently, the powerful database systems run on large computers that are accessed by DSS users from remote terminals. Database management systems are now beginning to appear on microcomputer systems, but these do not yet have the sophistication of those available on the larger computer systems. Data management subfunctions such as report generation and query are especially important for DSS applications.

Software products are beginning to appear on the market that are oriented toward database management and designed with DSS-type applications in mind. Examples of these products are: FOCUS, RAMIS II, NOMAD2, and EXPRESS.[9] The MIS manager should be aware that these products are often quite expensive to buy and to run (they do so much for the user that they often use substantial amounts of computing resources) on an in-house computer. For this reason, most of these products are available from computing service bureaus. However, a result of using external computing services to obtain access to the software products is that integration with the internal database is awkward.

Analytical Methods

Decision support systems often need analysis and modeling procedures. Statistical procedures are one good example of this sort. A user may need to do something simple such as computing the average of a column of numbers or something more complex such as testing two sets of numbers to see if they are statistically the same or different. Other applications of this type would include the statistical projection of time series data and correlational analysis.

Another analytical capability utilized by decision support systems is data projection or simulation. In this area of application, answers to

---

[9]FOCUS is a trademark of Information Builders, Inc.; RAMIS is a trademark of Mathematica Products Group; NOMAD2 is a trademark of National CSS; EXPRESS is a trademark of Management Decision Systems, Inc.

"what if" questions are the focus of attention. The financial planning languages available on almost all microcomputer systems are examples of this type of capability.

As is true in the case of database management systems, very sophisticated projection and simulation systems are available that run on large general-purpose computers. The Interactive Financial Planning System (IFPS) is one such example.[10] As with database-oriented systems, the software tools can be purchased to run in-house or are available from vendors of computing services. Because the data feeding the modeling systems is often limited in volume and frequently "special-purpose," the limitation of integration with data in organizational databases is not as severe in this area of application.

Of less frequent application, but important nevertheless, are optimizing models. These models, usually based upon mathematical programming algorithms, can be invoked in special instances.

Whereas data management systems provide the data functions described in the previous subsection, model management systems of a DSS provide the user with the models needed to support various kinds of decisions. These two functions can be thought of separately, but they frequently need to be integrated in practice. The modeling function provides *aids* to the decision process and the database function provides *input* to the decision process.

Interactive Computing

The implementation of decision support systems requires a heavy degree of interaction between the user-decision maker and the computing system. This implies that "interactive computing capabilities" must be available. When decision support systems are implemented on large-scale general computers, the user access to the DSS is from a terminal and performed in an interactive mode. Another version of interactive computing that is becoming more common in the development of decision support systems is to run the DSS software on a dedicated minicomputer. In this way, a number of users can be involved in different DSS applications at the same time. Their access to the system is through terminals. By using this approach, the special DSS software does not bog down the computing mainframe. A disadvantage of this approach is that in order to access central data, selected central data often must be transmitted to the minicomputer system. This transmission is usually indirect (e.g., through magnetic tape) and is slower and more awkward than is desirable.

The use of personal computers to host decision support systems of modest size is also growing in popularity. The advantage of their use is easy accessibility for the user. In this case, the interactive processing occurs at the terminal used by the decision maker. One present

---

[10]IFPS is a trademark of EXECUCOM Systems Corporation.

shortcoming of this DSS implementation is that the power of the DSS software is far less than is available on mainframes or minicomputers. Another limitation of the use of today's personal computers for DSS is that often the secondary storage available for data is not of great capacity (unless one has a hard-disk system, which increases the cost of the system substantially). Finally, the abstraction of central data and its loading on the microcomputer are even more awkward than in the case of the minicomputer-based DSS hardware. In most cases, data to be accessed by the microcomputer-based DSS must be loaded into the system at the keyboard. There are some products appearing on the market that provide downloading of data abstracted from mainframe systems, but selection capability from central files and local storage capacity at the microcomputer are current limitations (see the discussion of the "management support facility").

Expert Systems

A concept which is gaining some popularity in decision support systems is to offer aid to decision makers by placing an "expert" at their disposal. The way this is done is to program the expert's decision-making approach on the system. Recall from the previous discussion that one way of improving a person's decision-making *process* is to provide process aids such as statistical procedures and models. Another is to build into the system the process used by an expert to solve the same problem being explored by the decision maker.

To build such a system, the expert's decision-making process is studied in depth (in a given problem situation) and a computer program is written that behaves as much like the expert as possible. Then, when faced with a problem of this sort, the less-skilled decision maker can use the computer system to call upon the expert's knowledge and expertise.

Expert systems have been built to support decision making in medical diagnosis, in the analysis of core samples to determine whether to drill for oil, in computer chip design, and in the analysis of faults in complex equipment. In the business area, expert systems have begun to be explored to assist decision making in auditing, to help bankers make commercial loans, and to assist in personal financial planning.

The Management Support Facility

An outgrowth of today's personal computer will be a device that is called a management support facility (MSF).[11] In the early 1990s, these devices will be very pervasive in organizations throughout the world

[11] This discussion is based upon a Delphi study conducted by the Management Information Systems Research Center at the University of Minnesota. Approximately 25 leading practitioners and academicians were involved in three rounds of questioning involving the technical attributes of the MSF of 1990.

because of their technological attributes and their relatively low cost (about $7,500 in 1983 dollars for a basic unit). Many managers and professional workers will have a unit in the workplace and one at home. Of course portable models will be available.

The basic MSF of the 1990s will have memory sizes in the range of 1 to 2 megabytes, and secondary disk storage on magnetic disks with capacities on the order of 30 megabytes. Internal processing speeds will be in the range of a million instructions per second. They will have keyboard input plus touch-sensitive screens. It is likely that many of the basic units will have high-resolution color-graphic capability. Direct hard-copy output will be provided by matrix printers, but these devices will be connected to other hard-copy-producing devices such as plotters and duplicating printers for use when higher quality printing is required. The basic MSF which will be available 8 to 10 years from now will have attributes similar to the currently very popular IBM 4341-2.

Advanced models of the MSF will have special applications. These facilities will offer special features such as larger memories, more secondary storage, large screen capability, and special software. Speaking of software, all of the devices will offer very user-friendly fourth-generation languages which integrate computing, modeling, data management, and text processing. The software cost is included in the projected $8,000 cost.

The availability of large, unshared memories, coupled with high-capacity secondary storage and high-speed data communication by local networks, makes possible a number of exciting applications. Some obvious functions will be, for example, support for writing memos and reports. These outputs can then be directly transmitted through the communication network to distribution lists in the manner commonly discussed under the topic of electronic mail.

More interesting functions of the technology are related to the decision support function. First, the databases associated with the organization's transactions processing system can be interrogated and large subdatabases created at the MSF. The capacity of the MSF secondary storage and the high speed of data communication by local networks make this possible. These local databases can then be interrogated as described above, with the abstracted data being used to feed locally developed models. In addition, certain systems may be developed to work with these local databases in a "problem-finding" mode to alert the manager to potential difficulties. The use of expert systems to locate problems is one mode of this type of operation.

APPLICATIONS OF DSS

Numerous applications have been made in the last 15 years of decision support systems and more are being developed all the time. Presentation of several examples should help solidify the concepts that have been presented above.

DSS in Marketing

In 1979 the Nestle Company, a worldwide producer and marketer of food products, became concerned with the information flows between its various functions. A study indicated that, although massive quantities of data were generated internally and purchased outside, it was available only in hard copy. This was difficult to manage and transform into accessible information. The study team found that much of the data was therefore unused.

An internal consulting group was directed to develop a prototype decision support system for analysis of factory shipments, chain-store warehouse withdrawals, and store purchases on a regional basis. Several of these data types were purchased from outside sources, e.g., SAMI and Neilsen. The DSS was to be online with strong graphical capabilities. Market response models were to be developed and embedded in the system. The design objective was that all outputs were to be generated by the company's marketing professionals. Another objective of the test system was to develop a system that would allow the users to train themselves so that central staff support would be limited.

The system that was developed was a model-based DSS. The system provides for the recognition of problems and opportunities plus review and analysis (what? when? where?). It provides for investigation of cause-and-effect relationships. It also allows for study of alternatives through simulation.

Six weeks after management's approval to proceed with development of the test system, a first database system was implemented and manager training initiated. Usage grew rapidly with approximately a dozen users in the pilot group becoming advocates of the system. Soon top-level managerial backing for the system was forthcoming, and approval was given to expand the system from a one-division test to cover all the company's product lines.

DSS in Financial Planning

In 1977, the Coca Cola Company decided to explore the use of decision support systems for financial planning. The first step at Coca Cola was to purchase a financial planning language to run on its in-house computer to support the DSS activity. They had already decided that common languages like COBOL or PL/1 were inappropriate to such activity.

A search for the financial planning language that best suited the company's needs was conducted. The first step in this process was to set up a set of criteria against which to judge competing languages.

Several alternatives were evaluated in the light of the criteria and one selected. The selected language was installed on the company's computer on a lease-purchase agreement. It was leased for 2 years and purchased in 1979.

The first application developed was a benchmark system to test the planning language and to measure the degree of user acceptance. This system was the gross profit generator system. The system was composed of a series of models which generated the following outputs:

- Gross profit by brand and by product
- Gross profit by various levels of consolidation
- A profit-and-loss statement for all products consolidated
- An input listing showing all the assumptions

The benchmark system proved valuable, and soon a second application was initiated. This was used by the financial analysis department and given the title, the "peel-the-onion" system. This system is composed of a series of models, report generators, and data files which, when run in combination, produce several reports:

- Profit and loss by brand
- Profit and loss by line item and by brand
- Annual profit and loss
- Gross margin
- Operating profit
- Variance analysis reports

The peel-the-onion system allows for interactive analysis of different profit-and-loss scenarios with varying performance levels, using the "what if" and "goal-seeking" commands in the financial planning language that was selected by Coca Cola.

With the purchase of the planning language and the development of applications, the use of the language spread to a number of departments. From two users in 1977, usage increased to ten in early 1979, and to forty-five by late that year when the software was purchased.

Some of the areas into which use of the DSS generator spread were present-value models to evaluate cash versus lease versus loan alternatives for financing bottler plant expansions, investment analysis, cash flow analysis, and internal rate-of-return analysis. Other major areas of application are pro forma profit-and-loss statements in the fountain sales department and the bottler operations department. Finally, the development and testing of operating budgets using the financial planning language have gained widespread acceptance at Coca Cola. The use of the system has even spread to the Brazilian and Argentine regional offices of the Coca Cola Company and to the European offices.

DSS in Transportation

The American Airlines information management system (AAIMS) began as a personal information system for developing forecast models and then evolved into a DSS to assist the planning, finance, marketing, and operating functions. Its current users include other airlines, engine and airframe manufacturers, airline financial analysts, consultants, and the Air Transport Association.

AAIMS consists of two complementary parts: (1) a language which enables the user, a nonprogrammer, to use the system for the calculation and retrieval of data and (2) an expanding data file on almost every scheduled U.S. airline. The database contains approximately 150,000 time series measuring the activity of the scheduled U.S. carriers. The historical data goes back to 1968. The file consists of financial data, aircraft data, and other data such as crew and maintenance records listed by carrier.

The system language employed is APL. User communication with the system, with the exception of data loading, is done through a terminal using English language commands. Examples include DISPLAY, PLOT, CHANGE, and QUARTERLY.

Forecasting was the original design objective of the AAIMS. Many econometric models have been developed by forecasting air travel demand. Development of forecasts remains an unstructured task which can be greatly enhanced by close interaction of the forecaster and a computerized database.

One application involved forecasting the patterns of airline demand as it recovered from economic downturn. Another application of the system was analysis of the impact of deregulation of the airline industry before it occurred. A third application has been extensive investigation of the overall economics of the air transport industry, with emphasis on the industry's revenue and expense structure. The fuel crisis in 1974 was modeled in depth to analyze possible patterns of revenue and expense.

Overall, applications have included analysis of the following factors: load factors, market share, seating configuration, aircraft utilization, traffic and capacity growth, unit costs, and financial ratios. AAIMS is highly regarded by its users whether employed in a data management mode, in a statistical analysis mode, or in combination. Its limitations seem bounded only by the imagination of its users.

DSS for Human Resources Management

RCA, like many other organizations, had several systems dealing with the management of its personnel, among them systems for payroll, pension plan administration, insurance, labor relations, affirmative action programs, and general personnel management. Each subsystem existed on a stand-alone basis. The conclusion was that these nonintegrated stand-alone systems had little chance of supporting management decision making. Therefore, a decision was made in 1975 to develop a DSS for human resources management that would provide for clerical processing and would allow the integration and ease of interaction to support decision making. The system was called "industrial relations information system" (IRIS). It is in regular daily use in a highly diverse industrial enterprise as a transaction-driven data system, but it is designed for the non-computer-oriented manager in a problem-solving situation.

The system was designed to deal with questions that (1) are largely unanticipated, (2) will never again recur in exactly the same form, and (3) must be answered within 1 hour of their occurrence. IRIS was built on an interactive computer system using a commercial database management system coupled with a query capability. An extensive command language was designed and implemented to stand between the end-user and the data management system.

The system is used on four levels. One is ad hoc analysis of existing data. A second is to receive prespecified reports. The third use is to evaluate the consequences of proposed decisions. The fourth use is the most infrequent: the retrieval of isolated individual data items, say a salary rate for a particular employee.

Over its years of operation, IRIS was subjected to extensive cost/benefit analysis. This analysis was facilitated by the fact that some of RCA's divisions were using IRIS and others were not. These analyses showed that the IRIS system had a 60 percent rate of return on the investment made to develop the system.[12]

SUMMARY

Back in 1958 when the use of computers was first being discussed in an organizational context, much emphasis was placed upon using this technology to assist management. In actuality, the first computer applications were not directed at managing but assisted the processing of data. Still, many had hopes that managing could be supported by computer assists. We have seen, since the beginning in the late 1970s, that these goals have been reestablished through the mechanism of decision support systems.

It is likely that over the next decade decision support systems will receive a great deal of attention from both a theoretical and a practical viewpoint. On the practical side, the forecasts are that two basic directions will be taken over the next few years.

---

[12]Franz Edelman, "Managers, Computer Systems, and Productivity," *MIS Quarterly,* vol. 5, no. 3, September 1981, pp. 1-19.

One approach will be to build decision support systems on large general-purpose computer systems. This approach will have several advantages. The first is the great computer power that will be available to support very sophisticated fourth-generation software and rapidly handle very large databases. The second advantage of this approach is that access to the data in the system will be centrally controlled and managed, with the result that a great deal of integration will be possible. The major disadvantage of this approach is that these systems will be sharing resources with other applications and that a substantial amount of system overhead will be present. Further, the use of these systems implies that a large central computer is in place or available.

A second approach is to take advantage of the MSF. In these systems, decision support systems will be based upon local data or upon data that is abstracted from corporate databases (either central or distributed), and loaded upon secondary storage facilities at the MSF. This approach will lead to more flexibility than the centralized approach and will cause less system overhead on central computing facilities. The cost, of course, is in data communication and the fact that much of the data traffic will be limited to a "read-only"-like function. Otherwise, maintaining the integrity of the data becomes a very large problem. User friendliness and system reliability are advantages of the MSF approach. In practice, since all the systems will be integrated, some functions will undoubtedly be performed centrally and some will be downloaded to the MSFs.

The conclusion is virtually inescapable that, given the forthcoming technology, there will be a trend to DSS. The MIS manager should begin to explore DSS applications using either the mainframe approach, or the personal computer system approach, or both. This experience will assist in planning for future evolution.

SUGGESTED READINGS

Alter, S. L., *Decision Support Systems: Current Practices and Continuing Challenges*, Addison-Wesley, Reading, Mass., 1980.

Bennett, John L. (ed.), *Building Decision Support Systems*, Addison-Wesley, Reading, Mass., 1982.

Carlson, Eric D. (ed.), "Proceedings of a Conference on Decision Support Systems," *Data Base*, vol. 8, no. 3, Winter 1977.

Dickson, Gary W. (ed.), *DSS-82 Transactions*, Execucom Systems Corporation, Austin, Tex., 1982.

Edelman, Franz, "Managers, Computer Systems, and Productivity," *MIS Quarterly*, vol. 5, no. 3, September 1981, pp. 1-19.

Fick, G., and R. H. Sprague, Jr. (eds.), *Decision Support Systems: Issues and Challenges*, Pergamon Press, London, 1980.

Keen, P. G. W., and M. S. Scott Morton, *Decision Support Systems: An Organizational Perspective*, Addison-Wesley, Reading, Mass., 1978.

_____, and G. R. Wagner, "DSS: An Executive Mind-Support System," *Datamation*, vol. 24, no. 12, November 1979, pp. 117-122.

Rockart, J. F., and M. E. Treacy, "The Chief Executive Goes Online," *Harvard Business Review*, vol. 60, no. 1, January-February 1982, pp. 82-87.

Sol, H. G., "Processes and Tools for Decision Support," *Proceedings of the 1982 IFIP/IIASA Working Conference on DSS*, North-Holland, Amsterdam, 1982.

Sprague, R. H., Jr., "A Framework for the Development of Decision Support Systems," *MIS Quarterly*, vol. 4, no. 4, December 1980, pp. 1-26.

_____, and E. D. Carlson, *Building Effective Decision Support Systems*, Prentice-Hall, Englewood Cliffs, N.J., 1982.

Young, D., and P. G. W. Keen (eds.), *DSS-81 Transactions*, Execucom Systems Corporation, Austin, Tex., 1981.

DATA COMMUNICATIONS SYSTEMS

INTRODUCTION

Information systems (IS) managers have, since their emergence in the organizational hierarchy some 25 years ago, always been challenged to keep up with advancing technology. At the present, meeting this challenge is more serious than ever before. Technologies are evolving and new technologically based concepts are emerging that make it imperative that the IS manager keep up to date and make sound decisions regarding the use of these concepts and technologies in the organization. Decision support systems, the office of the future, telecommuting, distributed systems, and electronic funds transfer systems are but a few of the concepts which are emerging. The underlying technologies supporting these concepts include those of processing, storage, and communication of data.

For years IS managers have had to become knowledgeable about processing and storage technologies because of the fundamental role the technologies have played in data processing. Data communications, on the other hand, has been an area that many IS managers have delegated to others or have ignored because they were not using it or contemplating applications requiring its use. This state of affairs is being altered dramatically. The concepts listed above all require data communications as an integral mechanism. Even more important, many observers of the information processing scene believe that there is an inexorable trend toward a merging of data processing and teleprocessing, so that they will be part and parcel of the same thing by the end of the 1980s.

It is very clear that telecommunications is becoming ever more important to the IS manager, even for those IS managers already involved in teleprocessing. This statement is supported by the fact that teleprocessing costs are increasing as a percentage of the overall data processing budget. Additionally, organizations not yet involved in teleprocessing (including smaller organizations) are now considering applications which will require this technology. The result of these conditions is that the total expenditures for data communications in the United States is expected to reach the $10 to $25 billion range by the mid-1980s. Uncertainty as to how fast the applications and the industry will grow is the reason that the total market estimates have such a wide variation.

Mention was made of the notion that many IS managers are presently uncomfortable when dealing with the data communications area. One reason for this condition is that such terms as "modem," "multiplexor," "network architecture," "SDLC," and "packet switching" are unfamiliar. In addition, the IS manager must often deal in this area with unfamiliar equipment and vendors, differences in characteristics between data processing and data communications facilities (e.g., speeds and/or resistance to errors), and a confusing milieu of arcane and frequently arbitrary rules and practices of communications carrier organizations.

One result of this situation is that many IS managers have avoided matters regarding data communications by not engaging in applications requiring this technology. In other cases, the IS manager has attempted to play the role of the data communications specialist, often with the result that reliance is placed on one vendor or outside consultant. In still other cases, the manager has depended on nonmanagerial technical employees, with the result that technical matters have received undue importance in decision making. In a few organizations, the position of data communications manager has been created and staffed, but the availability of this type of person is very limited. It is inescapable that, as time goes by, the data communications area will become inseparable from data processing. Thus it is increasingly important that the IS manager become more comfortable with this area and, although reliance still may have to be placed upon technical experts for detailed analysis, understand the basic concepts of data communications as well as gain an appreciation of the basic issues which are primarily managerial in nature.

This chapter is intended to be a primer on the topic of data communications as it relates to the IS manager. First, a bit of history will be given in order to provide an appreciation of the current state of affairs in the area of data communications and how it was reached. The presentation will next turn to the technology of data communications. An emerging area of data communications, local area networks, will be the final topic of discussion.

HISTORY

Reading about the history of data communications, one gets the impression that writers and other visionaries have made forecasts that, in many cases, have either taken far longer than anticipated to be realized or have not yet come to pass. Similarly, it will become evident that many in the data communications industry itself have made business forecasts that have been overly optimistic. Yet, as was emphasized in the introduction to this chapter, there is little doubt that the area of data communications will have a profound impact on our organizational environment, and any questions in the area will deal primarily with how fast the impact will be realized.

Early Data Communication

Samuel F. B. Morse, the inventor of the telegraph, can be said to be the father of data communications. He stated in 1832 that "If the presence of electricity can be made visible in any part of a circuit, I see no reason why intelligence may not be transmitted instantaneously by electricity."[1] By 1852, Western Union was formed as a business whose purpose was to carry messages in coded form from one person to another over a privately controlled but publicly accessible network. It was only 20 years later that the device which is still the backbone of our data communications system, the telephone, made its appearance.

Electronic digital computers, of course, did not come along until much later. Moving from a laboratory device in the 1940s to a commercial product in 1954, digital computers began to find fairly widespread organizational use by the early 1960s. One might say that the integration of computers and data communications took place as peripheral devices such as printers, card readers, and tape drives were connected to central processing units by cables. However, in the opinion of the authors, this is too limited a definition of data communications. Yet, from some of the statistics that will be given later, a few writers appear to classify this limited use of technology as data communications. It is more realistic to say that data communications began in the late 1950s as teletypewriters were connected to processors as remote input-output devices. They were located perhaps 100 feet away from the processor, and transmission was at speeds of 45 bits per second (bps).

About this time the first large network was begun which integrated a computer with remote devices. This was the SAGE (semiautomatic ground environment) system, which was a military command and control system. In this system, the inputs were digital radar signals directed to a central computer. New York became the first operational site in

---

[1]R. A. McLaughlin, "Piecing Together the Datacom Industry," *Datamation*, vol. 25, no. 7, July 1979, p. 110.

1958, and a nationwide network was in place by 1963. It was also in the early 1960s that industrial applications of data communications began to appear. The airline industry was very influential in this movement with the American Airlines SABRE system serving as a well-known pioneer. This system had a central computer with 2000 nationwide terminals connected to it. The banking industry also began development of primitive online systems in the late 1950s; and they were operational on a limited basis by the early 1960s.

In these early days, organizations pioneering in data communications had little choice concerning transmission services. They went with a common communications carrier, usually AT&T. In most cases, they were forced to use what are termed "voice-grade" communications on a "dedicated" (leased) basis. The speed of transmission was low (less than 4800 bps), and the leased lines were vastly underutilized. As a result, the data communication costs per amount of data transmitted tended to be very high. One must keep in mind here that the transmission services employed were not designed with data transmission in mind, but were voice-oriented. In the latter case, the requirement is long "connect times" (message lengths) and slow transmission rates. The communication of data, on the other hand, requires exactly the opposite, that is, high transmission rates and (typically) short messages.

As large-scale communications systems began to be implemented, a number of problems began to arise, partially because of the complexity that users began to encounter as they developed and implemented data communications systems. At this time, of course, individual users were responsible for all the communications functions that had to take place at each end of the communication line provided by the carrier. Control mechanisms had to be developed to allow for selection of different terminals on the same line, and techniques had to be developed to protect data and to resolve contention and queuing. Many of the steps taken to solve problems such as these as well as to provide effective line utilization and reliability involved attempts to separate communications functions from computer processing functions. The notion of a communications "front end" evolved in which hardware devices and special-purpose software provided the communications functions and isolated them as much as possible from the data processing functions.

By about 1970, systems were common in which the computer provided the intelligence and communication hardware, and software provided the interface with common carrier data transmission services. Most of the larger networks employed "circuit switching," in which a complete physical link was established and dedicated to a single user. Circuit-switched networks, however, pose problems for computer data communications because it takes a long time to establish a circuit, and bandwidth that is not used cannot be shared with others. For these reasons, circuit-switched systems are not economical for computer traffic which is typically of short duration. Computers need short connect times and high data transfer rates, and in noninteractive applications, delays between the transmission and the receipt can be minutes or even hours.

Network designers were able to take advantage of the allowable delay times in batch systems by developing "message switching" systems in which a complete message would be sent from one node in a network to another. At each node, the message would be stored until capacity became available to send it on to the next node. This concept is called "store and forward." Recognize that a message would commonly be routed through many nodes and that, although the transmission rate of data from node to node could be high, there would be delays because of the storage time at the nodes. Under this process, network utilization is higher than with dedicated transmission lines because circuits are shared by many messages and the cost per message is reduced.

Such systems were in place in the early 1970s, but the facilities provided by the common carriers did not accommodate very well the need to support interactive systems, which require rapid transmission of short messages at low cost. The private networks developed by large organizations were custom designed. This often resulted in great expense and underutilization. Additionally, they were frequently incompatible with other networks. These conditions partially explain why standards activities have evolved in the data communications area and why "value-added" network systems have come into being.

The Evolution of Transmission Services

Consistent with the statement made in the opening paragraph of this section of the chapter, an examination of the evolution of the data communications industry and its practices in the 1970s shows that much progress and activity were forecast, but actual performance has come nowhere close to realizing the predictions. In the early 1970s, a number of organizations became committed to entering the data communications industry and some already providing services planned substantial expansion. Many of these organizations were committed to providing services beyond the circuit and message-switching capabilities available from common carriers. Some intended to compete even in the transmission of voice.

Organizations such as Datran, Microwave Communications Inc. (MCI), ARPA, AT&T, ITT, Telenet, Tymnet, Xerox, and IBM (Satellite Business Systems) all promised network services capable of providing switching and other functions. These networks would, in most cases, provide alternative services to those provided by the common carriers. One function to be provided would be "packet switching," in which complete messages would be broken into small pieces (packets), the pieces transmitted, and the total message reconstituted at the receiving location. In this manner, many users could share the network and the problem of nondelayed transmission of short messages as required by interactive systems would be solved. Even more importantly, a number of the networks would be "digital" networks in contrast to the then standard "analog" networks designed to carry voice communications. The digital networks would not only be be better designed for data transmission, they could carry voice as well.

The forecasts for the data communications industry in the early 1970s were very optimistic. Not only were many firms entering the industry or planning expanded services, but total industry revenues were estimated as being high. Telenet (along with Tymnet, a packet-switching network), by itself, predicted revenues of $2 billion by the 1980s. Similar predictions were made by other prospective and actual network vendors and by computer vendors. Users were told again and again that the answer to all their networking needs was just around the corner. The market value of these public network services was to approach $5 billion for data transmission by the early 1980s.

Unfortunately, something happened on the way to accomplishing these goals. Datran died. MCI became a voice network.. ARPA remained primarily a research network for universities. AT&T's network, ACS, was sent back to the drawing board and, as of this writing, has just been reintroduced but without details. IBM's networking concept, SNA, has been delayed. The XTEN network of Xerox can best be described as "on hold." So, where do we stand?

Currently there are several classes of carriers. These are listed in Table 10-1 along with specific current organizations in each class. The 1979 estimates were that these carriers would still get a good deal of revenue, but nothing like the forecasts shown earlier. Current estimates are that 1979 carrier revenues amounted to approximately $2.4 billion. It is also acknowledged that some "voice" revenue is included in this amount, so that the revenue associated with data transmission is less. The reason that industry revenues are less than forecast and that a number of industry entrants have given up involves technical, economic, political, and legal factors.

The reader must be aware that the data communications industry and segments of the industry are changing extremely rapidly. As of this writing, there is an effort underway by General Telephone and Electronics (GTE) to acquire the data communications service offered by Southern Pacific. Because of the dynamics of the industry, Table 10-1 should only be taken as an approximation of the actual state of affairs at the time this book is being read.

COMMUNICATIONS TECHNOLOGY

The primary decisions concerning data communications that must be made in an organization involve the selection of the attributes of equipment employed in the network and the types of communications

Table 10-1 Classes of Data Communications Carriers

Classes of Carriers	Data Communications Companies
Common:	Bell System, independent telephone companies
International common	ITT
Domestic record	Western Union (telegraph)
International record	ITT, Worldcom, RCA, Globcom, Western Union International
Airborne (satellite)	American Satellite Corp., Western Union, RCA Americom, Communications Satellite Corporation (Comsat), Southern Pacific Communications, GTE Satellite, Hughes Communications, Inc.
Specialized	Tymnet, Telenet, MCI

carriers that will be involved in transmission of data between organizational units. Figure 10-1 is a schematic of a simple data communications system. The goal of the host organization is to configure a system that is satisfactory in terms of performance, reliability, evolvability, and cost.

Achieving these objectives is difficult because the technologies and issues involved in data communications are complex. In order to operate within this area effectively, the information systems manager

Figure 10-1 A Typical Data Communications System

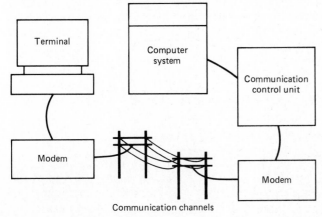

must be comfortable, at least, with the technologies involved. This section provides a primer on the technologies, including (1) transmission media (the communications links shown in Figure 10-1), (2) communications hardware (terminals, modems, communications control units), (3) communications software, (4) network concepts and control procedures, and (5) standards.

Before going on to discuss the details of data communications technology, a brief discussion of a few basics will contribute to a complete understanding. The perspective to be taken is that the information systems manager should be involved to some degree in decisions made by his or her organization as choices are made regarding the five areas listed above. Consequently, a threshold-level understanding of the vocabulary and fundamentals of data communications is necessary for the information systems manager.

Technological Basics

The key to achieving the objectives listed above is to select the communications link (or links) that is most suitable and to balance the other components of the network accordingly. Figure 10-2 is an illustration of the types of communications links or types of services that are available. Note that the major categories of services are switched vs. leased (with a combination or hybrid category added).

Examination of the switched category shows that what is being referred to is "dial-up" service which transmits data at up to 4800 bps. The advantage of this type of communications link is that the user pays only for time connected to the communications link and transmitting

Figure 10-2 Types of Communications Services (Some Examples)

SWITCHED	HYBRID	LEASED
Direct Distance Dialing (0 to 4800 bps)	Value Added Data Services	Subvoice Grade (0 to 150 bps)
WATS	MCI	MCI, So. Pacific
	Tymnet	AT & T Series 1000
TELEX AND TWX	Telenet	Western Union
		Voice Grade (300 to 9600 bps) AT & T Series 3000 Satellite (WU, RCA) Western Union DDS (2400-9600 bps) MCI, So. Pacific
		Broadband DDS (56 kilo bps & 1.5 mega bps) AT & T Series 5000 & 8000 Western Union Satellite (WU, RCA) MCI, So. Pacific, ITT

data. The disadvantages are that the transmission rates are relatively slow and that costs can be high if a great deal of data is to be transmitted. The alternative is to "lease" a line which is dedicated solely to one user. Note from Figure 10-2 that several categories of leased lines exist and are differentiated by the rate at which data can be transmitted. The high-speed or broadband links utilize technologies which will be discussed more fully later (microwave, fiber optics, and satellite).

Another fact to which attention should be paid is that most of the services shown in Figure 10-2 are analog services in which the signal varies constantly. Recall that these links were designed basically for voice communications. As time goes by, more links are taking a digital approach to transmission (the Bell System DDS is an example), in which discrete pulses are transmitted. *Computerworld* reports that currently about one-third of the trunks in the Bell System are digitized and that most all will be by 1990.[2] This approach is better suited to data transmission (although voice may also be transmitted in this form), and certain conversions required in going from the computer to the communications link are avoided (see the discussion of modems below). There are a few additional considerations of which the reader should be aware: (1) transmission rates, (2) switching types, and (3) forms of transmission.

Transmission Rates. Voice-grade circuits can transmit data at rates as high as 4800 or 9600 bps if the line is "conditioned" by the addition of electronic components which minimize interference. If higher speeds are desired, broadband, or wideband, services must be used. High-speed channels transmit data at 10,000 to 230,000 bps. These channels must employ microwave, satellite, or fiber-optic transmission media. Such speeds are usually employed in cases in which the communication is from computer to computer. These services are shown under the broadband section in Figure 10-2. (The specific firms providing broadband services are constantly changing, and a few are listed for purposes of illustration.)

Switching Types. The reader may recall from the section of this chapter dealing with the historical perspective that switched circuits can be of three basic types: message-switched, circuit-switched, and packet-switched. Most switched circuits shown in Figure 10-2 are of the message type. Under this form, complete messages are sent from one point in a network to another. Getting the complete message to its ultimate destination may require passing the message through many points

---

[2]"CCIA Charges Users 'Raped' By Decision Bell," *Computerworld*, September 14, 1981, p. 71.

in the network. At each point, the message is held (stored) until capacity exists to send (forward) it to its next routing point in the network. Naturally, substantial delays can occur because of the storing process. Circuit switching involves the temporary direct electrical connection of two or more channels between two or more points in order to provide the user with exclusive use of an open channel with which to exchange information. "Line switching" is another term for this concept. Packet-switching networks (in Figure 10-2, Telenet and Tymnet are examples) break the message up in "packets" and send each packet from its originating point to its final destination without delay. The message is reconstituted at the final point. Under this form, packets from many different messages may share a communication line, with the result of high line utilization and a reduction for users in the cost of sharing the line. These types of networks are called "value-added" networks because the carrier (e.g., Telenet) gets basic leased lines from an existing carrier and adds value by sharing lines with packet-switching minicomputers.

Forms of Transmission. Other terms which will be seen below include "half-duplex" and "full-duplex," and "synchronous" and "asynchronous" communication. A "simplex" communications line transmits data in only one direction at a time. Such lines are rare. A "half-duplex" line transmits data in both directions, but not at the same time. A "full-duplex" line permits simultaneous transmission of data in both directions at once. Full-duplex lines are more expensive and are usually used for computer-to-computer communications. One reason the half-duplex and full-duplex lines are used is for error checking to ensure that the message sent is received correctly. Full-duplex, in addition, increases the amount of work that can be done in a given period of time. Until recently, most lines were half-duplex, but with advanced line control procedures a switch to full-duplex may be expected.

Data is usually transmitted between points on a communications link in what is called "bit-serial" fashion. Most applications up to 1200 bps transmit bits in what is called the "asynchronous" mode. In this mode, the data bits of each character are preceded and followed by special start and stop bit sequences. "Synchronous" transmission, on the other hand, is usually employed for applications involving speeds of 2000 bps and higher. Here, a constant rate clock determines the exact time instant at which bits are sent and received, eliminating the need for the special start and stop bit sequences associated with asynchronous transmission. Synchronous transmission is thus more efficient in utilizing a given amount of available line capacity.

Finally, the reader should be aware that the possibility exists to transmit data according to various "codes." Some of the codes one hears about are ASCII, BCD, EBCDIC, and Baudot. At this point, the reader need simply be aware that the various codes exist and that IBM uses EBCDIC whereas most other computer vendors utilize ASCII. The section on standards later in the chapter will treat codes in greater detail.

Communication Transmission Media

Data or voice signals are transmitted over communications lines in either an analog or a digital form. "Analog" transmission refers to the transmission of a continuously variable signal and is best suited for voice signals. "Digital" transmission refers to the transmission of a discretely variable signal represented as digital pulses. Data signals, unlike voice signals, are discrete and must be converted into continuous signals before being sent over analog transmission facilities such as the telephone system. A device called a modem (modulator-demodulator) is used to perform this task.

Different kinds of communications lines or channels can be used to connect terminals and computers: (1) standard telephone lines, (2) coaxial cables, (3) microwave transmission, (4) satellite communications, and (5) fiber optics. The following sections discuss these various communications channels.

Telephone Lines. Standard telephone lines are widely used as communications channels. The major advantage of the use of the voice or analog telephone system is the universality of its facilities. Using an already existing complex network of lines, access can be established to essentially any location in the world at speeds of up to 9600 bps.

Telephone networks, however, are primarily designed for voice communications purposes, and a number of their technical properties impose important limitations on data communications applications. An example is the requirement for signal conversion devices to change the two-level digital signals of business machines into continuously varying (analog) signals that effectively use the capacity of the voice network.

With the recent trend toward distributed processing, however, increasing attention is being directed toward digital transmission facilities which are needed to accommodate business traffic. Newer transmission facilities such as coaxial cables, microwave links, and particularly satellites and fiber optics are infinitely more compatible with the requirements of data communications than are telephone lines. As a result of the installation of these newer media, even voice traffic is gradually being digitized to take advantage of the considerable traffic control and routing efficiencies that can be realized in an all digital medium. The Bell System's Digital Data System (DDS) offers service at 56 Kbps and 1.5 Mbps, but this service does not employ the technology of the analog voice telephone system.

Coaxial Cables. Coaxial cables are high-quality communications lines that have been laid under the ground or under the ocean. The electrical characteristics of the coaxial cable are such that data can be transmitted at a much higher rate than with standard telephone lines. They are also subject to very little distortion, cross talk, or signal loss. Coaxial cable is commonly used for analog transmission. However, it can also be used for digital transmission with a technique called "pulse code modulation" (PCM). The PCM technique offers a means of integrating voice and data transmission, as voice is digitally encoded. The major disadvantage is that each digitized voice circuit requires a 64 kHz bandwidth while an analog circuit requires only 4 kHz.

To date, significant technical and economic problems have inhibited major progress in the area of cable technology. The potential for this medium is very great, and recent increases in development activities in this area should lead to products which can exploit the capability of this wideband channel capacity.

Microwave Transmission. Microwave systems transmit signals through open space much like radio signals. They provide a much faster transmission rate than is possible with either telephone lines or coaxial cables. Microwave systems transmit data on a line-of-sight path between microwave towers that are usually spaced 25 to 30 miles apart. For long-distance transmission, signals are amplified and retransmitted from one station to the next.

Today, microwave facilities support transmission of both analog and digital signals. Microwave has a channel capacity comparable to coaxial cable. Its chief advantage is low cost per channel mile, especially in high-capacity systems, and its chief disadvantage is signal fading during poor propagation conditions. The cost advantage is the result of fewer amplifiers per channel mile than coaxial cables. Distortion induced by climactic conditions and interference with the line-of-sight path by foreign objects are other disadvantages of microwave transmission.

Microwave systems are used not only by the common carriers for long distance circuits but also by large individual users for wideband communications over a limited area such as a city. The outlook for microwave growth is excellent. The forecast is that from a 1970 level of 8500 long-haul microwave stations, the number of stations will grow to 11,600 in 1980 and 19,000 by 1985.

Communication Satellites. Communication satellites provide a special form of microwave relay transmission. Positioned in space in geosynchronous orbits 22,300 miles above the earth, satellites serve as relay stations for the transmission of signals generated from the earth. The first of the communications satellites, Intelsat I (Early Bird) was launched in 1965. Between 1965 and 1971, four generations of communications satellites (Intelsat I to IV) were launched.

The first U.S. domestic satellite was not launched until 1974, but in 1973 the RCA Corporation began U.S. service by leasing two "transponders" (channels) on Canada's ANIK II, using its own earth stations in New Jersey and California. Western Union launched the first domestic satellites in 1974. When these were operational, the U.S. Federal Communications Commission (FCC) ordered RCA to switch to the Western Union system, Westar. RCA later launched its own satellites in 1975 and 1976.

Today, there are eighty operating satellites orbiting in space. Sixty-four of these handle domestic, international, and military communications. The rest perform scientific, meteorologcommunical, or experimental duties. A study recently conducted for the National Aeronautics and Space Administration (NASA) concluded there would be a tenfold increase in the international demand for communication satellite circuits between 1982 and the year 2000. Of the communication satellites, twelve are totally dedicated to commercial communication as of this writing. The owners and their numbers of satellites are (1) Comsat General, four; (2) Satellite Business Systems, two; (3) RCA Americom, three; and (4) Western Union, three. Twenty more satellites are approved for launch as of this writing, and several more firms are now allowed by the FCC to enter the satellite communications business, among them Hughes Communications Services, GTE, and AT&T.

The principal advantage of satellite communications is in long-haul service with wide bandwidth where lower cost and higher reliability are required. Besides providing the wideband channels, satellites offer a number of additional capabilities:

Distance insensitivity: Because of the distance that signals must travel to the satellite and back, communications charges are not based on the mileage between facilities on earth. This means that a data processing facility can be established where it is most functionally useful and not, as has been the case, where existing terrestrial communications are available and overall network costs minimal.

Broadcast capability: With their point-to-multipoint, or broadcast capability, satellites also facilitate electronic mail, teleconferencing, and other business applications. The broadcast capability may also be used for the simultaneous update of distributed databases.

Integration: Satellites have the capability of integrating voice, data, video, and image communication. This capability will have a major facilitating impact on the office automation movement.

Networking: Another important feature of satellites is that they provide users with an integrated network and not simply a group of circuits. With private circuits from conventional carriers, a user must implement a network in stages. In contrast, since satellite service provides simultaneous and full interconnectivity among all earth stations, a user can implement an organizationwide private network overnight.

Although satellites have striking advantages over the transmission media discussed previously, they also suffer from a number of important disadvantages, including the following:

Transmission Delay: Although the distance between two communication stations on earth becomes irrelevant when using satellites, the actual distance that the signal has to travel to get to these two points can be large. Using satellite communications results in a higher transmission delay than would be the case were a terrestrial link between the two points employed. This delay is referred to as a "propagation delay" and is typically in the millisecond range for terrestrial circuits but is increased to several hundred milliseconds on satellite channels. Timing and data-throughput problems caused by such delays can now be resolved through the use of special compensation devices or new protocols.

Earth station cost: A problem with using satellites for communications is the very high cost of earth stations. Although here, as in most areas of the computer communications industry, costs have dropped dramatically, substantial sums are still involved. For example, the first earth station for AT&T's Telstar satellite cost $50 million to build, but a powerful contemporary transmit-and-receive station can be constructed for approximately $100,000.

Launching cost: The overall cost of using satellites must include the cost of putting them in space. With the availability of the space shuttle, the launching cost is expected to decrease dramatically. With its large payload, the space shuttle can carry larger satellites than those used presently. In general terms, the larger and more powerful the satellite is, the smaller and less expensive are the earth stations required.

Miscellaneous: Two other problems worth mentioning are that there is beginning to be spectrum congestion (which is interference between frequencies) in the frequencies used by satellites, and some persons are concerned about the vulnerability of satellites in the light of international tensions.

Fiber Optics. The developments in the area of fiber optics are as significant as those that have occurred in the area of communications satellites. Persistent research efforts over the past 15 years at the Corning Glass Works, Bell Laboratories, and Western Electric are responsible for much of the progress in the field of fiber-optic transmission.

Fiber-optic transmission systems offer powerful advantages over conventional coaxial cable and metallic wire links. Increased bandwidth, smaller diameter, lower weight, lack of cross talk, complete immunity to inductive interference, and the potential ability to deliver signals at lower costs are bringing fiber-optic systems out of the laboratory and into practice. This medium is coming into strong competition with conventional systems in telecommunications, computers, military systems, and many other areas.

Fiber-optic technology is based upon the ability of smooth, hair-thin strands of transparent material to conduct light with high efficiency. The major advantages of fiber optics over wire cables include substantial weight and size savings and increased speed of transmission. For example, 1 1/2 pound fiber-optic cable can transmit the same amount of data as 30 pounds of copper wire. A standard coaxial cable can carry up to 5400 different voice channels, while a single fiber-optic cable can carry up to 50,000 channels. There are several other advantages of fiber optics:

1. *No electric current:* Fiber optics is the transmission of light or optical signals, not electric current or voltage. The absence of a potential spark makes fiber optics particularly well suited for industrial process controls in explosive environments such as grain elevators, petrochemical operations, distilleries, and refineries.

2. *No EMI or RFI:* Unlike electrical signals transmitted over copper wire, optical signals are impervious to electro-magnetic interference (EMI) and radio-frequency interference (RFI); similarly, they do not generate EMI or RFI. This characteristic is advantageous to users in the data transmission industry, where induced fields may generate erroneous data or cause serious systems malfunctions. Optical links between peripherals, microprocessor and mainframe, or within terminals, can eliminate these problems.

3. *Secure communications:* Absence of EMI or RFI characteristics gives fiber optics unmatched data transmission security. Since generation of electromagnetic fields is the basis for remote "bugging" or homing in, this technique is useless on fiber-optic lines. The only way to steal information would be to physically tap into the light-carrying fiber, and this would immediately produce a noticeable light or signal loss.

The boom in fiber-optic technology is coming sooner and faster than many expected. The technology no longer is a laboratory curiosity but a viable applied technology expected to generate $2 billion in industry revenues in the United States alone by 1990. The Bell System planned to spend $80 million on fiber-optic systems in 1981 and $141 million in 1982. Projections of U. S. telephone company annual purchases of fiber optics have been boosted for the year 1990 from $450 million to $750 million.

Although the telephone companies, the government, and the military are the largest consumers of fiber-optic technology, there are also many smaller firms moving toward optical fibers and away from copper cables. Today, computer makers, peripheral equipment manufacturers, and instrument makers are actively evaluating fiber-optic data bus systems and may very well be the first substantial users of fiber-optic technology in the 1980s.

Communications Hardware

A data communications network consists of a number of different elements, each with a distinct role to play in enabling the network as a whole to meet its objectives. At its simplest form, a data communications facility consists of some form of input (source) or output (sink) unit, a communications link, and a host processor. Most networks contain many units of each type, but it is important to remember that they are all designed to facilitate, expedite, or make more efficient the basic functions of inputting, transmitting, processing, and outputting data. The basic network hardware elements considered in this section are (1) terminals, (2) modems, (3) line sharing devices (concentrators and multiplexers), (4) control units, and (5) front-end processors.

Terminals. In a communications system, a terminal provides an interface between the user of the system and the computer. Thus, a terminal may be a means for the user either to submit input into the computer or to receive output from it. Alternatively, the terminal may fulfill both of the functions.

In recent years, a substantial new array of different terminal devices has become available in the marketplace. These types of devices go well beyond the traditional functions of a teletypewriter in network applications. They provide certain types of intelligence and, hence, the ability to execute programs and store data at distant points from host processors.

There are a number of ways in which terminals may be classified, but the most useful approaches are to define them by function or use. There are five major categories of teleprocessing terminals:

  I. Low-speed teleprinter.
     A. Buffered or unbuffered.
     B. Limited intelligence.
     C. Used on dial-up or dedicated lines, but mostly dial-up.
     D. Popular applications: time sharing, message switching.
  II. Low-speed and medium-speed visual display (CRT).
     A. Alphanumeric or graphic (limited numbers).
     B. Mostly buffered with moderate intelligence.
     C. Popular applications: fast response, database inquiry.
     D. Used in stand-alone configurations.
 III. Batch processing terminals.
     A. Card reader, printer, operator console in minimal configuration.
     B. CRT display (tape cassette, diskette capability optional).

    C. Mostly buffered, frequently programmable.

    D. Either dial-up or dedicated lines.

    E. Popular applications: extend card reader, line printer, access to batch job queue to distant locations.

IV. Transaction terminals.

    A. Low cost workstation driven by buffered shared controllers.

    B. Use mostly dedicated lines.

    C. Mostly buffered and designed around particular industry applications.

    D. Popular applications: retail point of sale, banking, credit checking.

V. Intelligent workstation terminal.

    A. Usually involves a cluster controller to handle local peripherals and perform other functions.

    B. Buffered, highly modular, programmable (always by vendor, sometimes by user).

    C. Substantial functional capability independent of host processor (e.g., local data entry, transaction editing and verification, and database inquiry independent of host processor).

    D. Cluster controller can function as remote data entry station controller, remote display controller, communications concentrator for polling and code conversion, and applications processor.

    E. Can control such devices as teleprinters, CRTs (both local and remote), transaction terminals, tapes, diskettes, cassettes, disks, and online storage as well as other communications lines.

    F. Uses either dial-up or leased lines and can perform many functions without connection to host processor.

Modems. Modems (modulator-demodulators) are devices that provide the translation between the digital signals used by computers and terminals and the analog signals used on analog communications links. Effectively this means loading the digital signal (in binary representation) onto the normal carrier wave (the latter usually being in sine wave form). This process is reversed at the receiving end of the link, where the digital signal is "stripped" from the carrier wave. The digital signal can be loaded onto the carrier wave in one of three ways: by amplitude modulation (AM), by frequency modulation (FM), or by phase modulation (PM). Each of these techniques refers to the manner in which the basic carrier wave is modified (modulated) so that the receiving unit is aware that it is carrying information. Amplitude modulation tends to be the most susceptible to interference.

From the user's point of view, however, a modem is a "black box," in that the technique used for transmission need not be known. What is of paramount interest to the user, however, is the specifications of the link or of the modem. The two vital criteria are the speed of transmission and likely error rates. Although it is usually the speed of the communications link that is referred to, it is really more accurate to refer to the speed at which the modem can load signals onto the communications link.

Modems can also be characterized by the method employed in timing: asynchronous or synchronous. Asynchronous modems are the least complex from a technological standpoint. Virtually all modems operating at speeds up to 1800 bps are of the asynchronous or start-stop variety. Most asynchronous modems. using simple frequency modulation, or frequency-shift-keyed (FSK) modulation, transmit a signal at one frequency to indicate a space and at a different frequency to indicate a mark. These modems operate asynchronously in the sense that they transmit the appropriate frequency for exactly the length of time that the mark or space condition is present; the design of the modem imposes no special timing constraints.

Synchronous modems, on the other hand, are capable of operating at speeds up to 9600 bps over conditioned private voice-grade lines. Because these modems encode several bits in one signal element, they must receive bits from the data terminal at predefined time intervals, and conversely, they must know at what time intervals to present decoded bits to the terminal. This timing requires strict synchronization of the modem and the data terminal. The normal means of achieving synchronization is to have the modem "clock" the terminal. The modem sends a clock pulse to the terminal with every data bit and generates another set of clock pulses to control the output of data from the terminal to the modem. Terminals used with synchronous modems must be able to accept a clock to control their data transmission.

Modems can also be classified according to other two-valued characteristics: (1) high-speed (more than 2400 bps) or low-speed (2400 bps or less), (2) short-haul (limited distance) or long-haul (extended networks), (3) two-wire or four-wire, (4) full-duplex or half-duplex, (5) originate or answer, (6) FCC-registered or unregistered, and (7) Bell-compatible or Bell-incompatible.

In general, the major criteria for choosing a modem are transmission rate, turnaround time, error susceptibility, reliability, cost, and maintainability. The modem transmission rate must be sufficient to handle the basic system data volumes. Modem turnaround time is the length of time that is required for a modem transmitting in half-duplex to shift from sending to receiving or vice versa.

Error rates on modems depend basically on speed and the type of modulation used. Phase modulation is less error-prone than frequency modulation. When the speed of a modem is in the range of 4800 to 9600 bps, older modems require conditioned voice-grade lines to reduce errors during transmission. ·Conditioning is the electronic balancing of line characteristics by the common carrier and is supplied at extra cost.

Some modems dynamically balance the line to reduce the error rates, although this too is an added cost feature in the modem.

The cost of a modem is directly proportional to its speed or its rate of transmission. Reliability and maintainability are fundamentally important to the success of a data communications network. Most manufacturers provide information about the history of mean time between failures (MTBF) for their equipment. Availability of maintenance service in the locality where the modem is installed is also an important factor in evaluation. Some modems offer an alternative lower transmission speed to help overcome errors produced by a line that has become "noisy." Another similar option for private-line modems is the capability to transmit over the dial network in the event of failure.

Most modems are attached directly to the communications link in use and remain permanently in one location. However, some modems are constructed instead as "acoustical couplers," which makes them more portable. Acoustic couplers are often combined with a simple keyboard and hard-copy printer unit to provide a terminal of average briefcase size and portability. Such acoustically coupled terminals are being increasingly used because of their convenience. They can operate in offices, meeting rooms, or anywhere a telephone is available.

Line-Sharing Devices. Conceptually, the simplest way of connecting a number of remote locations to a single host processor is to provide a separate communications link to each remote location. The costs of the communications links in this type of network can quickly become prohibitive, and various line-sharing devices and procedures exist today to overcome the problem. Basically, the motivation for line sharing stems from economies of scale in the cost of the bandwidth and from the increased channel utilization such devices can produce when serving a large terminal population with predominantly unscheduled requests for service. Two of the main line-sharing approaches are the use of concentrators and multiplexers.

Concentrators. A "concentrator" is normally a minicomputer located at the terminal side of a long-distance line. As its name implies, it concentrates the data traveling to or from a number of remote locations into "bulk loads." A concentrator reduces line costs by collecting data from a number of terminals over relatively low-speed lines and transmitting the data to the host processor over a higher-speed line.

Being programmable, concentrators may also be used for a variety of tasks such as data validation, output formatting, and some backup and fail-safe functions. A concentrator may perform sufficient processing to enable its part of the network to continue essential processing if one or some of the communications lines become inoperable. Furthermore, it may store essential data if a line or device on either the host processor or the terminal side of the line fails.

Multiplexers. Compared with a concentrator, a "multiplexer" is basically an unintelligent (nonprogrammable) unit that performs the role of reducing total communications line costs but has no other function in the network. In this sense, the role of a multiplexer is solely economic, whereas, as mentioned previously, a concentrator may have a functional (backup, validation, etc.) as well as an economic role in the network. This distinction, however, will become less clear as an increasing number of multiplexers become based upon programmable minicomputers.

A multiplexer divides a communication line of a certain speed into multiple channels of a slower speed. For example, a line between a remote terminal and a computer may be capable of transmitting 9600 bps but this may be much greater than is required. A multiplexer allows the communication line to be divided, or multiplexed, into a number of slower-speed lines. This would allow a number of terminals to be connected to the line.

There are two main techniques used in multiplexing: frequency division and time division. In frequency division multiplexing (FDM), a transmission facility is divided into two or more channels by splitting the frequency band transmitted by the channel into narrower bands, each of which is used to constitute a distinct channel. Time division multiplexing (TDM), on the other hand, allots the common transmission channel to several different information channels, one at a time.

The primary disadvantage of FDM is the limited number of low-speed channels that can be combined into a high-speed trunk. The cost per low-speed channel for FDM is generally lower than for comparable TDM. This cost advantage is primarily evident when only a small number of low-speed channels are to be multiplexed. Another advantage of FDM is that it does not require the sychronization needed with TDM. The major advantage of TDM is its high multiplexing capacity. While a significant amount of common electronics are used by all the low-speed channels, present TDM generally represents a level of reliability comparable to FDM.

Communications Control Units.

Even though many modern data communications channels are capable of being operated at high speeds, there remains a significant difference between the rates of transmission and the speeds at which processors are able to process the data. Thus there is almost invariably a need for some type of buffering device between the channel and the processor. Moreover, most data is actually transmitted in "bit-serial" form (a sequential pattern of binary characters), whereas processing is typically carried out on parallel characters (or bytes).

A communications control unit thus performs the role of buffering the data transfer between the computer and the data communications network, as well as converting the bit-serial form into character form to be transmitted to main computer storage. These devices, although normally located centrally, may also be distributed throughout the network.

Some communications control units perform functions beyond just interfacing between the computer system and the communications channels. These functions may include error recovery when a signal is lost or when noise distorting a signal is detected on the line. They may interpret and process control information sent down the line, such as a character indicating the end of a message. They can also interface with many communications channels and control each one so that the computer system need not use resources to perform these functions.

Front-End Processors. A "front-end processor" is, in essence, a separate computer interposed between a data communications network and the host processor to perform a substantial part of the communications-oriented (as contrasted to applications-oriented) processing. These units can thus be programmed to edit input records for invalid data, to control the network traffic and only allow authorized users to have access to the system, and even to provide a fairly extensive set of standby processing capabilities in the event of host processor failure.

The advantage of a front-end processor is that it relieves the main computer system of performing communications-oriented tasks and allows the system to concentrate on applications programs and to produce useful output. It has been found that with large data communications networks up to 20 percent of the processing time can be spent in monitoring the communications lines and performing the same functions which can be performed by the front-end processor. Thus, in large networks, the use of a programmable front-end processor can significantly increase the processing capacity of the main computer system.

Line Control Procedures and Network Types

Having an appreciation of the basic facts about methods and equipment for data communications, the information systems manager can turn his or her attention to how that equipment interconnects with networks. The concepts and control procedures utilized in the design of data communications networks depend upon both the network functional requirements and the hardware employed. Appropriate configurations and controls can reduce costs and improve network efficiency and throughput. The following sections will consider the various network configurations and control techniques of which information systems managers need to be aware in order to better manage the establishment of a cost-effective network.

Line Configurations. Regardless of the type of communication channel, the speed at which data is transmitted, the mode of transmission, or the particular coding used for the transmission of characters on the channel, the terminals and computer systems must be arranged in some type of line configuration. There are three major types of line configurations: (1) point-to-point, (2) multipoint or multidrop, and (3) loop.

Point-to-Point Lines. A direct line connecting a terminal and a computer system in a communications network is called "point-to-point." In a point-to-point configuration each terminal sends data to and receives data from a computer system by means of an individual line, with no other terminals on the line. Point-to-point lines may be either switched (dial-up) or leased (dedicated) with a switched line; a common carrier such as the public telephone network establishes a connection only for the duration of a single call. Dedicated or leased lines, on the other hand, provide a permanent connection path between a terminal and the computer system. Point-to-point lines are expensive because only one terminal can use a line into the computer system. Thus, this type of line configuration has limited applications in data communications networks and can only be justified if the computer system and the terminal require communication on an almost continuous basis and fast response time is necessary. In many cases, point-to-point lines are used with computer-to-computer communications.

Multipoint or Multidrop Lines. To reduce the cost of the communications network, it is often desirable to attach more than one terminal to a single communication line. A line with several terminals, or "drop points," is called a "multidrop" or "multipoint" line. On multidrop lines, only one terminal can transmit at any one time unless multiplexing is used. More than one terminal on the line, however, can receive data at the same time.

This line configuration is normally used in inquiry systems with multiple CRT terminals because each terminal uses the line for only a short period of time. A leased line is almost always used for multidrop line configurations. Note that multidrop lines reduce the number of modems, ports, and line charges in comparison to point-to-point structures. Multipoint networks, however, require more software to control access to these lines. The following section, on line control procedures, will consider the methods used for establishing contact between the terminals and the computer system.

Loop Lines. Still another type of network configuration becoming popular in contemporary systems is the "loop" arrangement. This form of multidrop line configuration uses a short (approximately 1000 to 2000 feet) loop line; therefore, no modems are required. In this configuration, a data stream is transmitted around the entire loop at speeds of approximately 50,000 bps. Messages are preceded by the address of the terminal to which they are directed. These messages circle through the loop and, as a terminal recognizes its own address, it deletes its messages from the loop and processes it. Local loop lines are very effective in limited-distance applications where many individual terminals must be connected in a relatively small geographic area such as a grocery store, a bank, or a department store. Here, it might be prohibitively expensive to run separate point-to-point or multipoint lines to each remote terminal site. Furthermore, adding new stations or moving existing ones might be very costly and cumbersome, since it may involve rewiring of buildings. Major disadvantages of loops are their relatively inferior reliability and response time properties when connecting large numbers of terminals at traditional common carrier speeds of up to 10,000 bps. For this reason, loops are likely to remain popular primarily in local networks not involving a common carrier service.

Control Procedures. The method of establishing contact between terminals and the computer system primarily depends upon the type of line configuration used. The following paragraphs will consider some of the existing methods.

On a switched point-to-point line, the terminal establishes contact with the computer system by dialing the telephone number of the computer system. The modem at the computer site "answers" the call and establishes the connection. The modem also informs the terminal, through the use of a control character sent down the line, that it is ready to receive data. The computer system can, in turn, initiate contact with the terminal by appropriate commands which "dial" the number of the terminal. The terminal modem then responds in the same manner as described above.

Contact between a terminal and a computer system on a leased point-to-point line is normally accomplished by merely entering a control character or flipping a switch on the terminal or by the computer addressing a message to the appropriate line. Since the connection is dedicated via one leased line, the computer system "listens" for a request from the terminal to send data for a short period of time, and then the line is changed so that the terminal "listens" for a request from the computer system. In this way, the connection can be established almost immediately by switching the key or entering the control character.

When a multipoint configuration is used, several terminals are placed on one line, and thus efficient system operation requires some type of discipline or control for the access and utilization of shared network resources. There are several general categories of control which can be adopted to each applications environment, depending on traffic levels, response time requirements, and other factors. These alternatives range from virtually no control (contention-based systems) to strong centralized control methods such as polling by a master station on the line.

Contention. The simplest form of line control is called "contention." With contention control, terminals effectively compete for access to the line. If a terminal with a message to send requests a free line, transmission of the message proceeds. If the line is busy, the terminal has to wait until the line becomes free. The communications control software in the main computer may build up a queue of output service requests by remote terminals and fill these orders either on a first-come-first-served basis or according to a prescribed sequence.

Contention is relatively uncontrolled since terminals may tie up the line for long periods of time, even though no transmission is taking place. Hence, contention is not an effective method for heavily loaded multipoint line networks such as those typically used within business organizations. Contention is also often used on point-to-point or loop configurations where facility utilization is relatively low and in some cases is the only viable alternative.

Polling. Polling is performed by the computer system and the associated communications control unit. Each terminal is selectively queried according to a predetermined sequence or "poll" table, to learn whether it has data to send. If a terminal has nothing to send, it replies with a "nothing-to-send" control code and the next terminal on the line is polled.

Polling is usually performed under the control of vendor-provided software. Each station (terminal) on a multipoint line has a unique address and may respond only to polls preceded by this address code. The order and relative frequency of address entries in the polling list determine the polling sequence of each station. With this approach, the frequency of polling may be changed via software modification of the entries in the poll table to suit the particular traffic volume needs of applications. For example, to poll one station twice as often, its address is merely inserted twice as often in the poll list.

One disadvantage of polling is that once a terminal gains control of the line, the polling does not continue until after the message is fully transmitted. Thus, the danger exists that a terminal can keep control of a line for a long period of time. To overcome this condition, some systems include a programmed "time out" which allows the terminal to control the line for a specified period of time and then breaks the connection so that other terminals are not excluded from using the line. Another disadvantage of polling is that terminals can only send messages when queried. This is the reason why polling is seldom used for applications where terminal users require an immediate and continuing connection to the distant computer.

Typical link procedures or protocols which employ a polling procedure are binary synchronous control (BSC) and system data link control (SDLC) of IBM, Uniscope procedure and universal data link control (UDLC) of Sperry Univac, and high level data control (HDLC) of the International Standards Organization (see the section on fundamentals of network controls, below, for a detailed description of these protocols).

Selection (Addressing). Polling procedures, in general, are techniques utilized for gathering input from remote stations. A complementary function known as "selection" or "addressing" is used to accomplish output transmission to remote stations. The selection procedure may be accomplished in two basic ways. The first and more traditional approach is called "select-hold," where a remote station is asked to verify its ability to receive before any messages are sent to it. The second approach, known as "fast-select," involves sending the output message immediately without prior verification of the station. The latter approach is more efficient in line utilization, but requires more complicated error recovery procedures. As an example, the widely known BSC protocol implements the select-hold approach, whereas newer protocols such as SDLC enable the fast-select output procedure to be used.

Network Configurations. The various elements in a data communications system discussed thus far must be organized into a structure, or network, in order to accomplish the tasks for which they were designed. Although a network may be defined as any system composed of one or more computers and terminals, most networks are composed of multiple terminals, and possibly multiple computer systems, to allow the network to operate most efficiently and productively. The structure of a network depends primarily on the data flow organization of the network and the control of the data flow. There are six distinct pure network structures: (1) star, (2) hierarchy, (3) ring, (4) linear, (5) fully connected, and (6) network.

Star. A "star" structure involves one or more "nodes" connected on a point-to-point basis to a central node (Figure 10-3). An example of this structure is the connection of one or more terminals to a central computer via communications lines. The terminals may be on the same line (multidropped) or separate lines (single-dropped). A star configuration with both point-to-point and multipoint lines would be used when the central computer contains all the required data, and some terminals have more traffic than others. Note that in this configuration the organization of the network is strictly centralized.

Figure 10-3 Star

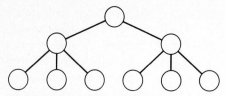

Figure 10-4 Hierarchy

Hierarchy. The "hierarchy" structure, also called a "tree," is an extension of the star structure concept. The star can be considered as a one-level hierarchy. The hierarchy structure is a cascading of the star structure, with control centered at the "root" node and reduced at each node away from the center (Figure 10-4). An example of the hierarchy structure is the connection of terminals to a central computer through a front-end processor.

The strengths of the hierarchy lie in their low cost and good performance properties as well as in the delegation of processing and control to the lower level nodes, which removes some or most of the burden from the central node. Failsoft characteristics, however, become more of a problem because a single failure can deny access to an entire subtree in the system.

Ring. The third pure network structure is the ring structure. A "ring" structure involves two or more nodes connected on a point-to-point basis with two adjacent nodes. Each node has the same level of responsibility for data flow control (Figure 10-5). An example of the ring structure is a series of computer systems communicating with each other. This structure is useful when not all of the processing is done at a central site, but rather some processing is done at local sites.

The ring has a lower cost than the star or the hierarchy structure because of line sharing. It also has lower performance because communication passes through several nodes.

Linear. The "linear" configuration may be thought of as an open ring and exhibits many of the properties of an open ring (Figure 10-6). This structure is common in nationwide communications systems because of its low cost in connecting widely dispersed nodes. Unless the lines are redundant, however, this structure is highly vulnerable to failure.

Figure 10-5 Ring

Figure 10-6 Linear

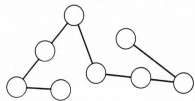

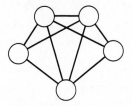

Figure 10-7 Fully Connected

Fully Connected. The final pure structure is the fully connected structure, which is an extension of the ring concept. The "fully connected" structure allows the nodes to be fully interconnected while maintaining the equality in data flow control among the nodes (Figure 10-7). An example of the fully connected structure is several computer systems interconnected by telecommunication services into a network.

This configuration has the advantages of high performance because of no line sharing, and good failsoft properties because of considerable redundancy. It is also very expensive, especially if the number of nodes is large. For this reason, fully connected configurations are rarely used in this pure form, but more commonly some lines are omitted.

Network. The network configuration, shown in Figure 10-8, is the completely general form and includes all other configurations as special cases. Note that the term "network" is used here to refer to a topological configuration and not as a synonym for a communications subsystem.

Fundamentals of Communications Network Control

Having presented communications concepts, media, and equipment and having gained an appreciation of the basic network design alternatives, we will now discuss these concepts as parts of a working communications network. As will shortly be seen, various vendors adopt different approaches to creating a network, each taking a somewhat

Figure 10-8 Network

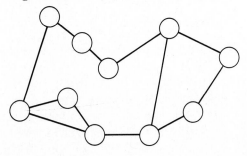

different view. In this section, the focus will be upon how the components of the network establish contact with one another. Since there are many ways of connecting the components together, various standards have been developed. The first subsection will deal with this topic. The second and third subsections will present two areas, codes and protocols, which are the subject of standards. The fourth subsection will cover the complex area of communications software. The final subsection will cover the way in which some of the vendors create a framework for their communications network, called a "network architecture."

Standards. Standardization efforts came about as a result of incompatibilities existing between various telecommunications systems. These incompatibilities occurred because there are a variety of choices for coding data and for formatting and timing the transmission of data. To cope with these issues, various organizations were formed to create standards to which vendors could adhere. Unfortunately, as will be demonstrated shortly, a number of different standards are available.

The International Standards Organization (ISO) was established by joint agreement to define standards for interconnection of international facilities and services. By agreement, each country would conform to the standards but would be allowed to add additional capabilities as a national option. The International Telecommunications Union established the Consultative Committee on International Telephone and Telegraph (CCITT) to make recommendations for future standards to ISO.

The United States agreed to work with ISO and CCITT for international compatibility, but national standardization was fragmented because of the federal, state, and industry structure of telecommunications. American industry has established two cooperative organizations to establish basic standards for interconnection and services: the American National Standards Institute (ANSI), sponsored by the Computers and Business Equipment Manufacturers Association (CBEMA), and the Electronic Industries Association (EIA). Fundamental standards to support federal and state regulation are produced by the National Bureau of Standards (NBS).

Codes. Data is transmitted over a communications line in one of a number of codes. These codes represent the data in the form of a string of binary digits and also enable certain essential instructional information to be passed over the line. The codes available break the stream of binary digits (bits) into groups of 5 to 8 bits. Each group represents a data character or a control character. A 5-bit coding structure enables 32 possible bit combinations; a 6-bit code, 64 combinations; a 7-bit code, 128 combinations; and an 8-bit code, 256 combinations. For most purposes, it is desirable to provide combinations of bits for the 10-digit decimal system and the complete alphabet (possibly in both upper- and lowercase), a number of special characters (punctuation marks, the dollar sign, or other currency signs), the control characters (e.g., carriage movements), as well as the control of the line itself. It might therefore appear that the number of combinations or codes required would preclude the use of anything less than a 6-bit code. In practice, however, the number of combinations in even a 5-bit code can be rendered sufficient by the use of so-called "shift codes." These special codes modify the value of succeeding characters until another shift character is encountered. Effectively this means that the same 5-bit code can represent as many characters as there are shift characters.

The most commonly used example of this principle is the CCITT alphabet No. 2, known as the Baudot code. Although widely used for telegraphic purposes, the Baudot code is not ideal for data communications purposes, and a number of alternative codes have been developed. Most of these newer codes employ six or seven bits to represent a character, and an additional bit for checking errors, commonly called a "parity" bit. To avoid a profusion of different data transmission codes, the American Standards body settled on a 7-bit code, which is termed ASCII (more properly known as USASCII-U.S.A. Standard Code for Information Interchange).

Hollerith coding on an 80-column punched card has long been in use. The binary-coded decimal (BCD) code is an extension of the Hollerith code that is used on magnetic tape and in computer storage to avoid the large numbers involved in pure binary systems. BCD (a 6-bit code) serves as the basis for several other codes, most notably one used by IBM, which employs an extended version of the code utilizing 8 bits and is known as EBCDIC, or extended binary-coded decimal interchange code.

Protocols. A protocol can be defined as a set of agreements stipulating the formatting and relative timing of messages exchanged between two processes communicating across a network. Another way of looking at protocols is to say that they are a formal set of conventions governing the format and control of information transfer between computer systems. Two machines can communicate only if they observe the same criteria concerning the formation of individual characters and commands, identical error-checking procedures, same-sized blocks of data, matched transmission speeds, and similar critical parameters. Providing these criteria is the function of a protocol.

The need for a set of agreed upon rules is further necessitated for two reasons. First, efficiencies can be achieved by reducing the amount of information transferred. For example, by presetting certain conditions for error checking, the extra information required to identify the type of error-checking technique need not be included in each transfer because the receiving end already knows what technique will be used. Second, every communications process requires the exchange of a set of control information. This is difficult in a communications line because only one path exists. Therefore, there must be a set of rules that allows the receiving terminal to distinguish control information and data when they are intermixed on one information path. A protocol thus provides a method for the orderly exchange of data by establishing rules for the proper interpretation of controls.

Protocols exist in hierarchies. The lowest level of protocol is at the electrical or physical level which specifies the establishment, maintenance, and disconnection of the physical communications link. An example of a physical level protocol is found in the Electrical Industries Association (EIA) RS-232C for connection between data terminal equipment (DTE) and data communication equipment (DCE). The next level might be called the "link level," which is responsible for the procedures to establish, maintain, and control the link between one computer or terminal and another. Examples of link level protocols are high level data link control (HDLC), developed by the International Standards Organization, and synchronous data link control (SDLC), which is part of IBM's systems network architecture (SNA).

There are still higher levels of protocols for system control and user communications and for the exchange of user data between operating systems and applications programs. These higher-level protocols are usually referred to as "host-level protocols." An example of the host level protocol is the seven-layer reference model developed by ISO's Technical Committee 97 (ISO/TC97). In addition to the first three levels of protocols described above, this model includes four other levels: (1) the transport control layer, which allows reliable end-to-end transfer of data across a communications network, (2) the session control layer, which provides for structured message exchanges between two work-stations or devices on a network, (3) the presentation control layer, which provides required format transformation such as translation of languages, data formats, and codes, and (4) the applications layer, where the computerized processes generate or receive and interpret the messages handled by the lower levels.

Although standards have been developed for some protocols, there are so many arbitrary factors involved that almost every computer vendor has adopted a somewhat unique set of protocols. The final part of this section will return to this issue as networks are discussed.

Communications Software. Data communications software can carry different meanings in various environments, and the overall definition of the term "data communications software" can be confusing not only to the newly initiated, but even to many of the·more experienced people in the industry. Rather than providing a specific definition of the term, this section focuses on some of the factors that are involved in describing data communications software. One should understand that data communications software must interface the user's applications programs with the access method that has been selected to control the network, keeping in mind that the telecommunications access methods themselves are control programs of a sort. In addition, all of this software must operate under the control of the operating system used in the host computer or in the user's data communications network.

Thus, data communications software must interface multiple application programs or routines not only with the chosen telecommunications access method, but also with the file-access methods, the database management system (if used), the remote terminals, and the front-end processor, as well as with the operating system. It must include a line control facility that accommodates the protocols within the network, and it must address the specific terminal characteristics of the devices employed in the network. In summary, data communications software must provide the means of controlling the specific data communications environment defined by the user.

Software in a data communications network can reside almost entirely in the central computer, or part of it can be located in the front-end processor, in a remote concentrator, in the communications control unit, or in an intelligent terminal. As networks get larger and more complex, it becomes more economical to migrate the network control functions away from the central processor and outward into the network. The following are normally included in the basic functions of the control software:

- Activation and deactivation of the links and stations
- Establishment of logical connections over physical links
- Processing of network commands
- Detection and correction of line errors and polling
- Recording of network status

An example of a familiar and highly developed set of communications software packages is that employed for the IBM 360/370/30xx/43xx series, some of which have been used since the late 1960s. There are four such packages in the IBM environment which represent examples of the range of products available to the designer of a data communications network:

- basic telecommunication access method (BTAM)
- queued telecommunication access method (QTAM)
- telecommunication access method (TCAM)
- virtual telecommunication access method (VTAM)

BTAM is the earliest and least sophisticated of the four packages. It provides basic facilities for sending and receiving messages and also for polling and addressing terminals. When using BTAM alone, the application programmer must be concerned with all the message control functions of the system.

QTAM is somewhat more sophisticated, providing additional facilities such as scheduling and resource allocation, queuing of messages on disk, and message logging. There is a macro language available which the applications programmer can use to ease the task of handling network control functions by means of macros incorporated into the applications programs.

TCAM, the successor of QTAM, is still more sophisticated in nature. In addition to all the features of QTAM, TCAM offers a message control program to handle message and network control functions. It also has facilities for system recovery, checkpoint, restart, and control of system shutdown.

VTAM is IBM's most advanced data communications software package and is intended to support the virtual computer systems using IBM's Systems Network Architecture (SNA) conceptual framework. VTAM basically incorporates all the facilities of TCAM and additionally allows the user to interface dynamically with a variety of application programs. VTAM is usable only with IBM's newer DOS/VS and OS/VS operating systems.

Network Architecture. A network control architecture is simply a reasoned method of holding together all the pieces of a communications system by imposing some order on the way one piece of equipment "talks" to another and on the way messages are composed and routed throughout the network. An architecture consists of two components, protocols and software. Protocols are covered by standards, but several are available to choose from. Software is not covered by standards, and therefore, a wide variety of architectures exist depending primarily on a vendor or a body responsible for setting standards. Figure 10-9 is a summary of the state of affairs. With the exception of DEC (Digital Equipment Corporation), each of the protocols employed is synchronous and bit-oriented. There are also asynchronous protocols used for teletypes and a synchronous character-oriented protocol used by IBM called "binary synchronous."

IBM's SNA is one example of a network architecture or framework. It contains three basic structures: an access method interface, a communications protocol, and a communications control program. The access method is VTAM. The communications protocol is SDLC. The network communications control program is called NCP, which stands for "network control program." As mentioned under the section on communications software, SNA employs a layered structure involving an applications layer, a function management layer, and a transmission subsystem layer. There are network-addressable hardware units, a path control element, and a data link control element. The latter is where SDLC is involved. SDLC employs a specific format for each data transmission block, called a "frame." Obviously, the SDLC frame is different from those used in other protocols. Similarly, the use of VTAM and the overall method by which the NCP operates set the IBM way of conceptualizing and implementing a network architecture apart from others.

It is beyond the scope of this chapter to go into great detail on any architecture, but it is worthwhile pointing out that the various systems listed in Figure 10-9 differ substantially from one another and are by and large incompatible. The ANSI standard protocol, for example, while bit-oriented, differs from SDLC in important ways. Some vendors employ the HDLC protocol, which also differs from others. Finally, the international standard, X.25, also differs from SDLC and HDLC. X.25 is similar to SDLC, but it allows for different modes of operation, whereas SDLC does not.

LOCAL AREA NETWORKS

Up to this point, our discussion of data communications has dealt with transmission of data and voice between points that were geographically separated by long distances. There is, however, another application for data communications that is of great importance: very high-speed transmission of data over relatively short distances, say, within a building or within an office park. The applications for this sort of transmission are those that are typically associated with the "office of the future": facsimile transmission, electronic mail, video conferencing, and the movement of large databases. What is required for these applications are very high rates of transmission over relatively short distances coupled with the ability to hook large numbers of "devices" into the network.

This connection of a number of devices is referred to as a "local area network." The transmission speeds in local networks can be as low as 9600 bps if the devices are connected by twisted-pair telephone wire, but typically much higher transmission speeds are involved. The speeds

Figure 10-9 Protocol Summary

Vendor/Organization	Architecture	Protocol Type
IBM	Systems Network Architecture (SNA)	Bit
ANSI	Advanced Data Communications Control Protocol	Bit
CCITT	X.25	Bit
Burroughs	Burroughs Data Link Control (BDLC)	Bit
NCR	BOLD	Bit
CDC	Control Data Communications Control Program (CDCCP)	Bit
DEC	Digital Network Architecture	Byte

to be employed in local area networks are typically in the range of 56,000 bps up to gigabits (billions of bits) per second. If the direct connection of devices using simple telephone wire is excluded, then there are three methods that can be used to form local area networks: twisted-pair wire, coaxial cable, and fiber optics.

Twisted-Pair Wire

Private branch exchange (PBX) or computer branch exchange (CBX) technology is of the type commonly found in today's telephone switchboards. These devices can transmit, using twisted-pair telephone wire, at 56K bps and, on newer devices, at 128K bps. The AT&T Dimension service and its "System 85" are examples of switchboard-based local area networks. Several other firms are competing in this market: Northern Telecom, Rolm, and United Technology's Lexar. Another firm that provides a hybrid PBX and baseband service is Datapoint through its ARC system. In general, the PBX approach does a better job of voice transmission than it does of data transmission. This is reflected in the transmission rates.

Coaxial Cable

There are two forms of local area networks employing coaxial cable technology: baseband and broadband. A baseband local area network uses a coaxial cable having a center conductor surrounded by a dielectric insulator. Surrounding these is a woven copper mesh. A polyvinyl jacket is placed over the mesh to protect against weather and handling. This approach provides for transmission speeds up to 50M bps over distances of up to 1.5 kilometers. An example of the baseband approach is Xerox's Ethernet, which is also supported by DEC and Intel. It also *appears* that IBM will favor a baseband approach. Critics of baseband technology claim that the narrow bandwidth means that high-performance computers may not be able to function at capacity with baseband systems. These persons also mention high cost and the inability to handle intrabuilding communication as limitations of the baseband approach to local area networking.

A local area network based upon the "broadband" approach also employs a coaxial cable having a center conductor surrounded by a dielectric insulator. Instead of a copper mesh, however, an extruded-aluminum jacket is used. The broadband approach has greater immunity to electromagnetic interference than baseband. Connection of devices to a broadband network is often accomplished using "splitters," which are used in the cable television industry. Broadband technology allows transmission across distances up to 50 kilometers and at speeds up to 100M bps. Wang's Wangnet is an example of a system employing broadband local area networking technology.

Fiber Optics

Fiber optics may be used in local area networks. All the advantages listed in the previous section on this technology are present if fiber optics are used in local area networks. One major advantage of this approach is that extremely high transmission rates are possible. Transmission speeds on the order of a billion bps are possible with fiber optics. A technical disadvantage at present is the lack of suitable splitters which will allow other than point-to-point connection of devices. For this reason and for economic reasons, the use of fiber-optic technology in local area networks is likely to be further in the future than the other approaches.

Some Final Considerations

As this is being written, there are several issues concerning local area networks that are under consideration. One is a technical issue regarding the development of standards as to how data will be passed around the network. There are at least three competing methods for performing this function, and the method used has serious cost implications. One device controller, for example, costs $1200 whereas another employing another approach to passing information costs $300 per device. Thus, consistent with what we have observed in other areas of data communications, various manufacturers choose different ways of doing things, with the result that no real standards exist.

Another current issue concerns the handling of both voice and data in local area networks. Some observers are suggesting that, at least in the short run, local networks will be hybrid operations with one method handling data transfer and another handling voice transmission. The data system would be connected to the voice system for connection to the systems available for long-distance communication.

Local area networks are a relatively new phenomenon, but they will be extremely important in the future. This technology, coupled with the evolution of today's personal computer, will enable the "office of the future" to become a reality. The MIS manager *must* closely watch developments in these two areas and be willing to experiment in order to prepare for the future we all know is coming.

SUMMARY

The position taken in writing this chapter is that many information systems managers would be well served by some material which provides a basic level of acquaintance with the field of data communications. This chapter has provided a historical perspective of data communications and an overview of the technology involved in the area. The overview has been highly detailed because of the importance of this basic technology to the field of management information systems in the next decade. An attempt has been made throughout to view technical matters primarily from a descriptive or definitional perspective. By reading this material, a person not well versed in data communications should be better able to communicate with vendors and/or technical personnel.

Before leaving this topic, some mention should be made that as of January 1983, AT&T is allowed to compete in the data processing industry. Under the name of AT&T Information Systems, this very large and powerful corporation will not only be able to supply communications services, but also will enter the computing equipment marketplace. One communications product that has been announced is the rebirth of the intelligent data communications network, ACS, under the new name of NET/1000. Exactly what AT&T will do for computing and/or combined computing and communications products is uncertain at this writing, but this is an area that should be monitored by the astute MIS executive.

The challenge facing the IS manager relative to data communications is not to decide whether to employ data communications, but rather how to employ this technology. As can be appreciated from reading this chapter, a myriad of data communications options exist. These options involve choices of how much to communicate and how to do so. The latter involves picking equipment or components that not only are cost-effective and reliable but also are compatible with one another.

SUGGESTED READINGS

Bingham, J. E., and G. W. P. Davies, *Planning for Data Communications*, Macmillan, London, 1979.

Champine, G. A., *Computer Technology Impact on Management*, North-Holland, Amsterdam, 1978.

Cypser, R. J., *Communications Architecture for Distributed Systems*, Addison-Wesley, Reading, Mass., 1978.

Doll, D. R., *Data Communications: Facilities, Networks, and Systems Design*, John Wiley, New York, 1978.

Edwards, M., "Battle of the Satellites," *Infosystems*, vol. 28, no. 5, May 1981, pp. 54-60.

Fitzgerald, J., and T. S. Eason, *Fundamentals of Data Communication*, John Wiley, New York, 1978.

Frank, H., "LAN's: Who Needs One?" *Management Technology*, vol. 1, no. 3, July, 1983, pp. 24-30.

Gardner, D. W., "Solving the Local Network Puzzle," *Datamation*, vol. 28, no. 8, July 1982, pp. 46-51.

Gibson, R. W., "A Primer for Evaluating and Purchasing Today's Local Area Networks," *Data Communications*, June 1982, pp. 147-156.

Hoard, B., "Local-Area Networks," *Computerworld OA*, vol. 16, no. 13a, March 31, 1982, pp. 67-69.

McLaughlin, R. A., "Piecing Together the Datacom Industry," *Datamation*, vol. 25, no. 7, July 1979, pp. 110-114.

Rockhold, A. G., "Fiber Optics: A New World of Communications," *Infosystems*, vol. 28, no. 8, February 1977, pp. 2-8.

Rosenberg, A. P., "The Quick and Dirty Way to Implement Datacom Nets," *Datamation*, vol. 25, no. 3, July 1978, pp. 48-54.

Sanders, R. W., and R. A. McLaughlin, "Networks at Last?" *Datamation*, vol. 26, no. 3, March 1980, pp. 124-128.

Sherman, K., *Data Communications: A User's Guide*, Reston Publishing, Reston, Va., 1981.

Smith, F. G., *Data Communications and the Systems Designer*, University Microfilms International, Ann Arbor, Mich., 1980.

Withington, F. T., "Sizing Each Other Up," *Datamation*, vol. 28, no. 7, July 1982, pp. 10-15.

ELEVEN

DISTRIBUTED DATA PROCESSING

INTRODUCTION

This chapter defines and historically examines distributed data processing (DDP) and evaluates the impact of DDP on organizations. Problems associated with DDP are discussed and a framework for planning and controlling DDP is presented.

DEFINING DDP

One of the serious obstacles to sustained discussion of DDP technology is the lack of clear definition of terminology. The term "distributed data processing" has been used to refer to highly centralized computing systems with remote terminals at one extreme, and to totally decentralized collections of stand-alone minicomputer systems at the other. This is because distributed data processing is an ambiguous term. It may include distribution of processing to remote sites, distribution of data collection, distribution of applications development, distribution of software programming, distribution of data itself, distribution of computer operations, and distribution of control of computing resources. Each of these can be more or less centralized or decentralized depending upon organizational requirements. For the purposes of this chapter, distributed data processing is defined as the decentralized use of hardware, software, and data that may or may not be technically or organizationally linked to major centralized or other decentralized hardware, software, or data.

The distribution of data processing functions can take many forms. One convenient framework for considering distribution of computing is in terms of a continuum with centralized computing at one extreme and decentralized computing at the other. The implementation of DDP in a specific organization should be determined by the specific requirements within that organization. The type of DDP which is selected would then lie somewhere between centralized and decentralized computing.

For example, a large bank in New York has implemented its version of DDP as a group of minicomputers which are independent and fully decentralized. A major oil company in Los Angeles has decided to develop a DDP telecommunications network in which the nodes in the network are classified according to one of three "levels": the first level is the large central computer center in Houston; the second level uses small computers for processing of remote data; and the third level encompasses the spectrum of functionally oriented intelligent terminals which connect to the level 1 and level 2 computers.

The preceding two examples illustrate the diversity of possible approaches caused by widely differing information requirements. Many other examples exist in which other corporations have developed their own DDP strategies based upon their own needs.

Besides the diversity of approaches to DDP, there is also a great deal of diversity in the roles DDP plays in organizations. DDP is one of the most pervasive phenomena occurring in organizations today. Performing roles as varied as word processing, electronic mail, engineering calculations, manufacturing process controllers, energy use controllers, programmer work stations, automated graphics, and executive decision support systems, DDP has become a major factor in modern organizations.

Why the move to DDP? The incredible advances in chip technology have virtually eliminated the traditional economy-of-scale arguments for large-scale centralized computing. Not that there is no longer a need for centralized computing, but there is the opportunity to decentralize when it fits organizational requirements. In many situations, DDP has come to the rescue of overloaded centralized computers by allowing them to off-load functions that were causing too much overhead.

With the proliferation of DDP, organizations are experiencing increasing difficulty in planning and controlling the effective use of DDP within organizational units. Without proper planning and control, DDP becomes a fragmented, piecemeal activity with potential contributions to organizational objectives substantially compromised.

Historical Perspective

Before discussing the impact of DDP on organizations and approaches for planning and controlling the implementation of DDP, it is helpful to review the organizational and technological evolution that set the current stage for DDP.

1950s and 1960s. Implementation of computer technology in most organizations occurred with minimal planning and control relative to other major organizational activities. The general assumption was that application of computer technology was "good." Accordingly, it was to be implemented as rapidly as possible with minimal control. This laissez faire attitude often resulted in fragmented, disruptive implementation of a plethora of computer applications with directly associated escalating computing budgets.[1]

1970s. Alarmed and dismayed, in the early 1970s organizations began to seriously reevaluate the emergence of computer technology in their organizations.[2] Organizations attempted to "get their arms around" this runaway technology and its growing expense. This was commonly accomplished by organizations centralizing computing resources and personnel. Compelling arguments such as economy-of-scale of hardware, software, and personnel combined with less difficult planning and control made centralization an attractive strategy.

The centralization of computing resources often caused organizational instability and even trauma. Individual organization functions that had previously controlled their own computer services were placed into an environment in which they had to compete with other users for services from a centralized computer facility. This change to a single computing resource, although often more efficient, resulted in degradation of flexibility and responsiveness for users compared to what they had experienced when they had their own computers. However, the increased sophistication and capability that were often achieved by centralization tended to offset these losses to individual users.

After many organizations made a rather painful commitment to centralized computing for the sake of efficiency and control, new technology developments reversed one major argument for centralization of computing resources -- economies-of-scale. In the late 1960s and early 1970s, minicomputers and microprocessors started to offer alternatives to large centralized computers that, though not always as efficient, were often more effective.[3] In spite of this, DDP was generally not accepted. In fact, it was often resisted by organizations, particularly by those responsible for centralized computing who tended to view DDP as a threat to their centralized function. DDP, via minicomputers, was also unpopular with the major mainframe vendors. It was considered the "poor man's" approach to computing. But by the

---

[3] Richard L. Nolan, "Managing the Crises in Data Processing," *Harvard Business Review*, vol. 57, no. 2, March-April 1979, pp. 115-126.

[1] Robert N. Anthony, *Planning and Control Systems: A Framework for Analysis*, Harvard University, Boston, 1977.

[2] "Business Takes a Second Look at Computers," *Business Week*, June 5, 1971, pp. 59-136.

mid to late 1970s it was evident that technology had made DDP both more efficient and more effective for many applications. One key acknowledgment of the viability of DDP came with IBM's introduction of the series 1 in 1976. Up until that time, IBM did not publicly support DDP either in philosophy or with their product lines.

1980s. The 1980s show increasing pressure for greater decentralization of computing via DDP.[4] There is both "pull" and "push" pressure for such activity. Users "pull" existing applications or potential applications off of centralized computing as more specialized hardware and software provide "turnkey" systems to solve immediate problems. These are commonly applications that end-users are impatient to implement. When they perceive that they cannot get fast enough service from centralized facilities, they turn to DDP solutions for their problems. Applications may be more suitable for DDP than for a large centralized computer. For example, most attempts at word processing using centralized large-scale computers have failed severely compared with low-cost word processing minicomputers.

Centralized computing services are beginning to "push" applications off of centralized computing in an effort to maintain service levels and response time for constantly increasing and more diverse work loads. For example, organizations are commonly off-loading parts of databases onto minicomputers to allow for inquiry and data entry at remote sites. Access to the central computer is available only when local needs cannot reasonably be met locally.

Given the history and forecasted developments in DDP, what sort of organizational impact can be expected for typical organizations? To a great extent it depends upon the variables associated with an individual organization, but certain conclusions can be drawn which are noteworthy:

o As DDP technology proliferates, organizations will become increasingly dependent upon data processing in every aspect of business life, and associated problems in human engineering will surface as crucial issues.

o User data processing departments will gradually shift emphasis from applications programming to data administration, database design and control, and user education. A customer services function at user levels will grow in importance as the use of technology increases.

o End-users will become increasingly responsible for developing their own applications systems using specialized computer terminals, English query languages, and application generators.

---

[4]Charles K. Davis and James C. Wetherbe, "An Analysis of the Impact of Distributed Data Processing on Organizations in the 1980s," *MIS Quarterly*, vol. 3, no. 4, December 1979, pp. 47-56.

o Networks of data processing systems will evolve with some applications centralized and some decentralized on the basis of the needs of a specific organization. Data, voice, facsimile, and video communications will eventually be included.

o Access to timely information for operational and management decision making and forecasting will become ever more important as firms which have DDP become more competitive due to better decisions and better planning.

PROBLEMS WITH DDP: CASE STUDIES

Though the technology to support DDP is clearly available and the impact inevitable, organizations are having considerable difficulty absorbing DDP. Consider the following case studies:

DDP Disaster at a Hospital

A medium-sized hospital installed a minicomputer-based online system to support admissions and patient billing. They continued to use a large IBM system to handle related batch processing.

The primary advocate for the new system was a hospital administrator who had been sold on the system by a turnkey-software vendor. The system was a huge success -- initially. However, the hospital went through rapid growth during the next 2 years and exceeded the capacity of the minicomputer. The hospital subsequently faced two serious constraints. The minicomputer vendor did not offer a larger configuration, and the software vendor did not support other hardware types. The hospital held out for a year until the minicomputer vendor released a new, larger system. But the software vendor had to make extensive modifications to use the new computer, modifications the hospital was reluctant to make because of expense and perceived limited market potential. The hospital is now considering throwing out the whole system and starting over.

Word Processing Becomes Data Processing

A manufacturing manager installed some word processing (WP) equipment to support his office staff. The WP vendor demonstrated limited but useful data processing capabilities that were available on the WP equipment. Applications began to proliferate which quickly created two problems: The manufacturing manager exceeded the capacity of the WP equipment, and he needed to integrate his data with centralized databases to get the information he really required to do his job.

Both problems could have been easily resolved had the requirement for integration of the WP with centralized computing been recognized in the initial development of the system. Unfortunately, the only way to provide the manufacturing manager what he wants now is to virtually start over. Most of the software and hardware will have to be replaced to provide the interfaces and capabilities needed.

Cobwebs for DDP

A major university was suffering from high turnover and lack of qualified secretarial personnel. Faculty and administrators were complaining about the difficulty of getting manuscripts and correspondence completed.

Central administration decided word processing equipment was the answer. After evaluating a number of vendors' equipment, a system was selected and equipment purchased and distributed to various departments on campus. Training programs were conducted by the vendor.

Six months after implementation, a postaudit revealed the equipment was scarcely being used. One machine had never even been turned on and was sitting in a corner collecting cobwebs. The faculty continued to complain of poor typing support.

Other Case Studies

Organizations are becoming full of "war stories" where DDP implementations have become disastrous. Most disasters occur as a result of failing to:

- Select technology that is appropriate for the task in the short and/or long run
- Plan for integration requirements for hardware, software, and/or data
- Consider behavioral and organizational issues

The remainder of this chapter discusses issues in managing DDP and then presents a framework for planning and controlling DDP. The framework has been successfully implemented in a large multinational corporation.

ISSUES IN MANAGING DDP

DDP disasters can be avoided if implementations are properly planned, supported, and controlled. It is an oversimplification to say that DDP can be implemented better by use of more planning and control. However, planning and control of DDP are not trivial. Planning and control of large-scale systems are still a major challenge to most organizations. DDP systems are small and their implementation often goes undetected. They evolve quickly, and specific systems become obsolete sooner than larger computer systems.

DDP planning and control require careful coordination of short- and long-run strategies and of diverse technical and applications expertise.

Short- and Long-Range Strategies

The technology available and applications possible allow DDP to become extremely pervasive in organizations. A myriad of micro, mini, general, and hybrid computers are available for diverse applications.

By using telecommunications networking, these may be interconnected with other distributed systems or with large-scale mainframes. With somewhat minor upgrades to hardware or software, most distributed processors can be enhanced to do other functions beyond the scope of the originally intended applications. Consequently, the possibilities of developing incompatible systems, at one extreme, or of developing integrated interconnected systems, at the other, are equally feasible. Clearly, incompatible systems are unacceptable in the long term.

To address the issue of incompatibility, the approach proposed involves both a short- and long-range strategy. It is based upon the observation that organizations must build, in response to users' demands, information systems that solve today's problems, but will endure to meet long-range needs.

A short-range strategy may encourage the use of minicomputers to be used in areas where the cost/benefit ratio is highly compelling within a well-defined functional area. However, to control these applications and ensure future compatibility, the scope of these short-range applications must be tightly defined and controlled. Addition of applications to these minicomputers requires the same highly compelling short-range analysis as was required for the original applications. This short-range strategy allows the organization to respond to both "pull" and "push" demands for DDP without loss of control while a long-range strategy is developed and initiated.

The ability to respond to short-range requirements while a long-range plan is developed is critical. The end-users usually have administrative control over their DDP technology. DDP systems "belong" to end-users in the same sense that typewriters or photocopiers belong to various departments in an organization. If end-users feel that long-range planning efforts will be too constraining for their needs, they reasonably can be expected to resist centralized long-range DDP planning. If an adversary attitude develops, it can manifest itself as direct hostility or even as a series of power plays to gain independent control of DDP activities in various departments.

Therefore, until a solid long-range framework is established, many short-range, cost-effective decisions must be made with uncertainty about future design objectives. This is a necessary process to avoid loss of cooperation of end-users.

Sensitivity to long-range issues must be continually emphasized to end-users to reduce the probability of short-range decisions becoming long-range mistakes.

Expertise Requirements

Given that both short- and long-range strategies must be operative and coordinated, the next issue is who should conduct the necessary planning and control? Most organizations have some form of MIS steering committee or some other high-level group or individual to direct overall MIS planning. This group provides the broad, systemic organizational activities and interactions needed to accomplish organizational goals and objectives. However, specific technical expertise is also needed. The necessary technical expertise must be drawn from three areas:

- *End-users* have the expertise required to define the decision-making and operational support a DDP system is to provide.

- *Computer services (or data centers)* include highly specialized technical personnel who collectively have in-depth knowledge of hardware, software, and data communications technologies.

- *Information systems development* includes systems analysts and programmers who can design and develop application software systems. (This expertise may be centralized or decentralized according to the needs of the organization.)

These three groups must interact with others, as depicted in Figure 11-1, to ensure proper definition of user requirements, proper selection of DDP technology, and effective systems development for both the short and the long term.

FRAMEWORK FOR MANAGING DDP

With the need for short- and long-range planning described and the expertise requirements defined, it is now possible to construct a framework for selecting and implementing DDP systems.[5] Several key activities are required to select and implement successful DDP systems. These activities can be broadly categorized as

- Planning and control
- Processing environment management
- Requirements analysis

[5]Charles K. Davis and James C. Wetherbe, "Planning and Controlling Distributed Data Processing Systems," *Systems, Objectives, and Solutions,* McGraw-Hill, New York, 1981.

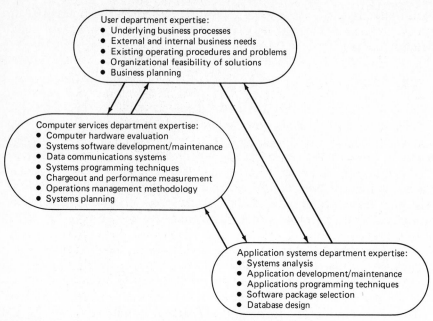

Figure 11-1 Areas of Expertise for Support of Systems Implementation Activities for DDP

- Systems development
- Implementation

Planning and Control

The centralized MIS steering committee, or a similar organizational entity, should assume primary responsibility for DDP planning and control. As discussed earlier, the MIS steering committee must draw from the collective knowledge of end-users, computer services personnel, and information systems personnel.

The MIS steering committee establishes both the systemic and the futuristic focus essential to managing DDP in an organization. Planning should be integrated with the long-range direction of the organization and define generic processing capabilities the organization will need in the long run. From this effort, the organization can develop a portfolio of DDP applications and set priorities for them for short-run projects. Once a strategic application becomes a project, it should be subjected to standard project management procedures and reporting for control.

The preceding discussion on planning and control is not dissimilar from a discussion on long- and short-run planning and control for any computer application. However, there are two important distinctions for DDP that require further consideration.

First, because of the rapid technological advances in DDP technology, technical, economical, and operational feasibility of applications can change dramatically with the introduction of a new product. For example, a new three-dimensional graphical microsystem is announced that can assist an organization's engineers. The application was not identified or included in the organization's DDP planning. There is a temptation to "put off" end-users because other applications come first. This can be a big mistake, causing loss of rapport with end-users and support for centralized DDP planning and control. When major technological developments occur, the MIS steering committee must be flexible enough to alter long-run plans for short-run advantages.

The second challenge to DDP planning and control is that application projects are not easily controlled. Most mature data processing organizations control applications development by controlling the activities of the organization's systems analysts and programmers (e.g., through project management) and by controlling computer utilization. However, end-users control their own DDP systems and often their own system development personnel, or they can buy system development services. Accordingly, DDP end-users can independently put on additional applications without regard to overall organizational considerations.

DDP has made it technically, economically, and operationally feasible to decentralize hardware, software, applications personnel, and data. However, organizations should not decentralize planning and control. Only through centralized planning and control can an organization maintain the systemic perspective necessary to properly manage the proliferation of DDP.

Initial and subsequent applications of DDP are reviewed and approved by the MIS steering committee like any centralized system project. End-user information systems and computer services will typically generate the ideas for DDP applications but no one group should proceed on their own, nor should one group be able to block a project. Project approval is the domain of the MIS steering committee, with technical assistance provided by end-users and by information systems and computer services personnel.

Processing Environment

The processing environment pertains to the hardware, operating software, and data communications that will be supported by the organization. The type of processing environment an organization has should be a function of planning and control and of existing and forecasted technology. Properly defining and managing the processing environment is critical for achieving compatible systems. With this effort fragmented, incompatible DDP efforts are virtually guaranteed.

The computer services group has the requisite expertise to manage the processing environment. Further, they can handle the necessary maintenance and enhancement activities to support DDP operating systems and data communication protocols. In this sense, the computer services group becomes a service organization to DDP end-users, which is the appropriate role for it. Too often DDP end-users are either neglected or considered adversaries of centralized computer services.

Requirements Analysis

The purpose of an information system is to support the decision making and operations of an organization. Accordingly, the impetus for acquiring a DDP system occurs when an organization recognizes an information need or operational situation that can be effectively supported by the use of computer technology. From a behavioral perspective, the best situation is when the impetus for a DDP system comes totally or partially from the end-user. This generates end-user commitment to a project. At a minimum, end-user personnel must be convinced of the benefit of a DDP project.

End-user personnel are in the best position to identify information or operational problems because they are closest to their problems and opportunities. However, additional useful support can be provided by the MIS steering committee and by computer services and information systems development personnel. The MIS steering committee has the broad organizational perspective needed to view information and operational problems that may not always be apparent to specific user departments. By virtue of resolving a broad spectrum of diverse organizational, informational, and operational problems, information systems and computer services personnel are usually highly innovative in requirements definition. These two groups are also the most familiar with the latest computer technology developments and can make suggestions that often have not even been considered by end-user personnel. They can also assist with feasibility analysis of possible solutions.

In summary, end-users will logically assume primary responsibility for informational or operational requirements with secondary support from the MIS steering committee and from information systems development and computer services personnel.

Systems Development

Systems development is concerned with developing detailed design specifications, defining a local and central data hierarchy, and developing the necessary software or selecting a software package.

Logically, these activities should be the primary responsibility of the information systems development group. They have the expertise to develop a logical and physical design and, in conjunction with database administration, can design the database.

The data structure for a DDP system must be carefully reviewed. Otherwise, redundancy and incompatibility occur that can set a DDP application back years when integration with a centralized or other decentralized database is attempted. Since data commonly transcends departmental and DDP boundaries, final data structure designs should be approved by the MIS steering committee.

Once the information-reporting capabilities are defined and the data structure resolved, the next question to be answered is whether to develop the system in house or purchase a package.

Purchasing packages has always been a risky proposition, but it offers considerable cost savings when done correctly. In the DDP environment, packages are even more complicated. Vendors are developing packages which, for all practical purposes, can be considered part of the operating software. The strong distinction between applications and operating systems software which exists for larger computer end-users is fading for smaller DDP systems.

Consequently, the ability to transfer and/or upgrade DDP packages can become a serious constraint. Computer services assistance is required when evaluating packages to avoid "painting oneself into a corner" with an application package. Once a decision between packages or in-house development is made, systems development can proceed.

Implementation

Implementation is perhaps the most neglected issue in non-DDP systems, so it comes as no surprise to find implementation neglected in DDP too. Implementation means change to everyone affected by the system. It is here that most behavioral problems occur. End-users exhibit dysfunctional behavior ranging from avoidance, or not using the system, to aggression, or deliberately fouling up the system.

We seem to accept that most people do not like change -- and behavioral resistance to change is a way of life. But some people do like change. If not, why do they buy the latest fashions, go to new restaurants, or voluntarily change jobs? People like change if they are controlling it and see that they will benefit from it.[6]

One lesson DDP should be teaching the centralized MIS professional is that end-users do like change if it is properly introduced. Some of the most successful DDP applications have occurred when end-users have bootlegged their systems into the organization. These systems are often technically and operationally inferior to systems that would have been

---

[6]James C. Wetherbe, *Systems Analysis for Computer-Based Information Systems,* West, St. Paul, Minn., 1979.

installed with the assistance of centralized MIS expertise. The end-users, however, are not about to be unhappy with the system, even when it is obvious the system was not the right choice. After all it is *their* system.

Ideally we would like to get this level of end-user commitment but with the advantages of information systems development and computer services expertise. How can we accomplish this? First, implementation must be under the direction of end-user personnel. The activities of implementation planning, end-user training, acceptance testing, and conversion should be directed by end-user management with assistance provided by information systems development and computer services personnel.

Second, implementation is not an activity to be considered after the system is developed. Rather, implementation planning and the implementation process itself should begin during the definition of informational and operational requirements analysis and parallel the entire systems development process. Only then are end-users able to see what is coming and able to influence it. Many decisions that will affect implementation are made during analysis, design, and development. These decisions result in changes, and end-users have the right to exercise some control over these decisions. Without such control, resistance can be expected.

APPLICATION OF THE FRAMEWORK

Table 11-1 summarizes the organizational interactions necessary to properly manage DDP. As indicated earlier, the framework presented in this chapter has been successfully implemented in a large multinational corporation. Since implementation, the company has not experienced the type of problems common to DDP proliferation.

Table 11-1 Organizational interaction for managing DDP

	End-user	Computer services	Information systems development	MIS steering committee
Planning & control	S	S	S	P
Processing environment	S	P	S	A
Requirements analysis	P	S	S	A
Systems development	A	S	P	A
Implementation	P	S	S	A

P = Primary responsibility.
S = Support role.
A = Approval.

Successful implementation of the framework is a good indication of its viability but it is not conclusive evidence. However, it is instructive to conduct an analysis of the case studies discussed earlier and postulate if the use of the framework could have been helpful in avoiding the problems experienced in these cases.

In the hospital case, a computer services review of the processing environment should have revealed the growth limitations of the minicomputer-based system. This information could have been used to either contractually obligate the vendor to provide for an upgrade or encourage the hospital to consider another alternative.

In the manufacturing case, a review by the information systems development group should have revealed that the systems and data structure being developed would be incompatible with the information systems eventually needed by the manufacturing group. A review by computer service personnel would have revealed the incompatibilities in the processing environment.

Finally, in the university case, end-users were not considered until implementation, and end-users did not control the implementation. A closer analysis of that case reveals that the end-users resented having a new system forced on them by central administration. The secretaries were threatened by the system; plus they had to leave their desks and go to another room to use the equipment. The system was never used because it did not support special symbols needed for mathematical notation.

Allowing end-users to plan for and manage implementation should have resulted in successful implementation. One department on campus that procured its own equipment through external funds was quite successful in implementing its system.

SUMMARY

DDP is, and will become even more of, a factor in the management and operation of organizations. There is clearly an important requirement for coordinating DDP activities within an organization. Each installation of a DDP system is an implementation of a large scale computing system in miniature. All of the traditional steps are included in varying degrees. Different organizational units have the expertise to support each step. Every implementation will have its own special problems and opportunities to be considered and evaluated within the team paradigm.

From a total organizational perspective, the major consideration in the implementation of DDP systems is not the distributed system itself. Rather, it is the development of an integrated, efficient, and effective DDP infrastructure capable of supporting data processing services in the future -- that is, the provision of systems that are flexible enough to evolve with changing corporate data processing needs, to grow to meet future needs of the end-user community, and to allow organizations to learn to use the technology effectively.

The development of integrated, or integrateable, distributed systems with a minimum of organizational disruption and confusion is therefore dependent upon teamwork among the various organizational units within which the enabling technical expertise resides. The team approach to planning and controlling DDP technology will allow organizations to reap the widely touted benefits of distributed technology -- that is, efficient and effective computing systems which can meet immediate needs now and which will continue to evolve and improve well into the future.

SUGGESTED READINGS

Anthony, Robert N., *Planning and Control Systems: A Framework for Analysis*, Harvard University, Boston, 1977.

Bostrom, Robert P., and J. Stephen Heinen, "MIS Problems and Failures: A Socio-Technical Perspective, Part 1: The Causes," *MIS Quarterly*, vol. 1, no. 3, September 1977, pp. 17-32.

_____and _____, "MIS Problems and Failures: A Socio-Technical Perspective, Part 2: The Applications of Socio-Technical Theory," *MIS Quarterly*, vol. 1, no. 4, December 1977, pp. 11-28.

Burnett, Gerald J., and Richard L. Nolan, "At Last, Major Roles for Minicomputers," *Harvard Business Review*, vol. 53, no. 3, May-June 1975, pp. 148-156.

"Business Takes a Second Look at Computers," *Business Week*, June 5, 1971, pp. 59-136.

Davis, Charles K., and James C. Wetherbe, "An Analysis of the Impact of Distributed Data Processing on Organizations in the 1980's," *MIS Quarterly*, vol. 3, no. 4, December 1979, pp. 47-56.

_____and _____, "Planning and Controlling Distributed Data Processing Systems," *Systems, Objectives, and Solutions*, McGraw-Hill, New York, 1981.

Gibson, Cyrus F., and Richard L. Nolan, "Managing the Four Stages of EDP Growth," *Harvard Business Review*, vol. 52, no. 1, January-February 1974, pp. 76-88.

Keen, Peter G. W., and Michael S. Scott Morton, *Decision Support Systems: An Organizational Perspective*, Addison-Wesley, Reading, Mass., 1978.

Lecht, Charles, *Waves of Change*, Advanced Computer Techniques Corp., New York, 1977.

McCosh, Andrew M., and Michael S. Scott Morton, *Management Decision Support Systems*, John Wiley, New York, 1978.

McFarlan, F. Warren, and Richard L. Nolan, *Information Systems Handbook*, Dow Jones-Irwin, Homewood, Ill., 1975.

McLean, E. R., "End Users as Applications Developers," *MIS Quarterly*, vol. 3, no. 4, December 1979, pp. 37-46.

Nolan, Richard L., "Managing the Crises in Data Processing," *Harvard Business Review*, vol. 57, no. 2, March-April 1979, pp. 115-126.

_____, *Managing the Data Resource Function*, West, St. Paul, Minn., 1977.

Wetherbe, James C., *Systems Analysis for Computer-Based Information Systems*, West, St. Paul, Minn., 1979.

Withington, Frederic G., "Coping with Computer Proliferation," *Harvard Business Review*, vol. 58, no. 3, May-June 1980, pp. 152-164.

TWELVE

ADVANCED OFFICE SYSTEMS

INTRODUCTION

This chapter is about advanced office systems. Increased capability, availability, and applicability of computing technology have resulted from reduction` in the cost and improvement in the efficiency of modern computers. Accordingly, many traditional organizational activities have become candidates for cost-effective support with computing technology. The changing economics of computers have created new applications of automation in office settings. Automating offices will be a great challenge for MIS professionals and organizations in the 1980s.

Productivity of office workers is currently receiving increased attention. In the 1960s, blue-collar productivity increased 83 percent because of various forms of automation.[1] During the same period, office-worker productivity increased only 4 percent. Capital investment per blue-collar worker averaged $24,000 during that decade. The corresponding figure for office workers is only $2000. The white collar proportion of the labor force is growing dramatically (reaching approximately 50 percent by 1980). The costs of operating offices are also increasing (often estimated at 10 percent of revenues for a large corporation). These figures, while they are only estimates, do indicate that a potential exists for improving an organization's economic standing through the implementation of systems to improve white-collar

---

[1] Alan Purchase and Carl F. Glover, "Office of the Future," SRI Long-Range Planning Service, no. 1001, April 1976.

productivity. Not too surprisingly, MIS managers have been advised to keep abreast of this automated office technology.

As with other kinds of computer implementations, effective use of office systems applications are lagging behind the availability of potentially cost-effective technology from vendors. This lag in successful implementation is due to three major factors that can be broadly categorized as technological, organizational, and behavioral. From a technological viewpoint, there is considerable confusion and misunderstanding surrounding the actual focus, capabilities, and degree of sophistication of various advanced office system offerings that are currently available. Similarly, due to the evolving nature of this technology, there are new approaches and new systems appearing continually. Within this proliferation of technology, a fairly wide consensus of opinion about the *basic* functions for advanced office systems is beginning to emerge. Accordingly, a functionally based taxonomy of the various office systems is now possible. Development of such a taxonomy is the first objective of this chapter.[2]

Beyond understanding office technology and its application, successful implementation of advanced office systems requires an understanding of the impact of this technology upon the work done in an office and the organizational and behavioral aspects of the office setting. Organizations are, for the most part, not prepared to assimilate advanced computing systems. There are essential educational, organizational, and behavioral dimensions to be considered before attempting the "office of the future." Examining these issues and relating them to the various functions of current and future automated office technology is the second objective of this chapter.

The taxonomy of advanced office systems and the organizational and behavioral issues addressed should help organizations to better plan, coordinate, and implement office automation technology.

TAXONOMY OF ADVANCED OFFICE SYSTEMS

The basic operating units for advanced office systems are "work stations." They may be any of several types of terminals for interfacing with a centralized mainframe computer or with a distributed minicomputer (which may be linked to larger mainframes or other distributed minicomputers, as appropriate).

Advanced office systems are used to describe many different kinds of systems. The underlying concepts tend to be unclear and confusing in

---

[2]The taxonomy presented is based upon work originally done by C. Dykman, C. Davis, and J. Wetherbe, "Taxonomy of Automated Office Systems and Critical Factors in Their Implementation," MIS Research Center Working Paper, April 1981.

practical applications. Thus, it is appropriate to take a functional approach when considering advanced office systems. Four categories of functions will be discussed in this chapter:[3]

- Document processing
- Electronic mail systems
- Executive support systems
- MIS interface

Document Processing Systems

Document processing systems consist of standard word processing applications. Included are correspondence preparation, forms preparation, general text-editing functions, an automatic spelling dictionary, and an electronic filing capability. These systems primarily augment the duties of secretaries (and are sometimes confused as encompassing all of office automation).

Correspondence preparation includes formal document preparation for a principal by a secretary, such as letters, memos, etc. This is the document or word processing function. Forms preparation includes a set of electronic video screens that are posted on a terminal as needed. These provide electronic forms for travel, training, personnel action, payroll history, etc.

A powerful text editor is a prerequisite for the creation, formatting, and updating function, and this area is often the focus of critical evaluation of available systems. Likewise, an electronic dictionary that can detect and identify misspelled words in the text is an important feature and has become a requirement in word processing systems.

A storage-and-retrieval system for electronic filing of documents provides a facility for filing standard paragraphs and work-in-progress documents and serves as an archive of documents with specified periods of retention.

Electronic Mail Systems

Electronic mail systems provide a facility for the composition and editing of messages, notes, and similar informal communications and for the transmission of electronic messages to other persons on the automated "mail-room" facility. Sending capabilities support transmissions to individual addresses and distribution lists or broadcast to all members on specified mailing lists. Standard messages can also be generated. Finally, a filing-and-retrieval capability manages the mail that is received and provides for access to correspondence by author, date, address, etc.

---

[3]This framework is based upon the work of C. Dykman, C. Davis, and J. Wetherbe, op. cit.

Executive Support Systems

Executive support systems consist of a series of online, storage-and-retrieval modules and files that support general executive functions with automated services used directly by executives to perform their work more effectively and more efficiently. These systems are presently available at various levels of sophistication. Simple executive support systems are often developed in house for particular applications. The executive support systems available include calendars, directories, tickler files, and calculator packages.

Automated calendar facilities commonly include three subfunctions: a personal calendar, a public calendar, and a calendar of events. The "personal calendar" is maintained by the executive to provide a chronology of planned activities. The "public calendar" is a planning vehicle that allows coordinators to efficiently schedule groups of individuals for participation in required activities. The "calendar of events" is another view of the scheduling data that must be tracked and involves entities external to the department.

The "directories" are retrievable (and modifiable) lists of key officials, important telephone numbers, and other basic listed data that is of use to the executive. Similarly, the "tickler files" are lists of projects to be done ("to do" lists), lists of staff assignments and deadlines, and lists of action items that are outstanding. The tickler file allows an executive to schedule future reminders. These listings support the executive in project control efforts and assist him or her in tracking progress on work efforts for which he or she may be accountable.

Finally, "calculator functions" are easily used modules for doing simple arithmetic calculations at the executive work station. The modules allow the executive to perform calculations as needed at the same work station that is used for the other support functions.

MIS Interface

Management information systems have, of course, been used prior to the advent of office automation. However, the advanced office concept provides for more tailored, local MIS support as well as links into traditional corporate MIS capabilities such as personnel or operational control systems. Consequently, advanced office systems are an extension of and an enhancement to existing MIS technology. These systems are sets of online computing programs and files that provide the executive with generally routine decision-making information.

Depending on their use, some programs and files may reside on a large-scale centralized computer, while others reside locally on a minicomputer. Whatever the physical arrangement of hardware and data, managers are provided, at their work stations, with easy and timely access to information that was previously unavailable or difficult to acquire. These information systems consist of business systems as defined below:

- *Organizational data systems* consist of records of budgets, personnel, property, and similar departmental data. This information may have been available to management previously; however, having the key information electronically on file and readily accessible increases the potential for effective use of the information.

- *Decision support models* are sets of programmed models and queries that manipulate current data files regarding business operations or planning forecasts and provide a basis for management decisions.

- *Project monitoring systems* provide periodic status reports and tracking information for assessing the progress of business projects. In the simplest form, these are project management and reporting systems, but they also include business systems for monitoring a wide range of ongoing business efforts.

- *Electronic filing systems* entail a simple and convenient facility for indexing, storing, and retrieving documents and correspondence that an executive decides to keep in his or her personal online files.

Table 12-1 provides a list of the basic functions of advanced office technology and their primary levels of use. It is important to properly define the organizational levels affected by the proposed automated technology. The economic justifications necessary for successful implementation of this technology differ according to the organizational level (e.g., management, staff, clerical, or secretarial) to be augmented by the systems proposed. Differentials in costs and types of work for personnel at various organizational levels support the rationale for incorporation of the organizational focus into any technical evaluations performed.

CRITICAL FACTORS IN OFFICE AUTOMATION

Technical evaluation and economic justification are only two steps to be performed in successfully introducing automated technology into the office. Though the office of the future is possible today, there are noneconomic considerations that often impede the successful implementation of this technology. Those responsible for office systems

Table 12-1 Taxonomy of advanced office systems

Application	Organizational level
Document processing systems	
Corresponding preparation	
Forms preparation	
Text editing	Secretarial
Spelling dictionary	
Electronic filing capability	
Electronic mail systems	
Composition of messages	
Editing of messages	
Electronic transmission of messages	Managerial/executive
Standard message generation	and secretarial
File and retrieval capability	
Executive support systems	
Calendars	
Dictionaries	Managerial/executive
Tickler files	
Calculator packages	
MIS interface	
Organizational data systems	
Decision support models	
Program monitoring systems	Managerial/executive
Electronic filing systems	
Electronic bulletin board	

implementation must focus on these elements and make the appropriate plans, decisions, changes, etc., in order to achieve success. These decisions differ according to the office functions to be automated as well as factors which are unique to the organization itself. This relationship is examined in the following analysis under two aspects: behavioral and organizational.

Behavioral Aspects

Advanced office systems often represent the first direct exposure of office workers to computing hardware and software. Automation is likely to change their daily work activities. Because of this, successful implementation demands that workers be motivated to use these systems and adapt to the technology and its impact on their work patterns. This motivation is made easier when there is a well-designed approach to implementation that considers the systems' impact on work groups, job definitions, and management styles. An overview of this impact follows.

Group Structure. A distinct advantage of advanced office systems is that they facilitate the communication of work groups. Important information can be easily disseminated to managers and their subordinates for timely action. However, in order for this to be successful, an accurate assessment must be made of the dynamism of such groups. For example, if group structure changes frequently, an electronic mail system should adapt to these changes quickly. System implementers must recognize that such mail systems will reduce the need for face-to-face contact among work group members. For groups where social contact is important, the impact may be negative. Conversely, groups where communication was seriously hindered by time commitments or distance may find that communication is much easier and control is potentially more effective.

The implementation of document processing systems often results in a pooled or clustered approach to classifying activities. A group may have previously consisted of a manager, his or her workers, and a secretary; however, with a pool or cluster, the group will need to rely on several secretaries to accomplish the work. Acknowledging such changes and assuring managerial personnel of a high level of service is important in generating their support for the implementation of document processing systems. Likewise, assisting secretaries in adjusting to work inputs from several sources is crucial to successful implementation of a clustered or pooled system.

Management Style. Office systems often serve as the foundation to provide information to managers in planning, organizing, and controlling activities. As such, developers of advanced office systems must address each manager's approach to these activities. For example, a manager who prefers to make decisions intuitively may not find statistical analyses or summarizations very helpful in his or her decision-making effort.

There is no one best way to design management information systems, which must enhance and complement the style that an individual manager uses in planning, organizing, and controlling activities. Understanding the way in which each individual performs managerial tasks allows the selection and development of systems that closely meet requirements as they exist, rather than expecting an executive to significantly change his or her management style and approach to match a new system.

Job Redesign. Job redesign or redefinition is a major element in automating office functions. Office automation can be expected to change the nature of daily work within organizations. At the secretarial level, workers will become involved in more technical computing-based work efforts. At higher levels in the organization, daily work activities will change as managers and staff personnel learn to use various information systems that will allow them to make better use of their time and make more informed decisions.

Systems designers must identify the components of each job that will be affected by office systems implementation. Documentation of the changes will result from automating the various functions, and recognition of these changes, by restructuring rewards, upgrading work status and titles, and providing necessary support, is a key issue to address in this area.

There is a learning curve effect associated with previously nontechnical users who begin to utilize newly automated facilities. As a result, employees must be motivated to expend the extra effort needed to learn and supervisors must be ready to accept less than optimal performance in the early stages of implementation. Effective motivation is more likely if those who are implementing office systems attempt to match the equipment to the work groups that exist and to the styles of managers. At the same time, job descriptions and remuneration should acknowledge the inherently higher skill levels needed, particularly at the clerical level.

Addressing the behavioral issues discussed will help to limit the demotivating factors associated with changes to work patterns and provide the incentive needed for success.

Organizational Aspects

Organizational considerations concern those attributes which are descriptive of the organization itself rather than of particular people within the organization. Research in complex organizations has resulted in an understanding that organizational structure and size, the organizational climate, and the distribution of power within an organization are all significant variables to be considered when major changes such as office automation are being introduced. The automation of office functions within an organization involves major change, and the following analysis illustrates the major impacts that must be anticipated.

Organizational Structure. The structure of an organization, centralized or decentralized, simple or complex, highly formalized or more informal, will often determine the type of system to be installed. For instance, a highly centralized, simple organization with formalized procedures may indicate that a time-sharing document processing system across the organization will be best; alternatively, a decentralized complex organization with little formalization may mandate stand-alone systems tailored specifically to meet departmental requirements. There is also a more subtle consideration related to organizational structures. The management personnel in charge of automating office functions should be located at the appropriate organizational level, which is normally the highest level affected by the implementation. If this level of management is aware of what is being done, its support of the project, which is crucial for successful implementation, is thereby secured.

Organizational Size. The size of the organization is most important because of the resources at its disposal for the implementation process. As a result, the cost-effectiveness of the various systems and the approach to system design and ongoing support may depend upon size.

A smaller organization may need to use consultants during the design process, contract externally for the necessary training, and use a time-sharing service to access organizational data systems and decision support packages. Such an organization may require a smaller volume of documents to be processed, filed, or electronically mailed. With the decreasing cost of computers, many small companies are increasingly capable of cost-justifying automated office systems. However, it will often be necessary to take a detailed but flexible approach to developing the potentially most cost-effective design with close monitoring of the cost savings realized.

A larger organization may have the resources needed for all steps in the process. In such organizations, a specific group may be charged with support and integration of office automation into existing manual and data processing systems. This type of group may be able to consider long-term investments, both in capital and in personnel, and cope with longer-term payback issues.

Organizational Climate. The climate of the organization -- the internal atmosphere of tension, stress cooperation, warmth, support, etc. -- affects the successful automation of various office functions. For example, an organization that exhibits a high degree of tension and distrust with little cooperation among organizational members may be impacted negatively by executive support systems that assist managers in tighter control of their subordinates' activities.

As a result, system designers must realize that organizational development and team-building efforts may be needed prior to the implementation of an office system. The climate may limit the types of systems which can be successfully installed unless there are serious efforts made to prepare the organization for these systems. The social system, including working groups and worker attitudes, and the technical system, including the facilities provided, training efforts, and user friendliness, should be coordinated for the implementation to be successful.[4] ,[5]

Power Distribution. The various types of power that exist in an organization can greatly affect the implementation of new systems. An organization may be formally centralized with legitimate power existing

---

[4]Robert P. Bostrom and J. Stephen Heinen, "MIS Problems and Failures: A Socio-Technical Perspective, Part 1: The Causes," *MIS Quarterly,* vol. 1, no. 3, September 1977.

[5]_____ and _____, "MIS Problems and Failures: A Socio-Technical Perspective, Part 2: The Application of Socio-Technical Theory," *MIS Quarterly,* vol. 1, no. 4, December 1977.

at a corporate level, but informal power may reside within component departments where various "experts" may influence the acceptance of the systems implemented. Analysis of this situation indicates that these "experts" must be involved in system design and implementation. The power nodes may not be readily apparent from studying the organizational chart; however, identification and use of the "opinion leaders" have been shown to be crucial to successful implementation of technological innovations.

Organizational Environment. Factors that are external to an organization are referred to as "environmental factors." There are two major environmental influences to be considered in the implementation strategy for automated office systems: the competitive environment of the organization and governmental regulations and influence.

The "competitive environment" concerns the issues of competitive advantage to be gained or lost as well as the knowledge and experience to be transferred as the result of the implementation of advanced systems technology. A planning strategy should concern itself with these issues in assessing office automation strategy. Competitive advantage assessments are concerned with identifying those competitors who are gaining or could gain significant advantages by implementing office automation. These advantages could be gained through increased productivity, cost reductions, faster and more effective response to customers, etc.

Additionally, it is important to understand the experiences of others with the new technology. Transfer of knowledge can prevent "reinvention of the wheel." When evaluating office automation, it is useful to determine what other organizations, particularly competitors, have done with these systems. Vendors as well as users of office automation are good sources of such information and systematic efforts to learn from others' efforts in this area of technology will be an important aspect of strategic planning.

The second organizational environment factor, governmental regulations, will also affect automated office systems, particularly in the areas of communications systems technology, privacy legislation, and antitrust actions against major vendors, such as IBM and AT&T. These actions by the government may limit the scope and change the basic rules for permissible office system technology.

Accordingly, it is important to systematically evaluate the regulatory situation as it will affect proposed systems. This evaluation should include tariff regulations related to communication capabilities and restrictions on electronic mail transmissions. Likewise, governmental actions may open new markets. An example can be seen in the approval of electronic funds transfer systems. Systems planners must design flexible systems which can adapt to changing regulations, and at the same time must predict these changes in order to position the organization to take advantage of new opportunities as they become feasible.

SUMMARY

This chapter has presented the basic functional structure of automated office systems, focusing on the implementation of these systems and the array of factors that must be considered in planning and executing such implementations. The prime conclusion to be drawn is that the implementation of advanced office systems must involve careful assessment of many factors besides the actual electronic technical feasibility of the office systems, including the lack of technical sophistication on the part of users at all organizational levels. The importance of these factors differs, depending upon the application being considered. A careful assessment and a systematic approach are necessary if successful implementation of these systems is to be reasonably anticipated by office managers.

SUGGESTED READINGS

Aldefer, Clayton P., *Existence, Relatedness and Growth,* Free Press, New York, 1972.

Argyris, Chris, "Management Information Systems, The Challenge to Rationality and Emotionality," *Management Science,* vol. 17, no. 6, February 1971.

Bostrom, Robert P., and J. Stephen Heinen, "MIS Problems and Failures: A Socio-Technical Perspective, Part 1: The Causes," *MIS Quarterly,* vol. 1, no. 3, September 1977.

_____and _____, "MIS Problems and Failures: A Socio-Technical Perspective, Part 2: The Application of Socio-Technical Theory," *MIS Quarterly,* vol. 1, no. 4, December 1977.

Burnett, Gerald J., and Richard Nolan, "At Last, Major Roles for Mini-Computers," *Harvard Business Review,* May-June 1975.

Canning, Richard G. (ed.), "The Human Side of Office Automation," *EDP Analyzer,* vol. 20, no. 5, May 1982, pp. 1-12.

Davis, Charles K., and James C. Wetherbe, "A Framework for Supporting and Controlling the Implementation of Distributed Data Processing Systems," *Systems, Objectives, Solutions,* April 1981, pp. 79-87.

Dykman, Charlene A., Charles K. Davis, and James C. Wetherbe, "A Taxonomy of Automated Office Systems and Critical Factors in Their Implementation," MIS Research Center Working Paper, April 1981.

Emery, F. E., and E. L. Trist, "The Casual Texture of Organizational Environments," *Human Relations,* vol. 18, no. 1, February 1965.

Fielder, Fred, *A Theory of Leadership Effectiveness*, McGraw-Hill, New York, 1967.

Gibson, James L., John M. Ivancevich, and James H. Donnelly, *Organizations: Behavior, Structure, and Process*, Business Publications, Dallas, 1976.

Guest, R. H., "Job Enlargement, A Revolution in Job Design," *Personnel Administration*, January 1957.

Hall, Richard, *Organizations-Structure and Process*, Prentice-Hall, Englewood Cliffs, N.J., 1977.

Herzberg, F., B. Mausner, and B. Syderman, *The Motivation to Work*, John Wiley, New York, 1959.

Hosage, Dan A., "The Advent of the Electronic Office," *Telecommunications*, September 1979, p. 57.

Ivancevich, John M., Andrew Szilagyi, and Marc Wallace, *Organizational Behavior and Performance*, Goodyear Publishing, Santa Monica, California, 1977.

Katz, Daniel, and Robert Kahn, *Social Psychology of Organizations*, John Wiley, New York, 1978.

Kircher, Jake, "Keep Abreast of WP, DP Managers Advised," *Computerworld*, vol. 14, no. 10, March 10, 1980.

Kleeman, Walter B., Jr., "The Future of the Office," *Environment and Behavior*, vol. 14, no. 5, September 1982, pp. 593-610.

Likert, Rensis, *The Human Organization*, McGraw-Hill, New York, 1967.

Litwin, G. H., and R. A. Stringer, *Motivation and Organizational Climate*, Harvard Graduate School of Business Administration, Boston, 1968.

Maslow, Abraham, *Motivation and Personality*, Harper and Row, New York, 1954.

"Office of the Future: Facts or Fantasy," *Infosystems*, vol. 23, no. 3, March 1980.

Pugh, Derek S., David J. Hickson, C. R. Hinnings, K. M. Lupton, K. M. McDonald, C. Turner, and T. Lupton, "A Conceptual Scheme for Organizational Analysis," *Administrative Science Quarterly*, vol. 8, No. 3, December 1963.

Purchase, Alan, and Carl F. Glover, "Office of the Future," SRI: Business Intelligence Program, no. 1001, April 1976.

Roberts, Karlene H., Chas. O'Reilly, Gen. Bretton, and Lyman Porter, "Organizational Theory and Organizational Communications: A Communication Failure?" *Human Relations*, vol. 27, no. 4, May 1974.

Rogers, Everett, and Floyd Shoemaker, *Communication of Innovations*, 2nd ed., Free Press, New York, 1971.

Scanlon, B., *Principles of Management and Organizational Behavior*, John Wiley, New York, 1973.

Schein, E. H., "Management Development as a Process of Influence," *Industrial Review*, vol. 2, no. 2, 1961.

Seashore, Stanley E., "Group Cohesiveness in the Industrial Work Group," Ann Arbor Institute of Social Research, 1954.

Terreberry, Shirley, "The Evolution of Organizational Environments," *Administration Science Quarterly,* vol. 12, no. 4, March 1968.

Wetherbe, James C., *Systems Analysis for Computer-Based Information Systems,* West, St. Paul, Minn., 1979.

_____, Charlene Dykman, and Charles K. Davis, "Implementing Automated Office Systems," *Journal of Systems Management,* August 1981.

_____, and Carlton J. Whitehead, "A Contingency View of Managing the Data Processing Organization," *MIS Quarterly,* vol. 1, no. 1, March 1977.

Wohl, Amy D., "Strategic Planning for Office Automation," presented January 14, 1981, University of Minnesota, Minneapolis.

THIRTEEN

ROBOTICS AND MIS

INTRODUCTION

A midwestern manufacturing firm had enjoyed a solid market share and respectable profitability since the creation of the firm over 50 years ago. Then, almost overnight, it lost both market share and profitability. Alarmed and dismayed, the president of the company ordered a study to determine what had happened. The study revealed that a foreign competitor was now supplying a lower-cost, higher-quality product. How could they do this? Robotics. The president wanted to know why his company had not exploited robotics technology to maintain its competitive advantage. Who was to blame? He decided that robots were essentially computers and since the MIS executive is in charge of that technology, he must be to blame.

As with telecommunications, advanced office systems, and personal computing, it is not clear with robotics who is responsible for corporate strategy, policy, and implementation. One thing is for sure: The MIS executive is ill-advised not to get "up to speed" on robotics and at least offer leadership in the emerging area of robotics.

The objective of this chapter is to review the basics of robotics. Specifically the chapter defines

- Robotics
- The trends in robotics
- The organizational and social impacts of robotics
- The recommended courses of action for MIS management

ROBOTICS

What do the jobs of a sheepshearer in Australia, a welder in Detroit, and a quality control inspector for calculators in Dallas have in common? Each can now be performed 24 hours a day, 7 days a week, without a mistake or a union. How? Each of the jobs is performed by an industrial robot.

The industrial robot, or "steel-collar worker," is the latest form of automation -- a programmable, flexible machine that can be taught anything from sheepshearing to welding. The application of robots is found primarily in the auto industry (50 percent) today, but it is expected to expand into virtually all industries by 1990. Technological improvements and growing experience with the use of robots are driving down robot prices and increasing their capabilities. Managers and workers at all levels of various-sized industries will be affected by robots at some time in the future.

Definition of "Robot"

What is a robot? Mechanical creatures that perform human functions have been in the science fiction literature for centuries. However, the term "robot" did not exist until 1921 when a Czech playwright named Karel Kapek dubbed the mechanical creatures in his play *robata*, which is the Czech word for "forced labor."[1]

The modern definition of robot varies from country to country. The Japanese broadly define a robot as any machine that has moving parts and is programmable. The Robot Institute of America defines a robot as a "reprogrammable multifunctional manipulator designed to move material, parts, tools, or specialized devices through variable programmed motions for the performance of a variety of tasks."[2] In simpler terms, the American definition means that a robot can be programmed many times to manipulate (grasp and move) things (e.g., parts, sheep, calculators) in different ways.

Description of Robots

Industrial robots are basically mechanical arms bolted to the floor. The power systems in robots are pneumatic, hydraulic, or electrical. Prices of robots range from $10,000 to $125,000 depending upon their

---

[1]Marvin Grosswirth, "The Robots Are Coming," *Datamation*, vol. 24, no. 12, Nov. 15, 1978, pp. 146-150.

[2]Leopold Froehlich, "Robots to the Rescue," *Datamation*, vol. 27, no. 1, January 1981, pp. 84-104.

Turret: A single arm swivels around a floor-mounted base and is capable of moving in and out and raising itself up or down. It looks much like a tank turret. Maximum capacity if 450 pounds.

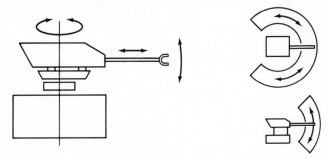

Figure 13-1 Illustration of Turret Robot

sophistication. There are basically two categories of industrial robots: nonservo-controlled and servo-controlled. Non-servo robots, also known as "pick-and-place" or "point-to-point" robots, are the simplest type of robots, accounting for one-third of all U.S. installations. Most models handle 5- to 30-pound loads and are used in materials handling--picking something from one spot and placing it at another. Freedom of movement is usually limited to two or three directions: in and out, left and right, and up and down. These robots are usually operated pneumatically and are electromechanically controlled. Prices range from $5000 to $30,000. Servo-controlled robots are the robots usually seen in car commercials welding cars. Servo robots contain one or more servomechanisms that enable the arm and gripper (or hand) to alter direction in midair. Five to seven directional movements are common, depending upon the number of "joints" in the robot's arm. These robots can move on a continuous path, which means it can follow an irregular (nonlinear) route. Prices range from $25,000 to $125,000.

Servo-controlled robots come in three basic types: turret, horizontal arm, and jointed arm. Each type of robot is illustrated in Figures 13-1 to 13-3.

Figure 13-2 Illustration of Horizontal Arm Robot

Horizontal arm: A rigid arm can be moved up and down, around a post, and in and out. Maximum capacity is 2000 pounds.

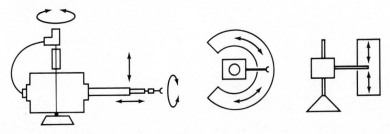

Jointed arm: The arm can lift objects up to 12 feet from the floor and can reach out from base. Maximum capacity is 225 pounds.

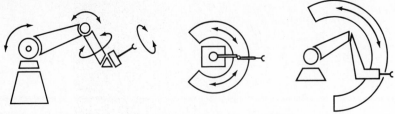

Figure 13-3 Illustration of Jointed Arm Robot

What really makes servo robots unique is the way they are programmed or "taught" to do their jobs. Servo robots can be trained using two methods:

- *Walk-through.* The user physically guides the robot's arm through the desired motions. The robot remembers the sequence and repeats it later.

- *Plug-in.* Using a push-button pendant or a data terminal keyboard the user tells the robot what motions to perform and the instructions are stored in the computer's memory for repetition later.

Teaching a servo robot can easily be accomplished in less than one hour per job; and once trained, the robot never forgets. Some servo robots can even be programmed to improve their own movements as required to perform a task.

History of Robotics

The industrial robot was the brainchild of George Devol, Jr., who patented his first robot in 1956. Devol teamed up with another robotics pioneer, Joseph Engelberger, and in 1958 formed Unimation Inc. Unimation installed its first robot in a General Motors plant in 1961.

In 1961, Engelberger felt the demand for industrial robots would be 1000 units per year.[3] He saw robots as the answer to declining U.S. productivity and quality. What suddenly made the concept of robots economical was a combination of rising labor costs and lower production costs, thanks to transistors and the digital capability of computers, which reduced the component cost and size while increasing reliability. The

[3]Bruce Hoard, "URI Researchers Set Sights on Robot Vision," *Computerworld*, vol. 15, no. 12, Mar. 12, 1981, pp. 37-38.

robot worked ideally under adverse environmental conditions doing jobs few workers desired. Unfortunately, in 1961 the world did not yet perceive the value of an industrial robot.

Several manufacturers, however, did see the potential for robots. AMF, Borg Warner, Hughes Tool, and General Mills all attempted to get into the robotics business in the 1960s, but failed. During the 1960s, most robots cost $60,000 to build and sold for only $25,000.

Despite early setbacks, the robot industry stayed alive, mostly overseas. In 1969, a Japanese firm, Kawasaki Heavy Industries, entered a licensing agreement with Unimation to produce and sell robots in Japan. The Japanese were clearly ready for robots. Kawasaki led Japan in its push to become the world's largest user of robots. Japan's success with robots sparked further interest in Europe, the Soviet Union, and the United States. The rest of the story is a robotics dream.

By 1974, the world wanted robots. Continuing advances in microelectronics and the experience gained with robots during the 1960s caused sales of Unimation, the world's largest robot manufacturer, to mushroom from $8 million in 1974 to $35 million in 1980. Encouraged by Unimation's success, dozens of smaller firms have joined the market and several corporate giants -- General Electric, IBM, and General Motors -- are forming robotics divisions.

Demand for robots is projected to grow at 30 to 40 percent per year in the 1980s. Robot sales worldwide are expected to exceed $3 billion by 1990. The next question is "What are the future trends in the robotics industry?"

TRENDS IN THE ROBOTICS INDUSTRY

Robotics Marketplace

Robots have made their greatest gains in the industry where the first robot was installed -- automobile manufacturing. American, Japanese, Italian, German, Swedish, and British automakers are doing their best to increase the productivity and quality of robots. The auto industry has a large number of simple, dirty jobs requiring a unionized, semiskilled laborer. The laborer costs about $15 an hour. The robot that replaces him or her costs $4.80 an hour to operate and does not complain or go on strike.

The primary functions where robots have successfully replaced workers are as follows:

- Palletizing material
- Forging
- Spraying

- Packaging
- Grinding, deburring, and polishing
- Simple assembly
- Machine loading and unloading
- Inspection
- Welding

Most robots in industry today are used in one of three areas: material movement, welding, or spraying.

Two factors have slowed the implementation of robots in other industries besides the auto industry: large start-up costs ranging from $50,000 to $120,000 and the lack of versatility of existing robots.

Costs of Robots

In spite of impressive cost reductions due to technology breakthroughs, most robot manufacturers are still small-job shops. What this means is that we have yet to produce robots in sufficient numbers to take advantage of the learning curve and economies-of-scale. So far, only the Japanese have begun using robots to produce other robots. Larger volumes and increased competition should drop robot prices by an order of magnitude in the next decade. In fact, there are already some $10,000 robots on the market.

Also, governments are stepping in to help firms purchase robots. In April 1980, the Japanese ministry of technology, MIRI, set up a robot-leasing company called JAROL to help promote the use of robots in Japan. Through JAROL, Japanese firms can lease robots to use in their facilities. During its first year of operation, JAROL leased over $5.5 million worth of robots. In the United States and Europe, tax incentives for investment in new capital equipment like robots have been discussed to boost productivity and keep up with the Japanese.

The bottom line is that robots are becoming cheaper, and we will see them not only in the auto industry, but in other industries as well.

Versatility of Robots

A robot that loads uniformly sized boxes on a pallet all day is fine, but not .of much use in assembly or any other operation. The point is that in the past robots were big, dumb hydraulic arms. They were effective only for a limited number of applications. Today's microprocessors are changing that. The welding robot on a General Motors line can now recognize the type of car coming down the line and weld accordingly. At Texas Instruments, a robot tests the functions on a calculator and "reads" the calculator display. The latest robots can be taught to do a variety of tasks accurately and quickly. In the United States, where 75 percent of all assembly jobs are made up of multiple tasks, this yields a great deal of potential for robots.

Robot Markets in the 1980s

Robots will probably continue to be most successful at simple jobs in harsh environments: spot welding, spray painting, forging, etc. The technology of such robots is proven and simple.

The Japanese, in fact, have chosen to continue with technologically very simple robots for most applications. The rationale is to start simple and gain experience in implementing and using robots before attempting to use a complicated state-of-the-art robot for a critical assembly.

Robots will most likely be used in the following types of jobs:

- Hostile or dangerous areas where injuries are a recurring problem
- Multiple-shift operations where one robot can replace several people
- Boring and repetitive jobs, where absenteeism is high because people really do not want to do the work
- Fatiguing operations where people get tired and dnot perform as well at the end of the day as they do at the beginning
- Problem areas where operator errors are frequent or where product damage is high

Beyond the 1980s, it is only a question of technology and imagination to guess how rapidly robots will advance into the workplace. Some industry analysts believe robots could replace 65 to 75 percent of the factory work force. Let's take a look at some of the trends in technology that could help make such a prediction reality.

TECHNOLOGICAL INNOVATIONS

The United States developed the first industrial robot and continues to hold the edge in new robotics technology, although the Japanese are quickly catching up. The primary objective in robotics development is to achieve a totally automated factory where humans do maintenance and supervision only. The Japanese plan to have their first prototype open in the 1980s. The Italians plan such a facility by 1990. In Japan, one robot manufacturer already operates three shifts with nothing but a skeleton crew of humans to help the robots.

The success of the automated factory depends upon the development of flexible and adaptable robots. In order to become adaptable, robots must respond to a continuously changing environment -- they must have senses and the ability to make decisions. This section reviews developments to date in the areas of sight, touch, and artificial intelligence and what can be expected in the decades ahead.

Sight

The most important sense according to robotic experts is sight. Sight will enable robots to adjust to small changes in their work environment, giving them greater flexibility. The challenge is to develop a vision system that will enable a robot to see a part in a bin, recognize it, and pick it up. Picking up parts out of a bin is trivial for humans, but it would be a giant step for a robot.

Artificial vision systems to date have no problem recognizing parts lying singly on a flat surface. Television cameras compare the image of what the robot sees to standard images stored in its memory. The television picture is digitized to reduce the number of bits of information required from 2.5 million to 10,000. The biggest drawbacks to these systems, besides their being two dimensional, are cost ($75,000 to $100,000) and speed (2 to 200 seconds to recognize a part).[4] Continuing advances in microelectronics should make sight cheaper and faster as more memory becomes available to store higher-quality images and the processors themselves become faster at recognizing objects.

The push to develop seeing robots is worldwide. Renault, the French automaker, has developed a robot that can recognize each of 200 parts for transfer to the appropriate operations. Hughes Aircraft Company introduced a semiconductor-chip imaging system, called "omneye," that has real-time recognition capabilities using a digital camera. Similar digital visual systems have been developed by the Stanford Research Institute (SRI), France's Laboratoire d'Automatique de Montpellier, and Machine Intelligence Corporation in Mountain View, California.

On the horizon, researchers are investigating fiber optics and stereoscopic and laser systems to develop robots that can see in three dimensions. As one researcher described the current efforts to develop robot eyes, "One thing is certain: Tomorrow's robots will have vision."

Touch

Robots have trouble knowing how hard they are gripping an object or if the object "feels" the way it is supposed to. A feeling robot could install a tiny light bulb in the dashboard of a car in one motion and tilt

---

[4]John Thackray, "The Robots of America," *Management Today*, July 1979, pp. 66-69.

the entire auto on its side to tighten lug nuts on the wheels for its next operation. Touch would also enable robots to inspect parts by feeling for rough edges or nonconformities.

Some robots already have the sense of touch. At Draper Labs in Cambridge, Massachusetts, a robot has been developed that can feel when a part is nonconforming and alerts its human supervisor. The robot can also jiggle parts until they fit, while assembling something.

Researchers at the Massachusetts Institute of Technology have developed artificial skin for robots that gives them a sense of touch. The skin is made of rubber sheets laced with wire. As the robot touches an object, differences in the voltage levels between the layers of skin determine the form of the object and amount of pressure applied to it. A microprocessor helps the robot interpret what it feels and how tightly it is being grasped.

Further touch research should make touch a reality for assembly robots in the future. Touch will help robots inspect and work with objects of various sizes, shapes, and weights.

Artificial Intelligence

What has made robots functional and economical is the computer -- the robot's brain. Sophisticated robots require a computer to integrate their sensory capabilities, communicate with their human coworkers, and remember what they have been taught.

The intelligent robot of the future will be linked to the totally automated factory. In fact, it may someday be possible to design a part or assembly with a computer ("computeraided design," or CAD), and for the computer to then determine how best to manufacture it and instruct the machines and robots in the factory accordingly ("computer-aided manufacture," or CAM).

Creation of such a facility is a massive, worldwide research effort of which (the computer's) intelligence is the main target. The Japanese have a national program called Methodology for Unmanned Manufacturing (MUM) to encourage the development of "smart" robots with microprocessor brains.

Successes to date include Hitachi Ltd.'s development of a robot that a user need physically lead through the operations to be performed only once. The robot then remembers them and determines the most efficient procedure for doing them.[5] At Nissan Corporation, robots turn out a completely assembled car body every 64 seconds; further, they can recognize the next model coming down the line and adjust their operations accordingly.

---

[5]"Robots Join the Labor force," *Business Week*, Industrial ed., vol. 2640, June 9, 1980, pp. 62-73.

In the United States, research under grants from the National Science Foundation (NSF), the National Bureau of Standards (NBS), and the U.S. Air Force is under way to develop the Integrated Computer Aided Manufacturing Facility (ICAM). Developments to date include a robot at MIT that can jump forwards and backwards and balance on one leg. The robot can actually improve its performance by generalizing upon the stored sequences in its memory and deducing what to do if it comes upon something new. Another robot at the University of Florida can be taught to deliver parts between assembly areas and remember if it encounters an obstacle, as well as determine how to get around the obstacle.

U.S. and foreign researchers view the programming of these robot brains as the key to turning robots into assemblers. More advanced robots like Unimation's PUMA (Programmable Universal Machine for Assembly) can be told what to do by typing in commands in a language that includes human words such as "here" and "move". IBM's new robot can be told what to do by writing a program in IBM's AML (A Manufacturing Language) on a personal computer that controls the robot. Researchers at the Stanford Research Institute have even developed a robot that will respond to one sentence commands such as "Assemble the carburetor."

Advances in artificial intelligence in the years ahead should allow robots to perform a larger variety of assembly and inspection tasks as well as become easier to instruct in those tasks.

ORGANIZATIONAL AND SOCIAL IMPACT OF ROBOTS

With all the projected advances in robotics capabilities and the massive migration of robots into the workplace, a number of social questions arise. This section reviews several of the major organizational issues related to the use of industrial robots and some of the unanswered questions we will face in the future.

Robots are sold primarily on the premise that they can replace expensive workers. However, the question arises whether robots just replace workers or create newer and better jobs in different areas for those same workers.

Job Enrichment

Robots have been touted by their manufacturers and some academics as the saviors of common laborers. No longer will humans be forced to do mindless, repetitive, physical labor 8 hours a day. Robots will do what robots do best: mindless, simple assembly and inspection tasks. Workers will be freed to do what humans do best: creative planning and decision making functions. The quality of working life and productivity will improve.

Jobs in the automated factory of the future will be more challenging and satisfying. According to Joseph Engelberger of Unimation Corp., robots will improve the self-worth and dignity of workers as "the guy looking after five robots becomes boss."[6] The other workers displaced by robots will be able to move to the better, newer jobs robots create, i.e., programming the robots.

Job Replacement

Current robot manufacturers and users proudly point out the fact that most robot-displaced workers are promoted or retrained. General Electric, one of the leaders in robot implementation in the United States (with over 200 robots installed to date), claims not one worker has been laid off because of a robot. However, even General Electric admits that using robots has allowed it to decrease the total size of its labor force. Rather than laying people off, General Electric has paid the cost of retraining those workers replaced by robots to date, but will all firms have the resources and desire to do the same? Also, what happens when the net number of factory jobs declines because of the use of robots, while the number of people seeking work continues to rise?

Auto industry representatives respond to such questions by stating that if they do not automate and trim labor costs, there will be fewer manufacturing jobs in the United States. (In recent years U.S. automakers have lost 400,000 jobs to foreign competitors already.) If the Japanese automate their industries and can underprice U.S. cars while increasing their quality, they will make up for lost jobs by the increased number of jobs created when they sell even more cars. It is quite simple: A firm either automates and stays competitive or goes out of business.

Union Reactions

As the headline on the October 26, 1981, issue of the *Wall Street Journal* proclaimed: "As Robot Age Arrives, Labor Seeks Protection against Loss of Work." Unions are awakening to the fact that robots eliminate union jobs. Douglas Fraser, UAW president, summarized union feelings as follows: "Nobody puts robots in because they think they're going to end up with the same or more workers." To date, unions have taken few actions to actually prevent automation of factories, since most jobs

---

[6]Subrata N. Chakravarty, "Springtime for an Ugly Duckling," *Forbes*, vol. 100, no. 12, Dec. 17, 1979, pp. 90-96.

lost so far have been undesirable anyway. However, as robots take more jobs, labor will demand protection.

Union officials have declared protection of jobs from automation a top priority in their bargaining talks. So far, unions at General Motors and General Electric have contract clauses that require management to:

- Give employees advance notice of automation plans
- Retrain displaced workers
- Include union employees on planning committees dealing with new technology[7]

Union officials stress that they are not Luddites trying to break machines and prevent automation. Unions realize new technology is essential to increase productivity, but unions also refuse to give companies a "blank check" to automate their operations.

Local union members agree with automation in principle as a means of keeping their firms competitive, but as a painter at General Electric who was replaced by a robot commented: "At first I was bitter. How would anyone feel when a bucket of bolts comes in and takes your job away?" The same painter also said that he felt he was lucky to have a new job. Seventeen hundred employees are currently on indefinite layoff at General Electric. General Electric claims it is the economy, and not the robots, that is causing the layoffs.

As the robots become "smarter" and replace ever increasing numbers of union workers, unions will undoubtedly increase their opposition to automation. The real question is "What will unions or the work force they represent do to stop technology?"

Information Revolution

Advances in microelectronics and computer technology are expected to allow the development of skilled, intelligent robots in the decades ahead. These robots could take over as many as 3 million manufacturing jobs by 1990. Today we are at the edge of a great social revolution.

Just as agricultural jobs were eliminated by the tractor and our population migrated from farm work to factory work, during the decades ahead robots and computers will eliminate factory work and our population will migrate to information work. Problems we face with this new information revolution are enormous and have yet to be adequately addressed:

- Work-ethic culture, but declining number of jobs combined with growing number of potential workers

---

[7]Joann S. Lublin, "Steel-Collar Jobs: As Robot Age Arrives, Labor Seeks Protection," *Wall Street Journal*, Oct. 26, 1981.

● Automation of middle-skilled jobs, leaving a large gap between low-skilled, low-paid workers and high-skilled, high-paid workers and making employee advancement from low-skilled to high-skilled jobs increasingly difficult

● Concentration of economic and political power among a small number of large corporations

It is important to emphasize that these problems need to be carefully thought through if we are to succeed in moving from a labor-based industrial society to an automated postindustrial society. As one author commented, "A foresight of the social consequences of robots and automation is most badly needed."

Anthropologist Sir Josiah Charles Stamp, in this passage from his book *Science of Social Adjustment*, perhaps summarized best the dilemma we face:

> All these discoveries, these scientific infants duly born and left on the doorstep of society, get taken in, variously cared for, but on no known principle, and with no directions from the progenitors. Nor do the economists usually acknowledge any duty to study the phase, to indicate any series of tests of their value to society, or even methods and regulation of the optimum rate of introduction of novelty. These things just "happen" generally under the urge of profit, and of consumer's desire, in free competition, regardless of the worthiness of the new desires against old, or of the shifts of production, and therefore, employment with their social consequences.[8]

RECOMMENDATIONS FOR MIS MANAGEMENT

Considering the potential of robotics to address the most pressing organizational issue today -- productivity -- MIS executives should take an opportunistic role in the use of robotics in their organizations.

At a minimum, MIS management must become literate in the area of robotics, particularly as it pertains to their industry. As a second step, they should set up a robotics consulting group, as many companies have. Such a group functions in the spirit of a personal computer consulting group. They "help users help themselves."

As a third and more aggressive step, MIS executives should spearhead the movement of robotics in their organizations by working with user areas to define and propose use of robotics in their organizations.

[8]Josiah Charles Stamp, *Science of Social Adjustment*, Macmillan, London, 1937.

SUMMARY

Robots, with the aid of computers, can do things few people would have dreamed would ever be possible several years ago. Decreased prices and further advances in sensory capabilities and intelligence will make automated factories an economic necessity in the future.

This chapter has discussed what the state of the art of industrial robots is today and what advances in robot technology are expected in the decades ahead. The social ramifications of this new "steel collar" work force were also briefly discussed. Manufacturing firms will be faced with the dilemma of purchasing large numbers of robots to stay competitive, unions will face a decline in jobs and power, and governments will face the question of jobs versus growth in the GNP.

The governments of western countries have taken a passive stance on development of social legislation to deal with the human side of technological development. The problem of obtaining measurable gains in productivity and quality can be solved with robots and technology. However, there is a hard problem of fewer jobs for everyone and a shift in the nature of the society in which we live. Thus, whether or not robots take over our jobs, automation will affect us. It will determine what types of jobs will be available to us in the future.

SUGGESTED READINGS

Brady, Michael, "Seeing Machines: Current Industrial Applications," *Mechanical Engineering*, Nov. 11, 1981, pp. 52-59.

Bylinsky, Gene, "Those Smart Young Robots on the Production Line," *Fortune*, vol. 100, no. 12, Dec. 17, 1979, pp. 90-96.

Chakravarty, Subrata N., "Springtime for an Ugly Duckling," *Forbes*, vol. 127, no. 9, April 27, 1981.

Conrad, S. J., and Wetherbe, J. C., "What the MIS Executive Needs to Know About Robotics," *Journal of Systems Management*, May 1983, pp. 38-42.

Cornish, Blake H., "The Smart Machines of Tomorrow: Implications for Society," *Futurist*, vol. 15, no. 4, August 1981, pp. 5-13.

Edson, Lee, "Slaves of Industry," *Across the Board*, vol. 18, no. 7, July/August 1981, pp. 5-11.

Froehlich, Leopold, "Robots to the Rescue," *Datamation*, vol. 27, no. 1, January 1981, pp. 84-104.

"From Japan, a Surprise Invasion of Robots," *Business Week*, vol. 2674, Feb. 9, 1981, pp. 64D-64J.

"GM's Path with Robots: From User to Maker," *Business Week*, Industrial ed., vol. 2691, June 8, 1981, p. 66F.

Grosswirth, Marvin, "The Robots are Coming," *Datamation*, vol. 24, no. 12, Nov. 15, 1978, pp. 146-150.

Harvey, David, "When Robots Take Over -- What's Left," *Chief Executive Monthly (U.K.)*, December 1979, pp. 43-44.

Hoard, Bruce, "URI Researchers Set Sights on Robot Vision," *Computerworld*, vol. 15, no. 12, Mar. 23, 1981, pp. 37-38.

_____, "Larger Memories Seen Fuel for Future Robotics," *Computerworld*, vol. 15, no. 22, June 1, 1981, p. 24.

_____, "Robotics Won't Replace Humans: Consultant," *Computerworld*, vol. 15, no. 22, June 1, 1981, p. 27.

"IBM Entry Is Expected Soon in Expanding Robot Industry," *Wall Street Journal*, Oct. 31, 1981, p. 25.

"IBM's One-Armed Robot," *Dun's Business Monthly*, April 1982, p. 44.

"Industrial Robots: Better than a Man -- Sometimes!" *Modern Materials Handling*, vol. 35, no. 4, April 1980, pp. 90-97.

Lublin, Joann S., "Steel-Collar Jobs: As Robot Age Arrives, Labor Seeks Protection," *Wall Street Journal*, Oct. 26, 1981.

"Machines That See Go to Work: Why Three Men of Vision Are Turning Entrepreneur," *Business Week*, Nov. 30, 1981, p. 62.

Morris, Dave L., "An Inexpensive Robot Guidance System," *Interface Age*, vol. 5, no. 4, April 1980, pp. 70-71.

"Now Everybody Wants to Get Into Robots: Filling the Gap in Robot Training," *Business Week*, Feb. 15, 1982, p. 52.

Ottinger, Lester V., "Robotics for the IE," *Industrial Engineering*, November 1981, pp. 30-35.

_____, "Robotics for the IE: Evaluating Potential Applications," *Industrial Engineering*, December 1981, pp. 80-83.

_____, "Robotics for the IE: Finding Opportunities for Robot Applications," *Industrial Engineering*, December 1981, p. 27.

"Robots Join the Labor Force," *Business Week*, Industrial ed., vol. 2640, June 9, 1980, pp. 62-73.

"Russian Robots Run to Catch Up," *Business Week*, vol. 2701, Aug. 17, 1981, p. 120.

Schrank, Robert, "Horse-Collar Blue-Collar Blues," *Harvard Business Review*, vol. 59, no. 3, May-June 1981, pp. 133-138.

Stamp, Josiah, *Science of Social Adjustment*, Macmillan, London, 1937.

Teresko, John, "Robots Come of Age," *Industrial Week*, Jan. 25, 1982.

Thackray, John, "The Robots of America," *Management Today*, July 1979, pp. 66-69.

Villers, Phillippe, "CAD/CAM Link May Make Robot Use Practical in High-Precision Production Tasks," *Industrial Engineering*, April 1982, pp. 80-85.

Yasaki, Edward K., "Japanese Push Robotics," *Datamation*, vol. 27, no. 7, July 1981.

Zippo, Mary, "The Robot in Industry: Friend or Foe of Workers," *Personnel*, vol. 57, no. 6, November-December 1980, pp. 51-52.

PART SIX

MANAGING MIS DEVELOPMENT

FOURTEEN

SYSTEMS ANALYSIS AND DESIGN STRATEGIES AND PROCEDURES

INTRODUCTION

The development of information systems is a key process in the overall scheme of MIS management. The systems development process results in production information systems that support the decision making and operation of organizations.

The concepts and techniques of information systems development have been poorly understood and poorly used over the short history of MIS. One problem has been the lack of knowledge and experience with developing information systems. Systems development is still a new, infant art and science. A second problem is that the technology available to support information systems has changed and continues to change at such a rapid pace that systems development techniques lag behind technology by 5 to 10 years. For example, just as a good technique was developed for batch-oriented technology, online technology became a major factor. Once techniques were refined for online systems, database technology and then distributed data processing came along. The advent of high-level user languages and advanced office systems all significantly affect the way information systems should be developed.

This evolutionary, or revolutionary, characteristic of information systems technology greatly complicates good systems development. When systems development deficiencies are resolved in one era of technology, a new era of technology begins.

Fortunately, experience has allowed more insight into systems development, which allows differentiation between systems development concepts and systems development techniques. Concepts transcend technology eras, while techniques may need to be redesigned.

For example, a major concept in systems development is determining what information a decision maker requires. As is illustrated in this chapter, the technique for doing that when using batch technology is different from the technique of using online database technology with high-level query languages.

This chapter focuses on managing the systems analysis and design process. The systems development life cycle (SDLC) is discussed as are several of the commercial methodologies available for managing the SDLC. Structured techniques for analysis and design are presented, strategies for information requirements analysis are discussed, and finally advanced techniques for systems design and development are reviewed.

SYSTEMS DEVELOPMENT LIFE CYCLE

SDLC is a framework for developing computer-based information systems that has emerged over the past 30 years. Though it is defined and portrayed in slightly different ways by different authors, the SDLC is generally easy to recognize and well-acknowledged.

Components of the SDLC

Figure 14-1 provides the conceptual model for discussing the components of the SDLC. The basic components of the SDLC are defined as follows:

- *Analyze problems and opportunities.* Determine and define problems and opportunities related to information systems and organizational processes.

- *Design system.* Design the information outputs, inputs, file structures, programs, procedures, and hardware and software necessary to support the information system.

- *Develop and test system.* Write the software necessary tsupport the system and test its accuracy. Install and test any needed hardware and operating software.

Figure 14-1 Components of the Systems Development Life Cycle

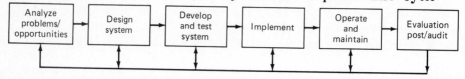

- *Implement.* Convert from the old system tthe new system, providing the necessary training and assistance.

- *Operate and maintain.* Support the production of the information system.

- *Evaluate.* Assess how well the system was developed and how well it operates.

The steps in the cycle are not necessarily discrete or a one-time process. Rather, the SDLC can be iterative, evolutionary, and overlapping. The steps in the cycle, however, retain a general sequential flow from the first step to the last. At any step in the cycle, previously unidentified problems and/or opportunities may be discovered. In such cases, it is important to ensure proper integration of the new solution with the other systems development activities resulting from the SDLC. Making even a minor change to the system without proper consideration of what has already been established can cause unanticipated and undesirable ripple effects.

For example, in a department store chain a decision support system to assist with budget decisions was progressing through an SDLC. During the design stage it was agreed that the system would be online. But during system development the programmers had difficulty making the system operate properly online. They independently switched the system to batch processing. The ultimate result was that after the system was implemented, no one used it because it was too inconvenient and time-consuming to get the information from the model.

Each component of the SDLC must be considered and integrated with previous and subsequent components. Therefore, as Figure 14-1 shows, all components of the SDLC allow for returning to the point of origin (analysis) and require walking through each component before reaching the last component (evaluation).

Formal System Development Methodologies

There are many pitfalls that can cause problems while progressing through the SDLC. To address these problems, a number of comprehensive packages have been developed that consist of training programs and procedures manuals to carefully lead organizations through an SDLC. These methodologies include extensive checklists and checkpoints that facilitate the management of an SDLC.

The following discussion provides a general overview of the major commercial SDLC packages -- PRIDE, SDM/70, CARA, and Spectrum. Though these four methodologies are not inclusive of all methodologies, they are the better known, and they are collectively representative of other methodologies.

PRIDE. PRIDE is a systems development methodology from M. Bryce & Associates, Cincinnati, Ohio. This methodology encompasses project management, design activities, data management, and supporting documentation for management, maintenance, operations, and users.

Life cycle phases of PRIDE are as follows:

- *Phase 1: Systems Study and Evaluation Activities.* The first phase is composed of a feasibility study, studying the existing system, determining the problem, and establishing the user information requirements in terms of outputs. It also includes a cost/benefit analysis. Report output: systems study and evaluation report.

- *Phase 2: Systems Design Activities.* This phase explores the design in terms of processes, outputs, inputs, and files by frequency. Report output: systems design manual.

- *Phase 3: Subsystem Design Activities.* The third phase is a further refinement of these processes, delineating who will do what with what data and in what sequence, with heavy emphasis on frequency. Report output: subsystem design manual.

- *Phase 4: Administrative and Computer Procedures Design Activities.* The writing of administrative procedures and the preparing of computer procedures, job specifications, and program specifications are covered in this phase. Report output: administrative procedures manual and computer run book.

- *Phase 5: Program Design Activity.* The programs are coded and tested during the fifth phase. Report output: program documentation.

- *Phase 6: Computer Procedure Test Activity.* The final phase covers testing the system as a whole, conversion from the old system to the new, and actual implementation. Report output: additions to the systems design manual.

SDM/70. SDM/70 is a systems development methodology marketed by Atlantic Software, Inc., and developed in conjunction with Katch and Associates. Each life cycle phase has a preface, methods guidelines (the individual task instruction), methods supplements, documentation guidelines, and a section reserved for the insertion of departmental standards. Life cycle phases for SDM/70 are as follows:

- *Systems Requirements Definition* (SRD). This phase has as its principal objective the analysis of existing systems and the determination of user requirements and objectives for the proposed system.

- *Systems Design Alternatives* (SDA). The objectives of this phase are to determine the viable alternatives for the system that is being developed and to present an analysis for those alternatives for management consideration.

- *Systems External Specifications* (SES). The objectives of this phase are to document all external design specifications which allow the users to agree that the system to be designed will meet the requirements of the organization.

- *Systems Internal Specifications* (SIS). SIS, by describing how the agreed upon design specifications are to be developed and implemented, goes beyond SES.

- *Programming Development* (PD). In this phase, the SIS is converted into a program by expressing the specifications in a computer language.

- *Testing* (TST). This phase spans several of the previous phases as the specifications and program code are tested.

- *Conversion* (CNV). This phase involves conversion of input files and recovery efforts to get the system up.

- *Implementation* (IMPL). All tasks necessary to fully implement the system are complete.

CARA. The CARA Corporation, which is located in Lombard, Illinois, markets systems development standards (SDS, commonly known as CARA). It is a formal methodology which can be used in all phases of systems development.

Life cycle phases for CARA are as follows:

- *Phase 1: Feasibility Study.* The current system is analyzed and problems are identified. After initial approval to continue is received, a general design of the proposed system is completed. A cost/benefit analysis and a schedule for the four remaining phases are prepared at the end of phase 1 and are submitted for approval in order to continue.

- *Phase 2: Details of System Design.* This phase seeks tfinalize with the user the various system inputs and outputs. Also, a final assessment is made of the technical impact the system will have upon total system resources. Schedules and costs are revised for the remaining phases of the project, and formal approval is obtained.

- *Phase 3: Programming and Procedures.* During this phase the programs are written and tested, and procedures for using the system are developed and approved. At this time, user training of the new system is initiated, which will continue on into the fourth development phase. Finally, an integrated system test is performed and the required approvals are again obtained.

- *Phase 4: System Acceptance.* Phase 4 yields the final version of the procedure manual. In addition, formal training for user personnel is conducted. The system is tested in the environment in which it will be operated, and final user approval is obtained.

- *Phase 5: Implementation and Support.* The final phase is concerned with formal user training at additional locations, implementing the system at these new locations, and performing a postinstallation audit.

Spectrum. Spectrum is a complete project management and system development methodology supplied by Spectrum International, which is located in Westlake Village, California. The system includes separate life cycles and standards for maintenance of small projects and larger development projects.

Life cycle phases for Spectrum are as follows:

- *Problem Definition and Project Proposal.* This phase covers the capturing of the project proposal that is given to the executive management group for approval. Also included are tasks necessary to activate the proposal, prepare a detailed estimate using estimating guidelines, and convert this to a budget request.

- *User Requirements Definition.* A set of procedures is followed teducate the project team on how the present system operates in this phase. It is assumed that the user knows what he or she wants but has difficulty articulating it in a form useful to data processing personnel.

- *Systems Definition.* This phase brings the basic outline of the new system into focus. A rough conceptual design is documented, and a group of alternative designs are identified. A list of factors related to the system's benefits and costs is developed and reviewed by the users for approval.

- *Advisability Study.* During this phase data is gathered, and the advantages and disadvantages of each of the design alternatives are identified. Users participate in choosing the appropriate alternative.

- *Preliminary Design.* An overall systems flowchart is drawn up, and the subsystems are designed. Detailed report layouts, all input forms, screens, and finalized database designs are completed. In addition, all of the controls for the system are identified. This information is reviewed by auditors and users.

- *Program Design.* During this phase all of the functions relating directly to the structuring of programming runs are isolated, and the programs and modules within programs that make up the computer processing are identified.

- *Programming and Program Testing.* The programming proceeds in this phase, and plans of tests to be performed on the computer are developed. Information is reviewed by qualified personnel to ensure each program and module will operate satisfactorily.

- *System Implementation Planning and Development of User Manuals.* This phase, which begins after the systems design has been fixed, runs parallel with the programming activity. Detailed conversion and training schedules and supporting materials are developed. Users review this material and commit themselves to schedules for required training and conversion.

- *System Test and Start-up Preparation.* During this phase the programs are assembled into systems and extensive test data is entered into test systems.

- *Operations Turnover.* During this phase the operations documentation is assembled and thoroughly reviewed with the operations group to make sure that the handoff from development to production will be smooth.

- *User Training and Start-up.* During this phase the schedules for implementation are finalized, the users are given their manuals and are trained in the operation of the system, and the files are set-up or converted to the operational system.

● *System Acceptance and Project Wrap-up.* Once the system is under way, the project team is responsible for monitoring it during parallel or simulation periods and for assisting the users in areas where attention is required. Users certify that the training, documentation, and results are consistent with their original requirements and that the system performs satisfactorily.

Summary of Systems Development Methodologies

The four systems development methodologies described above have important similarities and differences. The main thing they all have in common is that they are based on the traditional systems development life cycle.

There is no scientific, comparative analysis of the methodologies and, therefore, no conclusive evidence of one methodology being better than the others. One criticism they all share occasionally is that they are so comprehensive and require so much attention to details and procedures that progress may be impeded -- particularly on short, simple projects. The steps and procedures should be considered as a checklist, but not every step or procedure is necessary in each SDLC. In general, the methodologies are quite helpful, and they are used by many organizations.

SYSTEMS ANALYSIS AND DESIGN USING STRUCTURED TECHNIQUES

The preceding discussion on the systems development life cycle provides an overview of the entire systems development process. That discussion set the stage and provided the context for the remainder of this chapter, which focuses on systems analysis and design -- the first two components of the SDLC. The remainder of the SDLC is discussed in the next two chapters.

Analysis of Problems and Opportunities

The impetus for initiating an SDLC appears as a problem or opportunity arises. Note that once an *opportunity* arises, the *problem* capitalizes on it. For example, a wholesale distributor receives customer complaints concerning late deliveries of orders. These late deliveries result in loss of business and loss of customer goodwill. Action is necessary. On the other hand, if a distributor finds most customers would like better delivery than is generally available from other distributors, improving delivery is an opportunity to gain a competitive advantage. The problem is still how to make that improvement. Action is not necessary, but it is opportunistic to act.

When analyzing a problem or opportunity, care must be taken to differentiate between symptoms and problems. Often symptoms are diagnosed as the problem. What is the difference? Problems cause symptoms. Therefore the only way to resolve symptoms is to find their cause(s). Orders being received late is the symptom; analysis should uncover the problem.

Orders could be received late for a number of reasons:

- Salespersons not promptly turning in orders
- Order entry clerks making errors
- Order entry terminals having poor response times
- Order entry operations being inadequately staffed
- Poor training of order entry clerks
- Inventory not keeping adequate stock
- Vendors not promptly supplying the distributor with inventory
- Poor management in the shipping department
- Inadequate shipping capacity
- Credit department delaying approval of orders

The list could go on. If the problem is in the shipping department, improving response time on order entry terminals will not eliminate the symptom.

Note that many of the potential causes listed above are not necessarily information system problems. When analyzing a problem, both information system and non-information system issues should be investigated.

Fundamental Activities of Analysis

Analysis is the process of separating a whole into its parts to allow examination of the parts. The examination leads to an understanding of their nature, function, and interrelationships. Considerable effort is required to analyze an information system. The overall system must be defined. Then it must be separated into its subsystems or processes for further analysis. For example, an order processing system may be

Table 14-1 Analysis activities

Activity	Explanation
Review of documentation	Reviewing recorded specifications that describe the objectives, procedures; reports produced, equipment used, etc., in an information system
Observation	Watching the object system and/or the information system in process to note and record facts and events about their operation.
Interviews	Meeting with individuals or groups to ask questions about their roles in and their use of an information system
Questionnaires	Submitting questions in printed form to individuals to gather information on their roles in and use of an information system

separated into subsystems of order collection, entry, editing, posting, shipping, and reporting.

The four basic activities used to gather information about an information system are listed in Table 14-1. A review of available documentation is a logical starting point when seeking insight into a system. A documentation review allows project team members involved in systems analysis to gain some knowledge of a system before they impose upon other people's time. Unfortunately, documentation seldom completely describes a system, and it often is not up to date. The current operation of the system may differ significantly from what is described. Therefore, after a review of available documentation, a logical next step is to observe the operation of the system. Observation provides a more tangible perspective of what is described in the documentation. It also brings to light aspects of the documentation that are incomplete and/or outdated.

Having gained as much knowledge as is reasonably possible without imposing on other personnel, those involved in systems analysis can intelligently use interviews and/or questionnaires to gather additional information. Techniques of interviewing and questionnaire design are topics for extensive study. However, a few key concepts should be noted.

Application of Analysis Activities

The techniques of documentation, observation, interviews, and questionnaires are used in varying degrees during the following steps of analyzing the existing system:

1. Review organizational process or system.
2. Define decision making associated with the organizational process or system.
3. Analyze existing information system support of decision making.
4. Define the problem(s).

During the review of the organizational process or system, a working knowledge of the physical processes associated with the area under study can be developed. A clear understanding of the objectives of the organizational process and the means used to achieve the objectives can be developed.

After an operating knowledge of the organizational system under study has been acquired, the next step is to define the decision making associated with managing the system. A definition of the decision-making system provides the framework for determining what information is required. This is one of the most neglected aspects of systems analysis. Since the utility of information is its ability to support decision making, such negligence is somewhat surprising. Managers are frequently asked what information they would like to have or are offered copies of reports that are currently being produced or will be produced for other managers. This approach tends to encourage managers to ask for more information than they need. Research in the area of decision making and use of information indicates the following points:

1. Decision makers tend to ask for and feel more comfortable with more detailed information than they need. However, they appear to make better decisions with summarized information and exception reporting.[1]

2. The less knowledgeable decision makers are about the decisions required to properly manage a process, the more information they tend to request (presumably, hoping to find something of value). However, much of the information they request is irrelevant to their decision making.[2]

By basing information requests on the decisions they have to make, managers can be more discriminating in their information requests. This

---

[1] Norman L. Chervany, and Gary W. Dickson, "An Experimental Evaluation of Information Overload in a Production Environment," *Management Sciences*, June 1974, pp., 1335-1344.

[2] Izak Benbesat, and Roger G. Schroeder, "An Experimental Investigation of Some MIS Design Variables," *MIS Quarterly*, March 1977, pp. 37-47.

reduces the tendency of managers to create information overloads for themselves. Such overloads are both dysfunctional and expensive.

Defining the decision system is not a trivial process. Considerable discipline and effort on the part of managers is required to define such a system. Techniques for eliciting information requirements more accurately are discussed later in the chapter under "Advanced Systems Development Techniques." Managers often make decisions so routinely that it seldom occurs to them how often they make decisions and what types of decisions they make. Consequently, they are understandably tempted to take a "shotgun" approach to defining their information requirements rather than a more time-consuming, but more specific, "rifle" approach.

Decision Centers

The decisions made in an organization tend to be clustered into decision centers. A decision center generally consists of one or more decision makers, decision procedures, and an activity for which decisions must be made.[3] Accordingly, the decisions made in a decision center tend to pertain to the management of a particular organizational process.

Viewing the organization in terms of decision centers is particularly useful in systems analysis. Decision centers are areas where organizational processes may potentially be improved by the provision of more relevant, timely, and accurate information. In organizational terms, a decision center combined with an activity center constitutes a functional unit or department. For example, Table 14-2 assumes that an existing order processing system is being analyzed. It shows the decision center and major decisions likely to exist in the organization.

Another advantage of defining decision centers, as well as major decisions, is that doing so provides an overall profile of decision making within an organization. This profile often reveals discrepancies and redundancies in decision making. For example, if salespersons are under the impression that they can commit inventory, but they really cannot, this discrepancy should be cleared up. Otherwise, inventory may be committed to customers in error.

If the same decision is being made by two or more decision centers, this too should be resolved. Consider, for instance, a situation where all

[3]Sherman C. Blumenthal, *Management Information Systems: A Framework for Planning and Development*, Prentice-Hall, Englewood Cliffs, N.J., 1969.

Table 14-2 Decision centers involved in order processing

Decision center	Activity	Examples of major decisions
Salespersons	Selling merchandise	Which customers to call on What to sell customers What is available to sell
Credit department	Accounts receivable management	Which customers to allow credit to How much credit to allow Which customers need past-due notices Which customers' credit should be discontinued
Ordering department	Inventory management	What inventory to stock When to unload slow-moving inventory Which customers to allocate available inventory
Shipping department	Packing and shipping orders	What merchandise to send to what customers What orders can be shipped together to save delivery cost

orders must be approved for credit by the credit department before they are sent to the order processing department. However, the order processing department is unaware of this procedure, so a second credit check is made using an exact copy of the credit rating report used by the credit department. Such duplication of effort is not uncommon in organizations. It may go unnoticed until identified by someone aware of what both departments are doing. Requiring that information received by a department be justified for decision making should expose discrepancies and duplication of decision-making processes.

Analysis of Existing Information Systems

Analyzing the existing information system and its support of the decision system involves determining the collection, processing, storing, and reporting functions within the existing system.

Some form of documentation of the existing information system is generally available and is the logical starting point for analysis. Perhaps the most useful form of documentation for reviewing an information system is a systems flowchart. A flowchart is a graphical representation of the system, using symbols to represent operations, data flow, files, equipment, and so on. Figure 14-2 illustrates the various symbols used in system flowcharts, and Figure 14-3 depicts a system flowchart.

Processing		**Input-output**	
A major processing function.		Any type of medium or data.	
Punched card		**Perforated tape**	
All varieties of punched cards, including stubs.		Paper or plastic, chad or chadless.	
Document		**Transmittal tape**	
Paper documents and reports of all varieties.		A proof or adding-machine tape or similar batch-control information.	
Magnetic tape		**Disk, drum, random access**	
Offline storage		**Display**	
Offline storage of either paper, cards, magnetic tape, or perforated tape.		Information displayed by plotters of visual-display devices.	
Online keyboard		**Sorting, collating**	
Information supplied to or by a computer utilizing an online device.		An operation on sorting or collating equipment.	
Keying operation		**Clerical operation**	
An operation utilizing a key-driven device.		A manual offline operation not requiring mechanical aid.	
Auxiliary operation		**Communication link**	
A machine operation supplementing the main processing function.		The automatic transmission of information from one location to another via communiacation lines.	
Flow			
The direction of processing or data flow.			

Figure 14-2 Flowchart Symbols

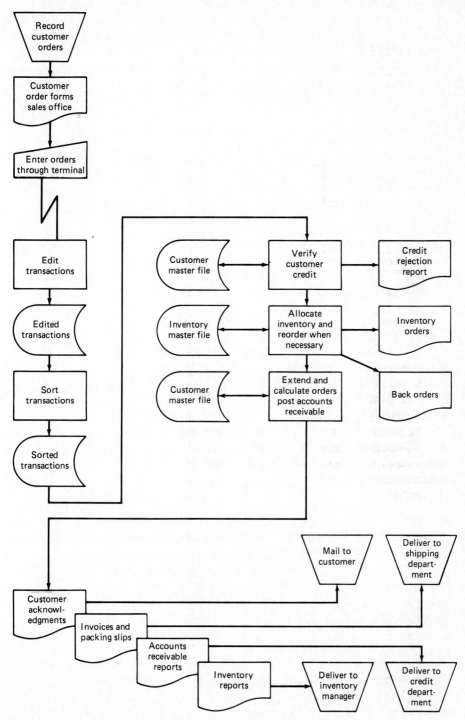

Figure 14-3 Flowchart for Order Processing

Isolation of Deficiencies in the Information System. The next step of analysis involves contrasting the needs of the decision system with the information generated by the information system. The objective of this contrast is to identify discrepancies between the information required and the information available. Deficiencies in the information system can then be identified. Operational problems in both the information system and the organizational process are also defined.

Project Proposal

The development of a project proposal for management review is the next step. The contents of the report would include such things as

- Project name
- Problem or opportunity definition
- Project description
- Feasibility of solution (technical, economical, and operational)
- Expected benefits
- Resource or Requirements
- Alternative solutions
- Authorization

This document should be brief (ranging from 2 to 5 pages) and focus on organizational and managerial issues. Review and approval of the document lead to the systems design component of the SDLC.

DESIGN SOLUTIONS

Perhaps the most ill-defined component of systems development over the years has been systems design. This process should generate the specifications, or "blueprint," that will be used to develop an information system to solve the problems defined during analysis.

Systems design suffers from a devastating lack of technique. Most early and many recent systems design specifications consist of sample reports, input layouts, file layouts, a flowchart, and a 100- to 500-page narrative description of what the system is to do. The main problem is that the narrative descriptions generally lack sufficient detail to generate design specifications that articulate with sufficient precision how the system is supposed to work. Such design specifications are typically redundant, verbose, voluminous, and tedious to write and to read. This lack of precision results in too many incorrect assumptions, contradictions, errors, and omissions when the specifications are translated into an operational system.

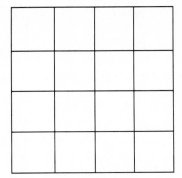

Figure 14-4 Problem Solving Square

Structured Techniques

A major development in systems design and to a certain degree in systems analysis is what is generally referred to as "structured techniques."[4]   ,[5],[6],[7]   (There are also structured techniques for pro- gramming, but they are discussed in the next chapter.)   Structured techniques are a set of tools that collectively provide more of an engineering discipline for systems analysis and design.

To illustrate the value of using structured approaches to problem solving, consider Figure 14-4.   Without reading any further, determine how many squares are in that figure.   If you only come up with 16, look again.

Most people will quickly estimate 16.   After more consideration, the count ranges from 17 to 36.   Also, people approach counting the boxes in a variety of ways -- many of which are disorganized.   Confidence in a first estimate is usually high, but the more the figure is studied, the lower the confidence becomes.

However, if we use a structured technique we can readily solve the problem with a high level of confidence.   The technique consists of creating a frequency distribution for each configuration of squares as follows:

$$
\begin{array}{rcl}
1 \times 1 \text{ squares} & = & 16 \\
2 \times 2 \text{ squares} & = & 9 \\
3 \times 3 \text{ squares} & = & 4 \\
4 \times 4 \text{ squares} & = & 1 \\
\hline
\text{Total} & = & 30
\end{array}
$$

[4]DeMarco, Tom, *Structured Analysis and System Specification*, Yourdon, New York, 1978.

[5]Orr, Kens, *Structured Requirements Definition*, Ken Orr and Associates, Topeka, Kan., 1981.

[6]Edward Yourdon and Larry L. Constantine, *Structured Design*, Yourdon, New York, 1978.

[7]Wetherbe, James C., "A Systems Specification Model for Instruction in Systems Analysis and Design," *Journal of Data Education*, July 1978.

Note that using this technique we can expand the number of squares included in Figure 14-3 and, though it would take longer, the solution to the problem would still be straightforward. Also, note that all people would solve the problem in the same way. This consistency would allow a person to complete the problem for someone who had started but did not finish (e.g., if the 1 x 1's and 2 x 2's were done, only the 3 x 3's and 4 x 4's would need to be done). The consistency in technique also allows for more than one person to concurrently work on the problem (i.e., one person could do the 1 x 1 count, another the 2 x 2 count, etc.). The introduction of a standard structured technique to even a simple problem like counting squares is quite useful. For something as complex as systems analysis and design it is vital.

Tools for Structured Techniques

The tools commonly used for systems design are

Flowcharts	Decision tables
Data flow diagrams	Decision trees
Structured English	Data dictionary

Flowcharts. The flowchart symbols and an example of a flowchart were presented in the discussion of systems analysis earlier in the chapter (see Figure 14-2). This earlier use of a flowchart makes an important point: Flowcharts are a tool for both analysis and design.

Data Flow Diagrams. Data flow diagrams use the symbols defined and illustrated in Figure 14-5. Data flow diagrams offer a more efficient, and in some ways, more profound way of showing data flow and relationships than a flowchart offers. Data flow diagrams are easier to work with, since they are less formal than flowcharts. Like flowcharts, data flow diagrams can be used as an analysis tool if existing documentation does not provide them, or they can be used as a design tool. In either case, it seems very easy to communicate with data flow diagrams.

Structured English. As a structured way to describe a process, structured English can usually be translated directly into program code and resembles COBOL code. An example follows:

    If hourly employee,
            If hours worked less than 40,
                    Produce absence report
                    Compute wages by multiplying hours worked x rate
            If hours worked equal 40,

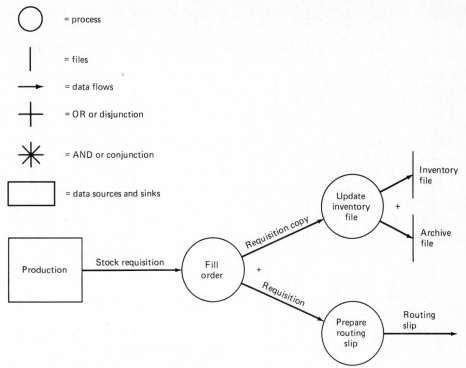

Figure 14-5 Data Flow Diagrams

> Compute wages by multiplying hours worked
> x 40 and 1.5 rate x
> hours worked over 40
> Else (salaried employee)
> If hours worked less than 40
> Produce absence report
> Pay salary
> Else (no absence)
> Pay salary

Decision Tables. A decision table is a powerful nonnarrative tool for describing complex relationships. It is a matrix containing columns and rows that define relationships. There are three major components of a decision table: conditions, courses of action, and decision rules. Possible decision rule entries and their definitions and an example of a decision table are provided in Figure 14-6.

Decision Tree. Decision trees offer an alternative to structured English and decision tables as a means to define complex relationships. An example of a decision tree is provided in Figure 14-7.

Decision Table for Airline Reservations

Conditions/courses of action	Decision rules							
	1	2	3	4	5	6	7	8
First-class request?	Y	Y	Y	Y	N	N	N	N
Economy-class request?	–	–	–	–	Y	Y	Y	Y
First-class available?	Y	N	N	N	–	–	–	–
Economy available?	–	Y	Y	N	Y	N	N	N
Alternative acceptable?	–	Y	N	–	–	Y	Y	N
First-class available?	–	–	–	–	–	Y	N	–
Reduce first-class available	x	●	●	●	●	x	●	●
Issue first-class ticket	x	●	●	●	●	x	●	●
Reduce economy available	●	x	●	●	x	●	●	●
Issue economy ticket	●	x	●	●	x	●	●	●
Refer to alternate flight	●	●	x	x	●	●	x	x

Note: double bar separates conditions from course of action

Legend:
Condition entries:
Y = yes, condition must apply
N = no, condition must not apply
– = indifferent
Course of action entries:
x = activate course of action
● = do not activate course of action

Figure 14-6 Decision Table for Airline Reservation

Data Dictionary. The data dictionary is at the heart of structured techniques. It plays the biggest role in eliminating the voluminous, hard-to-maintain narrative system descriptions that preceded structured techniques. It provides an individual entry for every data element in the system. Components of and an example of a data element dictionary entry are provided in Figure 14-8. Data element dictionaries are usually maintained on the computer.

Figure 14-7 An Example of a Decision Tree

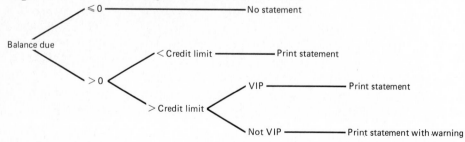

Components of Data Element Dictionary Entry

Name: Unique data name
Definition: Field format, narrative description, and code, if applicable
Source: Input source or computation and validation rules
Where Used: Reports, computations, and program using the data element
Maintenance: Procedures for updating a data element
Storage: File(s) data element is stored in

Example

Name: DEPARTMENT

Definition: The code of the department an employee works in
                Format is 999

                Code values are as follows:
                    101 - Administration
                    201 - Production
                    301 - Sales
                    401 - Engineering

Source: Input: New employee transaction
                Validation rule: Code value must be equal to a valid
                department code.

Where Used: Payroll Check
                Validation Error Report
                Department Payroll Report

Maintenance: Originated from new employee transaction when employee
                is hired.
                Updated whenever an employee changes departments.

Storage: Payroll Master File

Figure 14-8 Components of and Example of Data Dictionary Entry

Using Structured Tools for Design Specifications

Given a set of tools for doing structured design, the next issue is to integrate them into comprehensive design specifications. A framework for integrating these tools is discussed below.[8]

Systems Design and Specifications. When structuring information for an information system, a systems analyst may not know what specific hardware and software will be best suited to support the system. Therefore, systems design techniques and procedures should be as hardware- and software-independent as possible. This allows the systems specifications to be implemented with whatever hardware and software turns out to be most cost-effective in supporting the information structure. The relationship between information structure design and hardware and software is similar to the relationship between architectural design and building materials. In both cases, the specifications should articulate with sufficient precision what the final product should be without unduly restricting the selection of the best available means for constructing the final product. Achieving a balance between design techniques that are both hardware- and software-independent and yet

---

[8]James C. Wetherbe, *Systems Analysis for Computer-Based Information Systems*, West, St. Paul, Minn., 1979.

specific enough to be practical presents somewhat of a dilemma to systems analysts. The process of structuring information involves the following systems design specifications:

● Output definitions describe the printouts or terminal displays to be provided by the system.

● Input definitions display the format of each data field or element coming into the system.

● Data element dictionary defines all data fields that are to be inputted, computed, stored, and reported.

● Logic definitions illustrate complex logical relationships necessary for input, computation, and reporting of information by using structured English, decision tables, or decision trees.

● Systems flow provides a graphical representation of the system, using symbols to represent operations, data flow, files, equipment, etc., by use of flowcharts and/or data flow diagrams.

● File layout defines file structures and contents.

The various design specifications are linked together in such a way that the input, computation, logical processing, storage, and reporting of each item of information can be traced forward or backward from its point of origin to its final uses. This link is the result of using unique data names so that a data element in a report, data element dictionary, input layout, logical process, or a file can be traced to all documentation on that data element as portrayed in Figure 14-9.

Upon completion, the specifications should provide sufficient documentation to guide the required computer programming. Though organizations may have systems design procedures that differ from the procedures presented in this chapter, the differences will generally be cosmetic rather than conceptual in nature. Readers who master the techniques presented in this chapter should experience a comfortable transition to other systems design procedures. In summary, structured design tools combined into a well-disciplined framework allow the systems analyst to develop precise design specifications that are relatively hardware-, software-, and personnel-independent.

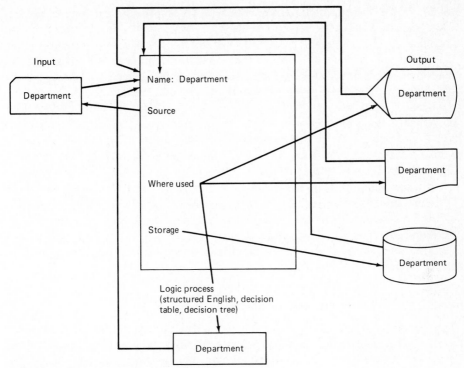

**Figure 14-9 Linking Design Specification
Using Unique Data Names**

ADVANCED SYSTEMS DEVELOPMENT TECHNIQUES

The use of the structured techniques introduced in the previous section addresses the problem of analyzing and designing a system "right." However, there is still one remaining problem -- designing the right system. The main purpose of an information system is to provide information to support the decision making and operations of an organization. No matter how sophisticated the programs, if management does not get the information needed for decision making, it did not get the right system.

Information Requirements Analysis

There is a saying among systems analysts: "What users ask for is not what they want, and what they want is not what they need." Therefore a critical step in systems analysis and design is determining management's information requirements. This chapter has discussed, in relation to systems analysis, the approach of focusing on decision making to determine information requirements.   This approach is an improvement over focusing directly on information.   IBM uses this approach in its Business Systems Planning (BSP) methodology.[9] Rockart proposes that managers should focus on critical success factors and from those determine what information is necessary to ensure successful management of those factors.[10] In spite of the improvements realized by focusing on decision making and critical success factors, getting a precise definition of management information requirements by using interview techniques has limitations.   The best evidence of the problem is the amount of revisions systems go through after implementation before management gets all the information it really needs.

At the beginning of the chapter, we pointed out the manner in which systems development technique lags behind technology.   The collective effect of several recent, and several not so recent, technological developments -- online systems, database technology, user languages, and decision support systems -- has significant implications for the manner in which systems are developed.

Problems with Traditional Approaches

Traditional systems development methodologies force user management during the system design phase to define in detail exactly what information would be needed in reports and terminal displays once the entire development cycle is complete, months or even years later.   The system has to be planned this way because the technology used to support the system is not flexible or forgiving.   Though the traditional approach to defining user requirements may be sensible in the view of the designers and earlier technology, it fails to recognize the dynamic nature of management.   Users are not trying to be difficult when they ask for changes once the system is complete.   It is simply a difficult task for a manager to define his or her information requirements in the abstractions -- flowcharts, file layouts, logic definitions, and report formats -- used by systems analysts.

This process is analogous to asking a home buyer to make all decisions about the details for a house from an architect's blueprints. Architects indicate that people having homes built, like users having systems built, are continually making design changes during "implementation." And few custom built homes, like information systems, provide what is really needed when they are first completed.   Indeed

---

[9] *Business Systems Planning -- Information Systems Planning Guide,* IBM Corporation, Publication No. GE20-0527.

[10] John F. Rockart, "Chief Executives Define Their Own Data Needs," *Harvard Business Review,* March-April 1979, pp. 81-93.

experience shows most people will build an average of three homes before their "ideal" house is built.

The fact that users ask for changes once a system is in place suggests that defining user requirements needs to be a heuristic, or learning, process. Managers should be given the opportunity to work with the output of a new system before massive development effort goes into the final system.

In our home-building analogy, consider the advantage of an approach to home building that would allow a model home to be developed, and families to move their furniture in and temporarily live in the house. Based upon what they liked or disliked, a new version of the home would be generated and the process repeated until the family is satisfied. On the basis of architects' experiences, three versions would allow a proper definition of a family's requirements. Unfortunately, housing construction technology is not yet flexible enough to make a heuristic approach to home building feasible.

Heuristic Development and Prototyping

One major constraint with which information systems development has had to cope over the years is that the prototype system, with all its flaws and shortcomings, becomes the production system. However, information systems technology is now flexible enough to make a prototype[11] or heuristic[12],[13] approach to information system building feasible. Online technology makes user interaction with the system more practical than it is with batch produced reports. Further, the state of the art in easy-to-use information retrieval (query) languages has improved dramatically and is continuing to improve. Database management systems -- especially those approximating or achieving the relational model -- allow significant improvement in data manipulation. More directly in support of management decision making, there is a proliferation of application-oriented models and easy-to-use modeling languages for decision support systems. Although all these technological advances increase support of management decision making, they impose overhead on their computer systems; but the continuous improvement in hardware cost and performance has made high overhead software practical.

---

[11]Richard C. Canning, "Developing Systems by Prototyping," *EDP Analyzer,* vol. 19, no. 9, September 1981, pp. 1-14.

[12]T. Berrisford and James Wetherbe, "Heuristic Development: A Redesign of Systems Design," *MIS Quarterly,* vol. 3, no. 1, March 1979, pp. 11-19.

[13]Don Leavitt, et al., "Heuristic Development Eases Strains," *Computerworld,* no. 26, June 25, 1979.

Heuristic or prototype development is a radical departure from traditional systems development that addresses the conceptual flaw existing in traditional systems development and exploits advanced technology.

Heuristic Development Overview. Figure 14-10 depicts the basic model of heuristic development. The activities associated with each stage of the model are as follows:

1. During the "Analyze problems and opportunities" step of systems development, develop a broad understanding of data currently used to support the decision making and operations of the organization activity.

2. Collect samples of whatever machine-readable data or manual data is available and load it into a database using a simple sequential physical structure for each file.

3. On the basis of the understanding of the data obtained in step 1, postulate key fields in each file and establish them as indexes. If multiple files are involved, any obvious relationships between files can be established by using whatever technology is provided by the DBMS.

4. Using a query language, develop screen formats and reports for information currently required by the user. Postulate and develop additional screen formats or reports that could be useful in the future.

5. Train users in the operation of the system, and have them spend time interacting with it. The experience gained by the users' interaction with the system technologies and capabilities functions as a catalyst which allows them to more fully envision and articulate their information requirements.

6. On the basis of the information gained in step 5, revise the system by making user modifications, such as adding new fields, creating new data relationships, and modifying screen formats. Eliminate indexing of data fields that are seldom used as keys for performance considerations. Any queries used frequently may be coded in a higher performance language such as COBOL to increase response time.

7. Repeat the sequence of steps 5 and 6 until the system is relatively stable.

8. Design an input system to provide edit and update capabilities for the data structure and output system, and proceed with the remainder of the systems development cycle.

Figure 14-10 Systems Development with Heuristic Development

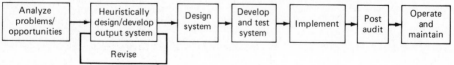

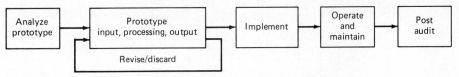

Figure 14-11 Systems Development with Prototyping

Heuristic development allows the systems analyst to define users' information requirements while *designing* and *developing* an output system. This approach provides managers with an opportunity to have tangible, realistic exposure to the new system as they learn the capabilities of the new technology and refine their information requirements. Once the output system is shaped to accurately fit user requirements, an input system is designed and developed.

The design and development of an input system after the development of an output system is a logical sequence. The development of an input system with data collection, transaction processing procedures, and a proper edit and update system is usually a major effort. The design requirements for an input system are easier to define and less susceptible to change if a stable output system is already defined.

Prototyping. The process of prototyping, like heuristic development, allows concurrent evolution of user requirements and system design (see Figure 14-11). The basic steps of prototyping are as follows:[14]

1. Identify users' basic requirements in terms of information and operating requirements.

2. Develop a working prototype that performs only the most important, identified functions, using a small representative database.

3. Allow the user to test the prototype by first demonstrating how the prototype works and how it responds to requested changes by making them as soon as possible or by documenting them and making the changes later.

4. Refine the prototype by discussing requested changes and deciding which ones should be included in the next version of the prototype. After the next prototype is created, steps 3 and 4 are repeated until the system fully achieves the requirements of the users. Proceed with demonstrations for other users (if necessary) or with system development.

Summary of Heuristic Development and Prototyping. Heuristic development and prototyping share a great deal in common. They both recognize the cognitive-style issue, require advanced technology, and are

[14]A. M. Jenkins, "A Framework for MIS Research," *Proceedings of the 9th Annual Conference: American Institute for Decision Sciences,* Chicago, Oct. 12-21, 1977, p. 573.

major revisions of systems methodology. There are, however, significant differences between them. Prototyping advocates developing a simple system that is refined through an iterative process. At some point a decision may be made to discard the prototype after having learned what is needed, and a formal system development process may be initiated. Alternatively, the prototype may become the production system.

Heuristic development, on the other hand, advocates developing an output system on an interactive basis only. The output becomes part of the production system. Once the output system is developed, heuristic development returns to a disciplined engineering approach to develop the input or file maintenance system, using conventional structured techniques.

In other words, prototyping advocates a creative trial-and-error process, including editing and updating, for developing the whole system. Heuristic development advocates this strategy for the definition of system outputs only.

The structured techniques developed in the past decade all stress that system design specifications must be output-oriented or output-driven. In structured design, the "right" output definition should lead to a system that works "right." The problem is that we have difficulty defining the right system. ` To that end, heuristic development ensures that the right system is defined (outputs from the system), and is thereby compatible with structured techniques, which ensure that the system works right (inputs and processing).

Application of Heuristic Development and Prototyping. Advanced development techniques have been successfully used in a wide variety of applications, in diverse organizational settings, with the following benefits:

- Shorter development
- More accurate determination of user requirements
- Greater user participation and support
- Less threatening process to users
- Greater user satisfaction

Companies that are working with the heuristic or prototype approaches associated with the MIS Research Center include National Car Rental System, Donaldson Company, Inc., General Mills, Inc., and Super Valu Stores.

Dave Johnson, vice president of information systems at National Car, says, "We have found the heuristic and prototyping approaches to be very successful, having developed several systems that way. The largest project we undertook using prototyping was to develop our national online network. Once that system went in, we had only a few minor changes. A big breakthrough."

Jim Throckmorton, director of data processing for Donaldson, looks at it this way: "In order to reduce the backlog of systems waiting to be implemented, we *must* shorten the system development time. Heuristic development has been one of the most successful methods we have used. We plan to expand its usage to many more systems. Another advantage to it is that there are significant dollar benefits to the company because the systems begin to provide deliverables far earlier than in standard system development approaches."

Sue Eastes was formerly director of systems development and currently is director of control and administration at General Mills. She states: "We are new at this process, but we have used it successfully in several applications. Now we are finding we cannot get the concept implemented fast enough. It has been a real eye opener for us. We have never had such user acceptance or made such rapid progress with systems. But we are still learning. We are not yet sure we can do this with all systems but we are definitely going to continue working with it."

At Super Valu, Rod Davis, director of methods, reports: "We have got to develop systems quicker and to more accurately get at user requirements. We think the heuristic and prototyping approaches are the answers."

The simplicity of heuristic development and prototyping relative to the problems to be solved is perhaps alarming. However, the simplicity of a concept can be its greatest asset. To illustrate the point, consider James Martin's statement on the effect of relational DBMS technology:[15]

> Throughout the history of engineering a principle seems to emerge: great engineering is simple engineering. Ideas which become too cumbersome, inflexible, and problematic tend to be replaced with newer, conceptually cleaner ideas which compared to the old, are aesthetic in their simplicity.

Martin's statement is particularly appropriate to use in this context because the relational concept is pivotal to heuristic development and prototyping. Heuristic development appears to be the means to more fully exploit the capabilities of the relational concept.

Integrating Heuristic Development and Prototyping into the SDLC. Given the promise of heuristic development and prototyping a question often raised is how to integrate heuristic development and prototyping into the formal development methodologies, such as PRIDE, SDM/70, CARA, and Spectrum, that are in use in many organizations. Table 14-3 provides guidelines on how this can be accomplished.

---

[15]J. Martin, *Principles of Data-Base Management*, Prentice-Hall, Englewood Cliffs, N.J., 1976, pp. 95-110.

Table 14-3 Traditional life cycle and phases of PRIDE, SDM/70, CARA, Spectrum, and Heuristic Design Activities

Traditional life cycle phases	PRIDE life cycle phases	SDM/70 life cycle phases	CARA life cycle phases	Spectrum life cycle phases	Heuristic design activities	Prototyping
Definition stage • Feasibility assessment • Information analysis	Phase 1: System study and evaluation activities *Plus* Phase 2: Design of outputs and files only Phase 5: Programming of outputs only	SDR: Systems requirements definition SDA: System design alternatives SES: System external specifications *Plus* PD: Programming of outputs	Phase I: Feasibility study Phase II: Detail systems design and file for outputs Phase III: Programming of outputs Phase IV: Acceptance of outputs	• Problem definition/ project proposal • User requirements definition • System definition • Advisability study • Preliminary design • Program design and testing for outputs	1. Develop understanding of data to support decision making and operations 2. Collect samples of data and load into database 3. Establish initial indexes and interfile relationships 4. Using DBMS query, develop screen formats/reports 5. Train users to work with these outputs 6. Modify system based upon what users discover in 5 7. Repeat 5 & 6 until system is relatively stable	1. Identify basic operating and information requirement

Physical design					
• System design	Phase 2: Complete system design activities for inputs and processes	SIS: System internal specification	Phase II: Detail systems design for inputs and edits	• Preliminary design • System/subsystem design	8. Design input system to edit and update capabilities for system
• Program development	Phase 3: Subsystem design activities Phase 5: Program design activity for inputs and edits	PD: Program development phase for inputs and edits	Phase III: Programming and procedures for inputs and edits	• Program design for inputs and edits • Programming/program testing for inputs and edits	2. Develop working prototype 3. Demonstrate prototype 4. Refine and make new versions of prototype and repeat step 3 onward until system is complete
• Procedure development	Phase 4: Administrative and computer procedure design activities			• System implementation planning/user manuals	
Implementation					
• Conversion	Phases 6 & 7: Computer procedure and system test activities	TST, CNV, and Impl: System testing, conversion and implementation phases	Phase IV & V: System acceptance and implementation/support	• System test/startup preparation • Operation turnover • User training/startup	
• Operation and maintenance • Post audit				• System acceptance/project wrapup	

351

SUMMARY

Systems analysis and design theory and techniques have evolved continuously since computer-based information systems were first used in organizations. Over the years the systems development life cycle (SDLC) has become the anchoring framework for systems development.

Within that framework, formal systems development methodologies such as PRIDE, SDM/70, CARA, and Spectrum have emerged to further refine and define the procedures for systems analysis and design.

Structured techniques represent a major breakthrough in systems analysis and design by providing an engineering-oriented discipline to address the otherwise vague, ambiguous, and contradictory process of articulating design specifications.

The development of advanced techniques like heuristic development and prototyping represents a major conceptual breakthrough in the elusive area of information requirements analysis. Systems developed using these advanced techniques have greater effectiveness in determining and serving user requirements. By exploiting the advanced technologies of DBMS, online systems, query languages, etc., systems are developed faster and with more user interaction and satisfaction.

SUGGESTED READINGS

"A Study Guide for Accurately Defined Systems," National Cash Register Company, Dayton, Ohio, 1968.

"Accurately Defined Systems," National Cash Register Company, Dayton, Ohio, 1968.

Ackoff, R. L., "Management Misinformation Systems," *Management Science,* vol. 14, no. 4, December 1967, pp. 147-156.

Alter, S., "A Taxonomy of Decision Support Systems," *Sloan Management Review,* vol. 19, no. 1, Fall 1977, pp. 147-156.

Argyris, C., "Management Information Systems: Challenge to Rationality and Emotionality," *Management Science,* vol. 17, no. 6, February 1971, pp. 275-292.

Benbasat, I., and R. G. Schroeder, "An Experimental Investigation of Some MIS Design Variables," *MIS Quarterly,* vol. 1, no. 1, March 1977, pp. 37-48.

_____and R. N. Taylor, "The Impact of Cognitive Styles on Information System Design," *MIS Quarterly,* vol. 2, no. 2, June 1978, pp. 43-54.

Berrisford, T., and J. Wetherbe, "Heuristic Development: A Redesign of Systems Design," *MIS Quarterly,* vol. 3, no. 1, March 1979, pp. 11-19.

Canning, Richard G., "Developing Systems by Prototyping," *EDP Analyzer,* vol. 19, no. 9, September 1981, pp. 1-14.

Chervany, N. L., and G. W. Dickson, "An Experimental Evaluation of Information Overload in a Production Environment," *Management Science,* vol. 20, no. 10, June 1978, pp. 1335-1344.

Couger, J. D., "Evolution of Business System Analysis Techniques," *ACM Computing Surveys,* vol. 5, no. 3, September 1973, pp. 167-198.

_____and R. W. Knapp, *Systems Analysis Techniques,* Wiley, New York: 1973.

Date, C. J., *An Introduction to Database Systems,* Addison-Wesley, Reading, Mass., 1977, pp. 73-196.

DeMarco, Tom, *Structured Analysis and System Specification,* Yourdon, New York, 1978.

Dickson, G. W., and J. K. Simmons, "The Behavioral Side of MIS," *Business Horizons,* vol. 13, no. 4, August 1970, pp. 1-13.

Hancock, J. L., "User Requirements and Systems Productivity," *Proceedings of the Ninth Annual SMIS Conference,* Los Angeles, CA, Sept. 26-28, 1977, pp. 13-20.

Head, R. V., "Automated System Analysis," *Datamation,* vol. 17, no. 16, Aug. 15, 1971, pp. 22-24.

Herron, Thomas J., Reagen Ramsower, Joseph V. Tolva, John R. Van Hook, James C. Wetherbe, and Edward C. Willems, "Incorporating Heuristic Development Into Formal System Development Methodologies," Management Information Systems Research Center, University of Minnesota, Minneapolis, 1981.

Jenkins, A. M., "A Framework for MIS Research," *Proceedings of the 9th Annual Conference: American Institute for Decision Sciences,* Chicago, Ill., Oct. 12-21, 1977, p. 573.

Keen, P. G. W., and M. S. Scott Morton, *Decision Support Systems: An Organizational Perspective,* Addison-Wesley, Reading, Mass., 1978.

Leavitt, Don, et. al., "Heuristic Development Eases Strains," *Computerworld,* no. 26, June 25, 1979.

London, Keith R., *Decision Tables,* Auerbach, Pennsauken, N.J., 1972.

Lucas, Henry C., *The Analysis, Design, and Implementation of Information Systems,* McGraw-Hill, New York, 1976.

_____, "The Evolution of an Information System: From Key-Man to Every Person," *Sloan Management Review,* vol. 19, no. 2, Winter 1978, pp. 39-52.

Martin, J., *Principles of Data-Base Management,* Prentice-Hall, Englewood Cliffs, N.J.: 1976, pp. 95-110.

Munro, M. C., and G. B. Davis, "Determining Management Information Needs: A Comparison of Methods," *MIS Quarterly,* vol. 1, no. 2, June 1977, pp. 55-67.

Nolan, R. L., "Systems Analysis for Computer-Based Information Systems Design," *Data Base,* vol. 3, no. 4, Winter 1971, pp. 1-10.

Nunamaker, J. F., Jr., "A Methodology for the Design and Optimization of Information Processing Systems," *Proceedings SJCC,* Montvale, N.J., 1971, pp. 283-294.

Orr, Ken, "Structured Requirements Definition," Ken Orr and Associates, Topeka, Kan., 1981.

Peters, L. J., and L. L. Tripp, "Comparing Software Design Methods," *Datamation*, vol. 23, no. 11, November 1977, pp. 89-94.

Prywes, N. S., "Automatic Generation of Software Systems," *Data Base*, vol. 6, no. 2, Summer 1974, pp. 7-17.

Renaud, D., "Current Implementation of Relational Systems -- ADABAS and the Relational Model," *Concepts and Planning*, Auerbach, Pennsauken, N.J., 1977, pp 1-12.

Schussel, George, "The Role of the Data Dictionary," *Datamation*, June 1977.

Simon, H. A., and A. Newell, "Human Problem Solving: The State of the Theory in 1970," *American Psychologist*, vol. 22, no. 2, February 1971, pp. 145-159.

Smith, H. R., and C. Knuth, "A Computerized Approach to Systems Analysis: A Technique and Its Application," *8th Annual Conference, American Institute for Decision Sciences Proceedings*, San Francisco, Nov. 10-12, 1976, pp. 549-551.

Snuggs, M. E., G. J. Popek, and R. J. Peterson, "Data Base Systems Objectives as Design Constraints," *Data Base*, vol. 6, no. 3, Winter 1974, pp. 11-20.

Taggard, W. M., and M. O. Tharp, "Dimensions of Information Requirements Analysis," *Data Base*, vol. 7, no. 1, Summer 1975, pp. 25-30.

Teichroew, D., "Problem Statement Languages in MIS," *Proceedings, International Symposium of BIFOA*, Cologne, West Germany, July 1970, pp. 253-279.

_____and H. Sayani, "Automation of System Building," *Datamation*, vol. 17, no. 16, Aug. 15, 1971, pp. 25-30.

Thall, R. M., "A Manual for PSA/ADS: A Machine-Aided Approach to Analysis of ADS," ISDOS Working Paper No. 35, Department of Industrial Engineering, University of Michigan, Ann Arbor, Mich. 1971.

Thomas, I. M. H., "Data Base Concepts for Systems Analysis," *Proceedings of the National Conference on Information Systems Development*, Western Periodicals, North Hollywood, Calif., 1978, pp. 39-46.

Wetherbe, J. C., "A Systems Specification Model for Instruction in Systems Analysis and Design," *Journal of Data Education*, July 1978.

_____, "Development and Application of Industry-Based Cases in Systems Analysis and Design," *Journal of Data Education*, October 1978.

_____, *Systems Analysis for Computer-Based Information Systems*, West, St. Paul, Minn., 1979.

Yourdon, Edward, and Larry Constantine, *Structured Design*, Yourdon, New York, 1978.

FIFTEEN

SOFTWARE DEVELOPMENT

INTRODUCTION

This chapter provides a management overview of key issues in software development. Problems, and techniques for solving them, are reviewed for software development, quality assurance, testing, and user-developed systems.

MANAGING SOFTWARE DEVELOPMENT

Software development primarily pertains to the structuring or programming of application software to support the information system. Good software development results in software that effectively and economically processes information.

Problems in Software Development

Application programming has a rather controversial history. Such factors as shortages of computer programmers, frequent and enormous cost overruns on program development, and calamities caused by "bugs" in large, complex computer programs have done little to enhance the potential contributions of computer technology.

In most organizations, computer programming has not been subjected to traditional management measurements of quality and quantity. Rather, the mystique and glamour of computer technology have often caused management to take a "hands-off" approach to the specialized and often undisciplined activity of computer programming. The standards and quality control so essential to uniformity and reliability are often not enforced. Programs developed in such environments are difficult to understand, test, debug, and modify.

The computing industry is plagued with unfortunate stories of information systems that have been crippled or become useless with the turnover of critical programmers. In many of these cases, the program code was so complex and confusing that it was easier to write new programs than to figure out how the old ones worked.

Fortunately, considerable progress has been made in the area of computer programming standards and control. The major emerging concepts are

- Structured programming[1]
- Top-down development[2]
- Development support libraries[3]
- Chief programmer teams[4]
- System development methodologies

These concepts are discussed in the following subsections.

Structured Programming

Surprisingly, the programming of complex computations does not represent the major cause of software problems. Rather, the major contributor to confusing and error-prone program code is nonstandard and undisciplined use of control (branching) logic. In such cases, the logic flow can erratically jump about in the program code in such a way that it is extremely difficult to follow.

The main culprit of undisciplined coding is the unrestricted use of unconditional branches (e.g., GO TO statements or their equivalents). The application of structured programming standards to control logic can resolve this problem. Programs can be written in such a fashion that they are straightforward and readable. The complexity and confusion involved in tracing undisciplined branching can be eliminated.

Structured programming is based on a solid theoretical foundation. Bohm and Jacopini have formally proved that only three basic control structures are necessary for computer programming:[5]

---

[1]Harlan D. Mills, "Top-Down Programming in Large Systems," *Debugging Techniques in Large Systems*, 1971, pp. 41-56.

[2]Clement L. McGowan and John R. Kelly, *Top-Down Structured Programming Techniques*, Mason/Charter, New York, 1975.

[3]Harlan D. Mills and John J. Naughton, "Programming Standards and Control," in *The Information Systems Handbook*, 1975, pp. 568-591.

[4]"Improved Programming Technologies — An Overview," *Installation Management*, IBM, White Plains, N.Y., 1974, p. 3.

[5]C. Bohn and G. Jacopini, "Flow Diagrams, Turing Machines, and Languages with Only Two Formation Rules," *Communications of the ACM*, 1966, pp. 366-371.

1. The SEQUENTIAL structure: Statements are executed one after the other.

2. The DO WHILE structure: One or more statements are repeated as long as a condition is true.

3. The IF THEN ELSE structure: One of two statements is branched to, based on whether a given condition is true or false.

The logic within these three structures is presented in Figure 15-1. The three structures can be combined with each other to define program logic from beginning to end. Though unconditional branches are not necessary, on occasion they may be used for purposes of programming practicality. However, such branches should be made on an exception basis and should be carefully documented and justified.

Note that each of the structures has a single entry and a single exit. This single-entry-single-exit property can be maintained as the structures are combined to build program modules or segments. For example, Figure 15-2 shows a logic flow that contains all of the structures and has the single-entry-single-exit property.

The use of the single-entry-single-exit structure in organizing logical structures allows the clustering of program functions into single-entry-single-exit modules or subsystems. Assigning program functions to specific modules allows the modules of a complex program to be independently programmed by separate programmers. Because each module has only one point of entry and one point of exit, the interfacing of these modules in one program or system is simplified. Since each module's function is clearly defined before it is programmed, the modules fit together to form a complete program.

Besides allowing program functions to be programmed independently, modularization simplifies program testing, debugging, and modification.

Figure 15-1 Basic Control Structures of Structured Programming

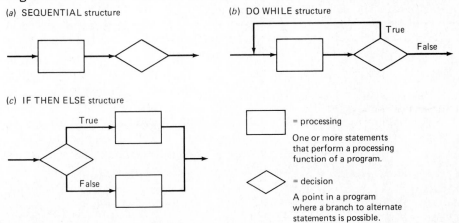

(a) SEQUENTIAL structure

(b) DO WHILE structure   True   False

(c) IF THEN ELSE structure

True   False

= processing

One or more statements
that perform a processing
function of a program.

= decision

A point in a program
where a branch to alternate
statements is possible.

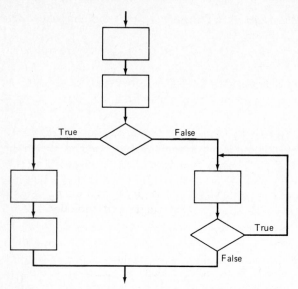

Figure 15-2 Logic Flow with Single Entry/Exit and Multiple Control Structures

Since program functions are defined in specific modules, they can usually be tested, debugged, and modified as separate modules of a program code. This reduces confusion caused by program statements branching into or out of modules at points other than those at which the modules are designed to be entered or exited.

Top-Down Development

Program development has traditionally been a "bottom-up" procedure. The lowest-level functions are coded first. They are then tested and prepared for integration with other program functions.[6] This approach often results in data definition and interface problems during integration of the functions. Consequently, integration is delayed until these problems are resolved. Another major drawback of the bottom-up approach pertains to debugging program malfunctions after the functions have been integrated. It may be extremely difficult to determine which of the many program modules combined during integration is the source of a particular problem.

A bottom-up approach philosophically contradicts the manner in which a system evolves. The systems development process evolves from a broad and conceptual level to an increasingly detailed and operational

[6]"Improved Programming Technologies," op. cit.

level. Much of the low-level detail required for a bottom-up approach is not available until late in the systems development cycle.

"Top-down" program development is a procedure in which program requirements are factored from the top to the bottom. Top-down development is sometimes referred to as an outside-inside approach. The program to be developed is first considered in its broadest sense. This involves considering the program in terms of its inputs and outputs (i.e., what is to happen *outside* the program). The program is then factored into the progressively smaller functional units required to achieve the desired transformation of inputs to outputs (i.e., what is to happen *inside* the program).

Structured programming is a means for conveniently factoring large, complex programs into manageable single-entry-single-exit modules. The factoring continues until modules are defined at a level directly transferable to program code. The factoring process is illustrated in Figure 15-3. Each module (A through O in Figure 15-3) can be independently programmed, tested, debugged, and, if necessary, modified.

During the testing and debugging of a program module, other modules to be integrated may not yet exist. Dummy units called "program stubs" are used to simulate such modules. Program stubs do not usually perform meaningful computations; however, they send acceptable responses back to another module so that it can continue processing as if real modules were already in place. The eventual integration of the various program modules is not a problem because well-defined data definitions and interfaces are inherent to the top-down approach.

Three guidelines have proven useful for top-down program development:

1. Use indentation in source code to highlight the DO WHILE and IF THEN ELSE structures.
2. Keep the program modules to 50 or fewer statements.
3. Code a program module only after the higher-level module that invokes it has been coded and tested. (For example, in Figure 15-3, module A should be coded and tested before modules C and D.)

Structured Software Design Techniques

A variety of commercially developed products are available which further refine and operationalize the concepts of structured programming and top-down development. Though these products often have cosmetic differences, there is a great deal of similarity in how they work and how they are used. Some of the more common techniques are reviewed below. The review is designed to provide a general understanding of the

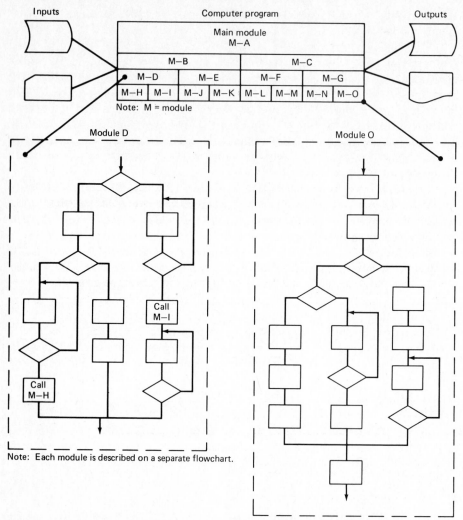

Figure 15-3 Top-Down Approach of Software Development

various techniques, but it is beyond the scope of this book to provide skills training in each of the techniques. However, with the conceptual understanding provided in the preceding discussions and the review below, it should be easy to grasp the specifics of any of the following techniques in any organization within which they are used.

The specific techniques reviewed are:

1. HIPO: -- Hierarchy plus input, process, and output
2. SADT: -- Structured analysis and design techniques
3. W/O: -- Warnier/Orr technique
4. SDD: -- Structured decomposition diagram

HIPO. IBM has developed a system of procedures and forms called HIPO (hierarchy plus input process output) that is designed to facilitate effective and efficient top-down program development. HIPO provides excellent discipline and a structure to factor complex programs into individual single-entry-single-exit modules. Each module is defined in terms of its inputs, processes, and outputs.

HIPO provides a visual representation of software that serves as both a design tool and documentation. Completed HIPO forms (or charts) provide a blueprint for program code and reduce the need for program flowcharts. The HIPO charts partition all program modules, define the hierarchy and organization of the modules, and define the communication between modules. HIPO has been criticized because it does not usually define the sequence of execution (i.e., conditional branching or iterations) as flowcharts do. However, when necessary, HIPO specifications can be augmented with flowcharts.

The actual HIPO chart looks much like an organizational chart, hierarchy showing how functions or activities are composed of more elementary functions (see Figure 15-4). The process of factoring down, or functional decomposition, continues until a function has been reduced

Figure 15-4 HIPO Hierarchy Chart

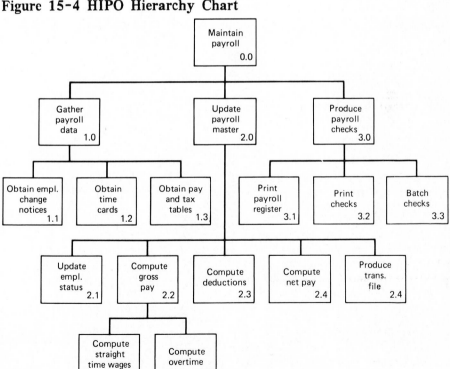

located at the appropriate level on the hierarchy chart and is labeled with a "noun-verb" action statement. For example, the function of "compute gross pay" may be factored or decomposed into "compute straight time wages" and "compute overtime." Each box or function within the chart is numerically labeled referring to the next higher function so that organization can be maintained.

The noun-verb action statement labeling each function in a HIPO chart is further described through IPO (input/output charts), and shown in Figure 15-5. IPO charts consist of three boxes showing the input, process, and outputs. For higher-level functions, the process may be the control statements for one or more subfunctions. As lower-level functions are described in an IPO chart, the process becomes very close to the actual code to be used in programming the function.

HIPO is generally regarded as a good technique for limited analysis work. However, it is criticized for lacking the characteristics that would allow it to be useful in complex system structures. Specifically, the relationships between functions or data elements that are critical to any system are not evident due to processes being analyzed separately. Also, the consistent use of the technique and its iterations are controlled.

SADT. SADT is a product of Soft Tec Incorporated and was developed as a complete methodology for the use and control of the tools used in analyzing and designing a system. It provides a graphical representation of the hierarchy functions and data within a system (see

Figure 15-5 HIPO Input, Process, Output

From: Update payroll master (2.0)

I	P	O

SALARY
EMPL-STATUS
	1. IF EMPL-STATUS = SALARIED
	   THEN SAL-GROSS-PAY =
	   SALARY/24
	   ELSE PERFORM "COMPUTE
	   STRAIGHT-TIME WAGES"
		SAL-GROSS-PAY

EMPL-STATUS
HRS-WORKED
	2. IF EMPL-STATUS = HOURLY
	   AND HRS-WORKED > 40
	   THEN PERFORM "COMPUTE
	   OVERTIME"	

To: Compute straight time wages (2.2.1)
Compute overtime (2.2.2)

Box no. 2.2

Diagram: Compute gross pay

Figure 15-6). As illustrated in Figure 15-6, SADT displays the inputs, processes, outputs, controls, mechanisms, and relationships between the functions and data in the system.

Note that in Figure 15-6 there is a macro diagram at the top of the figure which is then, as with HIPO, factored down into more detailed

Figure 15-6 SADT Diagram

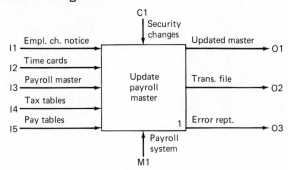

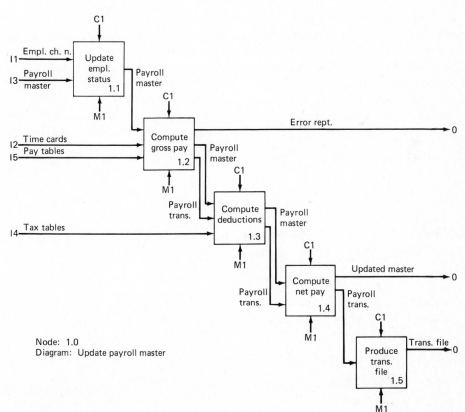

Node: 1.0
Diagram: Update payroll master

to its most basic activities. Each function is placed within a box and boxes conveying a specific operation to be performed to achieve processing. The arrows connecting the vertical faces of functions in a SADT diagram represent data interfaces and are labelled appropriately. The other arrows on the horizontal faces of the SADT diagram represent the external constraints on the function and the mechanism used to perform the function.

Beyond specifying the tools involved in the SADT technique, SADT also includes comprehensive procedures and rules for using SADT.

Implementation of SADT requires a strong management commitment due to its high cost, extensive training requirements, and the high volume of work automation which is often required for complex systems.

Warnier/Orr Technique. The Warnier/Orr technique (W/O) is a systems design and program design technique. The W/O technique is unique in that in it uses graphical displays consisting of a hierarchy of brackets to portray activities or data elements. Figure 15-7 illustrates a W/O diagram and defines the symbols used.

The W/O technique consists of several steps which ultimately end in the programming of the system. The first step of the technique involves the diagramming of system outputs. System outputs, including reports and files, are then decomposed and a hierarchy is shown by brackets which enclose data or functions supported. Parallels are used to show how the data or function is controlled -- sequentially, logically, or repetitively.

W/O diagrams can be used to schedule when data is required to achieve the production of the desired outputs. For example, the reporting cycle (yearly, quarterly, monthly) can be shown with its

Figure 15-7 W/O Diagram

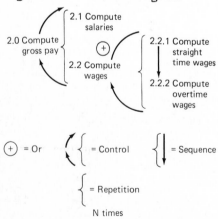

scheduled output. This ensures that the data needed to produce the output is available on time.

Another feature of the W/O diagram that is particularly useful is called "change analysis." During change analysis, all possible occurrences that would cause a data element, function, or reporting cycle to change are investigated. If the design cannot handle the occurrence, appropriate changes are made. This allows the design to encompass predictable changes in the environment.

The final stage in the W/O technique consists of translating diagrams into program code. Each bracket in the W/O diagram becomes a module in a computer program. (Note that each bracket in a W/O diagram is similar to a decomposed box in a decoposed IPO or SADT chart.) The arrows in a W/O diagram represent the control statements while the functions become the working statements. The W/O diagrams which show the working statements as derived from the functions are duplicated. This program diagram can then be pseudo-coded (i.e., structured English) showing the control statements as derived from the arrows. Pseudo code can then be translated directly into program code and structured walk-throughs at control points within the entire process to complete the technique.

W/O diagrams are very useful for data structuring techniques as the diagrams come very close to programming code. However, they are criticized for not providing adequate functional analysis. In other words, while the W/O diagrams clearly show composition, they lack the links between the various functions.

SDD. SDD is a hybrid structured analysis technique developed by CTEC Incorporated. It is derived from the previously discussed SADT and the W/O technique and attempts to "borrow of the best" of both techniques. SADT diagrams are used for analyzing functional hierarchy and W/O diagrams are used to describe the function. Figure 15-8 illustrates an SDD version of SADT. Note that the data interfaces (arrows) of SADT are circumvented, but the decomposition of the data remains. Mechanism arrows are also not used in this version of SADT. Diagramming is completed by showing the data interfaces in a modified W/O diagram, as illustrated in Figure 15-9. This hybrid version of SADT and W/O technique decomposes both functional activities and data elements without the voluminous diagramming required in the SADT technique.

The analysis phase of SDD is completed with a data/function matrix, as illustrated in Figure 15-10, which is also a hybrid of the decomposition of data elements and functions. The data function matrix depicts the role, if any, that each data element plays within each function. Note that in Figure 15-10 each intersection of a data element

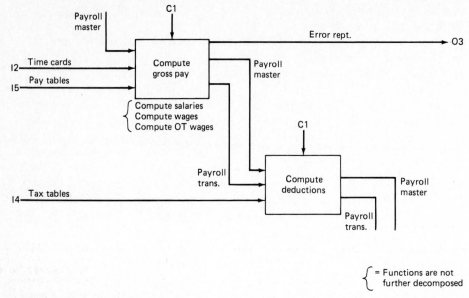

Figure 15-8 SDD Truncation of SADT

and a function is labeled with an "1" for input and/or "0" for output or "C" for constraint, if appropriate. The result of this matrix is a complete diagram showing the lengths between data elements and functions.

SDD has three advantages over SADT and the W/O technique when used separately. First, the combining of W/O technique with SADT provides "shortcut" notation without disturbing the flow of SADT diagramming. Second, the voluminous diagram required in SADT can be circumvented without losing the hierarchical structure. Third, the data function matrix provides a link between data elements and functions that is not found in either SADT or W/O diagrams.

Figure 15-9 SDD Modified W/O Diagram

			Inputs	Outputs
	1.1 Update empl. status		Empl. ch. notice Payroll master	Payroll master
	1.2 Compute gross pay	1.2.1 Comp. sal. 1.2.2 Comp. wages 1.2.3 Comp. OT	Payroll master Time cards Pay tables	Payroll master Payroll trans.
1.0 Update payroll master	1.3 Compute deductions		Payroll master Payroll trans. Tax tables	Payroll master Payroll trans.
	1.4 Compute net pay		Payroll master Payroll trans.	Updated master Payroll trans.
	1.5 Produce trans. file		Payroll trans.	Trans. file

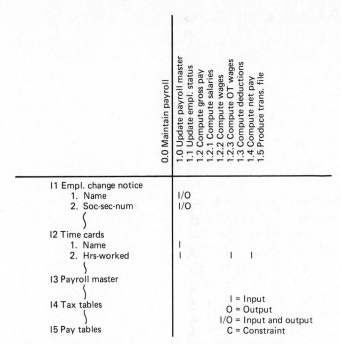

Figure 15-10 SDD Data/Function Matrix

Review of Structured Software Design Techniques

There is a great deal of similarity between the structured techniques discussed above. They are all graphical representations of functional and data hierarchies. They start at a higher conceptual level and factor down to detail, ultimately providing enough definition to be readily translated into computer programming instructions.

There is no research indicating which techniques work the best. Rather, there is only anecdotal information from people who have worked with different techniques. These comments were worked into the discussion of the techniques as appropriate.

At the beginning of the discussion of these techniques it was pointed out that the idea is to provide familiarity with a variety of techniques available, recognizing that different techniques have different characteristics and different strengths and weaknesses. Again, keep in mind that the theory behind the techniques is to provide a more closed/stable/mechanistic disciplined approach to software development. Also, note that all techniques draw extensively on the theoretical framework of general systems theory.

Development Support Libraries

Traditionally, the productivity of programmers has been low because of the necessity of their handling clerical activities that are peripheral to program development, such as filing and maintaining program listings, and creating, updating, and backing up program libraries. If such activities do not interfere with program development, it is often because they are being neglected, which is even worse. Failure to perform these tasks jeopardizes the integrity and operation of an information system.

To address the issues of programmer productivity and integrity, many organizations have implemented a development support library (DSL) function. A DSL is software for maintaining continuous documentation of major activities associated with developing a system. Operation of the DSL is usually the responsibility of one or more program librarians who are not under the supervision of those programming the system.

The DSL consists of two basic components: an internal library and an external library. The internal library is stored on computer files and contains all programs, test data, linkage-editing statements, and job control statements. The external library is maintained in human-readable form and describes the contents and the status of the internal library. Machine procedures are required to operate the internal library, and clerical procedures are required to operate the external library. The basic procedures required for each library are listed below:

INTERNAL LIBRARY	EXTERNAL LIBRARY
1. Creating, updating, and deleting libraries	1. Documenting directions marked by programmer
2. Retrieving program modules	2. Using internal library
3. Excuting programs	3. Filing status listings
4. Backing up and restoring libraries	4. Filing and replacing pages in systems documentation
5. Producing library status listings	

The DSL reduces the number of clerical activities that have to be done by programmers. It also defines sole responsibility for the DSL functions. Accordingly, both programmer productivity and control of the development process are improved.

Chief-Programmer Teams

Because of the increasing size and complexity of major programming efforts, a team effort is often required to complete a system on schedule. The coordinating and interfacing of the efforts of several computer programmers have traditionally proved to be a cumbersome task. The advent of structured programming, top-down design, and DSLs has provided the necessary framework for a team approach to program development. Coordination and integration of activities are simplified by the modularity of tasks that these interrelated techniques afford.

The use of a team of programmers headed by a chief programmer has proved to be highly productive. It is also a means of achieving high-quality program development.[7] The chief-programmer team concept involves a team effort. The team members perform specific functions, as follows:

1. *Chief programmer:* The chief programmer is a highly proficient programmer who has overall responsibility for the program design and coding. He or she defines and assigns program modules to be coded by other team members. He or she reviews all code and supervises the testing and debugging of code. The chief programmer informs management of the project status and arranges for additional team members when necessary.

2. *Backup programmer:* The backup programmer is an experienced programmer who works closely enough with the chief programmer to assume his or her responsibilities, if necessary. He or she also participates in the coding of program modules.

3. *Program librarian:* The program librarian is a clerical person who handles the DSL functions described in the preceding section.

4. *Others:* Additional team members (primarily programmers) are assigned to the team as necessary. These team members generally have specialized skills (e.g., coding speed, application knowledge, or knowledge of unique coding techniques).

Chief-programmer teams provide increased control and integrity to the development process. They also provide for professional growth and technical excellence in programming. Clerical activities are done by the program librarian, thereby releasing programmers to devote their technical skills to developing programs. Inexperienced programmers are exposed to senior-level programmers in an environment that prepares them for leadership roles on future teams.

---

[7]F.T. Baker, "Chief Programmer Team, Management of Production Programming," *IBM Systems Journal,* vol. 11, no. 1, March 1972, pp. 56-73.

Systems Development Methodologies

Formalized systems development methodologies that pertain to the entire systems development life cycle (i.e., PRIDE, SDM/70, CARA, and Spectrum) were discussed in Chapter 14. Each of these methodologies was described in a section providing procedures and checklists for software development and covering such topics as program design, external and internal design specifications, and program testing.

These methodologies provide good templates to use to manage and control software development. They impose discipline and structure on what can become an unwieldy, disorganized effort to manage and provide a framework for structured, top-down development.

QUALITY ASSURANCE

Quality, or the lack of it, has become a major issue worldwide. Besides increasing productivity, perhaps no other general management issue has received so much attention. As many quality experts are quick to point out, a major cause of lost productivity is poor quality. Poor quality can cause production delays, cost overruns, and unacceptable products.

The development of quality assurance in application software has traditionally been one of the most neglected activities in industry. The software industry is laced with stories of million dollar errors in checks printed on computers, lost customer accounts, online systems being down more than they are up, etc. There has been so much emphasis on meeting deadlines that there is little time for quality assurance. It seems that, as so often happens in MIS, "urgency drives out importance." No recipient of an information system would knowingly pressure for a deadline to be met if meeting that deadline would result in unacceptable quality. But deadlines can become so urgent that the importance of quality is overlooked.

Recently, more "street-wise" management has placed greater emphasis on quality in software development. Starting with quality-oriented management attitudes, MIS organizations have been able to significantly increase quality in software development by using technologies including design overviews, detail reviews, and code inspections. Besides increasing quality, these techniques provide a potent educational process. The techniques are discussed below.

Management Attitudes

The right place to start with quality assurance is with the attitude of management. Management should insist on *economic* quality, that is, quality that is cost-effective. Quality that costs more than it is worth is not economic.

For example, an online system that is up 98 percent of the time may be acceptable for a wholesale distributor's online order entry system. In general, it would not make economic sense to add a backup computer to provide 99.8 percent up time. However, such reliability does make economic sense for an online airline reservation system.

Management must establish quality standards that are reflective of the organization's requirements, communicate these attitudes, and support and reward quality performance.

A particularly popular process used to establish an attitude of quality is the "quality circle." In a quality circle, organizational participants who play key roles in a process are freed from their regular duties to have collective discussions on ways to improve quality. This allows "importance" to get some leverage over "urgency." It shows that management places enough importance on quality to take time away from production. Also, the energy that is generated by group discussions with individuals having different perspectives often results in outstanding ideas.

Quality circles can be established to focus on programming techniques, documentation, use of new technology, etc. They often have a training orientation, where more-skilled personnel share their techniques with less-skilled personnel.

Design Overview

A more specific, but still macro, level of quality assurance is the design overview. A design overview should be incorporated into the MIS function's systems development methodology. It consists of a peer evaluation of the designer's overall approach to software development for one or more programs in an information system.

The designer's peers critique the design but generally do not offer suggestions for improvement (this would put the reviewers into the role of designer). The designer responds to the criticism with explanations or suggested improvements. If satisfactory responses to criticism cannot be provided at the first meeting, subsequent meetings are scheduled.

This process continues until the designer's peers are willing to approve the software design.

Detail Reviews

Once the design overview is complete, the systems designer begins detail design of the software. Upon completion of this effort, the next level of quality assurance is the detail review, or what IBM calls a "structured walk-through."

During this stage of quality assurance, the systems designer steps through the logic of their software in a presentation to qualified peers. The designer's peers check for use of good structured techniques and top-down design as well as specific logic. As with a design overview, the detail design is critiqued and, if necessary, an iterative process of explanations and corrections follows until the peers agree to approve the detail design.

Code Inspection

The final stage of quality assurance prior to system testing is code inspection. During code inspection, a programmer other than the original coder inspects the instructions line by line in a clearly compiled computer program to see if everything seems correct and coding conventions have been followed.

As mundane as this task may seem, it has proved to be a powerful way to check for errors. It has been estimated that isolating and resolving an error at this stage of software development is 50 to 100 times easier than when the system is complete.

TESTING

After quality assurance is complete, computer programs and program modules are tested. As the programs are integrated into the total information system, overall testing of the system is possible.

Testing is a critical stage of the systems development cycle. It is the major checkpoint prior to the actual implementation of the system. The consequences of system malfunctions are minimized when they are discovered and resolved during testing, rather than during implementation.

Validation

System problems are discovered by subjecting the system to extensive validation. The major system processes to be validated are

1. *Clerical processing:* The data collection and preparation procedures must be performed correctly.
2. *Input processing:* Transactions must be properly checked for errors and must be applied to the right records in the right files.
3. *Computational processing:* The proper variables must be computed by using the proper arithmetic.
4. *Logic processing:* Decision rules must be executed with the correct sequencing and branching.
5. *File access:* Records must be stored in and retrieved from the right locations.
6. *Output processing:* The correct variables must be printed in the right places on printouts and displays.

These processes can be validated through the processing of real or fabricated transactions that represent normal and abnormal conditions. The outputs resulting from transaction processing can be validated by checking to see if they are correct. For example, the amount due on a loan can be computed on a calculator and compared to a corresponding output provided by the computer system.

An information system must be able to handle exceptions (i.e., abnormal transactions). To validate this aspect ' of the system, transactions that deviate from the normal transaction form should be prepared and processed. For example, payroll transactions with invalid department codes, a missing social security number, pay rates below the minimum wage rate, or hours worked that exceed the allowable limit should be prepared. A properly developed information system should detect such errors and report them on error reports.

Debugging

The process of correcting system malfunctions is called "debugging." The source of an incorrect output can exist anywhere in an information system. The problem can occur during data collection or preparation, during input processing, in the computational or logical processes of one or more computer programs, or at any other point. Therefore, to debug a malfunction, the source of its occurrence must be isolated before the problem can be resolved.

Malfunctions occur somewhere between the initial entry of data into the system and the final output. In other words, if the data entering the system is correct, but the information leaving it is incorrect, then the malfunction resides somewhere between entry and exit. The specific location of the malfunction can be isolated by working backward from the output to the input and/or forward from the input to the output. Each point in the system where the data is used can be checked to determine where the malfunction occurred. That is, the data can be displayed before and after each system process until the specific process causing the problem is isolated. In many cases, the data is not reported or displayed before or after a process (e.g., before and after a sort). In such cases a special program may have to be written or a simple dump of the file made for debugging purposes. Figure 15-11 illustrates a system with identified checkpoints for isolating a system malfunction.

Once isolated, a system malfunction can be resolved -- say, by a change in program code, data collection procedure, or keypunch procedure. If the malfunction exists in a computer program, the use of structured programming facilitates debugging. Since the function of each module is defined, each module that uses the data in question can be determined and checked for the malfunction. Once isolated, program modules can be corrected and integrated back into the system.

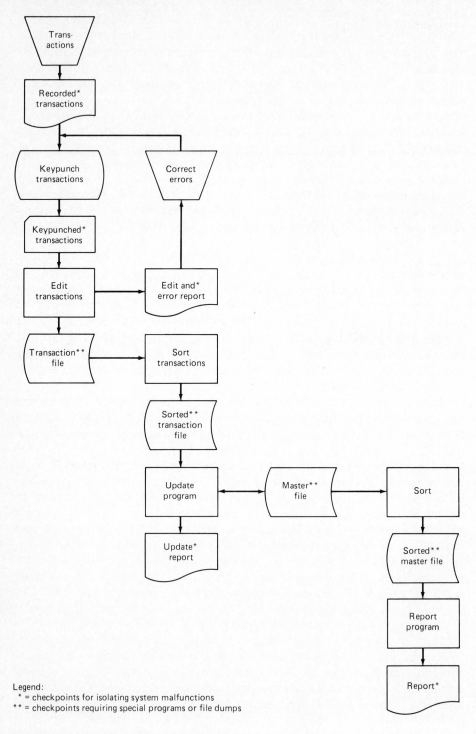

Figure 15-11 Standard Checkpoints for Debugging an Information System

USER-DEVELOPED SYSTEMS

One thing is clear: Given the insatiable demand for more and better information to support decision making and operations of organizations, enough computer programmers cannot be graduated from our colleges and universities to handle the workload.

The situation is not dissimilar to the one faced by the telephone company years ago. Had the telephone company not automated as it did, everyone in the work force would have to be a telephone operator to handle today's telephone workloads.

What did the telephone company do? They *did* make all of us telephone operators. In the early days of telephone use, we had to go through a telephone operator to do everything, including making a local call. Gradually, via automation, the telephone company shifted more and more of the work load to us. First, we could make local calls by ourselves, then long distance, then credit card calls, etc. Today we only get assistance from a telephone operator when we can't make a call on our own, and often that assistance is provided by a computerized telephone operator. There are not fewer telephone operators. The telephone company is simply able to provide more service without adding substantial numbers of people. As a result, costs per transaction have gone down.

The evolution of telephone use is analagous to what is happening with computer use. In the early use of computers, managers or users of computer services were totally dependent upon the computer technician for everything. The gradual evolution of user-friendly languages is allowing managers to do more and more on their own. The computer technician's role, like that of the telephone operator, is becoming one of "helping users to help themselves."

Evolution of Programming Languages

Early computer languages of the 1950s looked like this:

```
011011   0111011   0111101
011100   1100110   1010111
110000   1110000   1110010
```

By the late 1950s and early 1960s they looked more like this:

```
LD   A    R1
AD   B    R1
ST   R1   C
```

In the mid- to late 1960s and 1970s they more commonly looked like this:

    READ PRODUCT-FILE
        INVALID KEY PERFORM BAD-KEY ROUTINE.
    MOVE PRODUCT-NUMBER TO O-PRODUCT-NUMBER.
    MOVE P-DESCRIPTION TO O-DESCRIPTION.
    MULTIPLY UNITS-ORDERED BY SELLING-PRICE
    GIVING TOTAL-PRODUCT-LIST.

Today, user-friendly languages look like this:

    SELECT PERSONNEL-RECORDS WHERE JOB-
        CLASSIFICATION IS ACCOUNTANT, SALARY
        IS LESS THAN 35,000, AND COLLEGE
        DEGREE IS MASTERS.

Today's advanced programming languages allow a manager to learn enough skills in a day or two to satisfy most of their immediate and ad hoc information requirements, if properly collected and organized data is stored on the computer.

Computer technicians and information systems professionals will still be needed to manage and control the increasing complexity of hardware, software, and databases necessary to support this new environment. However, managers will not have to explain everything they need to a technician. They will have direct access to the computer, so overall productivity should increase significantly.

Managing User-Developed Systems

The trend toward managers as programmers is a good trend. However, if it is not handled properly, it can have negative consequences. Possible problems are listed below:

- Systems may be developed that cannot be integrated with other systems or corporate databases.

- Users may purchase mini- or microcomputer systems to do their own programming, which may not be capable of handling the job for which they were purchased.

- Users may develop programs that are not subjected to adequate quality assurance checks to ensure that accurate, reliable processing has been performed.

- Systems may be developed without adequate documentation, thereby rendering the system useless when its developer leaves the organization.

To avoid the types of problems listed above, as well as to provide an environment that supports and encourages user-developed systems, the following actions are recommended:

- The information systems function should set up a user assistance or information center to support end-user computing and programming.

- This group should be service-oriented. It should propose solutions to user problems and then "help users help themselves."

- This group should keep current on new technological developments in the areas of micrographics, personal computers, software packages, etc.

- A uniform commitment should be made by this group to provide consulting support in the use of certain types of micro- and minicomputers.

- This group should maintain proficiency in the use of all major user facilities and provide one-on-one user consulting when needed.

- A user hotline should be established to provide instant response to users having questions about, or difficulty in the use of, end-user computing.

- Procedures should be established for quality assurance and documentation checks on user-developed systems that are to become available for general use or will become an integral part of any department's operation.

Medtronic Inc. is a progressive company in terms of using managers as programmers. Besides properly managing users as programmers, it is actually encouraging them to program. To facilitate the proliferation of programming among managers, Medtronic provides a small financial bonus to managers who develop proficiency in the use of programming languages pertinent to their areas of responsibility.

Tom Morin, director of information systems, says, "We're convinced that the 'carrot' approach is the way to go. We are providing the best consulting service we can to our user managers, and top management has been supportive enough to reward those managers who develop the skills."

SUMMARY

Software development has been plagued by delays, cost overruns, and errors. Techniques that have improved the development of software include structured programming, top-down development, development support libraries, chief-programmer teams, and systems development methodologies.

Beyond improving the process of developing software, quality assurance strategies have proved effective. Quality assurance starts with a quality-oriented attitude on the part of management and employs techniques such as design overviews, detail reviews, and code inspections.

Testing of software follows quality assurance. Testing includes validation and debugging of software. The problems and the magnitude of testing have been reduced with the advent of better software development and quality assurance techniques.

A major trend in software development is user-developed systems. Advances in programming languages have made it possible for users to develop much of their own software. However, good management of user-developed software is critical to protect both the users and the organization.

SUGGESTED READINGS

Baker, F. T., "Chief Programmer Team, Management of Production Programming," *IBM Systems Journal,* vol. 11, no. 1, March 1972, pp. 56-73.

_____, "System Quality through Structured Programming," Fall Joint Computer Conference, 1972.

Bohm, C., and G. Jacopini, "Flow Diagrams, Turing Machines, and Languages with Only Two Formation Rules," *Communications of the ACM,* vol. 9, no. 5, May 1966, pp. 366-371.

Dahl, O. J., E. W. Dijkstra, and C. A. Hoarde, *Structured Programming,* Academic Press, London, 1972.

Dijkstra, E. W., *Structured Programming,* Academic Press, New York, 1972.

Elspas, B., K. N. Levitt, R. J. Waldinger, and A. Waksman, "An Assessment of Techniques for Proving Program Correctness," *ACM Computing Surveys,* vol. 4, no. 2, June 1972, pp. 97-147.

"Improved Programming Technologies -- An Overview," *Installation Management,* IBM, White Plains, N.Y., 1974, p. 3.

Knutsen, K. Eric, "Business Systems Analysis: Program Design," in F. W. McFarland and R. L. Nolan (eds.), *The Information Systems Handbook,* Dow Jones-Irwin, Homewood, Ill., 1975, pp. 539-567.

_____, and Richard L. Nolan, "On Cost/Benefit of Computer-Based Systems," *Managing the Data Resource Function,* R. Nolan (ed.), West, St. Paul, Minn., 1974, pp. 253-276.

McGowan, Clement L., and John R. Kelly, *Top-Down Structured Programming Techniques,* Mason/Charter, New York, 1975.

Mills, Harlan D., "Top-Down Programming in Large Systems," in Randall Rustin (ed.), *Debugging Techniques in Large Systems,* Courant Computer Science Symposium 1, New York University, New York, 1971, pp. 41-56.

_____, "Mathematical Foundations of Structured Programming," IBM Report No. FSC 72-6012, 1972.

_____, and John J. Naughton, "Programming Standards and Control," in F. McFarlan and R. Nolan (eds.), *The Information Systems Handbook,* Dow Jones-Irwin, Homewood, Ill., 1975, pp. 568-581.

Nolan, Richard L., and Henry H. Seward, "Measuring User Satisfaction to Evaluate Information Systems," in R. Nolan (ed.), *Managing the Data Resource Function,* West, St. Paul, Minn., 1974, pp. 253-276.

Parnas, D. L., "On the Criteria to be Used in Decomposing Systems into Modules," *Communications of the ACM,* vol. 15, no. 12, December 1972, pp. 1053-1058.

Sammet, J. C., "Perspective on Methods of Improving Software Development," *Software Engineering,* vol. 1, 1970.

Weinberg, Gerald M., *The Psychology of Computer Programmming,* Van Nostrand Reinhold, New York, 1971.

Wetherbe, J. C., *Systems Analysis for Computer-Based Information Systems,* West, St. Paul, Minn., 1979.

_____, *Executive's Guide to Computer-Based Information Systems,* Prentice-Hall, Englewood Cliffs, N.J., 1983.

SIXTEEN

IMPLEMENTATION

INTRODUCTION

In common use in data processing, the word "implementation" refers to the stage in the systems development life cycle in which computer programs are developed. This topic was addressed in the two previous chapters. Here, our use of the word implementation is different and is associated with getting a newly developed or significantly changed system used by those for whom it was intended. Furthermore, their use of the system ought to be without significant "people" problems. Our discussion of implementation therefore deals with the behavioral aspects of information systems.

Building management information systems and introducing new technologies into organizations are classic examples of change. Yet, few information systems managers view these processes from the perspective of accomplishing change. Despite a growing awareness that comes in part from a good deal of writing about "people" problems in MIS, too many systems builders still focus only upon the technical aspects of creating new or modified systems.

The implementation of computer-based information systems can be viewed as a three-stage process. The first stage is an awareness that many behavioral problems can occur when systems are introduced into organizations or existing systems are changed. Associated with this stage is an understanding of the specific kinds of dysfunctions that can occur. The second stage concerns an understanding of *why* these problems happen. In essence, this stage involves diagnosis. The third stage involves the treatment of the problems identified in the second stage. This, of course, is the most difficult task associated with implementation. As the reader will see, substantial work has been done on proposing solutions to implementation problems. Unfortunately, much of this work is very general in nature, and it is hard to find details on how to operationalize many of the suggested approaches.

Before we go on to present some of our experiences with implementation problems, it is instructive to say just a bit more about what we mean when we use the word "implementation." Implementation, in our context, is involved whenever a computer-based information system is installed in an organization or when an existing system is modified in nontrivial ways. When a system is truly implemented, it means that the installed system is used by the persons for whom it was intended, without significant problems.

It is also appropriate to discuss what we mean by the word "use." A system is used if without the system the users would have trouble doing the job which is supported by the system. In other words, a system is used when it is integrated in the work which it was developed to assist. This may be a clerical system to process invoicing transactions or a marketing information system to assist brand managers. In the former case, clerks would *use* the system in their day-to-day activities in invoicing customers and would feel hamstrung in their job if the system were suddenly unavailable. Similarly, the brand managers would *use* their system when it became integrated into their decisions concerning brand management, and they too would feel handicapped in doing their work should the system become unavailable.

A system is not successfully implemented unless it is used. Furthermore, as was said above, it must be used without significant problems. A number of these problems, associated with avoidance, projection, and aggression, were discussed in Chapter 2. How these behaviors manifest themselves in specific symptoms is described in the following case examples.

AWARENESS

Almost everyone who has read about computer usage in organizations or who knows people who work with computers has heard horror stories of some sort about nonuse or misuse of the computers. Recounting these episodes can be instructive. In the first place, it calls attention to what can happen when people and computer-based information systems interact. Second, we can learn from our mistakes. Unfortunately, in many cases it seems as though each new systems installation creates a new set of mistakes. In other words, it is difficult to generalize from previous situations.

Most importantly, narrating case examples of implementation problems creates an awareness of what can happen when proper consideration is not given to the behavioral side of management information systems. MIS managers, systems developers, and users involved with systems need to be aware of the symptoms of behavioral consequences involved with the organizational use of computers. The following vignettes are offered to raise the reader's consciousness regarding systems implementation.

Case A

One of the best-known and most dramatic examples of dysfunctional behavior associated with implementing a computer-based system occurred when the U.S. Post Office Department installed the postal source data system (PSDS). This system was designed at Post Office headquarters in Washington, D.C., and developed by a computer vendor according to the design specifications. The system was to measure post office productivity, forecast work loads, and perform the payroll function.

A test of the PSDS was made at two Post Office locations which seemed to be ideal. The workers at these two locations had high morale, relatively high educational levels, and stable work histories. The test locations were Minneapolis, Minnesota, and Milwaukee, Wisconsin. Equipment was installed in these two locations and the test was begun. Right from the start, problems occurred which had little to do with the technical design of the system, because the system did what it was supposed to do.

A group of university researchers studied the PSDS test at the Minneapolis site and they found that:[1]

1. During its first few months of operation, the system was plagued with errors. Out of 4300 transactions, 400 had some sort of error. Interviews indicated that many of these were made by postal workers "on purpose."

2. Interviews concerning what the workers' peers thought of the system showed that they didn't like it. "There was much grumbling, confusion, and fear," and "It was terrible. They wanted to go back to time cards," were typical statements attributed to coworkers.

3. Operating management said that worker reaction to the system included physical sabotage, threats, and union resistance. There were reports that workers used the system to make popular foremen look good and unpopular ones look bad.

---

[1]G.W. Dickson, J.K. Simmons, and J.C. Anderson, "Behavioral Reactions to the Introduction of a Management Information System at the U.S. Post Office: Some Empirical Observations," in D. Sanders (ed.), *Computers and Management*, 2d ed., McGraw-Hill, New York, 1974.

4.   The reports of physical sabotage included cases in which honey was poured into badge readers and an instance of a badge reader being "accidentally" run over by a forklift truck.

5.   The managers, when questioned about system usefulness, never responded positively.

Following the test periods in the two locations, the decision was made to install the PSDS on a national basis.   A few years after this, *Computerworld* reported:[2]

> Washington   D.C.   --   The   Post   Office   Department's computerized   management   information   system   (MIS)   costs more   and   is   less   useful   than   previous   manual   systems, according   to   the   General   Accounting   Office   (GAO).

The   GAO   report   on   the   Post   Office   Department   is   virtually   a textbook of how not to develop an MIS.

When   the   Post   Office   Department   started   developing   the   system   in 1966,   it   said   the   system   would   reduce   paperwork   and   at   the   same   time produce   more   timely   and   accurate   reports.   Employees   producing   manual reports   were   to   be   reassigned   to   other   tasks   at   a   saving   of $4.5   million per year.

But   inadequate   planning,   insufficient   testing,   and   excessive   haste,   the GAO said, resulted in a system that:

● Was over 2 years late
● Will cost $60 million, almost twice as much as expected
● Requires more rather than fewer people
● Has "substantially increased costs"
● Has a high error rate
● Produces useless reports

Despite   the   difficulties   with   the   system,   it   is   now   being   expanded   to   35 additional   post   offices,   an   action   that   drew   particular   GAO   criticism.

Although   the   GAO   attributed   many   of   the   PSDS   difficulties   to   poor planning   and   hasty   development,   the   researchers   were   of   the   opinion   that many   of   the   problems   were   compounded   by   poor   implementation   planning and   procedures.   Many,   if   not   most,   of   the   problems   highlighted   in   the GAO   report   could   have   been   avoided   if   the   system   implementation   had been properly handled.

---

[2]J. Janion, "Post Office Shows How Not to Develop Information System," *Computerworld*, Aug. 4, 1971.

Case B

A large university had a research group studying marketing which was funded by a number of local businesses.[3] Over the years, the research group would do projects for the funding businesses. One of these projects was for a very large retail organization. In this case, the retailer's department store division expressed interest in having the research group build a decision support system to help its merchandise planners. The goal was to develop a system that the planners would use to remove some of the drudgery of calculation from the process of creating an annual buying plan.

The research group, working with the head of the buying organization, identified three key buyers. These buyers worked with the research staff to design the computerized planning system. According to the buyers' specifications, the system was developed on the university computer system and tested by the three buyers. They were enthusiastic. So was the manager who wrote a nice letter to the research group telling of his plans to use the system at the department store.

It was surprising when one of the members of the research group contacted the store 3 years later and could find no trace of the system. The manager and the three buyers were gone and no one there had ever heard of the system. It was even more surprising to the researcher who, upon describing the system in an attempt to locate it, heard that the management and the buyers would be extremely interested in having a system just like he was describing to support their planning. He could only smile when he was asked if the research group would like to get involved in developing such a system.

Case C

This example is similar to the previous one. It involves an energy forecasting system developed for a state energy agency. The system involved the use of a statistical model to forecast energy consumption in a large number of buildings throughout the state. Again, working with state personnel, an outside agent built the model and set up a system to gather data for energy forecasting.

This system is not being used, and the model is gathering dust on the shelf. The personnel in the energy office say that the system to gather the data required by the model is too expensive and cumbersome. Furthermore, according to these sources, the data is inaccurate anyway and thus the model is invalid.

---

[3]C. W. Rudelius, G. W. Dickson, and S. W. Harley, "The Little Model That Couldn't: How a Decision Support System Found Limbo," *Systems, Objectives, and Solutions*, August 1982.

Case D

George Johnson worked in the administrative group at the headquarters of a large national computer software company. He reported directly to the financial vice president of the firm and held the title of project control systems administrator.

His company specialized in developing software systems under fixed price contracts and had branch offices in several large cities in the United States. The firm's president determined that a key to his firm's success was the ability to measure and control project costs. He and the financial vice president put George in charge of developing a system for project cost control. Shortly after receiving this assignment, George attended a three-day workshop on successful use of computer systems which emphasized systems planning. Upon returning to work, George spent a few weeks developing an administrative computing systems plan which featured project cost control. The system would be based upon input data from all the project managers located at headquarters and in the branches.

George convinced his company to engage an external consultant to assist in selecting a mechanism for creating the system based upon the plan. Many alternatives were considered. They included building the system in house with the company's computers, obtaining a packaged system for project cost control, and using a nontraditional approach involving the use of fourth-generation software to build a system on microcomputers.

After detailed analysis of the alternatives, the selection team recommended a microcomputer-based system utilizing new, fourth-generation software which took a database approach. The company's president concurred with the recommendation, being especially pleased with the cost of this alternative in relation to the others. The computer's vendor was hired to build the system and to work closely with George in doing so. In only 10 weeks, a prototype of the system was complete. Over the next few months, changes were made to the system based upon George's suggestions, many of which were enhancements that he became aware of the need for only after using the prototype system. The steering committee set up to oversee the project was very pleased by the system's cost and also was impressed by how well George thought the system would meet the company's needs. From the time the vendor started on the system, only 6 months had elapsed.

Soon after the system was finished, George was given the position of project manager and transferred to one of the company's branches. The project cost control system was never used by the firm's project managers, and the several microcomputers acquired to run the system either were not used or were used as word processors.

We have recorded many other very dramatic cases of computer abuse that are symptoms of implementation problems. Instances have been noted in which disk drives have been physically assaulted by persons wielding screwdrivers, keys have been dropped into disk drives, terminal keyboards on the production floor have been smashed with hammers, and employees have attempted to sabotage the system by putting in erroneous input. These, of course, are the most glaring examples of symptoms of behavioral problems regarding computers. More subtle and more common symptoms among the work force include nonuse of system output and general resistance to the system in one way or another.

The reader may think that these tales involve isolated incidents. Perhaps the cases of outright physical sabotage do, but systems plagued by nonuse and misuse are, unfortunately, more common than not. The MIS manager, the systems builder, and the user involved with computer-based systems ought to be aware of the types of behavioral problems that can and often do occur. By being conscious of the symptoms of such problems, one can look to their causes and attempt to take steps to avoid problems of the type that we have described.

DIAGNOSIS

Becoming sensitive to the fact that implementation problems can occur when an information system is changed or a new one is introduced and appreciating the symptoms of these problems is a first step in installing successful systems. A second necessary condition is to understand why implementation problems occur.

Unfortunately, there are a multitude of reasons why we have problems implementing systems. Few topics associated with the information systems area have received as much treatment as implementation. The volume of literature on implementation is the reason why this chapter has the most footnotes of any chapter in this book. Undoubtedly, the problems that have been noted have led to this volume of study. The difficulty is that the hypothesizing and research results available to us provide a long list of potential causes and conflicting evidence as to what may or may not be important. If one clear message comes from the work available, it is that almost every situation is different and there are many things that can cause difficulty.

Various observers of implementation have attempted to encapsulate all that is understood about the subject and to develop a general framework which displays the factors affecting successful system use. One such model, suggested by Lucas,[4] is shown in Figure 16-1. The Lucas model

[4]Henry C. Lucas, Jr., *Implementation: The Key to Successful Information Systems,* Columbia University Press, New York, 1981.

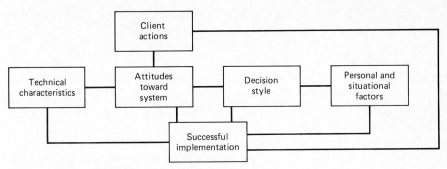

**Figure 16-1 The Lucas Model of Factors
Influencing Implementation Success**

is one of many, but it is typical in that it begins to reflect the
complexity associated with systems implementation. Further, it serves to
identify a number of variables thought to be associated with
implementation success or failure.

Factors Associated with Implementation Problems

One method of studying systems implementation has been to examine
failures and attempt to learn from them. The difficulty with this
approach is that almost every observer comes up with a different reason
for a failure. Furthermore, the failure cases support the position that
almost every installation is different. The failure cases are useful in
that they do generate a list of potential causes of implementation
problems.

Another approach to studying failed systems implementation is to
conduct factor studies. This approach is more formal than the failure
study approach in that specific hypotheses are generated as to what
factors may be associated with successful versus unsuccessful systems.
These hypotheses are then tested by gathering rather large amounts of
data in organizations that have implemented systems and testing to see
which factors led to success and which led to failure. Formal factor
studies have been criticized because they have generated conflicting
results. Again, they are useful in generating a list of issues to consider,
but serve to add evidence to the situational nature of systems
implementation.

Other research approaches have been taken which postulate methods
which can be used to bring about successful systems installations. These
approaches often involve an implementation *process* which attempts to
overcome certain underlying causes of implementation problems. Several
of these processes will be discussed in some detail in the next section of

this chapter, but here they will only be used to point out the hypothesized causes of failure which the processes attempt to overcome.

Thus, we have a variety of causes or factors from the abundant literature, which may explain implementation problems. The word "factor," as used here, differs from its meaning in the term "factor studies." As we use the word, it is defined as an underlying cause or an explanation of dysfunctional behavior associated with systems implementation. The word "factor" as used in association with the term "factor studies," is more specific, and usually refers to a condition present in the organization at the time of systems implementation. A project team used to design a system would be an example of the latter meaning. Another example of this type of factor would be the presence or absence of the support of top management. The factors, or underlying causes, which we will now discuss are more basic in nature and come from a wide variety of sources, many of which describe differing points of view as to what it takes to successfully implement systems.

Before going on to present our discussion, we want to make it clear to the reader that the underlying causes of implementation problems are not mutually exclusive and independent. Many of the factors which will be discussed are related to one another, and many may be present in any given systems implementation. Where appropriate, we will point out important relations among the factors we have identified that seem to cause the problems of which we are speaking.

Technical Issues. User problems may be caused, or certainly influenced, by a variety of technical factors associated with the system, a few of which are:

- *Ease of use:* The degree to which the intended users see the system as being "unfriendly" or difficult to use, will add to the psychological cost to them of using the system. A high perceived cost of using the system requires its perceived benefits to be great.

- *Cost and time:* If the system was delivered over budget and/or later than promised, users tend to get negative feelings about the system.

- *System response and reliability:* Situations in which the system reacts too slowly, crashes, or is unavailable when needed have been known to create great problems of user dissatisfaction.

- *Previous systems experience:* There have been cases in which previous bad experiences with systems have carried over to new systems activities in a negative manner.

- *Data problems:* If the data in the system is felt to be inaccurate or incomplete, users tend not to use the system.

We saw in the case of the decision support system for retail buyers an example of technical factors contributing to system failure. In that case, the interactive system implemented by the university research group on its computer system was converted to a batch system by the department store. One reason the buyers did not use the system was that it was not responsive enough to address their problems. The system in case B involving the state energy agency is an example of a system plagued by data problems. The major reason given by the nonusers for ignoring the system was that the data going into the system was so bad that it produced useless results.

Perceived Need. For a system to be used, and used successfully, its users must perceive a need for it.[5,6,7,8] In other words, if the users of a system do not perceive that the system will help them do their jobs or help their organization run more efficiently or be more effective, then it is almost a foregone conclusion that the system will fail.

Consider, for a moment, how the perception of need for a system comes about. Either the user must expect and have demonstrated that a system will have personal or organizational benefit, or the user must have faith in the opinions of her or his superiors that such is the case. The perceived system benefit must exceed the perceived cost of using the system, or problems of a behavioral nature can be expected.

On a large system affecting an entire organization or a major part of it, senior management must perceive a need for the system. The concept of management support often shows up as a factor associated with system success. We would rather consider management support as a *necessary* factor associated with the perception of need. In other words, if senior management is perceived as being negative toward, or

---

[5]John D. Little, "Models and Managers: The Concept of a Decision Calculus," *Management Science,* April 1970.

[6]Michael Radnor and Rodney Neal, "The Progress of Management Science Activities in Large U.S. Industrial Organizations," *Operations Research,* March-April 1973.

[7]Randall L. Schultz and Dennis P. Sleven, (eds.), *Implementing Operations Research Management Science,* American Elsevier, New York, 1975.

[8]Edward B. Roberts, "Strategies for Effective Implementation of Complex Corporate Models," *Interfaces,* November 1977.

even not actively supportive of, a new system, then subordinate managers and operating workers affected by the system will quickly decide that there is no need for the system and act accordingly. Thus, management support is needed if the system is to have any chance of success, but management support will not automatically assure success of the system.

One factor associated with the need for a system is a positive rate of return. The use of cost/benefit analysis in deciding whether to go ahead with a system can be important.[9],[10],[11] Conducting studies of potential system costs and benefits is only one small part of proving the need for a system. Much more is required of senior management. Statements reflecting their attitudes, the allocation of resources to the system, and actions such as spending their valuable time on systems-related issues go a long way to show that senior managers perceive a need for the system.

In the case of a large system, even when it is obvious that the key managers truly support the system, there also must be some perceived need on the part of those directly affected by the system. These persons must feel that the system will benefit them or their organization in some way. Even if there is a perceived need for the system from the top of the organization and on the part of individuals involved with the system, it does not mean that systems success is assured. All that we can say is that if either or both of these conditions are lacking, then a successful systems installation is extremely unlikely.

In support of these observations, consider the situations described in the case examples at the beginning of this chapter. In the case of the Post Office, not only were the postal workers not convinced of the need for the PSDS, but they could see little formal support for the system on the part of senior postal management. A similar condition existed in the last case in which the software project managers were given a computer system based upon a process that they didn't use or want. The system was needed by one person, George Johnson. It was designed according to how he thought projects ought to be managed. When George was reassigned, with no real support from top management for the project management process supported by the system, it was not surprising that the system was not used. Finally, in the case of the system to support the retail buyers, there possibly was a perceived need for the system on the part of the three buyers involved in the system development, but this

[9]Michael J. Ginzberg, "A Process Approach to Conducting Management Science Implementation," doctoral dissertation, MIT, Cambridge, Mass., 1975.

[10]Steven Alter, "How Effective Managers Use Information Systems," *Harvard Business Review*, November-December 1976.

[11]Robert Blanning, "The Decision to Adopt Strategic Planning Models," The Wharton Working Papers, The Wharton School, University of Pennsylvania, Philadelphia, Penn., 1979.

need was not effectively communicated to their peers. Furthermore, there was little actual support for the system on the part of the organization's senior management.

To summarize, chances of a successful system installation are directly affected by whether the parties associated with the system perceive a need for it. Especially problematic are cases in which the perceived need is neutral or negative. In cases of systems which affect multiple parties and/or are dictated by senior management, it is of great importance to successful installation that a demonstration be made of top-level support (need) for the system. We want to emphasize that this demonstration of support goes far beyond tacit approval for the system or even the provision of resources for system development. We mean that senior management must demonstrate by their actions and attitudes that the system is really important (needed). How this can be done will be made clear in the concluding section of this chapter.

Control over Change. There is evidence to support the proposition that people do not resist change so much as they resist having no control over change.[12],[13],[14] This hypothesis has led to much of the work on change processes. These strategies will be discussed in more detail in the next section of this chapter, but mentioning a few of the tactics involved will help the reader to recall several familiar concepts.

Frequently, user participation is employed to facilitate change and to provide some control over the change to those affected by it. Use of project teams to stimulate involvement is one way to provide control over change to the systems user. To a certain extent, user training is another way. By understanding the system and the reason for it, the assumption is that the user will have greater control over changes brought on by the system. Finally, making a user responsible for a new system is another way of providing user control over change.

The U.S. Postal Service's PSDS is a classic example of a situation in which the workers had absolutely no control over the change caused by the system. In no way were the workers involved or consulted.

Mutual Understanding. One factor which appears to be associated with the implementation of systems is the frame of reference brought to the task by the technical designers in contrast to the frames of reference

[12] Warren G. Bennis, Kenneth O. Benne, and Robert Chin, *The Planning of Change*, Holt, Rinehart, and Winston, New York, 1963.

[13] Bernard M. Bass and Harold J. Leavitt, "Some Experiments in Planning and Change," *Management Science*, September 1963.

[14] Edgar H. Schein, *Process Consultation: Its Role in Organizational Development*, Addison-Wesley, Reading, Mass., 1969.

of the managers and other users associated with the system.[15] [,16,17] The argument is that designers tend to be more analytical in their view of systems, whereas managers tend to be more intuitive. Thus there may be a mismatch in their approaches to the solution of a problem. This mismatch may result in a solution that is inappropriate for the user and thus may generate a system that is not used or is used inappropriately.

The example given in case B involving the retail buyers and the university research group demonstrates a situation in which there was potential for differences between the frame of reference of the system developers and that of the users of the system. In this case, we do not see that this factor was involved, but the decision support system that was developed may still have been structured inappropriately for its intended users.

Expectancies. Expectancies, at first glance, may appear to be similar to the perceived needs. The concepts are certainly related but are not exactly the same. It has been suggested that the way users expect a system to contribute to their performance and their belief that performance is related to rewards they receive (in their job) are important to how these users will employ a system.[18] [,19,20] Expectancies may be particularly important in influencing the use of systems of a discretionary nature, such as decision support systems.[21]

Expectancies as to how valuable a system will be certainly relates to how one will perceive the need for a system. If users expect that a system will not enable them to do their jobs better and will not increase organizational efficiency, then the perceived need for the system is likely to be low. Similarly, if they expect that performing well on job tasks supported by the system will not assist them in achieving their goals, then they will be unlikely to use the system.

[15]C. West Churchman, "Managerial Acceptance of Scientific Recommendations," *California Management Review*, Fall 1964.

[16]Robert Doktor and William F. Hamilton, "Cognitive Style and the Acceptance of Management Science Recommendations," *Management Science*, April 1973.

[17]James L. McKenney and Peter G. W. Keen, "How Managers' Minds Work," *Harvard Business Review*, May-June 1974.

[18]Daniel Robey, "User Attitudes and MIS Use," *Academy of Management Journal*, vol. 22, no. 3, September 1979.

[19]Victor H. Vroom, *Work and Motivation*, New York, Wiley, 1964.

[20]Robert W. Zmud, "Locus of Control, Ambiguity Tolerance, and Information Design Alternatives: Correlates of Decision Behavior," *Proceedings of the American Institute for Decision Sciences*, vol. 1, 1979.

[21]Gerardine DeSanctis, "An Examination of Expectancy Theory · Model of Decision Support System Use," *Proceedings of the Third International Conference on Information Systems*, Ann Arbor, Mich. 1982.

Expectancies can be affected by training, experience, and the attitudes of others. It is possible, therefore, to use tactics associated with these areas to influence expectancies and thus to deal with this cause of implementation problems. In none of the case examples do we observe any attempt to influence expectancies.

Power and Social Change. Recently, attention has been focused on the roles of power and politics as causes of implementation problems.[22] [23] [24] Installing a new system or changing a current one is a political process, one that probably disrupts the power and/or social structures of an organization. Often involved are issues such as the following:

- *Rivalries and territorial threats:* The system can increase the power or influence of one department or group over another. Frequently a subunit will take a local perspective at the expense of the overall organization.

- *Fear of obsolescence:* The system can diminish job responsibilities or contribute to a feeling of loss of esteem.

- *Group cohesiveness leading to resistance to outsiders:* Systems specialists and/or consultants are resisted because they are not part of the local group and do not understand the "business."

- *Cultural factors:* The system is resisted because it does not fit in with present practice or goes against the experience of incumbent managers.

- *Job security:* These are concerns that jobs will be eliminated or that job duties will be diminished.

- *Information possessiveness:* The system will make information available to others that is presently closely held. Of special concern is the fact that subordinate managers may lose decision autonomy or excuses for poor performance based upon a lack of information. Further, having data and information is an element of power and must either be protected if currently present or sought if not.

---

[22] A. Pettigrew, *The Politics of Organizational Decision Making,* Travistock, London, 1976.

[23] Eugene Bardoch, *The Implementation Game: What Happens after a Bill Becomes Law,* MIT Press, Cambridge, Mass., 1977.

[24] Peter G. W. Keen, "Information Systems and Organizational Change," *Communications of the ACM,* January 1981.

● *Job pattern changes:* The system can change communication patterns with peers, present psychic rewards, and affect work group norms.

Frequently, these conditions will result in what have been called "tactics of counterimplementation." These tactics at the managerial level include (1) diverting resources from the project, (2) deflecting the goals of the project, (3) dissipating the energies of the project, and (4) neglecting the project with the hope that it will go away. At the operating level, tactics of counterimplementation take the form of (1) making errors on purpose, (2) using the system for purposes other than it was intended, (3) failing to use the system, and (4) relying on old manual procedures whenever possible.

The system failure at the software development company described in case D involved tactics of counterimplementation. The project managers ignored the project until, with the neglect of senior management, it did simply go away. Many political and social pressures were present in the situation which influenced the actions of the project managers.

MIS Organization and Project-Related Factors. The factor studies mentioned earlier identify a number of factors associated with the MIS organization and project development practices that may be associated with systems failing.[25],[26] Factors that have been found to be correlated with success in at least one situation are shown in Table 16-1.

Commitment. Ginzberg[27] has shown that two kinds of commitment are required to avoid systems that fail to be implemented successfully. The first is an organizational commitment to the project itself. The second is a commitment to change. "Commitment to the project" means that during the stages of system development, installation, and use, management must assure that the problem is understood and that the system developed solves that problem. Both users and management must develop this commitment as it increases the odds that they will take appropriate actions at each project stage to assure the project's success. Commitment to change means that the organization is willing to accommodate the change that is likely to be required to implement the system.

In the case of the project management system for software projects, there was little commitment on the part of management or project

---

[25]Michael Radnor and A. H. Rubenstein, "Implementation in Operations Research and R&D Organizations," *Operations Research,* November–December 1970.

[26]Richard Powers and Gary W. Dickson, "MIS Project Management: Myths, Opinions, and Reality," *California Management Review,* Spring 1973.

[27]Michael J. Ginzberg, "Key Recurrent Issues in MIS Implementation Process," *MIS Quarterly,* June 1981.

Table 16-1 Factors shown to be associated with MIS project success

MIS organization-related
Organizational location of MIS function
Influence and reputation of MIS group
Adequacy of MIS resources
Size of MIS organization
Technical capability of MIS staff

MIS project-related
Turnover of project staff
Integration of analysis and programming for project staff
Experience of project staff
Availability of trained people to implement project and act
  as "change agents"
Complexity and size of system being implemented
Degree to which a plan for change and project implementation
  has accompanied the traditional project/plan
Degree to which a project fits an organization's strategies
  and/or fits its "way" of operating

managers to the project. There was no commitment on the part of the project managers to change. Lack of both types of commitment contributed to the failure of the project. A similar lack of both types of commitment was present in the case of the decision support system for the retail buyers and again contributed to the failure of the system.

Design Assumptions. Some systems are built for a single user, but most are intended for a multitude of users. One cause of resistance is to design the system only according to the views of the systems builder as to what the user will need. This condition certainly existed in the case involving the U.S. Post Office. In situations in which users are involved in the system design, various groups of users can be identified, each having different needs.

Ginzberg[28] describes a decision support system in which a few users had little need for the system, a few had a need for some basic capabilities, and many had need for a system with advanced capabilities. Obviously, a system having only basic features or a system operating only on an advanced level would miss some of its potential audience. It should also be noted that to build a system for the "average" user might be less than satisfactory to any group of users. These comments certainly could apply to the case of the decision support system for the retail buyers described in case B.

[28]Michael J. Ginzberg, "Steps Towards More Effective Implementation of MS and MIS," *Interfaces*, May 1978.

Organizational Climate. There are some instances in which the organizational climate has been so hostile that it is difficult to accomplish change. If the attitudes of organizational members are poor toward one another or toward attempts to modernize, then any change is made that much more difficult. On the positive side, if there is an openness in the organization so that opinions and values may be shared, change can be facilitated. Researchers studying organizational change have spoken of a climate which supports mutual trust between the potential users of the systems and the systems developers.[29] In this way, a free exchange of ideas is encouraged.

In many cases, the influence of senior management is vital in determining the organizational climate. If the climate is poor, steps must be taken to improve matters in this area before any attempt is made to introduce change. The case of the attempted introduction of a system at the Post Office involved a hostile organizational climate. The university researchers reported that the relations between management and labor were as poor as they had ever seen. It was their opinion that almost any new system of any sort would be resisted by the work force under almost any circumstances. At the mere mention of a new system, a grievance was filed by the workers' union. This was done before the workers even knew what the system was for.

Change Process. Much of the understanding concerning the causes of resistance to organizational change comes from those suggesting a process for bringing about change. These persons argue that how the change is brought about is what is important. In other words, if one wants to successfully introduce an information system into an organization, it is the process by which the system is introduced that is important. The following section of this chapter will deal with the topic of introducing change, so at this point we will only mention this topic as one factor associated with successful systems introduction. The Post Office example amply demonstrates the importance of the change process. The Post Office system installation depicts a situation in which it would appear as though they took everything known about introducing organizational change and did exactly the opposite.

Formal Diagnosis

The discussion thus far should be convincing that, because of the factors that may be involved, introducing a new system into an organization is complex. On the basis of the findings of the various studies of implementation that have been highlighted, one could simply be aware of

---

[29]Robert W. Zmud and James F. Cox, "The Implementation Process: A Change Approach," *MIS Quarterly*, June 1979.

the various causes of implementation problems and, in any situation, informally attempt to scout out any circumstances that could cause problems. On the other hand, one could look for causes of systems implementation problems in a much more formal manner.

Alter[30] was one of the first to suggest that a formal implementation risk analysis be conducted. Knowing most of the potential causes of implementation problems, one could systematically check to see if any potentially dangerous conditions existed prior to beginning work on a system. Then by treating the environmental conditions and doing things right on the project, more successful systems ought to be able to be installed.

Anderson and Narasimhan[31] provide one very formal approach to conducting the risk analysis called for by Alter. These researchers demonstrate how, by using the statistical procedure called discriminant analysis, a search can be made for environmental factors that could potentially cause implementation problems. In a test of their procedure in eight firms involving 22 management science projects, 13 variables from the literature thought to be associated with implementation success were tested. Interestingly, in this study of the implementation of management science projects, the following items were found most often to be associated with success: (1) the appropriateness of the method used to solve the problem, (2) the felt need for a solution to the problem, and (3) the fact that top management was involved. The set of all factors was used to predict the success of the projects. All the projects were correctly classified by the procedure.

Up to this point, we have done three things. The first was to attempt to convince the reader that serious behavioral problems can exist as information systems are introduced or changed. The second was to dramatically illustrate some forms of the dysfunctional behavior that can happen. Our third point has been to acquaint the reader with some of the vast array of causes which underlie the symptoms of dysfunctional behavior. Understanding the causes of the problems and knowing what to look for (formally or informally), we can now develop some prescriptions to implement successful systems.

TREATMENT

There are two levels on which to address how to overcome the problems associated with implementing or changing systems in a major way. The first level is a conceptual one and involves an appreciation of the various schools of thought regarding the change process. The second

---

[30]Steven Alter, "Implementation Risk Analysis," Working Paper Series, University of Southern California, Graduate School of Business Administration, Los Angeles, Calif., 1976.

[31]John C. Anderson and Ram Narasimhan, "Assessing Project Implementation Risk: A Methodological Approach," *Management Science*, June 1979.

level translates the conceptual focus into practical suggestions for implementing systems change.

The Change Process

There are several views of how to manage change. The two most popular schools of thought are the planned-change approach and the innovation process. Some of the less common views are those of the sociotechnical-systems school and the communication approach. We will introduce the more common approaches first and provide only brief descriptions of the others.

Planned Change. The planned-change approach was introduced by Lewin and Schein[32],[33] and elaborated upon by Kolb and Frohman.[34] The theory behind the change process, according to these authors, is that various stages are involved in successfully bringing about change. Figure 16-2 shows the stages of each change model along with the stages of the more traditional systems design process. In the first stage, a climate for change must be created and a contract established on the part of the user for change. In this stage, goals are established and momentum for change is created. Other activities on this level include (1) establishing the nature of the user's problem, (2) making sure that the person or group serving as the change agent possesses the proper skills, (3) defining a person in the user organization to serve as champion for the project and ensuring that this person can provide the needed resources and leverage to support the project, (4) making sure a felt need for the project exists or taking action to establish such a need, (5) making sure that senior management is supportive of the change and defining the actions that are necessary on the part of this group to reflect this attitude, (6) making sure that the users understand and agree to the project's goals and objectives, (7) identifying measurable checkpoints in the project to see that these objectives are being met, and (8) working out an adequate psychological contract by agreeing upon roles during the project for the change agents and the users and identifying conditions for terminating the relationship.

The second stage involves mobilizing the technical, managerial, and organizational resources and doing the project. The system evolves from the initial design. Among the change-related activities at this stage are

[32]Kurt Lewin, "Group Decision and Social Change," in T. Newcomb and E. Hartley (eds.), *Readings in Social Psychology,* Holt & Co., New York, 1952.

[33]Edgar Schein, "Management Development as a Process of Influence," *Industrial Management Review,* May 1961.

[34]David Kolb and Alan L. Frohman, "An Organization Development Approach to Consulting," *Sloan Management Review,* Fall 1970.

Lewin/Schein	Kolb and Frohman	Traditional Design
	Scouting	Feasibility Study
Unfreezing		
	Entry	
	Diagnosis, Planning,	
Change	Action	Technical Analysis
		and Design
	Evaluation	
Refreeze		Installation
	Termination	

Figure 16-2 Process Views of Implementing Organizational Change

(1) determining that actual changes are occurring, (2) ensuring that the user is receiving the type of training that will be needed to successfully use the system, (3) measuring to see that the goals of the project are actually being met, (4) responding to any signs of resistance to change, and (5) making sure that the change agent has really built up personal credibility with the user.

The final stage establishes that the new system has meshed into the user organization and its ongoing practice. Here, one must (1) make sure that new behavior patterns have been adequately learned, (2) ensure that the user organization can use the system without the systems builders' presence, (3) establish that the users feel that they "own" the system, and (4) make sure that the users are committed to using the new system.

As can be seen, the planned-change approach is a cycle of stages which precedes and accompanies the activities that are more traditionally thought of as part of the systems development process. A key part of the process is that change can be managed by a consultant playing the role of a change agent, who acts as a guide during implementation. Many of those writing on the subject of implementing successful systems advocate employing the planned-change approach, and much of our understanding of the subject comes from studies using this approach.

Innovation Process. The innovation-process approach to change originated in the field of political science. The theory underlying this approach argues that much technological change is political in nature. Authors advocating this approach to change suggest various models which delineate a sequence of steps which should be followed in the process of adopting an innovation (in this case a new system). In general, the suggested models begin with a stage in which there is the recognition that a problem or opportunity exists. Next, an attempt is made to develop a potential solution. A trial of this solution is made and modified until a sustained position is reached.

An important facet of the innovation-process view is the role of "gatekeepers." These are persons or groups of persons that serve as links between the suppliers and users of new technology. The gatekeepers develop informal channels that facilitate communication. Another key role is that of "early adopters." These are persons of high social and/or political status who serve as missionaries for an innovation. Early adopters tend to be independent individuals, often outside the mainstream, whose demonstrated success with an innovation leads to its general acceptance.

The innovation-process approach, like the planned-change approach, views change as something subject to facilitation and management. This view concentrates on establishing a need for change, linking up with gatekeepers and early adopters, and emphasizing informal communication channels. The argument of this approach is that innovations are not well received by formal organizations having rigid procedures. Ways must be found to get small groups of people together to work on the change and to bypass formal communication channels. The role of senior and local managers is thought to be vital in supporting such a process.

Sociotechnical-Systems Approach.

The sociotechnical-systems approach to facilitating systems implementation is similar to the two approaches presented above. This view also is based upon the position that change needs to be managed. It stands in contrast with the other approaches in that its focus is different on what should be managed. Under this approach, two subsystems are identified -- the technical subsystem and the social subsystem. The argument is that both subsystems must be managed successfully for a technical system involving people to be effective. An information system is such a system.[35]

The sociotechnical-systems approach is participative in its nature. The notion is that no one has the right to design a job for someone else; thus, users must participate heavily in the system design. This approach also recommends the use of a sociotechnical-systems expert who helps the users with job design and generally facilitates the process of change.

The sociotechnical-systems approach focuses to a large extent on the consideration of job design and redesign associated with the new system. Other factors which should be carefully considered according to this view are the interpersonal social system (who interacts with whom) and the reward system.

Communication-Network Approach.

The communications-network approach to change is based upon the premise that the effects of a

---

[35]Enid Mumford, E. Mercer, D. Mills, and M. Weir, "Problems of Computer Introduction," *Management Decision*, vol. 10, no. 1, 1972.

system are those which measure the changes in potential users' task activities and their interactions with other people in carrying out those activities.[36] ,[37] It has been found that when people are presented with a task, they respond by performing certain task activities and forming communication structures for getting the work done efficiently and in a need-satisfying manner.

A management information system is argued to affect the most basic patterns of task activities and interactions. According to the communication-network view of implementation, consideration should be given to (1) the specific task activities the potential users actually perform, (2) the interactions and communications in which the users engage in performing the activities, and (3) the way users feel about each of the activities and interactions. These are the inputs which would be used by the change agent to facilitate building a successful system.

The reader can see that, no matter what theoretical view is taken to overcome the causes of problems that occur when change is implemented, it is a common argument that successful change requires managed change. In addition, there needs to be a competent change agent involved to manage the change. Having discussed the theoretical background and keeping in mind the previous discussion about the many seeming causes of implementation problems, we can now suggest some prescriptions for building successful systems.

A Practical Approach to Implementing Systems

Since we have discussed the causes of problems associated with introducing change and some of the theories as to how changes ought to be introduced, we can now turn to a practical example of how one might implement a system. First, assume that the system to be implemented is a large transaction processing system that affects both the managerial and clerical personnel of a major function of a large organization. Further, assume that the project was requested by the senior management of the function and given high priority by the organization's information systems steering committee.

Getting Started. The first thing to do is some scouting in the Kolb-and-Frohman sense. In this sort of activity, one would assess the general climate in the organization regarding information systems. In

---

[36]A. Bavelas, "Communication Patterns in Task-Oriented Groups," *Journal of the Accoustical Society of America,* November 1950.

[37]Edgar Schein, *A Theory of Group Structures vol. 1: Basic Theory,* Gordon and Breach, New York, 1976.

actual practice much of this information may already be available, but for our example, suppose that it is not. One should assess:

I. Organizational climate:
   A. The degree to which the organization is open and communication is facilitated. Does the organization encourage constructive change?
   B. The level of understanding in the organization regarding information systems, and what they can and cannot do.
   C. The previous history of experiences with introducing and using information systems.
   D. The general attitude of organizational members regarding the MIS organization and its abilities.
   E. Whether the organization is considering any major disruptive influences in parallel with the project, such as new building construction, changes in business practices, organizational changes, and mergers or acquisitions.

II. Role of senior management vis-a-vis information systems:
   A. The attitudes of senior management toward MIS as indicated by their actions and statements. In other words, do senior management have a demonstrated need for information systems?
   B. The adequacy of resources devoted to the MIS function.
   C. The degree to which senior management spends time on IS-related activities.
   D. The degree to which successful use of IS is rewarded.
   E. The expectancies of senior management of IS. Does senior management perceive that successful information systems will help managers and the organization achieve better performance, and will such performance be rewarded?
   F. The degree to which senior management makes the head of the IS function a part of the executive management team of the organization.

III. MIS and planning:
   A. The degree to which the effects of information systems are considered in the organization's planning process.
   B. Whether IS management is part of the organization planning process.
   C. The degree to which successful information systems are perceived to be needed to achieve the organization's strategic goals.

IV. The nature and role of the chief information officer:
   A. The perception on the part of others of this person as a manager.
   B. The degree to which this person is considered a part of senior management.

C. The overall degree of respect this person has in the organization.

The method by which much of this information will be collected is through interviews. The interviews should be conducted with senior management and with a sample of others in the organization. User perceptions related to the items listed above are especially important. The perceptions should be compared with the responses of the senior management to check for parallelism.

Many of the items listed above are uncontrollable (at least in the short run). Steps should be taken to improve those that are unsatisfactory yet controllable or semicontrollable. If the climate is judged as too hostile overall or if a key factor must be changed to avoid a high probability of project failure, then the project should be deferred until matters improve.

An environmental assessment will give those responsible for the project an overall feeling of how supportive the climate is in which they are to work. The poorer the organizational climate, the harder one must work on implementation of the project.

A final step in the scouting phase is to identify all those in the functional organization that will be affected by the system. It is not a bad idea to determine the level of perceived need of these persons for the potential system and their expectancies for the system. Again, this information is useful in deciding how much effort must be put into the implementation process.

The next activity is to get ready for entry. There are a number of things which ought to be done in this regard:

1. Senior management should announce the project to all affected users and make appropriate statements supporting the system.

2. Functional management should also announce its support for the system and describe in more detail the nature of the system and its purpose.

3. A project team manager should be picked from the user organization. This person should be someone who is recognized as a successful manager, and who is influential among his or her peers. It should be made clear that this person's career in the organization will depend on the project's success. Responsibility and *authority* to carry out the project should be given to the project manager.

4. A systems architect from the IS group should be appointed to work as the number two person responsible for the project. It is extremely important that the systems architect and the project manager respect one another and work well together.

5. Key users (managerial, professional, and clerical) should be appointed to the design team. Again, influential leaders should be selected.

6. Project goals should be identified, especially as they influence successful implementation. Measures of the degree of goal attainment should also be agreed upon and checkpoints set.

7. If they have not already had it, system builders and user members of the project team ought to get some training in organizational change and in interpersonal communications. They should also be trained in the system development methodology and in the project management tools to be used on the project. Special emphasis should be placed on understanding the roles various parties will be expected to play during the system development and installation.

8. The team member responsible for implementation should be identified. It is desirable that this person have substantial training and experience in implementation methods, although this is often not feasible.

Making the Change. We are assuming that, as much as possible, the systems personnel on the project are familiar with the function addressed by the system and have good communication skills for working with users during the design process. Thus, with good communication and the participation of users on the design team, there is mutual understanding between the user system and the technical system. The team now begins the entry phase of the project. At this point, a bit of user education is frequently useful. Often it is most effective to provide some education about computer systems and information about what to expect from the new system in regard to where the technology and its use are going. A short program for all users to be affected by the system is best. At this time it is possible to get the users to agree to (or commit to) change. Sometimes this is done in the form of a formal contract. After the education, it is helpful to remeasure user expectancies regarding the system.

Early in this stage, the project plan is developed. The implementation plan is a part of this document. Plans for further user involvement beyond participation on the project team and training plans are developed. It is usually too early in the project to begin the development of training material since the nature of the system is` still too undefined. The plan will specify what kind of training will be conducted and for whom. It will also state the schedule for the development of training material for the new system.

It is in this stage that the system design takes place. The users should be allowed to set priorities and make trade-offs for themselves in business terms. Feedback should be provided to the entire community of users as to how their influence has been felt in regard to the system to be introduced. Careful consideration is required during the design of nontechnical issues such as job changes, power system modifications, and changes in the social system. These issues should be openly discussed and taken into consideration during design.

Finally, as subsystem designs are completed, user walk-throughs should be conducted, and appropriate users should take responsibility for the adequacy of the design. We are assuming that the overall project has been broken into smaller packages of "deliverables" and that these packages will be implemented in a staged sequence.

As the designs of the subsystems are accepted by the user community, the subsystems move into programming, unit testing, and system testing. As a last step, there is an acceptance test in which the users are heavily represented. While the system is being developed and tested, training programs are being designed and developed and user documentation is being written by the implementation staff of the project team.

Installing the System. The system is installed by the implementation group of the project development team. User training, often conducted by user members of the design team, is undertaken. A member of the team stays with each affected user group for a period of time to make sure that the system is running smoothly and the operating personnel can run the system under all conditions. In many cases, a person in the user organization receives additional systems training and becomes the local expert on the system. This person is responsible for knowing the use of the system inside and out. If the system is rolled out from one user suborganization to another, the training material and the user documentation are improved (on the basis of experience) as the rollout takes place.

Some organizations have had success with appointing a user to be responsible for the ongoing use of the system after it has been installed. Among this person's duties are to measure goal attainment of the system and to continually monitor the system in order to suggest modifications or enhancements. Finally, this person continually measures user reaction to the system and expectancies for the system.

In concluding this discussion, it is appropriate to observe that for the implementation of single-user systems, such as decision support systems, or for the installation of smaller systems than the one in the example just presented, appropriate changes would have to be made in the recommended process. The approach, though, of a managed-change process would still be used. The reader should note how the suggested process addressed the issues of (1) perceived need and commitment, (2) mutual understanding, (3) expectancies, (4) power and social change, (5) technical-system issues, (6) organizational climate, and (7) project-related factors. Throughout the process each of these issues would be monitored, and if corrective action were called for, it would be applied.

SUCCESS STUDIES

One branch of the implementation literature is based upon what can be learned from implementation failures. The writings in this area are called "failure studies." We also can learn from successful systems implementation. The authors have been associated with several positive experiences with MIS implementation and offer two examples as "success studies."

Case X

Company X is a nationwide leasing company. This company is in a market dominated by three other companies besides themselves. The competition either had or was building counter support systems for servicing their retail customers. These systems were based upon terminals in the rental locations which speeded customer service and provided highly accurate data for purposes of management reporting.

The president of company X was noted for his use and support of the information systems function of the company. He, along with senior management, decided that to successfully compete in the industry his firm would have to have a counter support system at least as good as others in the industry. A feasibility study was conducted for a system that would have terminals in the more than 1000 rental locations owned by the company. It was determined that the investment in the project would total several million dollars and involve a project team staff of about 30 people at the peak level. In addition, many company personnel in the field and at the home office would be affected by the system.

Several years previously, prior to the current president's arrival, the company made a failed attempt to place some primitive automated equipment in rental offices. This equipment was intended to ease the rental clerk's job by automatically computing bills. It was never accepted in most offices and fell into disuse. The company president and his newly appointed head of MIS did not want to have another failure, especially in view of the magnitude of the investment being made.

A project team was set up, in this case mainly staffed by MIS personnel. One of the first actions, however, was to select key personnel from around the country in job positions that would be affected by the system and to bring these persons to the company headquarters for a week. These persons were influential leaders in that they were known to others having similar job titles. These user representatives worked with project team personnel to understand the various jobs and to identify ways in which the system could eliminate or reduce current difficulties in performing each job. All the user representatives were lodged at a luxury hotel where all meetings took place during the week. The company president and other officers met with the user representatives to stress the importance of the project to management and to the company. They also stressed how important it was to have the input of user views and how the meeting attendees represented their peers.

After the meeting, results were summarized for the attendees. In addition, the firm's newsletter was used to announce the project and to explain how the user representatives had influenced the way in which the new system would work. Specific examples were given.

As the project progressed, a number of these user representatives were brought back to headquarters to review the design. A few were even added to the training part of the project team to assist in the design of the training programs. Later, these people went around the country to assist with the training.

The system was first introduced in the rental locations in the firm's headquarters city. A few modifications were made, and then the system was introduced throughout the country one location at a time. An interesting technical feature of the system was that response time delays were built into the system so that in the early days, when not many locations were on the system, response time would be about 3 seconds. Later, as more locations were added, the response delays were reduced so that response time still did not exceed 3 seconds. This way, early users did not notice degradation in response time as the system became busier.

All in all, the counter support system was a great success. It met management's objectives and suffered little from any of the standard implementation problems. Even the rental clerks were heard to say that the system gave them more time to do their real job which was to provide service to the customer.

Case Y

The top management of company Y was convinced that its basic accounting systems were obsolete and that an effort should be made to rewrite them from scratch. This company was in a unique industry, so that installing packaged systems was not a viable option. It intended to install the new systems in seven domestic and five foreign office locations. The feasibility study estimated that to design, test, and install all the new systems would take at least 3 years.

A project team was created to design the systems and to build them as well. Since the project had such good support from the company's senior management, the best personnel from data processing were assigned to the project. In addition, many of the design team members came from user organizations located in both domestic and foreign offices. The project was widely publicized, and many users attempted to get assigned to the project to further their careers. Because of this condition, the project team had its pick of capable personnel.

A senior controller was selected to head the project, and a bright young manager from the controller's organization was appointed as chief architect for the project. The latter person was unique in that although he was technically a user, he had technical attributes that made him act more like a data processing person than would another person with his background. He knew the technology and had a good feel for the nuances associated with project management and dealing with computer vendors.

The project was primarily designed by user personnel on the project staff with heavy consultation with users in field locations. In the second year of the project, an organization was created to plan the systems implementation and training. One major impact of this group not too long after its creation was that the project was broken up into packages for installation. Thus, the project had several levels and implementation stages. For example, the first installation was domestic payroll in one field office. This package was then installed in other domestic offices. The next stage of installation involved the other accounting applications in domestic offices. About the time these packages were installed in about half of the domestic offices, the payroll application installation was begun in the first foreign office.

The installation teams consisted of user personnel from various job positions who had been appointed to the installation team. Some of these persons worked on the installation planning and on the development of training material, whereas others had been brought in relatively late in the project and were specially trained to assist with implementation.

Despite a few problems with training in the first few offices and cases in which user documentation needed improvement, the applications were successfully installed and ran with a minimum of user discontent. In fact, quite the opposite occurred. Users were very enthusiastic about the new system and generally agreed that it allowed them to do their jobs better and more easily.

SUMMARY

Both the success stories demonstrate how the implementation process was managed as part of the systems development life cycle. In addition, in both cases, the environment was generally conducive to systems development and implementation. Finally, senior management in both instances went out of its way to support the projects.

Perhaps case X shows better than case Y how the project team worked at implementation, but both project teams did concentrate on implementation aspects of the project. Perhaps both projects would have been successful even if implementation had not been stressed, but the authors are of the opinion that any potential problems were diminished by the care paid by each project team to implementation.

We have attempted to show how important it is to consider the behavioral aspects of systems along with the technical aspects. The MIS manager and the development team members should consider an implementation life cycle right along with the systems development life cycle. In fact these cycles support one another. In both of the successful implementations, the system design was heavily influenced by what was learned from user representatives. Not only did the representation give the user community a feeling of control over the change brought about by the system, but the user inputs resulted in a higher-quality technical system.

Awareness of the problems that may arise if implementation is ignored should lead the MIS manager to take the time to learn what causes problems of implementation. Approaches to implementation, of the sort described in this chapter, can be effective in avoiding problems, but problems may still occur. In such instances, the manager may want to call upon a behavioral specialist to suggest remedial actions. In any case, it is better to implement a system that will be used by those it is intended to support without any dysfunctional behavior. This is why we believe so strongly that the time and the effort put into systems implementation are well spent.

SUGGESTED READINGS

Alavi, M., and J. Henderson, "Evolutionary Strategy for Implementing a Decision Support System, *Management Science*, vol. 27, no. 11, November 1981, pp. 1309-1325.

Anderson, N. B., B. Hedberg, B. Mercer, E. Mumford, and A. Sole, *The Impact of Systems Change in Organizations*, Sisthoff and Noordhoff, Germantown, Md., 1979.

DeSanctis, Gerardine, and James F. Courtney, "Toward Friendly User MIS Implementation," *Communications of the ACM*, vol. 26, no. 10, October 1983, pp. 732-738.

Dickson, Gary W., and John K. Simmons, "The Behavioral Side of MIS," *Business Horizons*, August 1970, pp. 59-71.

Ginzberg, Michael, "Steps Towards More Effective Implementation of MS and MIS, *Interfaces*, vol. 8, no. 3, May 1978, pp. 57-63.

Keen, Peter G. W., "Information Systems and Organizational Change," *Communications of the ACM*, vol. 24, no. 1, January 1981, pp. 24-33.

Lucas, Henry C., Jr., *Implementation: The Key to Successful Information Systems*, Columbia University Press, New York, 1981.

Schultz, Randall, and Dennis Slevin, (eds.), *Implementing Operations Research/Management Science*, American Elsevier, New York, 1975.

Zmud, Robert W., and James F. Cox, "The Implementation Process: A Change Approach," *MIS Quarterly*, vol. 3, no. 2, June 1979, pp. 35-43.

PART SEVEN

MANAGEMENT OF PRODUCTION AND COMPUTER OPERATIONS

SEVENTEEN

COMPUTER CAPACITY PLANNING

INTRODUCTION

Computer capacity planning (CCP) can be a major dilemma for MIS managers. It is not uncommon to find an MIS executive faced with the embarrassing predicament of trying to explain why the multimillion-dollar computer system that was supposed to have adequate capacity for 4 years is overloaded and must be upgraded after 1 year.

This chapter defines CCP and proposes a four-phase model for CCP. The model contains the major steps needed for developing a comprehensive computer capacity plan. The requirements for capacity planning are defined in terms of people, hardware, software, and computing resources. Common tools and methodologies for each step in the planning process are described, including a discussion of the advantages and disadvantages of each. This chapter also provides guidelines for the development of a formal capacity planning function.

DEFINITION OF COMPUTER CAPACITY PLANNING

A problem in the literature and in communication among users is the inconsistent use of terminology to describe the concepts of computer planning. Prior to 1970, when concerns focused on technical performance issues, data processing managers used the terms "computer performance evaluation" and "capacity planning" interchangeably. As the hardware and performance monitoring tools became more sophisticated and data processing expenditures grew, "computer capacity planning" became an accepted term for describing all the functions related to computer planning.   Another term used today by MIS executives is "computer capacity management."   Although closely related, computer performance evaluation, computer capacity planning, and computer capacity management have distinct meanings.

Computer performance evaluation (CPE) is concerned with the efficiency of programs, hardware usage, and scheduling.   Ideally, systems personnel "tune" the system for optimum (and cost-effective) performance.   In reality, the system is tuned to reasonable limits of performance as cost and time allow.   Tuning is one way of extending the life of a system when capacity limits are reached, but it is not predictive of future capacity requirements.

Computer capacity planning (CCP) assumes that resources are tuned and adds the dimension of predicting future computer resource demand. Bronner of IBM defines CCP as "gathering a certain amount of performance data, and making certain predictions about what will happen when you increase the load on that 'system'."[1] A more generalized definition is given by the Institute for Software Engineering (ISE): "Capacity planning is that set of functions concerned with determining and maintaining the proper balance between the workload and equipment configuration at a minimum cost consistent with throughput, response time and reliability objectives."[2] Lipner states there is one basic objective -- "consistent acceptable end user service."[3] A good composite definition for CCP is obtaining computer capacity sufficient to meet user service requirements and projecting future computer resource demand in time to obtain additional computer resources at minimum cost.

What is computer capacity management (CCM)?   As stated previously, the term has been used interchangeably with CCP.   Yet it is more than CCP.   Sandez points to management decision making as a key factor that differentiates CCP from CCM.[4] Davis and Wetherbe discuss management of the chargeout procedure as a capacity management technique, but do not relate it directly to its impact on the capacity planning process.[5] Perhaps *EDP Performance Review* sums it up best with the statement, "To the best of our knowledge there is no standard,

---

[1]L. Bronner, "Overview of the Capacity Planning Process for Production Data Processing," *IBM Systems Journal*, vol. 19, no. 1, 1980, pp. 4-27.

[2]"Capacity Management and Software Physics," *EDP Performance Review*, vol. 7, no. 6, June 1979, pp. 1-8.

[3]Leonard Lipner, "Capacity Planning Simplified," *Computer Decisions*, vol. 11, no. 9, September 1979, pp. 54, 56.

[4]Lou Sandez, "A One Year Retrospective on Getting Started in Capacity Management," presented at the ICCCM, April 1981.

[5]Charles K. Davis and James C. Wetherbe, "DSS for Chargeout System Planning, Control in Large-Scale Environment," *Data Base*, Summer 1980, pp. 13-20.

Figure 17-1 Computer Capacity Planning Hierarchy

widely accepted definition of capacity management."[6]   The definition of computer capacity management used in this chapter is the management of the computer capacity planning process through management-level decisions affecting service, costs, budgets, scheduling, and related policy.

How is CCM different from CCP?   CCP takes a baseline case of current data (usage, service levels, and policy constraints) combined with future projections of growth, makes predictions of future capacity work-load levels, and points to capacity exhaustion.   CCM takes this information and manipulates usage and capacity levels through artificial constraints, for example, (1) by using a chargeout system but pricing below cost to encourage use when there is excess capacity, or pricing above costs and restricting user budgets when capacity is near saturation to discourage use; (2) by setting varying response time-cost relationships; (3) by intentionally degrading response times to make the response time consistent for both slack and high-usage periods; (4) by making priority-ranking decisions on applications to be used or removed; and (5) by determining scheduling windows for particular uses -- batch jobs, interactive time-sharing, testing, etc.   These are a few examples of management controls that can affect CCP and are, according to this definition, part of CCM.

Figure 17-1 depicts the hierarchical relationships of CPE, CCP, and CCM.

STAGES OF COMPUTER CAPACITY PLANNING

The confusion over what constitutes CCP leads to problems in finding an effective approach to planning computer resources.   Typically, businesses find themselves in the position of simply ordering more hardware resources when response time degrades to the point that users

[6]Phillip C. Howard, "Capacity Management and Planning," pt. 1, *EDP Performance Review*, vol. 7, no. 5, May 1980, pp. 1-7; pt. 2, *ibid*, vol. 8, no. 6, June 1980, pp. 1-7.

Table 17-1 Phases and activities in CCP

Phase I: *Identify the problem*
- Recognize the problem
- Develop a work plan
    Budget resources
    Assign responsibilities
    Make a time schedule
    Provide for training
    Develop procedures

Phase II: *Collect the data*
- Determine which measures and how often to measure
- Define major applications
- Establish service objectives
- Monitor the current environment
- Validate data collected

Phase III: *Model the workload*
- Forecast growth
    New, current, and latent demand
- Determine the base case
- Model the future environment
- Isolate probable cases
- Financially evaluate the best alternatives

Phase IV: *Review and control*
- Select and document alternatives
- Produce reports
- Present to management
- Compare planned versus actual utilization
- Refine and standardize planning procedures
- Make capacity planning an ongoing process

Table 17-1 Phases and Activities in CCP

are threatening to transfer their processing needs to an outside service bureau. The MIS manager battles with upper management to commit resources needed to provide better service to users, and with users who are frustrated by inconsistencies in their computer services. The four-phase approach to CCP described in this section aims to provide an appropriate planning approach to minimize these problems and provides a variety of tools and techniques that can be employed in each stage of planning (see Table 17-1).

Identify the Problem

Before CCP can begin, management must recognize the importance of this process. There are several convincing arguments in favor of CCP. Lipner of BGS Systems, a major supplier of CCP systems, mentions these three:

- As computers become the foundation for conducting day-to-day business, a firm cannot risk the possibility of poor computer performance due to overutilization of resources. CCP minimizes the risk of running out of capacity and, consequently, interrupting business operations.

● With budgets in excess of millions of dollars, top management demands that data processing managers justify all expenditures for new equipment. CCP provides detailed data to support these expenditures.

● Changing computer technology and long vendor lead times create problems in planning. A thorough CCP will allow the data processing manager to know when in the future a larger capacity will be needed, how much more will be needed, where it will be needed, without having to rely on vendor recommendations.

Top management commitment for CCP provides authority, independence, and resources to the planning process.

After management commits itself to forming a CCP function, the MIS manager must assign someone to coordinate the CCP activities. In most companies, one person is assigned as full-time capacity planner or two people share this responsibility on a full- or part-time basis. Using two people protects the project from loss of continuity if one person leaves.

There is little consensus on where to place the capacity planning function in the organization. The person assigned often has a systems background or comes from operations or applications development, areas that represent the technical skill requirements for CCP. Because there are few experienced computer capacity planners, it may be necessary to hire someone with a computer or math background and train him or her in CCP.

The planner's first job is to develop a work plan. This plan budgets the hardware, software, and computing resources needed for CCP and assigns responsibilities among systems, operations, applications development, user departments, top management, and the steering committee for conducting CCP functions. Although the exact hardware, software, and computing resources may not be known at this time, an estimate should be made to budget their expected cost.

In essence, this work plan provides a framework for studying current utilization, projecting future work loads, and matching growth projections to equipment resources in a cost-effective manner.

Collect the Data

In stage 2, the capacity planner collects data to define the current processing environment. Three types of measurements are required: system, work load, and application programs. "System measurement" tools capture data describing how the major hardware resources are used. Examples are operating status of the CPU, channel utilization, control unit utilization, storage device utilization, disk head movements, and data set contention. "Work-load measurements" evaluate the logical utilization of the computer by the work (jobs) run on it. Examples of work-load measures are number of jobs run concurrently and turnaround time. "Program measurement" is concerned with the individual uses of the computer resources, for instance, location of instructions being executed, percentage of time spent executing instructions, percentage of time spent waiting for completion of I/O activity for each data set, and the impact of paging activity. Three major areas are usually evaluated: CPU usage, I/O activity, and on virtual systems, paging activity.[7],[8]

In order to describe resource utilization, the CCP group must determine which factors to measure and how often to collect the data. Bronner of IBM suggests collecting the following kinds of data:[9]

- CPU utilization, utilization of software subsystems, and applications
- Number of utilizations and number of SIOs (start I/O instructions) for each channel control unit, head of string, I/O device
- Transactions per time period
- Total number of transactions
- Response time for each transaction
- Response time for each type or class of transaction
- Multiprogramming level
- EXCPs (execute channel program instructions) and SIOs for each transaction
- EXCPs and SIOs for each type or class of transaction

Examples of transactions are batch jobs, time-sharing interactions, and database transactions. In order to avoid information overload, the list should be limited to *key* variables, which may differ among data processing installations.

To collect meaningful data from users, the CCP group must divide the current work load into major applications or major systems. This division allows users to forecast growth for each application and facilitates translation of user estimates into data processing terms (CPU hours, number of input transactions, etc.).

---

[7]Thomas M. Hoger, "Hardware and Software Monitors — Are They for You?" *Canadian Datasystems,* vol. 11, no. 11, November 1979, pp. 70-72.

[8]"Results of the MISRC Capacity Planning Survey," issued to members of the Task Force on Capacity Planning, MIS Research Center, University of Minnesota, May 1981.

[9]Bronner, op. cit.

Next, as a CCM issue, the planning group should establish service objectives. "Service objectives" or "service levels" are the quantitative descriptions of the way in which services are delivered. The four categories of service objectives to consider are timeliness, accuracy, cost, and reliability.[10]

These objectives state service requirements in user-oriented terms such as response time or batch turnaround time. For example, a service requirement can be defined as follows: Time-sharing response time will be no longer than 5 seconds during peak periods, and batch turnaround will be less than 45 minutes.

Monitoring key variables should be an ongoing process. Historical logs allow planners to track the resource utilization for each application system as well as compare growth among applications. Historical data is also necessary for validating the data collected and verifying the appropriateness of the methodology for collecting that data.

Model the Work Load

Stage 3 focuses on forecasting growth and modeling the work load to estimate future capacity requirements.

The first step in this analysis is to forecast growth in new and current applications. Forecasts are solicited from users and application developers. Users forecast growth in existing applications, and application programmers and analysts work with users to estimate growth of new applications. Planners should also estimate latent demand, which is the unsatisfied current demand caused by constraints in computing resources; this should be satisfied after increasing capacity.[11]

The next step is to choose a modeling technique. The primary options are analytic modeling (which is based upon queuing theory), simulation, and benchmarking. These techniques are described later in this chapter.

Having selected a modeling procedure, planners work with systems and operations personnel to determine a "base case" for the model -- a valid representation of the current environment. Systems people provide data for the model while operations personnel fine-tune for optimum performance.

Once the base case is established, forecasted work-load changes are added to the model in order to predict future capacity utilization. It is advisable to vary the work load according to ranges in estimated growth and to analyze peak and average periods over several time intervals.

---

[10]Barry A. Stevens, "Audit and Control of Performance in Data Processing," *EDP Performance Review*, vol. 6, no. 1, January 1980, pp. 1-13.

[11]J. C. Cooper, "A Capacity Planning Methodology," *IBM Systems Journal*, vol. 10, no. 1, 1980, pp. 28-45.

There is general agreement that utilization should be stated in terms of service levels rather than 100 percent equipment capacity.[12,13,14] While a resource may be viewed as having potentially 100 percent utilization, in practice resources are constrained by service objectives. Hence, resource capacity varies among installations. The upper limit on resource capacity is the utilization level above which resources become bottlenecked, causing response or turnaround time to fall outside of the user service objective.

After modeling the work load, planners must isolate the bottlenecks to identify where and when computer resources need to be added or changed. Again, this decision is tied to the cost of meeting user service objectives. A review of these service requirements is necessary at this point to determine if any changes are warranted.

The final step in stage 3 is to financially evaluate the most feasible alternatives. The Institute for Software Engineering recommends setting up a master equipment and inventory schedule that contains information on equipment, configuration, and associated costs. This schedule facilitates cost analysis of each alternative.[15] Organizations find this kind of equipment inventory and schedule to be particularly useful in planning capacity changes.

Review and Control

The last stage in capacity planning involves documenting the best alternatives, selecting the best choice, and reporting to both technical and nontechnical management.

When choosing how and when to change resources in a computing installation, several factors need to be considered, such as financial constraints, organizational concerns, and strategic considerations. Planners must thoroughly cost-justify the final recommendation and make certain that it fits the organizational structure and is in accord with top management's long-range strategic business plan. Consequently, capacity planners have to coordinate this decision-making activity with business planners to ensure that the selected alternative is economically and operationally feasible, as well as technically superior.

Even though only one recommendation is given to top management, all feasible alternatives should be documented. This allows a brief

---

[12]"Capacity Planning: Predicting Your Future Computer Needs," *Computer Decisions*, vol. 12, no. 2, February 1980, pp. 64-70.

[13]"Fulfilling User Service Objectives," *EDP Performance Review*, vol. 8, no. 10, October 1980, pp.1-8.

[14]"Results of the MISRC Capacity Planning Survey," op. cit.

[15]"Effective Computing Management," Tutorial for 1981 International Conference on Capacity Management.

discussion of the alternatives considered and reasons for rejecting the alternatives considered inferior.

Several levels of management, both technical and nontechnical, need to be kept informed of CCP activities. Therefore, different reports must be prepared to meet these varying needs. Although all reports should be in business format, terminology must be keyed to the appropriate technical level. Leavitt suggests that, for top management, the unit of measure be no more complex than hours per month of CPU time with percentages of available total time.[16] A slightly more frequent and more technical report is appropriate for the MIS manager. The technical support manager requires frequent detailed reports that support findings reported to top management.

Regardless of the technical depth of the report, Partacz, of the Majers Corporation, suggests analyzing the report to see if it meets the following seven criteria:[17]

1. Easily understood
2. Reliable
3. Repeatable (i.e., consistently generate some results)
4. Expressed in meaningful numerical values
5. Usable for budgeting purposes
6. Useful in detection and solution of problems
7. Useful for predicting problems, not just for confirming them

Several authorities recommend making an oral report to top management, in addition to a written report.[18],[19] As in the case of the written document, the oral report should be presented in a business format. Leavitt recommends setting up the meeting in advance and making sure that managers are informed of the recommendation *in advance of* the formal presentation. By doing this, no surprises can come out at the meeting. Meaningful information is transmitted in the oral presentation, but more importantly, this format gives the planners the visibility they need, as well as experience in practicing communication skills.

CCP does not stop after the final report is presented to top management. On the contrary, CCP is an ongoing process. Current data must be stored for comparison against actual utilization. This data

---

[16]Don Leavitt, "Performance Measures Not Good Enough," *Computerworld,* vol. 12, no. 22, May 29, 1978, p. 27.

[17]"Fulfilling User Service Objectives," *EDP Performance Review,* vol. 8, no. 10, October 1980, pp. 1-8.

[18]Don Leavitt, "CPE Only Part of Capacity Planning," *Computerworld,* vol. 12, no. 51, December 18, 1978, pp. 21-26.

[19]"Results of the MISRC Capacity Planning Survey," op. cit.

should be provided as feedback to users who make frequent forecasts for the plan and to top managers who approve capacity expansion decisions based on the plan.

As the capacity planning effort matures, planning procedures need to be refined and solidified. As forecasting procedures improve, they should be standardized. And, as the level of sophistication in data collection and analysis rises, planners should evaluate using more sophisticated planning aids. Finally, as the planning procedures improve, this process can be incorporated into the major functions of the MIS department. Many firms have formed a capacity planning department.[20]

TOOLS AND METHODOLOGIES FOR COMPUTER CAPACITY PLANNING

In this section, the goals of each phase in CCP are reiterated and the tools and methodologies appropriate for achieving these goals are described. Table 17-2 maps these tools and methodologies into the four stages of CCP. Table 17-3 details the advantages and disadvantages of each tool and methodology.

Identifying the Problem

Stage 1 of capacity planning requires that the MIS manager recognize the need for capacity planning and assign a planner to develop a work plan for capacity planning.

There are alternative methods for implementing a work plan. The Institute for Software Engineering recommends implementing a software physics approach to capacity planning.[21] (Software physics is explained later in this chapter.) Lipner of BGS Systems describes another capacity planning methodology centered around a performance prediction model called BEST/1, an analytical model based on queuing theory.[22] Bronner and Cooper developed a planning methodology called USAGE (understanding your system and application growth environment).[23] USAGE is a comprehensive, step-by-step process for forecasting capacity requirements over a period of 1 to 2 years. Many homegrown

---

[20]L. Bronner, op. cit.
[21]"Effective Computing Management," op. cit.
[22]Lipner, op. cit.
[23]Cooper, op. cit.

Table 17-2 Tools and methodologies for CCP

Phases & activities	Tools & methodologies
I. *Identify the problem*	
Develop a work plan	Institute for Software Engineering
	BGS Systems
	USAGE
II. *Collect the data*	
Define the major applications	Business elements
Monitor and specify the current environment	Software physics
	Hardware/software monitors
	Job accounting packages
	Benchmarks
	Synthetic programs
III. *Model the workload*	
Forecast growth	
Determine what to forecast	Natural forecast units (KVIs)
Decide how to project	Predictor variables
	Linear projection
	Regression
	Applications profiling
	Clustering
Model the future environment	Analytic modeling (queueing)
	Benchmarking
	Simulation
IV. *Review and control*	Graphs

Note: Those steps for which no clearly defined methodology or tool exists are not included in this exhibit.

methodologies are described in journals.[24],[25] ,[26],[27] A good summary of the requirements for a complete methodology is contained in a two-part report entitled "Capacity Management and Planning."[28]

The keys to a successful work plan are keeping it as simple as possible and striving for a *minimum* amount of data collection and

[24]H. Pat Artis, "Forecasting Computer Requirements: An Analyst's Dilemma," *EDP Performance Review,* vol. 8, no. 2, February 1980, pp. 1-5.

[25]"Managing the Computer Workload," *EDP Analyzer,* vol. 18, no. 1, January 1980, pp. 1-13.

[26]Phillip C. Howard, "Capacity Planning at American Airlines," *EDP Performance Review,* vol. 7, no. 9, September 1979, pp. 1-6.

[27]Lou Sandez, op. cit.

[28]Howard, "Capacity Management and Planning," Pts. 1 and 2, op. cit.

Table 17-3 Advantages and disadvantages of CCP tools and methodologies

	Tools/ methodologies	Advantages	Disadvantages
Phase I	USAGE	Simple to understand Widely used Appropriate for getting started	Assumes the DP shop operates within USAGE guidelines, does not have bottlenecks or critical response time needs Can only be used as a basis for measuring total CPU capacity analysis Does not address long-range planning, simulation, or modeling
Phase II	Business elements	Allows user forecast of individual applications growth	Not all DP shops can effectively account for their resource utilization by specific dept. or application
	Software physics	Hardware-independent Analysis can be broken into meaningful categories such as work done each hour, each day, by entire workload Can measure the hardware as the software thinks it is being used (logical machine utilization)	Complicated procedure
	Hardware monitors	Machine-independent Do not impose any additional load on the system Good accuracy	Often difficult to install Limited number of data capture devices (probes) Difficult to verify High cost Some monitors do not allow breakdown in resource utilization by application Most depend on software to reduce and display data
	Software monitors	Portable Easy to start Can pinpoint bottlenecks, configuration inadequacies, poor data set placement, and other problems Variety of types	Uses up core and CPU Inflexible in terms of application systems and types of output Requires modifying the operating system

Table 17-3 Advantages and disadvantages of CCP tools and methodologies (continued)

	Tools/ methodologies	Advantages	Disadvantages
			Requires software for the reduction and display of data
	Job accounting procedures	Do not require changing the operating system	Not the same level of detail as software monitors
		Provide regular reporting of system utilization	
		Can use these for measuring utilization by each user and establishing user charge rates based on the same utilization measure	
	Benchmarks	Allow comparisons of utilization rates across equipment	Inflexible
			User must specify "typical" program or programs
			Time-consuming
	Synthetic programs	Allow comparisons of utilization rates across equipment	Time-consuming to write
			Difficult to isolate the "typical" program
Phase III	Natural forecast units (KVIs)	Meaningful to users	Must be translated into DP terminology
		Leads to establishment of standard costs for defined units of work	Some units are not so obvious
	Predictor variables	Can use to predict growth in areas for which measures are not available	May not want to disclose this information
			May identify the wrong "predictors"
	Linear projections	Simple to use	Does not account for complex relationships
	Regression	Can isolate key volume indicators	Lack of historical data on performance
		Allows plotting of lines for trend analysis	May not be able to identify any highly correlated indicators

Table 17-3 Advantages and disadvantages of CCP tools and methodologies (continued)

Tools/ methodologies	Advantages	Disadvantages
Applications profiling	Forecasts are tied to business forecasts rather than trending data	May be difficult to identify historical data
		No method for determining what level of detail is best for modeling a particular application
		Difficult to profile application mixes
Clustering	Useful for estimating growth in *new* applications	Sometimes difficult to isolate similar elements
Queueing theory models	Relatively quick application and calculation	Limited formulations
	Commercial packages available that are fairly easy to use	User has to specify load
Benchmarking	Provides accurate data on resource utilization	User has to specify the load
		Requires functioning hardware and software
	Forces the user to be explicit about workload, software, and hardware configuration	Results may become obsolete in a rapidly changing environment
		Time-consuming
		Inflexible

analysis. Most planners collect too much data initially. Over time, they have to weed out unessential information.

The methodology chosen for capacity planning should be as independent as possible of any specific product, because of the continually changing MIS environment.[29]

---

[29]Bronner, op. cit.

Collecting the Data

The goal of stage 2 is to collect data to define the current environment. Data collection activity requires users to estimate growth in current and new systems and MIS to estimate utilization, given user forecasts. Since these projections are complementary activities, Cooper suggests breaking down the work load into work units that are mutually understandable. He coined the term "business elements" -- units that are meaningful to both users and MIS professionals.[30] Business elements are usually major applications within production, testing, and operations support. One problem in using business elements is that MIS installations cannot always specify resource utilization by application.

The Institute for Software Engineering recommends using software physics to analyze the "work" of a computer system. In software physics, one unit of work equals one byte of data moved or acted upon -- essentially a hardware-independent work-load classification.[31],[32] Using this approach requires the use of hardware and system software. One problem commonly mentioned by people using software physics is that it involves a complicated analysis procedure.

Hardware monitors represent one type of data collection device. "Hardware monitors" are electric and/or electromechanical devices, external to the computer, that sense signals in the host system. These tools are machine-independent, provide good accuracy, and do not impose additional load on the system. However, they are often difficult to install and verify, have a limited number of data-capture devices (probes), do not allow breakdown in resource utilization by applications, and depend on software for the reduction and display of the data captured. Hardware monitors range in price from $350 to $12,000 and up.[33],[34]

The software monitor is another common device for collecting data. "Software monitors" are programs that measure resource utilization. These monitors are based upon an intercept or sampling concept. Intercept-type monitors insert additional coding at key data gathering points in the system control program or application program. Sampling-type monitors stop the program, at which point a measuring routine takes over, noting the time and status of events. Most software monitors in use today are sampling-based.[35]

---

[30]Cooper, op. cit.

[31]"Capacity Management and Software Physics," op. cit.

[32]"Quantitative Methods for Capacity Planning," *EDP Analyzer*, vol. 18, no. 7, March 1979, pp. 1-13.

[33]"Hardware Monitors," *EDP Performance Review*, December 1980, pp. 8-29.

[34]Hoger, op. cit.

[35]Ibid.

Software monitors are portable and easy to start and are good at pinpointing bottlenecks, configuration inadequacies, poor data set placement, and other performance problems. Despite these advantages, software monitors use up core and CPU time, are inflexible in terms of application systems and types of output, and require modification of the operating system. Like hardware monitors, software monitors have a wide price range -- from $500 to $50,000.[36],[37]

Job accounting procedures are used for collecting and analyzing data. These procedures are software packages that process accounting data files, producing a variety of cost- and performance-related reports. Although the information provided by these packages is primarily used for establishing user charge-back rates, this data can be used to analyze system utilization. An advantage of using this data collection technique is that job accounting packages do not require making changes to the operating system but they also do not provide the same level of detail as software monitors. Prices range from $2000 to $30,000.[38]

Most users rely almost completely on data gathered by accounting and performance-monitoring software packages to analyze resource utilization and to plan capacity.[39]

Two common techniques for analyzing operating efficiency are benchmarks and synthetic programs. "Benchmarks" are programs that are considered typical of the data center's work load. These programs are run on different machines to compare operating efficiency. Problems with benchmarks are their inflexibility and the time they consume in people and equipment resources.

"Synthetic programs" are programs that are written specifically for evaluating operating efficiency. As in the case of benchmarks, these programs allow comparison of utilization across equipment. The main problem with using synthetic programs is having to isolate a "typical" set of parameters and the length of time it takes to write the benchmark program.

Modeling the Work Load

Stage 3 focuses on forecasting growth and modeling the work load to estimate future capacity requirements.

Stating projection requests to users in business-related terms helps the users forecast growth in their applications. One way to obtain these projections is to have users forecast in natural forecast units, also known as "key volume indicators" (KVIs). KVIs are work units,

[36]"Hardware Monitors," op. cit.

[37]Hoger, op. cit.

[38]"Hardware Monitors," op. cit.

[39]"Quantitative Methods for Capacity Planning," op. cit.

specified in business terms, that correlate with actual system utilization. For instance, a KVI for an order entry system is the number of orders to be processed.

Predictor variables are related to natural forecast units. "Predictor variables" are key volume indicators identified as predictors of growth in resource utilization.

MIS planners translate user forecasts into MIS terminology. In the above example, "number of orders" translates as number of transactions, amount of storage space, number of I/O accesses, and CPU processing time.

One potential problem with using key volume indicators or predictor variables is that sometimes users do not want to provide an accurate estimate for reasons of confidentiality. They may also identify variables that are not truly predictive of growth in data processing terms, thereby leading to upgrade decisions based on faulty information.

A simple way to estimate growth is by using "linear projection," a method of extrapolating future levels of a single variable on the basis of historical data. One company found this technique to be very easy to use but not as accurate as time series analysis.[40]

A more sophisticated forecasting procedure is "regression." This technique depends on developing equations that relate resource consumption to a set of independent variables. Given the level of sophistication required to develop accurate multiple regression equations, this technique is most appropriate for experienced capacity planners.

Two forecasting techniques described by Artis are clustering and applications profiling.[41] "Clustering" identifies similar work-load elements. "Applications profiling" is a regression technique that relates user-stated predictor variables to resource requirements. Artis found that these procedures are particularly useful for projecting growth for new applications. However, it is sometimes difficult to isolate similar elements and to profile application mixes.

No matter which forecasting technique is used, the chosen methodology should match the abilities and requirements of the company and MIS installation. In other words, do not use techniques that you do not understand.

The next step in this phase is to model the work load. The simplest modeling procedure is based on queuing theory. This process focuses on the mathematical characteristics of interacting transactions to express resource utilization. Since commercial packages exist to implement this type of model, it can be used by systems people who do not have the math background to develop or fully understand queuing models.

---

[40]"Results of the MISRC Capacity Planning Survey," op. cit.

[41]H. Pat Artis, "Forecasting Computer Requirements: An Analyst's Dilemma," *EDP Performance Review*, vol. 8, no. 2, February 1980, pp. 1-5.

Simulation is another common modeling procedure. Dunlavey defines simulation as a process that "creates an analogy of the computer system by defining the numerical and logical characteristics of the resources and computing the step-by-step consequences (i.e., queues, transit times, etc.) of introducing a series of transactions (jobs, programs, execution calls, messages, etc.) through it."[42] In effect, this technique mimics the events that occur in the system.

Many simulation packages are commercially available. However, they are costly, time-consuming to use, and difficult to validate and maintain.

Another sophisticated modeling procedure is benchmarking. "Benchmarking" requires building a physical upgrade on a system in another location or inhouse and running a typical set of jobs on this system. Benchmarking provides accurate data on resource utilization, but requires that the future work load be explicitly specified and that the hardware and software be functional.

Reviewing and Controlling

The two goals in stage 4 of CCP are (1) to report the results of the capacity study to management and (2) to review and control the planning process. Companies agree that one of the most effective reporting tools is the graph.[43] A commonly used graph plots percentage utilization over time, by individual hardware resource. An effective addition to this graph is a line drawn at the percent of utilization beyond which service falls outside of the stated service objectives. Figures 17-2 through 17-7 are samples of the graphs used when reporting to management.

Capacity planners at 3M Company use computer-based aids (MICS, SAS) that produce graphs from the utilization data gathered. These graphs are displayed in an area called the "chart house." Anyone interested in utilization information has access to the chart house.

Stage 4 also represents the iterative part of capacity planning: review and control. Developing a computer capacity plan does not stop after the final recommendations are made to management. On the contrary, planners have to collect data to verify the accuracy of their projections and the reasonableness of the plan. Consequently, planners repeat the processes of collecting data (stage 2), modeling the work load (stage 3),

---

[42]Richard F. Dunlavey, "The State of the Art in Analytical Modeling," *EDP Performance Review*, vol. 6, no. 11, November 1978, pp. 1-6.

[43]"Results of the MISRC Capacity Planning Survey," op. cit.

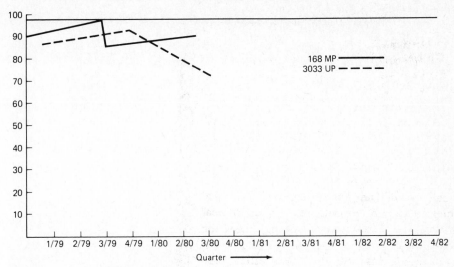

Figure 17-2 CPU Activity

and reporting to management (stage 4). In addition, the work plan detailed in stage 1 may be modified as planners gain experience in capacity planning. Therefore, planners should reiterate stage 1 annually, or as needed.

Figure 17-3 Meantime Between Hardware Failures

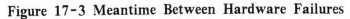

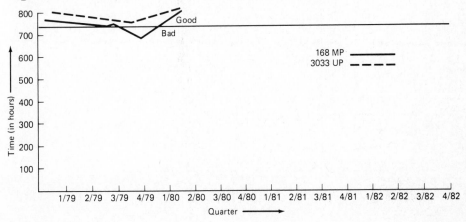

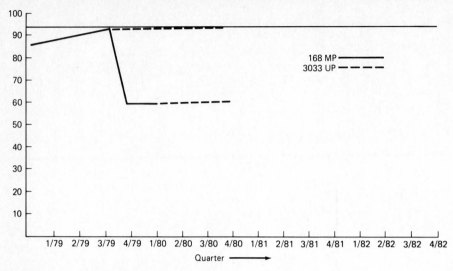

Figure 17-4 TSO Terminal Usage

ASSIGNING RESPONSIBILITIES

A good capacity plan depends on the cooperative efforts of users, management, and MIS personnel. Users provide information on the performance of their systems and forecast growth in new and current

Figure 17-5 Printer Usage

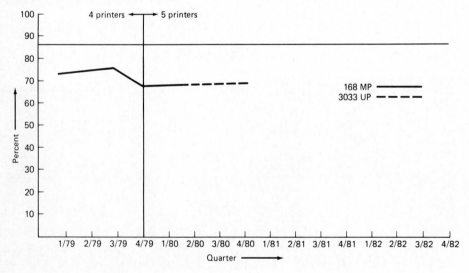

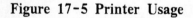

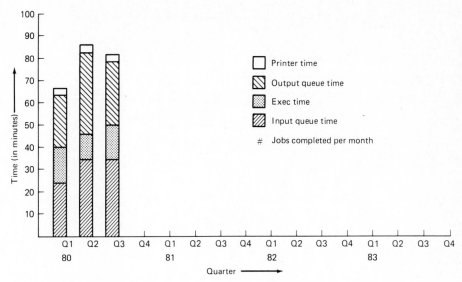

Figure 17-6 Batch Test Turnaround Regular First Shift

applications. Management influences service level decisions made between MIS and users. Top management or a steering committee may authorize MIS expenditures. Within the MIS department, operations people monitor the current work load, application developers translate

Figure 17-7 TSO Response (Sample Only -- Not Real Data)

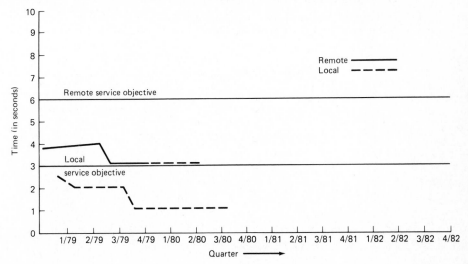
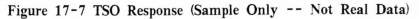

Table 17-4 Personnel responsibilities for CCP

Responsibility	I Identify the problem	II Collect the data	III Model the workload	IV Review and control
Users	Report satisfaction		Forecast growth in current applications Plan for new systems Define requirements for new systems	Report satisfaction State service requirements
Application developers	Report on user satisfaction		Forecast growth in new applications Estimate latent demand Translate user projections into DP terminology	Negotiate user service objectives Provide feedback to users on the accuracy of their forecasts
Operations	Report on schedule	Monitor the environment Maintain logs		
MIS managers	Gain commitment from top management for CCP Report to top management Assign responsibility for CCP			Contract with users for service objectives

Technical systems support* (computer capacity planning)	Investigate user complaints Develop a work plan	Select system parameters Determine tools to use to measure utilization Validate data collected	Model the current workload Validate the base model Model the future	Provide feedback to users on how well service objectives were met in last period Provide feedback to application developers who made forecasts Revise the capacity plan Select alternatives for meeting capacity Determine service objectives
Top management or steering committee	Commit resources to CCP			Approve the plan Authorize expenditures Evaluate alternatives for operational and economic feasibility
Outside specialists	Help develop a work plan			
Vendors		Collect utilization statistics	Model the future workload	
Cost accountants				Determine cost of meeting user service objectives

*This breakdown in job responsibilities assumes that the CCP function is contained within the technical systems support area.

user forecasts into MIS terms, and the technical support staff models the current and future work load.

The work plan should spell out these responsibilities so everyone will know what they are expected to contribute to the planning process. Table 17-4 provides one way of assigning these responsibilities.

SUMMARY

The phases and steps involved in developing a computer capacity plan are (1) identifying the problem, (2) collecting the data, (3) modeling the work load, and (4) reviewing and controlling. A variety of tools and methodologies appropriate for each stage in CCP are available.

The stages presented in this chapter are generalized for all MIS installations. However, the various techniques discussed may not be appropriate for every organization. The key in selecting planning techniques is that they match the needs and abilities of the company and people who will use them. In many cases, purchased tools or methodologies will have to be modified. For some companies, tools will have to be developed inhouse.

SUGGESTED READINGS

Artis, H. Pat, "Forecasting Computer Requirements: An Analyst's Dilemma," *EDP Performance Review*, vol. 8, no. 2, February 1980, pp. 1-5.

"B&B Planning Tools to Ease Capacity Planning Decisions," *Computerworld*, July 28, 1980, p. 41.

Bell, Thomas E., "Twenty-One Money-Saving Questions," *Financial Executive*, vol. 45, no. 12, December 1977, pp. 18-24.

Bronner, L., "Overview of the Capacity Planning Process for Production Data Processing," *IBM Systems Journal*, vol. 19, no. 1, 1980, pp. 4-27.

"Capacity Management Fields Performance Dividends," *Computer Decisions*, May 1980, pp. 64-65.

"Capacity Management and Software Physics," *EDP Performance Review*, vol. 7, no. 6, June 1979, pp. 1-8.

"Capacity Planning Methodology," *Computer Performance Measurement*, Auerbach, 45-01-07, pp. 1-12.

"Capacity Planning: Predicting Your Future Computer Needs," *Computer Decisions*, vol. 12, no. 2, February 1980, pp. 64-70.

Clawson, W. Kemp, "Software Physics Shows Managers What's Happening," *Computerworld*, vol. 11, no. 3, January 17, 1977, p. 25.

"Computer Performance Evaluation Users Group," *EDP Performance Review*, vol. 7, no. 11, November 1979, pp. 1-9.

Cooper, J. C., "A Capacity Planning Methodology," *IBM Systems Journal*, vol. 10, no. 1, 1980, pp. 28-45.

"CPE Effort Eases Manufacturer's DP Functions," *Computerworld*, vol. 12, no. 48, November 27, 1978, pp. 31-32.

"Data Processing: How to Buy Enough Computers," *Business Week*, December 8, 1980.

Davis, Charles K., and James C. Wetherbe, "DSS for Chargeout System Planning, Control in Large-Scale Environment," *Data Base*, Summer 1980, pp. 13-20.

Donohoe, Irene, "Virginia National Bank Cashes in on CPE Effort," *Computerworld*, November 12, 1979, p. 70.

Dunlavey, Richard F., "The State of the Art in Analytical Modeling," *EDP Performance Review*, vol. 6, no. 11, November 1978, pp. 1-6.

Dunn, Nina, "Getting the Most Out of Your Data Center," *Computer Decisions*, May 1979, pp. 68-73.

"Effective Computing Management," Tutorial for 1981 International on Capacity Management.

"Fulfilling User Service Objectives," *EDP Performance Review*, vol. 8, no. 10, October 1980, pp. 1-8.

"Hardware Monitors." *EDP Performance Review*, December 1979. pp. 14-52.

"Hardware Monitors," *EDP Performance Review*, December 1980, pp. 8-29.

Hart, Larry E., "CPM Program Can Boost Productivity," *Computerworld*, December 13, 1976, p. 25.

Heil, Stephen W., "One Approach to the Management of Computer Performance Data," *EDP Performance Review*, vol. 7, no. 1, January 1979, pp. 1-10.

Henkel, Tom, "Capacity Planning Called a Hazardous Business," *Computerworld*, October 20, 1980, p. 23.

Hoger, Thomas M., "Hardware and Software Monitors -- Are They for You?" *Canadian Data Systems*, pp. 70-72.

Holmes, Edith, "Performance Management Overdue: Kiviat," *computerworld*, June 12, 1978, p. 25.

"How to Prepare the Long Range EDP Plan," *EDP In-Depth Reports*, vol. 8, no. 7, March 1979, pp. 1-16.

Howard, Phillip C., "Capacity Planning at American Airlines," *EDP Performance Review*, vol. 7, no. 9, September 1979, pp. 1-6.

_____, "Capacity Management and Planning," pt. 1, *EDP Performance Review*, vol. 7, no. 5, May 1980, pp. 1-7; pt. 2, ibid., vol. 7, no. 6, June 1980, pp. 1-7.

Landon, Michele, "Capacity Plans Pay off for Shops of All Sizes," *Computerworld*, vol. 14, no. 37, September 15, 1980, pp. 41-45.

Leavitt, Don, "Performance Measures Not Good Enough," *Computer Decisions*, vol. 12, no. 22, May 29, 1978, p. 27.

_____, "CPE Only Part of Capacity Planning," *Computerworld*, vol. 12, no. 51, December 18, 1978, pp. 21-26.

_____, "MVS Planning Technique Taking Shape, Technician from Bell Labs Tells Meeting," *Computerworld*, vol. 15, no. 51, December 18, 1981, p. 25.

_____, "Performance Measures Not Good Enough," *Computerworld*, vol. 12, no. 22, May 29, 1978, p. 27.

Lipner, Leonard, "Capacity Planning Simplified," *Computer Decisions*, vol. 11, no. 9, September 1979, pp. 54, 56.

Lipovich, G. Jay, "DP Manager and Performance Measurement," *Journal of Systems Management*, vol. 28, no. 3, March 1977, pp. 22-27.

"Managing the Computer Workload," *EDP Analyzer*, vol. 18, no. 1, January 1980, pp. 1-13.

Mead, C. C., "Hardware Monitors Help Services Firm . . . Forecast, Budget Growth for 11 Data Centers," *Computerworld*, vol. 13, no. 48, November 26, 1979, pp. 54-55.

"Modeling the Queue," *Datamation*, vol. 25, no. 7, June 1979.

Nguyen, H. C., "The Role of Detailed Simulation in Capacity Planning," *IBM Systems Journal*, vol. 19, no. 1, 1980, pp. 81-101.

"Performance Highlights from the NCC," *EDP Performance Review*, vol. 7, no. 7, July 1979, pp. 1-8.

"Performance of Computer Installations: Evaluation and Management," *Data Processing Digest*, August 1979, p. 19.

"Products and Services and Evaluations," *EDP Performance Review*, February 1978, pp. 7-9.

"Quantitative Methods for Capacity Planning," *EDP Analyzer*, vol. 18, no. 7, March 1979, pp. 1-13.

"Results of the MISRC Capacity Planning Survey," issued to members of the Task Force on Capacity Planning, MIS Research Center, University of Minnesota, May 1981.

Sandez, Lou, "A One Year Retrospective on Getting Started in Capacity Management," presented at the ICCCM, April 1981.

Saxton, W.A., "Modeling Tool Expenses Teleprocessing Threat," *Infosystems*, vol. 26, no. 10 (pt. 1), October 1979, pp. 140-142.

Schiller, D.C., "System Capacity and Performance Evaluation," *IBM Systems Journal*, vol. 19, no. 1, 1980, p. 47.

Seaman, P.H., "Modeling Considerations for Predicting Performance," *IBM Systems Journal*, vol. 19, no. 1, 1980, pp. 68-80.

"Service Bureau Investigates Capacity Planning Methods," *Computerworld*, June 30, 1980.

"Software Physics Credited for Easing Upgrade," *Computerworld*, August 27, 1979, p. 43.

Stevens, Barry A., "Audit and Control of Performance in Data

Processing," *EDP Performance Review*, vol. 6, no. 1, January 1980, pp. 1-13.

Wetherbe, James C., I. Lynne Carper, and Susan Harvey, "Computer Capacity Planning: Strategy and Methodologies," *Data Base*, vol. 14, no. 4, Summer 1983, pp. 3-13.

EIGHTEEN

HARDWARE AND SOFTWARE ACQUISITION

INTRODUCTION

The acquisition of computer technology is one of the most difficult, complex responsibilities of MIS management. The alternatives available and the dynamic characteristics of alternatives are often overwhelming. Few technology decisions are made with complete confidence that they are the optimum decisions.

In this chapter the acquisition of hardware and software is examined. The process is discussed as a decision-making process progressing from intelligence to design and choice. The *intelligence* section reviews the means of achieving insight and understanding into technology alternatives. The *design* section focuses on the request for quotation (RFQ) and request for proposal (RFP) documents. Also discussed are contractual and financing issues. The *choice* section discusses proposal validation and the vendor selection process.

TECHNOLOGY INTELLIGENCE

"Technology intelligence" is gathered by considering MIS objectives and identifying and examining technology to contribute to achieving those objectives. In a technologically dynamic field such as computing, it is unfortunately common for those responsible for technology decisions to continue to use hardware and software with which they are familiar, rather than to thoroughly investigate and consider other technological alternatives. To illustrate, the use of minicomputers was a cost-effective alternative for online processing several years before most organizations considered implementing them as an alternative to large centralized computers. Even computer professionals are occasionally reluctant to change to technologies that differ from those that were current when they received their training. In other words, they tend to invest their efforts in structuring technology (e.g., by programming or organizing data files, and by tuning the operating system) with which they are familiar to accomplish something new, rather than back up to consider other technology alternatives that might be more effective and efficient.

The reluctance of a computer professional to capitalize on new technologies is not dissimilar to that of an accountant who resists changing from a manual accounting system to a computerized one. No amount of structuring of the manual system can provide the performance that is possible with computer technology. There exists somewhat of a paradox when computer professionals, who have brought so much change to others, are reluctant to endure change themselves.

Therefore, an important aspect of technology intelligence is to thoroughly examine new technologies that might be *included* to support an information system or systems prior to proceeding with *structuring* technology. It is far better to find the technology that can best perform the task required than to fit the task to a more familiar but less suitable technology.

Intelligence

To properly consider technology alternatives, the decision makers responsible for technology selection must know about the state-of-the-art hardware and software technology. Research into existing technology is therefore required. The primary sources of intelligence about technology are

- In-house expertise
- Vendor representatives
- Consultants
- Literature
- Other organizations

In-House Expertise

Computer professionals within the organization are a logical starting point in acquiring information about technology that may be included in an information system. In very simple or obvious cases, they may provide the only expertise required. For example, if an organization is implementing a new personnel information system in conjunction with an existing payroll information system, simply using the existing computing equipment may be a clear-cut decision. However, for more complex and sophisticated situations, such as redesigning several major information systems in order to use online technology, additional expertise may be desirable.

A limitation of using in-house staff is that they are not likely to be aware of the latest technological developments available from all hardware and software suppliers. They may also be biased toward hardware and software with which they are familiar.

Vendor Representatives

Representatives from the various manufacturers of hardware and/or software (e.g., IBM, Burroughs, NCR, Honeywell, Univac, CDC) are a major source of information on technology. Vendor representatives can be contacted and requested to give presentations and demonstrations of their company's available or forthcoming hardware and/or software relevant to the information system under consideration.

The major drawback of vendor representatives as an information source is that they tend to be biased toward the hardware and/or software they are marketing. It is important to acquire information from several different vendor representatives to ensure an objective perspective of alternative technologies.

Consultants

Consultants can be contacted to provide information on technology and to make recommendations on selection. Their insight can be helpful because they generally have a wide variety of experience with different organizations and technologies. This additional perspective can be highly beneficial.

On the negative side, consultants cost money; are subject to hardware and software biases -- as is any computer professional; and only make recommendations. They will not be around to live with the results of their recommendations.

Literature

The various professional and trade journals unique to the computing industry are an excellent source of information on technology as well as on other aspects of computing and information systems. It is worthwhile to subscribe to several of these publications. Some of the common publications are

- *Communications of the ACM*
- *Computer Decisions*
- *Computerworld*
- *Computing Reviews*

- *Data Communications*
- *Data Management*
- *Datamation*
- *Infosystems*
- *Mini-Micro Systems*
- *MIS Quarterly*

Two other very useful sources of information on technology are available through industry research services provided by DataPro and Auerbach. Both companies market subscription services that provide information on hardware and software supplied by different companies. These sources can be used to determine vendors that should be contacted for additional information.

The following are shortcomings of literature as a source of intelligence:

1. Articles in publications are generally a result of an author's decision to make a contribution in a certain area. Therefore, there may or may not be articles that specifically discuss technology pertinent to the information system under consideration. Also, the articles that are available may contain author biases.

2. Hardware and software information services, though extremely comprehensive, are, of necessity, generalized. They do not specifically discuss hardware or software as it applies to a particular organization's problems.

Other Organizations

Other organizations that have developed or are developing similar computer-based information systems can provide considerable insight into the advantages and disadvantages of technology. A common way of locating such organizations is through vendor representatives. It is quite appropriate to request a list of organizations to which the vendor has sold similar hardware and/or software. In situations where there is some question about the capability of a vendor's hardware and/or software, visiting with some of their other customers is highly desirable.

The following are disadvantages of information based on visits to other installations:

1. Other installations are not identical, so care must be taken not to inaccurately generalize.

2. The reasons for another organization's technology decisions may no longer apply because of new technological developments that provide better alternatives.

3. If the other organization is a competitor, the organization may not be willing to share all or any of the information about its environment.

General Selection Criteria

The intelligence phase provides a general understanding of what information systems capabilities are possible with existing technology. Determination can be made of the technological and economical feasibility of supporting the information system as desired. For example, in an online retail information system are there combinations of retail terminals and computers that can perform the necessary processing functions at a price that is realistic for the organization? If the technology does not yet exist or is cost prohibitive, it may be necessary to compromise the desired information system to strive for one that is realistic.

Such intelligence about current technology and its cost allows the organization to establish general selection criteria for the type of system desired. Examples of such criteria are whether batch or online processing is to be used, a general idea of processor size and speed, storage capacity needed, and, of course, a price range. Preliminary criteria as to the type of system required provide the framework for the design phase of the decision-making process.

TECHNOLOGY DESIGN

During the design phase, the information about technology is structured into specific alternatives. The objective of the design phase is to design the most economical alternative for properly supporting the information system. There is generally a wide variety of alternatives. It is easy and also tempting to get overly involved with the rather exciting technological elegance. For example, it is interesting to compare processor instruction sets and speeds, disk access techniques, and operating software architecture. But alternatives should be compared in terms of what they do, not what they are.[1] This perspective can best be illustrated by analogy. In purchasing a television set, the type of technology used to produce a quality picture, ensure reliability, and so forth, may be interesting, but the selection of a television set should be based upon its performance -- on what the television does -- and not purely on its technology. The value of technology is based upon the results it produces, not in how interesting or complex it is.

[1] Erik M. Timmereck, "Computer Selection Methodology," *Computing Surveys*, December 1973, p. 201.

Requests for Quotations and Proposals

The end result to be accomplished during the design phase is the creation of system specifications that can be used to request hardware and/or software proposals from vendors. These specifications are generally expressed in either a request for quotation or a request for proposal.

A "request for quotation" (RFQ) is used when the hardware and/or software to be procured is somewhat predetermined. This is usually the situation when an organization has existing computing facilities that need only to be expanded to accommodate a new information system. In such cases, an additional disk drive or additional computer memory may be all that is required. Therefore, an RFQ is prepared that specifies the exact hardware and/or software required. The vendor should respond with specific prices. Figure 18-1 illustrates an RFQ for CRT terminals. Some technical terms in Figure 18-1 may be unfamiliar to the reader. Familiarity with the terms pertinent to an RFQ is acquired during the intelligence phase of a "real" selection exercise. For the purposes of this discussion, such familiarity is not required.

A "request for proposal" (RFP) is used for more complex procurement activities. Generally, there is uncertainty as to the best hardware and/or software to procure. Such a situation may occur when an organization is installing its first computer system or replacing all or most of an existing one. An RFP is less restrictive than an RFQ in that an RFP indicates the functional capabilities required but allows latitude to vendors in configuring and proposing different hardware and/or software alternatives. In fact, the RFP approach allows vendors to participate in the design of alternatives to meet an organization's requirements. For example, one vendor may propose both centralized and distributed technology for an online system. The organization can

Figure 18-1 An RFQ for CRT Terminals

REQUEST FOR QUOTATION

Six CRT Terminals
   Specifications:

   1. Sixty-four Alphanumeric ASCII Characters, Upper and Lower Case
   2. Cursor Addressing
   3. Dual-Intensity Display Mode
   4. 1920-Character (24 X 80) Screen
   5. RS-232 Interface
   6. 300/2400 Baud
   7. Serial Printer Interface (include RS-232 Cable)
   8. Half-Full Duplex Mode
   9. Acoustic Coupling of Hardware Connections
   10. RS-232 Ten-Foot Cable
   11. Ten-Key Numeric Pad

take advantage of the technological creativity available from a wide variety of computer professionals working for different hardware and/or software suppliers. .

Mandatory and Desirable Specifications

Specifications for RFQs and RFPs are generally expressed in terms of mandatory and desirable specifications.

"Mandatory specifications" indicate hardware and software features and capabilities that must be available for an alternative to be considered. For example, a mandatory requirement for an online system might be the ability to concurrently support at least 30 terminals with an average response time of less than 2 seconds.

"Desirable specifications" indicate hardware and software capabilities that are of value but not essential to the operation of the system. Desirable specifications pertain to enhancements to mandatory specifications or introduce new features or capabilities not discussed under mandatory specifications. For example, it may be desirable, but not necessary, for an online system to support more than 30 terminals.

Care must be taken in specifying both mandatory and desirable specifications. The writer must not use specifications that are too vendor-oriented or unfairly restrictive. For example, it would be unfairly restrictive to specify that disk access time must be exactly 30 milliseconds if it were known that only one vendor's disk access time was exactly that speed. To avoid such unfairness, specifications should be expressed in terms of minimal acceptable levels.

Hard and Soft Dollars

The criteria by which RFQs will be evaluated should be defined in the systems specifications. Obviously, a major selection criterion is the cost, or "hard dollars," required to purchase the hardware and/or software. Any response to an RFQ or RFP that meets all mandatory specifications should be given a "hard-dollar evaluation." Any hardware or software that does not meet the mandatory specifications should be considered nonresponsive to the specifications and eliminated from further consideration.

Systems specifications that are desirable may be assigned soft-dollar values. A "soft-dollar value" is a subjective assessment of the economic worth of a desirable feature or capability of a hardware or software component. "Soft dollars" are a mechanism used to award vendors for features or capabilities provided above and beyond mandatory requirements. For example, vendors who can deliver hardware in advance of the mandatory delivery date might be given a soft-dollar credit against the hard-dollar cost of their equipment.

Vendors should be notified in advance as to what soft-dollar

MANDATORY SPECIFICATIONS

I. Main Storage (Memory)
  A. System must have minimum storage capacity of 4 million bytes.
  B. Fetch cycle for one word should not exceed 1 microsecond.
  C. Store cycle for one word should not exceed 2 microseconds.
  D. Memory should exhibit physical modularity to enable functional isolation for trouble-shooting and fault detection.
  E. Memory should permit the use of parity bits for error detection.

DESIRABLE SPECIFICATIONS

I. DELIVERY DATE
  Vendors will be awarded "soft-dollar" credits toward the cost of their proposals for bettering the mandatory delivery date. The schedule of credits follows:

Delivery Date	Credits
May 1981	$60,000
June 1981	40,000
July 1981	20,000
August 1981	-0-

Figure 18-2 Mandatory and Desirable RFP Specifications

evaluations will be made of their quotations or proposals. Providing this information allows vendors to assess the importance and, therefore, the need to address desirable specifications.

Figure 18-2 illustrates how mandatory and desirable systems specifications can be expressed. Note that vendors may be awarded different amounts of soft dollars, depending on the levels at which they satisfy a desirable specification.

Preparing an RFP

An RFP is more involved and difficult to prepare than an RFQ. Therefore it is worthwhile to discuss how to prepare one. There are many ways to structure an RFP; a general outline is provided in Figure 18-3 and discussed below.

1. Introduction
The introduction provides the basic information necessary for vendor orientation.
  a. Confidentiality. A great deal of proprietary and confidential information about an organization's structure can be revealed in an RFP. To protect the organization's interests, it is wise to clearly state to vendors what information contained in the RFP is confidential and clearly define restrictions of its use.
  b. Purpose of RFP. The purpose of the RFP should clearly state why the RFP was developed. The focus should be on high-level business and MIS issues.

REQUEST FOR PROPOSAL
FOR
MEAD MANUFACTURING

I. INTRODUCTION
   A. Confidentiality Statement
   B. Purpose of RFP
   C. Background Information
   D. Summary of Requirements
II. GENERAL INFORMATION AND REQUIREMENTS
   A. Schedule of Selection Process
   B. Proposal Deadline
   C. Vendor Contact with ACME Manufacturing
   D. Alternative Proposals
III. APPLICATIONS TO BE SUPPORTED
   A. Production Scheduling
   B. Material Requirements
   C. Financial Systems
IV. SPECIFICATION
   A. Representative Hardware Configuration and Listing
   B. Representative Operating Software
   C. Representation Application Software
V. CONTRACTUAL EXPECTATIONS
VI. EVALUATION OF PROPOSALS
   A. General Approach
   B. Hard-Dollar Evaluation
   C. Soft-Dollar Evaluation
VII. SPECIFICATIONS FOR VENDOR PROPOSALS
   A. Vendor Reply Format
   B. Vendor Cost Schedule

Figure 18-3 An Outline for an RFP

c. Background information. Background information should provide a brief historical review of the evolution of computing use in the organization and lead up to the current state of computer utilization relevant to the RFP.

d. Summary of requirements. The summary of requirements should provide a general overview of the applications and of the anticipated hardware and software required to support them.

2. General Information and Requirements

a. Schedule of the selection process. This schedule should define specific events and timetables leading up to the awarding of the contract. Typical events include (1) presentation and distribution of RFP to vendors and (2) interviews by vendors.

b. Proposal deadline. To ensure fair treatment of vendors and prompt progress with the RFP, the RFP should contain a firm deadline for vendors to submit a proposal.

c. Vendor's contract with the organization. There is often considerable money (sometimes many millions of dollars) involved in an

RFP. Consequentially, there is a great deal of incentive for a vendor to get the contract. But more vendors are going to be disappointed by the results of the RFP than are going to be pleased. This competition can lead to a lot of covert political activities throughout the organization on the part of the vendor representatives. It is therefore wise to establish who they can contact should they have questions or need additional information. Otherwise they will feel free to contact whomever they please, including the chief executive officer and the board of directors of the organization.

d. Alternative proposals. If alternative proposals are acceptable, the RFP should so indicate. For example, it might be acceptable to have a vendor propose a large single computer as one alternative and a distributed system as another. Also, a vendor might want to collaborate with one or more other vendors in proposing different configurations of hardware and software.

3. Applications to be Supported

This section of the RFP should list and describe the applications to be supported by the system proposed by the vendor. Within each application, information on file storage requirements, transaction volume, lines printed, number of terminals, etc., should be detailed.

4. Specifications

On the basis of the intelligence gained in preliminary discussions with vendors, a general, but thorough understanding of system specifications can be developed. The vendors should be provided with as much specificity of system requirements as is reasonably possible to direct them in preparing a responsive RFP.

a. Representative hardware configuration and history. A generic configuration and description should be provided of the computer components and of the dollar performance attributes perceived necessary to support the applications described under point 3. A graphic configuration should be provided, and items such as computer memory size and cycle timer, the number and the speed of printers, the number of terminals to be supported, and the number, storage capacity, and access time of disk drives should be detailed.

b. Representative operating software. This topic should generically detail the operating software (operation system, job control, utilities, communication monitors, database management systems, etc.) required to support the applications described under point 3.

c. Representative application software. If any application software (e.g., accounting purchases) is part of the RFP, the specifications should be outlined and related to the applications described under point 3 of the RFP.

5. Contractual Expectations

Many organizations accept the vendor's standard contract. This can be a mistake.[2] Vendor contracts are written by the vendor's attorneys and usually protect the vendor's interests better than the customer's. For example, vendor contracts typically will make statements like "the vendor promises to provide good maintenance." The term "good" is not precise enough to protect the customer's interests. It is more precise to say "the vendor will guarantee 98 percent uptime on the system." This is an improvement, but it is still not adequate because it does not state what penalties the vendor will incur if the 98 percent uptime is not provided. For example, the customer might want the vendor to incur a 1 percent reduction in equipment rental (or rental equipment) for every 1 percent the system is available less than 98 percent and want the vendor to incur a 5 percent reduction for every 1 percent less than 92 percent. Terms such as delivery date, performance, and reliability should all be contractually evaluated. However, two warnings are in order. Though most vendors will (begrudgingly) negotiate contractual terms, IBM generally will not. Also, if the customer organization's attorneys get involved, they may tend to make contractual stipulations that no vendor will accept. Judgment must be used.

6. Evaluation of Proposals

So that vendors may direct their RFPs at the criteria most critical to the customer, the evaluation criteria to be used by the customer should be explicitly stated.

a. General approach. This topic should give an overview of the philosophy behind the evaluation criteria, including a discussion of mandatory and desirable attributes, and hard- and soft-dollar evaluations.

b. Hard-dollar evaluation. The hard-dollar evaluation should list those aspects of the RFP that are mandatory and the means of hard-dollar cost analysis that will be used to evaluate RFPs.

c. Soft-dollar evaluation. The soft-dollar evaluation should describe how desirable aspects of the RFP will be evaluated.

7. Specifications for Vendor Proposals

Vendors generally have enough ready-made proposal material that they can easily produce a lengthy, impressive RFP. Unfortunately, when vendors respond to an RFP in this manner, it is difficult for the customer to relate his or her needs to the vendor's response. Therefore, to provide a uniform, straightforward approach to evaluating vendor proposals, the customer should specify the format for vendor responses.

---

[2]Barry L. Bateman and James C. Wetherbe, "Cost Analysis of Computer Maintenance Contracts," *MIS Quarterly*, December 1978, pp. 15-22.

a. Vendor reply format.   A detailed outline should be provided of how vendors are to respond to the RFP.

b. Vendor cost schedule.   Vendors should be instructed to provide a detailed cost schedule of all items in their proposal in order to allow the customer to select different components from different vendors and to associate specific costs with specific items in the RFP.

RFP Procedure

The procedure used in interacting with vendors once the RFP is written should establish that the customer . is capable and determined to manage the RFP process.   Otherwise the vendors may try to manage the customer.

Once the RFP is prepared, vendors capable of responding to the RFP should be invited to a formal overview of the RFP and receive copies of the RFP.   This formal setting establishes a professional atmosphere for the process.

Some vendors may ask for a private presentation, but this should not be allowed.   To do so would exhibit favoritism in what should be a fair, highly competitive process.

Vendors should be instructed to adhere to the schedule, company contract rules, confidentiality rules, and vendor reply formats.   They should also be notified that the proposal awarded the contract will be validated (as discussed in the next section) before final acceptance of the RFP will be given.

During the preparation of proposals by vendors, all vendors should be given equal access to any additional organizational information.   Once the vendors make their presentations and submit their proposals, the selection process can begin.

TECHNOLOGY CHOICE

The responses to RFQs and RFPs provide the information required to proceed with choosing an alternative.   The objective is to select the most cost-effective alternative.

Financial Analysis

In the simplest case, an RFQ or RFP may contain only mandatory requirements.   In such a case, all that is necessary is a hard-dollar evaluation.   The RFQ or RFP with the lowest cost is awarded the order.

In cases where desirable specifications are used, both hard-dollar and soft-dollar evaluations are required.   The hard-dollar evaluation is conducted to determine the actual cost of each alternative. The soft-dollar evaluation is then conducted as follows:

1.   For each desirable attribute provided by a vendor, the associated soft-dollar value is deducted from the vendor's hard-dollar cost.

2.   The vendor with the lowest cost after soft-dollar adjustments is awarded the bid. If the system is to be rented or leased (rather than purchased), soft-dollar deductions are prorated. For example, if a soft-dollar adjustment of $60,000 is prorated for a system renting for $20,000 a month for 5 years, the adjusted price is $19,000 a month.

In some cases, desirable specifications may have hard-dollar costs. For example, additional hardware may be required to support additional (desirable) terminals. This can be adjusted for by conducting separate hard-dollar evaluations for vendors capable of supplying the particular feature or capability.

The alternatives that are available for the acquisition of the system should also be considered in the financial analysis. There are several financial methods available for procuring a computer system. Generally, one of the following methods is used:

1.   Rent directly from the manufacturer or vendor. This method involves periodic payments (usually monthly) for use of the computer equipment. Rental provides the flexibility of short-term leasing, less than 24 months, and generally includes a maintenance contract.

2.   An operating lease from a third party. A leasing agency purchases the equipment from the manufacturers and supplies equipment from its own inventory. Again, there are periodic payments, usually monthly, for use of the computer equipment. Generally, longer agreements are required, greater than 24 months, and the longer commitments tend to reduce the monthly charges. Maintenance agreements may be obtained by the user directly from the manufacturer or vendor.

3.   A financial lease from a third party. The user agrees to make payments to the lessor over a period of time, usually 5 years or more. As with the operating lease agreement, maintenance agreements may be obtained by the user directly from the manufacturer or vendor. A portion of the user's lease payments is credited to the purchase of the equipment. Upon termination of the lease agreement, the user either owns the equipment or may purchase it at a previously determined price.

4.   Direct purchase from the manufacturer or vendor. This form of purchasing involves payment in full and the passing of a title. In the past, this method was widely used. However, technological improvements and rapidly changing user requirements have caused systems to become obsolete before their gains on investments could be realized. As a result, other methods, especially third-party operating leases, are now being used more commonly.

The following are other areas of concern that require investigation and evaluation when considering the acquisition of a computer system:

1. Maintenance. Prime-shift and overtime charges should be evaluated. Many vendors provide for a fixed price and an "on-call" price for overtime charges. This requirement should be investigated on the basis of the system's dependency on particular components.

2. Insurance. This area is normally covered under the vendor's insurance agreement. However, with purchased equipment, the responsibility belongs to the user.

3. Salvage value. Proceeds from the sale or disposal of purchased equipment will add to the cash flow for that year. Consideration for tax purposes should be given to the disposal price versus the depreciated value.

4. Investment tax credit. The 1972 tax law permits 7 percent of the purchase price of an investment to be used as a tax credit on newly purchased capital equipment, to be depreciated over at least 7 years. If the depreciation schedule of the item is between 5 and 7 years, then two-thirds of 7 percent is allowed. If the depreciation schedule of the item is 3 to 4 years, then one-third of 7 percent is allowed. The buyer or user accrues this tax credit on purchased equipment. When the equipment is rented or leased, the vendor or lessor may pass the tax credit to the user, but industry practice varies and depends upon the specific terms of the rental or lease agreement.

Proposal Validation

A vendor's response to a customer's proposal is a written document describing a system or systems that the vendor considers responsive to the customer's requirements. However, in an attempt to provide an attractive price, a vendor may propose a system that is inadequate; it may not be able to properly process the work load. Therefore, the customer should check whether each proposed system is indeed capable of handling the work load before a final choice is made.

A number of methods have been proposed for validating proposals,[3] some of which are not very practical. The least-used approaches include the following:

- *Effectiveness formulas* only measure the computing power of a machine. They do not relate the measured power of the machine to the applications that will utilize the computer.

- *Kernel evaluation* is a measure of the central processing required on a specific machine to enumerate a specific task

[3]Diebold Group (ed.), *Automatic Data Processing Handbook*, McGraw-Hill, New York, 1977.

(e.g., a matrix multiplication or a social security tax calculation). Kernel evaluations, like effectiveness formulas, do not provide evaluations that are representative of the actual work load to be performed by the customer.

- *Simulation* uses tools such as IBM's CSS (Computer System Simulator), Lockheed's LOMUSS II (Lockheed Multipurpose Simulation System), and Comress's SCERT (Systems and Computer Evaluation Review Techniques). To use the modules, characteristics of job mixes representative of the customer's applications are fed into a simulated model of the computer system under consideration.

- *Mathematical formulas* use queueing theory tools in the evaluation process. To use a model, parameters are provided with descriptions of the customer's job mix. The problem is finding a model that fits the customer's situation. There are general-purpose models available for such things as multiprogramming, time-sharing, and networks, but generally, finding a good fit between customer specifications and a model is difficult.

The most accepted and comprehensive means of validating a proposal is the use of a benchmark program.[4] A "benchmark" is a point of reference from which performance measurements of hardware and software can be made. Benchmark comparisons are most commonly made by running computer programs and/or mixes of computer programs that are the actual work, or are representative of the actual work, to be performed on the new system. The times required to process such work loads serve as the benchmarks, on the basis of which projections can be made as to the ability of the proposed system to process the total work load.

In order for the benchmark program to be effective, it should be capable of serving as a measure of normal and peak work loads, turnaround time for a batch environment, and response time for an online system. A library of standard benchmark programs would be useful for repeated testing. Such a library could provide a set of familiar programs whose functions the user understands. These would be helpful when performing benchmark runs on different machines because the user would be able to identify deficiencies or weaknesses on the proposed system.

---

[4]Erick M. Timmereck, "Performance Measurement: Vendor Specifications and Benchmarks," in F. Warren McFarlan and Richard L. Nolan (eds.), with the assistance of Esa-Jane Rapaport, *The Information Systems Handbook,* Dow Jones-Irwin, Homewood, Ill., 1975, pp. 365-367.

Benchmark programs can be used to validate and compare the performance of various systems or just to validate the performance of the most economical proposal. Comparative benchmark runs are advantageous in situations where the costs of different proposals are very close. In such cases, a slight performance advantage may be the deciding factor. If one proposal is substantially more economical than the others, a single benchmark run may be conducted. If that system performs satisfactorily, it may be selected. Otherwise, a benchmark comparison should be made for the next-lowest proposal. Benchmark comparisons are continued until a system that performs satisfactorily is identified. Because each benchmark comparison generally requires time and effort on the part of both the customer and the vendor, as few as possible to achieve a good evaluation should be conducted.

SUMMARY

Hardware and software acquisition is a decision-making process progressing from intelligence, to design and choice. During the intelligence phase, information can be obtained from in-house expertise, vendor representatives, consultants, literature, and other organizations.

Technology design consists of preparing either a request for quotation (RFQ) or a request for proposal (RFP) to elicit responses from vendors. RFQs and RFPs can use both mandatory and desirable specifications combined with hard- and soft-dollar evaluations to provide flexibility in requesting responses from vendors. An RFP is a more complex document than an RFQ and allows for more creativity on the part of the vendor. An RFP should include an introduction, general information and requirements, applications to be supported, system specifications, contractual expectations, evaluation criteria, and specifications for vendor proposals.

The selection of hardware and software involves a financial analysis including lease versus purchase considerations. It also includes validation of the proposal, usually by some form of benchmark comparison.

SUGGESTED READINGS

Auer, Joseph, and Charles Edison Harris, "Negotiating Computer Contracts Effectively," *Infosystems*, April 1978, pp. 79-87.

Bassler, Richard A., and Harold C. Demoody, *Computer System Evaluation and Selection -- An Annotated Bibliography and Keyword Index*, College Readings, Arlington, Va., 1971.

Bateman, Barry L., and James C. Wetherbe, "Cost Analysis of Computer Maintenance Contracts," *MIS Quarterly*, December 1978, pp. 15-22.

Culinguent, Peter, "System Performance Evaluation: Survey and Appraisal," *Communications of the ACM*, vol. 10, no. 1, January 1967, pp. 12-18.

Ferrari, Domenico, "Workload Characterization and Selection in Computer Performance Measurement," *Computer*, vol. 5, July-August 1972, pp. 18-24.

Fife, Dennis W., *Alternatives in Evaluation of Computer Systems*, MTR-413, Mitre Corporation, Bedford, Mass., December 1968.

Goff, Norris F., "The Case for Benchmarking," *Computers and Automation*, May 1973, pp. 23-25.

Hillegass, John R., "Standardized Benchmark Problems Measure Computer Performance," *Computers and Automation*, January 1966, pp. 16-19.

Howard, Phillip C. (ed.), "Measuring System Performance with Benchmarks," *EDP Performance Review*, vol. 1, no. 9, September 1973, pp. 1-7.

Ihrer, Fred C., "Benchmarking vs. Simulation," *Computer and Automation*, vol. 21, November 1967, pp. 8-10, 18.

Joslin, Edward O., *Computer Selection*, Addison-Wesley, Reading, Mass., 1968.

_____(ed.), *Analysis, Design and Selection of Computing Systems*, College Readings, Arlington, Va., 1971.

Lucas, Henry C., Jr., "Performance Evaluation and the Management of Information Services," *Data Base*, vol. 4, no. 1, Spring 1972, pp. 1-8.

McFarland, F. Warren, Richard L. Nolan, and David P. Norton, *Information Systems Administration*, Holt, Rinehart and Winston, New York, 1973.

Simon, Herbert, *The New Science of Management Decision*, Harper & Brothers, New York, 1960.

Timmereck, Eric M., "Computer Selection Methodology," *Computing Surveys*, vol. 5, no. 4, December 1973, pp. 199-222.

_____, "Performance Measurement: Vendor Specifications and Benchmarks," in F. Warren McFarlan and Richard L. Nolan (eds.), with the assistance of Esa-Jane Rapaport, *The Information Systems Handbook*, Dow Jones-Irwin, Homewood, Ill., 1975, pp. 365-367.

Wetherbe, James C., *Systems Analysis for Computer-Based Information Systems*, West, St. Paul, Minn., 1979.

COMPUTER OPERATIONS MANAGEMENT

INTRODUCTION

Chapters 17 and 18 provided managerial frameworks and techniques for capacity planning and hardware and software acquisition. This chapter discusses management of the day-to-day operations of a computer facility -- availability management, operating guidelines and procedures, problem and change management, and management reporting.

A successful computer facility must provide quality information systems to support the decision-making and operation functions of the organization. "Quality information" is defined in this context as timely, accurate, reliable, and accessible information. The many factors that may interfere with the delivery of quality information systems support from a computer facility may be broadly categorized as availability, procedural issues, problem management, and change management.

"Availability" pertains to having adequate computer capacity consistent with organizational information processing requirements. It requires prudent management of computer capacity and relationships with users.

"Procedural issues" pertain to the operating guidelines and procedures used to manage the operations of a computing facility. These procedures must be standardized, complete, and easy to understand to avoid confusion and errors.

"Problem management" pertains to identifying problems in computer operations and tracking them to their satisfactory resolution. Problems in computing operations can be numerous, complex, and elusive. Unless a disciplined procedure for tracking problems is used, problems tend to accumulate and become a serious constraint of quality in information systems.

"Change management" pertains to planning and control of modifications to computer operations. Computing facilities are constantly going through change. New hardware, operating software, and applications software require changes within a computing facility. Poorly managed change can cause problems and therefore must be managed through a viable change management process.

Each of these topics is discussed in the following sections.

AVAILABILITY MANAGEMENT

Organizations have become dependent upon availability of computer systems for continuity of their business operations. Accordingly, responsible management must seriously consider systems availability more than ever before.

Failure to maintain systems availability can have drastic effects upon an organization. In an extreme case, the complete loss of a computing facility (e.g., by fire or flood) could put a company out of business. In the more common instance, erratic availability of essential operational systems can result in significant productivity losses and bad management decisions.

"Systems availability "can be defined as the percentage of scheduled time that a computer service is fully operational. The management goal is to sufficiently ensure availability as it pertains to specific users so that users are able to maximize their productivity.

Defining systems availability in terms of percentage of scheduled time that a service is available provides a measure that makes it possible to establish service objectives, measure availability, observe trends, take corrective actions, and establish longer-term preventive measures with respect to recurring problems.

User Service Agreement

The first logical step of availability management is to determine availability required on a user-by-user basis for different services provided by computer operations. For batch-oriented applications systems, availability is typically defined in terms of such parameters as transactions processed and turnaround time. For online applications, parameters typically include response time and uptime for a system.

As stated earlier, service levels can be expressed in terms of percentages. For example, availability for a batch system can be defined by stating that 96 percent of all transactions will be processed on time, or turnaround for a batch job class will be 1 hour 90 percent of the time. Online applications might be defined as an uptime of 98 percent, with response time less than 2 seconds 95 percent of the time, and less than 5 seconds 80 percent of the time.

A definition of user service levels provides the framework for establishing a user service agreement. The service agreement minimizes the likelihood of a misunderstanding between users and computer operations.

Misunderstandings can occur for a variety of reasons. For example, a user's work load might significantly increase and exceed capacity allocated to a system, but the user expects the same level of service. Such developments can affect system availability adversely and cause problems between users and computer operations.

Therefore, for most customer-oriented transactions, it is advisable to have a formally documented agreement that defines the terms and conditions under which service is provided. The spirit of such an agreement should be positive and aimed at ensuring quality service without misunderstandings.

Typical contents of a user agreement include

- Contact points and procedures for both computer operations and user areas
- Scheduling guidelines and procedures
- Work volumes (e.g., transactions per time period)
- Chargeout rates, if applicable
- User responsibilities (e.g., data arrival deadlines, procedures for advance notification, documentation required, and procedures for making system changes)
- Computer operations responsibilities (e.g., response time and availability, turnaround time, schedules, and procedures for notifying users when delays or problems occur)

Computer Operations Performance

User service agreements provide the framework for establishing the computer operations performance criteria necessary to fulfill the user service agreements. To provide quality but cost-effective service to users, adequate computing resources and efficient use of those computing resources are required.

In other words, quality service can be provided by having an abundance of computing capacity, but such an approach is wasteful and irresponsible. Therefore, performance criteria for computer operations are needed that focus on efficient use of computer resources.

There are three major factors that can be used to evaluate computer operations performance: work load, resource utilization, and cost.

"Work load" pertains to the throughput achieved by computer operations and includes such measures as the following:

- Number of transactions processed by type
- Number of programs or statements executed

- Number of online connect hours provided
- Number of cards read and lines printed
- Number of data transfers between the processor and storage devices

"Resource utilization" pertains to how and to what extent computing resources are used. Examples of such measures are as follows:

- Percentage of utilization by system component
- Meter hours of utilization of system components
- Percentage of productive use of equipment (meter hours - available operating hours x 100)
- Work allocation (i.e., successful production by application runs, resumes, test jobs, scheduled and unscheduled maintenance, and downtime on hardware and software)

"Cost" pertains to the expense of providing different services to users. The purpose of monitoring costs is to ensure the addition or deletion of computing resources as necessary to maintain a high level of efficiency. Bottlenecks caused by under- or overutilization of resources in the system are wasteful.

Typical cost measures are as follows:

- Cost per line of output
- Cost to compile 100 statements of code
- Cost to enter 10,000 keystrokes of data
- Cost per hour of terminal connect time
- Cost per hour of CPU time
- Cost of reruns

By monitoring such cost data, management can spot cost trends. For example, is the cost for a service increasing or decreasing? What is a fair cost for a service?

Capacity Management

The task of computer operations management is to balance *effective* user-oriented performance requirements with *efficient* computer operations performance criteria. This process is called "capacity management."

Chapter 17 explained that capacity planning provides the foundation for capacity management. Capacity planning focuses on deriving the computing resources necessary to do a work load. Capacity management deals with defining the work load and making value judgments on how capacity is used to resolve conflicts in user requirements. The better the job of defining user service levels and the better the job of capacity planning, the easier the job of capacity management.

A helpful approach to capacity management in a way that ensures system availability is through a hierarchical allocation process similar to that used for budgeting. In a budgeting process, the overall budget is established and then allocated to lower-level units. As long as each unit within the hierarchy maintains its budget, the overall budget objective is met.

Similarly, as depicted in Figure 19-1, overall system availability (or other performance criteria) can be set, and then lower-level criteria can be established. Criteria are allocated so that if lower-level criteria are met, overall criteria are met. During any time period, actual percentages in one area might exceed limits, but that may be offset by better-than-average performance in another area.

By establishing hierarchical responsibilities for different dimensions of availability (e.g., batch jobs, applications), management can more readily monitor the system and evaluate problem areas that are interfering with availability.

Figure 19-1 Examples of Allocation of System Availability Responsibility

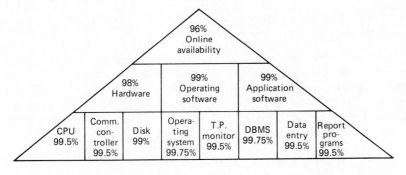

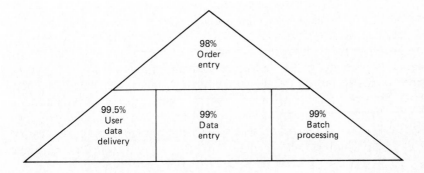

OPERATING GUIDELINES AND PROCEDURES

Establishing user service levels and ensuring computer capacity and performance criteria provide the foundation for the desired systems availability. Needed next are specific guidelines and procedures to manage the operations of a computing facility.

Operating guidelines and procedures for an organization can be a multivolume set of manuals. Therefore, the intent of the following discussion is not to provide an all-encompassing operations handbook. Rather, it is to provide a review of those areas that should be considered when establishing operating guidelines and procedures for a computing facility.

"Guidelines and procedures" can be defined as orderly and logical arrangements of goals and policies designed to support organizational objectives. In other words, guidelines and procedures do not exist on their own merit, but rather as operational extensions of corporate or departmental goals and policies. In this respect, guidelines and procedures are critical to effective operations because they provide a systematic method for achieving common direction, orderly operation, and control capability for both effectiveness and efficiency. Support for this contention lies in the fact that organizational units without established guidelines and procedures tend to behave in a mode opposite to that described above.

Establishing and Maintaining
Guidelines and Procedures

Given that guidelines and procedures are necessary for effective operations, the next step is to develop a method for establishing and maintaining guidelines and procedures (Gs & Ps). Because Gs & Ps are the means by which goals and policies are initiated, Gs & Ps can be viewed in terms of an "administrative hierarchy" as illustrated in Figure

Figure 19-2 Administration Hierarchy

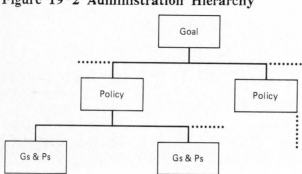

19-2. "Goals" represent generalized statements about the organizational unit's overall objectives, "policies" are more definitive statements about the goals, and Gs & Ps are concrete statements regarding the actual implementation of the policies. For example, user service levels and computer performance criteria provide the major goals and policies for developing operating Gs & Ps. The advantage of using this approach is that it provides some organization to what could otherwise be a rather chaotic and haphazard task.

A common method of establishing Gs & Ps is to modify existing operations manuals developed by other organizations. This approach has the advantage of reducing the somewhat overwhelming task of writing an operations manual from scratch; however, it has the associated disadvantage of not necessarily meshing with the organization's goals and

Figure 19-3 Content of a Guidelines and Policies Manual

1.0 GENERAL
   .1 Purpose of Manual
   .2 Numbering and Data Conventions
   .3 Distribution of Manual
   .4 Maintenance of Manual

2.0 DATA CENTER ADMINISTRATION
   .1 Organization Chart
   .2 Summary of Job Descriptions
   .3 Technical Library
   .4 Departmental Filing
   .5 Label Standards
   .6 Training History and Schedules
   .7 Job and Program Numbering Conventions
   .8 Computer Societies and Organizations
   .9 Work Environment and Practices

3.0 HARDWARE
   .1 Computer Configuration
   .2 Off-line Equipment
   .3 Hardware Housekeeping (P.M., head cleaning, etc.)
   .4 Back-up Computer Facilities (include contract)

4.0 CONTROL SYSTEMS
   .1 Utilization Recording and Reporting
   .2 Tape and Disk Library Procedures
   .3 Card File Procedures
   .4 Job Scheduling
   .5 Control of Work Flow
   .6 Forms Control (inventory and ordering)
   .7 Program Maintenance Progress Report

5.0 OPERATING STANDARDS AND PROCEDURES
   .1 Date Standards
   .2 Computer Start-Up and Shut Down
   .3 Program Documentation Standards
   .4 Software Standards
   .5 Program Testing Procedures and Standards
   .6 Preproduction Procedures and Standards
   .7 Data Center Operating Procedures

      Data Control Procedures
      Keypunch Instructions
      Unit Record Procedures
      Operator Instructions
      Output Distribution Instructions
      Program Maintenance Procedures

policies. A sample table of contents for a Gs & Ps manual is given in Figure 19-3.

Although a Gs & Ps manual is recognized as the conventional approach for establishing and maintaining procedures, it has a number of serious deficiencies:

1. Once the manual is developed, little effort is directed toward maintaining it.
2. Very little emphasis is placed on ensuring that operations personnel are acquainted with the procedures outlined in the manual.
3. The organization of a Gs & Ps manual can become so complex that its usefulness is severely hampered.

One method that is advocated for overcoming some of these problems is a technique referred to as "scripting." This technique uses a matrix scheme for identifying procedures and actions required. A "script" normally consists of a series of action steps matched against responsible personnel via some coding scheme. The "coding scheme" indicates which individuals should be notified, who should take action, who should approve the action, etc. The advantage of this technique is its simplicity and conciseness.

Regardless of the specific techniques used, Gs & Ps should be developed for the following general areas:

1. Computer system management
2. Production processing
3. General housekeeping
4. Disaster recovery
5. Security

Computer System Management

In general, "computer system management" deals with the operation and control of computing machinery and operating software in the computer center and at remote sites for which the MIS staff is responsible. Computer system management consists of equipment operation, equipment maintenance, inventory management, and emergency procedures.

Equipment Operation. General areas to be considered when developing guidelines and procedures for equipment operation are
 I. Hours of operation (general-use hours, restricted-use hours, operator-on-duty hours, etc.)
 II. System initiation (power-up procedures, initial checkout, etc.)

III. Checkout and diagnostics

IV. Performance monitoring (mainframe and peripheral monitoring on a scheduled basis)

V. Environmental monitoring (temperature, humidity, power consumption, etc.)

VI. Console operation (message initiation and response, logbook maintenance, etc.)

VII. Peripheral operation (printer quality, remote station accessibility, disk and tape drive operation, etc.)

VIII. Take-down procedures

IX. General cleanliness and orderliness

Equipment Maintenance. "Equipment maintenance" is concerned with ongoing maintenance activities as opposed to emergency procedures. Some general areas are

I. Scheduled preventative maintenance (regularly scheduled for all hardware)

II. Maintenance logs (kept on all maintenance performed)

III. Remote site maintenance

IV. Telecommunications maintenance

V. Facilities maintenance (water and air-conditioning, power backup, fire prevention, etc.)

Inventory Management. "Inventory management" deals with hardware inventory and supply inventory considerations:

I. Hardware inventory (central facilities and remote facilities)

II. Supply inventory (location, accessibility, usage, shelf life, etc.)

III. Ordering procedures

Emergency Procedures. "Emergency procedures" are established for equipment failure, software failure, environment failure, and security problems. Scripting is particularly useful in this area. Some considerations are

I. Notification procedures (for maintenance staff, operations staff, and users)

II. Record keeping (logging of all emergencies)

In summary, computer system management is concerned with keeping the system running so that production processing can occur.

Production Processing

"Production processing" deals with guidelines and procedures for effectively utilizing available resources. Areas such as job scheduling, job processing, system tuning, quality control, and library maintenance are generally considered to be a part of this function.

Job Scheduling. "Job scheduling" is an integral part of computer operations because of the requirements placed on computing and the importance of timeliness of the outputs associated with those requirements (payroll, general ledger, etc.). Job schedules should encompass the entire work flow associated with an application -- from the preparation of source documents to the distribution of final outputs -- so that both the users and the information systems personnel understand what to expect and what is expected of them. Schedules can be developed in a number of ways:

- As a critical-path network
- On a schedule board
- As charts and graphs
- In computer files

In addition to routine production runs, scheduling guidelines and procedures should be established for nonroutine requests, especially if these requests would place a heavy burden on resources.

Job Processing. "Job processing" involves the effective execution of scheduled jobs. Three general areas of concern are

I. Preprocessing (ensuring all material -- tapes, input cards, programs and files -- is available prior to execution)

II. Execution (having restart capabilities, abort procedures, and logging techniques)

III. Postprocessing (output distribution achieving validity, checking and updating job information files)

System Tuning. The problems associated with job scheduling and job processing have increased substantially with the advent of multiprocessing, time-sharing, and remote access. While large production jobs normally remain under the control of the computer, other functions (small jobs, development activity, etc.) are increasingly being handled by the user. This development has caused more emphasis to be placed on "tuning" the system to achieve improved resource utilization. System tuning can be accomplished in a number of ways:

I. Priority setting. Priorities can be assigned to different types of jobs or users.

II. Scheduling and dispatching algorithms. Most systems come with schedulers and dispatchers which can be adjusted to suit the individual environment.

III. Resource limitations. Limits on memory size, execution time, output requirements, etc., can be set for different classes of users and user jobs.

IV. Operating system. Operating systems normally have a number of parameters which can be altered to suit the particular environment.

Quality Control. "Quality control" in a computer usually centers on input, processing, and output controls as opposed to program or data validity controls. Input controls ensure that the proper data is used, maintain the integrity and safety of the inputs, and ensure that the inputs are stored securely. Processing controls include audit reports on what was run when, and log reports on normal and abnormal job activities. Output controls are concerned with ensuring that the proper forms are used, that print quality is maintained, and that distribution activities are correctly performed.

Library Maintenance. Computer center libraries can be divided into two parts:
  I. Physical libraries. Some important considerations for maintaining tapes, disks, cards, and documentation in physical libraries are
   A. Environment. Humidity and temperature should be regulated in storage areas to prevent warping, etc.
   B. Location. Locations should be safe but accessible.
   C. Aging. Tape, disk, and card libraries should be kept in good condition with old and worn materials being replaced. Documentation should be kept current.
 II. Software libraries. Maintenance for program and data storage, either on line or in a manual library, consists of
   A. Accurate documentation (version, location, usage, etc.).
   B. Appropriate backup.
   C. Adequate access security.

In summary, production processing is concerned with those aspects of computer operations that involve the effective utilization of computer resources to perform the functions assigned to the computer.

General Housekeeping

The area of general housekeeping is often ignored, but should be given proper attention as an integral part of computer operations. "General housekeeping" refers to the guidelines and procedures associated with machine room cleanliness, inventory storage, operator appearance, etc. Although a rigorous treatment of this topic is not necessary, it is important to recognize that from the standpoints of appearance and safety, a significant amount of attention should be directed toward developing and enforcing rules and regulations in this area.

Disaster Recovery

A tornado assaults a metropolitan area, demolishing the corporate computing facilities of a company. Tornado alerts allowed personnel to evacuate safely, but the computer hardware, data files, programs, documentation, and the whole computer facility itself are gone. What does the company do now?

If the company is a financial institution, it will need to have its computer operation back in business within 1 to 3 days to avoid financial ruin. If the company is a manufacturer, wholesaler, or retailer, it may have up to 2 weeks. In either case, if the company does not have a computer disaster recovery plan, it is in trouble.

Most organizations are so dependent on computer processing that they cannot operate without it. In the event of a computer disaster, they could not hire or train people soon enough to revert back to manual procedures. They would have to have a replacement computer in operation within days or face substantial losses. Consequently, a computer disaster recovery plan should exist in case it should ever be necessary.

Causes of Computer Disaster.

A computer disaster can result from any number of natural or accidental events such as storms, fire, power loss, or even sabotage. A fire would not have to directly destroy a computer to create problems. The effect of fire on a floor other than the floor housing the computer can cause water damage, eliminate air-conditioning or power, or prevent physical access to the computer. Independent of a fire, a substation can fail, interrupting power. As for sabotage, organizations have lost critical data files as a result of a disgruntled employee deliberately destroying data files, and there is always the danger of externally plotted sabotage.

Backup and Recovery.

It is not too difficult to maintain off-site backup copies of software or computer programs, data files, and documentation as protective measures. It is more difficult to ensure backup computer hardware and facilities.

Typically, access to backup hardware and facilities is secured through a reciprocal arrangement with another organization. The drawback to this arrangement is that few organizations have enough excess capacity to absorb much, if any, of another organization's processing. Also, maintaining processing compatibility among different computers is an ongoing problem.

Computer vendors have a reputation for being extremely cooperative in the event of a computer disaster. On more than one occasion after a disaster such as a flood, vendors have pulled the next computer off the assembly line and shipped it to their customer before the customer had even contacted them.

But if a computer facility is destroyed, what does the organization do when the replacement computer arrives? A number of organizations in the Twin Cities have come up with a good answer to this question. In a joint effort, companies have created a computer backup facility "shell" that has adequate power, air-conditioning, and space to house three large-scale computers.

For some organizations, even a backup facility is not good enough. For example, Norwest Information Services in Minneapolis supports over 500 affiliate and correspondent banks. An interruption of service in this situation is critical. Their readiness plans provide for a worst-case lapse in processing of 30 hours. They maintain totally separate computing facilities and computers that can back up each other in the event of a problem. The most critical applications can be supported until full processing can be restored.

Beyond the operational and survival issues of having a computer disaster recovery plan, there are also legal implications. Corporate officers and corporate directors are potentially liable to the stockholders if a corporation fails because of a computer disaster. A few years ago such liability would have not been the case. But today, enough corporations have developed computer disaster recovery plans that the leadership of an organization that fails to prepare can be considered not to have taken reasonable and prudent measures to protect the corporation.

Computer Security

An area of MIS management which is becoming increasingly important is computer security. As computers become more and more integrated into business and government activities, protecting the hardware, software, and data files becomes more and more critical. Five categories of security threats exist in relation to hardware:

1. Equipment failure
2. Environmental threats
3. Theft
4. Sabotage
5. Accidents

Equipment failure can be minimized by hardware redundancy, preventive maintenance, and diagnostic monitoring and analysis. Environmental threats refer to fire, floods, earthquakes, power failures, etc. Careful site selection, warning systems, fire and water protection systems, building design features, and prompt repair facilities are some of the measures which can be taken to reduce the danger associated with the environment. Theft and sabotage can be minimized by isolating the computer from general access and by providing controlled access to the computing facility. Accidents can be reduced by careful training and strict enforcement of general housekeeping rules and regulations.

With increasing amounts of corporate and individual data being stored in computer databases, it is important for information systems management to seriously consider methods for providing software and data security. These problems become greater as the level of technology increases. Time-sharing, remote-access computing systems pose the greatest threat to security because of the difficulty of controlling unauthorized access. Vendor-supplied security features are often inadequate, which require users to develop their own security measures at considerable inconvenience and cost. Some common methods of providing software security are

- Passwords and encoding techniques
- Check digits and check sums
- Parallel processing of highly sensitive data
- Redundancy and backup
- Detailed audit trails
- Off-line storage of critical information
- Prohibiting remote access during critical production runs

Different techniques can be used for establishing and maintaining security of software and data files; for example, a security committee can be formed or outside consultants can be brought in. Regardless of the techniques, the important consideration is that the issue of hardware and software security is of vital concern to computer operations.

PROBLEM MANAGEMENT AND CHANGE MANAGEMENT

Problems and changes are a way of life in a computing facility. Accordingly, it is critical to have effective and efficient means to identify, monitor, and control both problems and changes.

Problem management and change management fall under the umbrella of operating guidelines and procedures. However, they are fairly new concepts that have received considerable recognition in computer management literature. Therefore they are treated as major topics in this chapter.

The trend in most large-scale computing environments is to establish a quality assurance (QA) function with primary responsibility of ensuring quality information systems by managing problems and change.

Problem Management

Problems that occur in a computer processing environment are numerous and diverse. They range from a malfunction in operating software to a malfunction in a tape drive. To resolve problems that occur in computer operations, a problem management function (PMF) is established to monitor and control the day-to-day problems encountered. PMF meetings are normally held daily to review problems that have occurred since the last meeting and problems that are still in the process of being resolved.

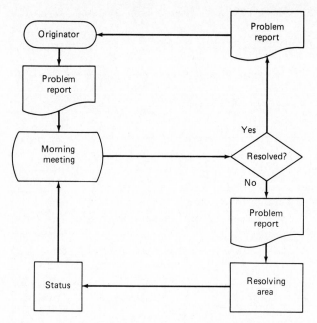

Figure 19-4 Problem Management Flowchart

PMF meetings may be chaired by the QA group and include participants from computer operations, technical services, communication services, systems development, and pertinent vendor representatives.

PMF Process. Figure 19-4 portrays the basic logic of a problem management process. When a problem is encountered, the person or department experiencing the problem records the required information on a problem report, as shown in Figure 19-5. The problem report is forwarded to the daily PMF meeting. A good procedure is to have the QA group review problem reports and assign priorities to them based upon how critical the problems are. An example of how priorities might be assigned is provided in Figure 19-6.

At each meeting, copies of new problems should be distributed and reviewed and any necessary corrections in problem descriptions or problem assignments made. Problems should be reviewed in priority order.

A problem should be closed only when a "permanent fix" (i.e., a fix that requires no further modifications) is implemented. When a problem is "closed," it means there is no further action needed concerning the problem. Preferably, the fix should have survived at least one processing cycle before closing occurs.

PROBLEM REPORT   DATE _____

LOG NUMBER _____

REPORTED BY	LOCATION	TELEPHONE	TIME OF CALL
JOB NAME/CUSTOMER	ABEND OR ERROR CODE	PROGRAM NAME	
WAS JOB A RERUN? YES ☐ NO ☐	PROCESSING DATE	PROBLEM TYPE SOFTWARE ☐ MISC. ☐	

PROBLEM DESCRIPTION

TEMPORARY FIX EXPLANATION   PROBLEM CODE

	DOCUMENTATION PROVIDED DUMP ☐ EXEC RPT ☐	OTHER	
TEMPORARY FIX BY	DEPARTMENT	TIME	DATE
UNABLE TO FIX — SENT TO	DEPARTMENT	TIME	DATE

PERMANENT SOLUTION — EXPLANATION

PERMANENT SOLUTION BY		TIME	DATE

**Figure 19-5 Example of a Problem Report
(Courtesy of Norwest Information Services)**

PRIORITY 1

A. A problem which is (or will be) causing a user to be without
 a scheduled service.

B. A Priority 2 problem that has caused a user deadline to be
 missed more than once.

C. All other Priority problems that have occurred more than 5 times.

> DE-ESCALATION
>
> Priority 1 problems may be de-escalated when the service
> has been restored.
>
> NOTE:
>
> Problems that have been escalated to a Priority 1 using the
> criteria stated in "B" and "C" above cannot be de-escalated.

PRIORITY 2

A. A problem (initially corrected with a temporary fix) that caused
 a user deadline to be missed.

B. A Priority 3 problem that has occurred more than once.

C. Failure of any on-line or real-time system (CPCS, TSO, TSS, CICS,
 TLMS) or any component (Hardware or Software) of such systems.

PRIORITY 3

A. A one-time problem that did not impact the user.

Figure 19-6 Problem Priority Criteria

When a problem is closed, the appropriate area representative should provide the QA group with a copy of the problem document that includes the following information:

  I. Explanation of the permanent fix
 II. Date the permanent fix was implemented
III. Authorized signatures of the person who resolved the problem and
      the manager who approved it

Occasionally, it may be determined that the original assignment of a problem for resolution was inappropriate, and the problem should be solved by another person or area. In such cases a procedure for transferring a problem is necessary. Such transfers should be approved by the receiving area and reported in the area meeting.

Responsibilities of PMF Members. To ensure proper communication and follow-through on assignments, PMF responsibilities should be based upon problem priority.

All PMF participants should notify their respective management of all priority problems immediately following the PMF meeting. Participants should also provide at the PMF meeting a daily status report of all priority 1 problems which the participants are currently assigned to resolve.

For priority 2 items, participants assigned problems should provide the QA group with an estimated completion date within a standard number of days (e.g., 2 to 3 days) from the date the problem was assigned. A status report should be provided to the QA group on the estimated completion date.

Disciplined adherences to PMF procedures allow computer operations to stay on top of and to resolve problems in computer operations. The QA group should provide management with reports on the activities and performance of the PMF effort.

Change Management

As problem management is designed to control and communicate problem resolution, change management is designed to control and communicate changes. Change is a way of life in computer operation, primarily because of problem resolution, software and hardware enhancements, and procedures and documentation changes. These changes can be minor or major, ranging from a change in procedures to a computer conversion. As with problem management, a good strategy is to assign responsibility of change management to the QA group or a similar function.

A key purpose of the change management function (CMF) is communication. Therefore a CMF committee should include participants from technical services, users or system development personnel, vendors, and computer operations personnel. Figure 19-7 portrays the

Figure 19-7 Coordination Considerations for Change Management

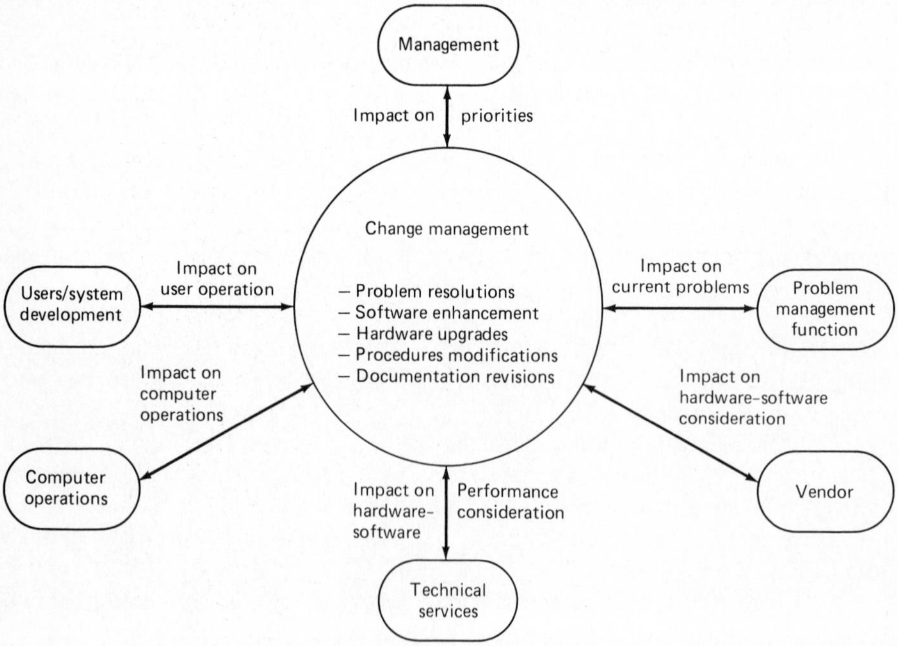

coordination considerations for change management. By having a member of the QA group chair both change and problem management committees, coordination between these efforts is ensured.

Change Management Process. The underlying theory behind change management is to isolate, test, and coordinate changes. If several changes are poorly coordinated and made simultaneously, problems can occur. And it is not easy to determine which changes caused the problem. Experience has shown that even minor changes can cause severe impact if they are not tested and communicated properly. Conversely, several changes can successfully be made simultaneously if they are carefully tested and coordinated.

Priority schemes are helpful to change management. A recommended priority scheme follows:

- *Priority 1:* Emergency change necessary to restore service or to prevent an immediate loss of service to one or more customers

Figure 19-8 Procedure for Priority 1 Changes

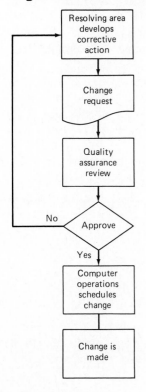

- *Priority 2:* Nonemergency change that is independent of any other change to the processing environment

- *Priority 3:* Nonemergency change that is dependent upon one or more other changes to the processing environment

Priority 1 Changes. Being of an emergency nature, priority 1 Changes need to be implemented quickly with only the absolutely necessary procedural steps required. A model of priority 1 changes is provided in Figure 19-8.

When an emergency situation arises, the resolving area should develop a corrective course of action and fill out a change request form. An example of a change request form is provided in Figure 19-9. The change request form should be reviewed by the QA group, who should ensure that the request is of an emergency nature and that the immediate impact of the change does not adversely impact the processing environment. Upon approval by the QA group, computer operations should schedule the change as soon as possible.

Priority 2 and 3 Changes. Priority 2 and 3 changes, which are not required for emergencies, should go through a more disciplined process. A model for priority 2 and 3 changes is provided in Figure 19-10. After being originated by a person or area and after being reviewed by the QA group, priority 2 and 3 changes can be reviewed at a weekly change meeting. If approved, the change is scheduled and assigned for installation. A weekly schedule should be generated from this process and distributed to all pertinent staff and management.

If a proposed change is not approved, an appeal process should be initiated. The decision to override a disapproved change should rest with the computer facility manager. The computer facility manager has ultimate responsibility for the successful operation of the processing environment. In the event that a disappproved change is overridden by the computer facility manager, the QA group should authorize the change and proceed accordingly.

In summary, the above-described change management process ensures that quality is maintained even though many changes must be absorbed in computer operations.

MANAGEMENT REPORTING

Like any management function, computer operations management requires management reports to support decision making associated with computer operations. Though the specific reports used in any organization will

PRODUCTION CHANGE REQUEST/NOTIFICATION

REQUESTOR			PHONE-HOME	PHONE-OFFICE	PRODUCTION DATE	DATE THIS REQUEST
APPLICATION/SINGLE SERIES	STEP NAME/SERIES ONLY	PROGRAM LOAD MODULE	PROGRAM USE FREQUENCY		TYPE OF CHANGE (CHECK ONE OR MORE)	☐ PROGRAM ☐ JCL ☐ OTHER

DESCRIPTION OF CHANGE, REASON REQUIRED

EXPLAIN IN DETAIL

_____

_____

_____

_____

_____

_____

_____

_____

_____

SPECIAL CONSIDERATIONS	YES	NO		YES	NO
WILL PROCEDURE CHANGE FOR JOB SUBMISSION			WILL REMOTE JCL REQUIRE CHANGES		
WILL PROCEDURE CHANGE FOR DISTRIBUTION			WILL JOB SCHEDULE CHANGE		
WILL INTERNAL DOCUMENTATION REQ. UPDATING			CHANGE IS TEMPORARY		
WILL JOB SET UP CHANGE			EXPLAIN ANY REMOTE CHANGES		
WILL USER INPUT CHANGE					
WILL USER OUTPUT CHANGE					
WILL USER HAVE TO BE NOTIFIED					
WILL USER DOCUMENTATION CHANGE					

STATE ANY PROGRAM ADDS, DELETES, MOVES, RENAMES OR MANIPULATIONS.

ORIGINAL NAME	ENDING NAME	ORIGINAL LIBRARY	ENDING LIBRARY	UTILITY USED	ACTION PERFORMED

STATE ANY MANUAL PROCEDURE CHANGES
MADE OR REQUESTED _____

FALL BACK PROCEDURES	MANAGER APPROVALS	TIME	DATE
1ST_____	PROJECT_____		
_____	JOB TECH SUPPORT_____		
_____	EDP SERVICES_____		
2ND_____	REMOTE SUPPORT_____		
_____	SECURITY_____		
_____	QUALITY ASSURANCE		

Figure 19-9 Example of a Change Request (Courtesy of Norwest Information Services)

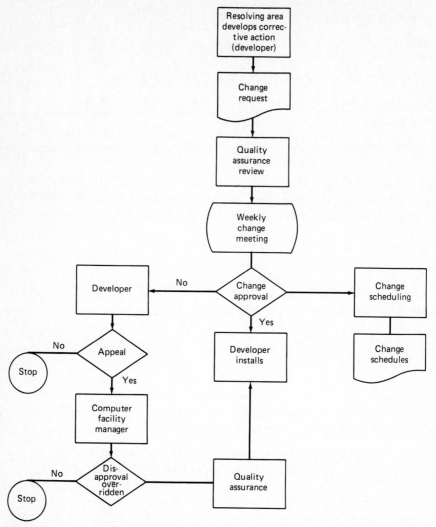

Figure 19-10 Procedure for Priority 2 and 3 Changes

vary, there are certain generic reports that are typical and appropriate for computer operations management. These reports concern

- Equipment utilization
- Problem and change activities
- User service levels

Each of these categories is discussed below.

Equipment Utilization

Equipment utilization reporting allows management to develop trend analyses of equipment usage so that potential overload situations can be detected early. Early detection helps to minimize the problems generally associated with long lead times for equipment delivery from vendors and the problems associated with rushing the change management process within the computing facility.

In essence, computer utilization reports are used primarily for computer capacity planning as discussed in Chapter 17 (and indeed are often identical to capacity planning reports). However, capacity planning cannot be accomplished solely on extrapolation of historical data. Major changes in user requirements must also be considered. The user-service-level analysis and user service agreement are helpful in identifying such development.

Equipment utilization reports generally focus on

I. Overall system utilization
II. Individual component utilization
III. Auxiliary storage media utilization

These activities are typically expressed as a percentage of actual utilization of total availability.

Problem and Change Activities

Problem and change activity reports are used to monitor some of the likely causes of operational errors and inefficiencies. The common symptoms of problems in problem and change management typically show up in the form of too many reruns of jobs and unscheduled downtime, or system failures. When the preceding occurences are excessive, they are generally accompanied by many problems and changes that are in an unresolved status.

Problem and change activities can thus be monitored by

- Review reports. These provide the total number of jobs run and percentage of reruns and their causes.

- Equipment failure reports. These record failures by component, showing times, length, and date of failure.

- Status reports on problems and changes. These provide an itemized list of changes and unresolved problems.

User Service Levels

User-service-level reports reveal how well computer operations are serving users. They allow management to determine deviations from service-level agreements made with users, or other irregularities so that corrective action can be taken.

As discussed at the beginning of this chapter, user service is broadly defined in terms of availability, but it can be further factored into

- Volume and cost of work (e.g., number and cost of transactions processed, jobs executed, lines printed, and number of online inquiries)

- Quality of work (primarily determined by number of errors made in processing and in terms of timeliness of processing)

SUMMARY

Computer operations management focuses on availability management, operating guidelines and procedures, problem and change management, and management reporting.

Availability management starts with determining user service levels and documenting user service agreements. User service agreements are translated into computer performance objectives, according to which a balance must be established between effective service to users and efficient use of computing resources.

Operating guidelines and procedures ensure the proper day-to-day use of computing facilities. They focus on computer equipment management, production processing, general housekeeping, disaster recovery, and computer security.

Problem management and change management provide management control over the identification and resolution of problems that arise and changes that must be made in the processing environment. Quality assurance and coordinating committees play a key role in the management of change and problems.

Management reporting provides the information necessary to plan and control computer operations. Key management reporting issues are equipment utilization, problem and change activities, and user service levels.

SUGGESTED READINGS

Aasgaard, D. O., P. R. Cheung, B. J. Hulbert, and T. C. Simpson, "An Evaluation of Data Processing, 'Machine Room' Loss and Selected Recovery Strategies," MISRC WP-79-04, MIS Research Center, University of Minnesota, 1978.

Albrecht, Leon, *Organization and Management of Information Processing Systems*, Macmillan, New York, 1973.

Allen, Brandt, "Computer Security," *Data Management*, January-February 1972.

Boyce, J., R. Belhumeur, P. Raimer, and T. Shute, "Tracking and Resolving Problems and Coordinating Changes," IBM Technical Bulletin, GG22-9000-00, Poughkeepsie, N.Y., 1975.

Brandon, Dick H., *Management Standards for Data Processing*, Van Nostrand, N.Y., 1963.

_____, Arnold D. Palley, and A. Michael O'Reilly, *Data Processing Management: Methods and Standards*, Macmillan, New York, 1975.

"Change and Problem Management Policies and Procedures," Northwest Computer Corporation Inc., Minneapolis, Minn., 1981.

Davis, C., and J. Wetherbe, "Decision Support System for a Chargeout System in a Large Scale Computing Environment," *Data Base*, July 1980.

Davis, G. B., D. L. Adams, and C. A. Schaller, *Auditing and EDP*, 2d ed., AICPA, New York, 1981.

Dickson, G., and J. Wetherbe, "Zero-Based Budgeting: An Alternative to Chargeout," *Information and Management*, November 1979.

Forman, J. L., "Problem Management in a Complex Systems Environment," IBM Technical Bulletin, GG-22-9150-00, Palo Alto, Calif., 1978.

Garrison, R., "An Availability Management System," IBM Technical Bulletin, GG 22-9155-00, White Plains, N.Y., March 1980.

_____, "The Availability Manager: An Approach to Improving DP Systems Availability," IBM Technical Bulletin, GG 22-9156-0, White Plains, N.Y., October 1980.

Gill, James, "Scheduling and Cost Control of the Data Center," *The Information Systems Handbook*, Dow Jones-Irwin, Homewood, Ill., 1975.

Hoffman, Lance J., *Security and Privacy in Computer Systems*, Melville Publishing, 1973.

Jancura and I. L. Lilly, "S.A.A. No. 3 and the Evaluation of Internal Control," *Journal of Accountancy*, March 1977, pp. 69-74.

Jucius, Michael, and William Schlender, *Elements of Managerial Action*, Richard D. Irwin, Homewood, Ill., 1960.

Litecky, C. R., and L. E. Rittenberg, "The External Auditor's Review of Computer Controls," *Communications of the ACM*, vol. 24, no. 5, May 1981, pp. 288-295.

Lobel, Jerome, "Computer Security," *The Information Systems Handbook*, Dow Jones-Irwin, Homewood, Ill., 1975.

"Managing, Planning System Capacity." *Data Management*, March 1978.

"Managing the Data Center," *Data Management*, October 1974, pp. 20-25.

"Managing the Data Processing Organization," *Installation Management*, GE-19-5208-0, White Plains, N.Y., 1976.

McFarlan, F., Richard Nolan, and David Norton, *Information Systems Administration*, Holt, Rinehart, and Winston, New York, 1973.

Neuner, John, and Lewis Keeling, *Administrative Office Management*, South-Western Publishing, Cincinnati, 1966.

Pritchard, J., *Computer Security: Risk Management in Action*, NCC Publications, 1978.

"Problem and Change Management in Data Processing -- A Survey and Guide," *Installation Management*, GE-19-5201-0, White Plains, N.Y., 1976.

Wofsey, M. M., "Effective Management of Computer Operations," *Data Management*, September 1975, pp. 22-31.

INDEX

Abraham, Nancy M., 11
Addressing in line control, 261
Administrative hierarchy of guidelines and
    procedures, 462–463
Advanced office systems, 290–300
Advisory groups, 42–43, 62
Alter, Steven, 397
Analog transmissions, 247, 248
Analysis:
  procedures for, 227–228
  types of (*see specific entries, for example:*
    Change analysis; Systems analysis)
Anderson, John C., 397
Anthony, R. N., 120
Application programming, 355–356
Applications profiling in forecasting, 423, 426,
    429
Aptitude tests, 67
Artificial intelligence, 311–312
Artis, H. Pat, 429
Asynchronous modems, 254
Asynchronous transmissions, 246
Attribution theory (Heider), 92–93
Auditors in MIS assessment, 176–177
Availability of systems, 457–461

Backup computer facilities, 468–469
Backup programmers, 369
Baseband local area networks, 270
Batch computer systems, 20
Behavior:
  in advanced office systems, 295–297

Behavior (*Cont.*):
  in computer use problems, 33–35
Behavior modification (*see* Reinforcement
    schedules; Reinforcement theory)
Benchmarks:
  in computer capacity planning 423, 425, 426,
    428, 430
  in proposal validation, 454–455
BIAIT (business information analysis and
    integration technique), 132–133, 140
Bohn, C., 356
Bottom–up program development, 358–359
Broadband local area networks, 270
Bronner, L., 414, 418, 422
BSP (business systems planning), 130–131, 140,
    149, 150
Budgeting:
  for computer use, 21, 23, 27–29, 40
  zero–based (ZBB), 136–137, 140
Burnstine, D. C., 132
Business elements in computer capacity
    planning, 424, 427
Business information analysis and integration
    technique (BIAIT), 132–133, 140
Business systems planning (BSP), 130–131, 140,
    149, 150
Buss, Martin D. J., 25

Capacity, computer (*see* Computer capacity
    management; Computer capacity planning)
CARA systems development methodology,
    325–326, 350–351

CBX (computer branch exchange), 270
CCM (computer capacity management), 414–415, 460–461
CCP (*see* Computer capacity planning)
Centralization of MIS development, 49–53
Change:
  coping with, 38
  in systems implementation, 391, 393–396, 398–401, 404–405
Change activity reports, 479
Change analysis, 365
Change management in computer operations management, 458, 474–478
Change management function (CMF), 474
Chargeout-based planning systems, 135–136, 140
Checking accounts, 190–192
Chervany, Norman L., 167–169
Chief-programmer teams, 369
Circuit-switched communications systems, 240–241, 245, 246
Clerical systems in systems hierarchy, 31–32
Closed/stable/mechanistic organization model, 75–84
Clustering in forecasting, 423, 426, 429
CMF (change management function), 474
Coaxial cables, 248, 270
Coca Cola Company, 231–232
Code inspection in quality assurance, 372
Codes in networks, 264–265
Commitment in systems implementation, 394–395
Communication:
  of data (*see entries beginning with the term:* Data communications)
  in reinforcement, 102–103
Communication control units, 256–257
Communication lines (*see entries beginning with the term:* Line)
Communication–network approach to change, 400–401
Communication networks for data (*see* Network view of data; Networks)
Communication satellites, 248–250
Communication services, 240–242, 244–246
Communication software, 266–268
  (*See also* Programs, synthetic; *entries beginning with the term:* Hardware; Program; Programming)
Computer-based information systems:
  expectations gap in, 4–5
  implementation of (*see* Systems implementation)
  software in (*see entries beginning with the term:* Software)

Computer branch exchange (CBX), 270
Computer capacity management (CCM), 414–415, 460–461
Computer capacity planning (CCP), 413–436
  defined, 413–415
  responsibilities for, 432–436
  stages of, 415–433
  tools and methodologies for, 422–433
Computer center libraries, 467
Computer equipment:
  distribution of, 49–53
  guidelines and procedures for, 464–465, 469
  utilization reports for, 479
  (*See also entries beginning with the term:* Hardware)
Computer hardware (*see entries beginning with the term:* Hardware)
Computer languages, 206, 207, 231–232, 375–376
Computer operations management, 457–480
  change management in, 458, 474–478
  management reports in, 476, 478–480
  operating guidelines and procedures in, 457, 462–470
  performance in, 459–460
    (*See also* Computer performance evaluation)
  problem management in, 457, 470–474
  systems availability in, 457–461
Computer performance evaluation (CPE), 414, 415
Computer programming (*see* Programmed systems in systems hierarchy; Programmers; Programs, synthetic; *entries beginning with the terms:* Program; Programming; Software)
Computer security, 469–470
Computer services, 281–286
Computer software (*see entries beginning with the term:* Software)
Computer systems:
  batch, 20
  choosing, 42–47
  management of, 35–39, 464–465
  (*See also* Computer-based information systems; Data communications systems)
Computers:
  budgets for, 21, 23, 27–29, 40
  conceptual frameworks for, 26–32
  history of, 20–21, 239–241
  issues involving, 23–26
  managerial expectations about, 35
  organizational use of, 19–40
  problems of, 32–39
  sabotage of, 33–34, 469

Computers (*Cont.*):
  standards for, 37–38
  technology for: acquisition of (*see* Hardware
      and software acquisition)
    rigidity of, 37–38
  trends in, 21–26
  types of: digital, 239
    micro- (personal), 21–23, 60, 208, 228–229
    mini-, 21–23, 208, 228, 229
  vendors pushing, 38
  (*See also* Data processing; *entries beginning
      with the term:* Data processing)
Computing, interactive, 228–229
Concentrators in data communication, 255
Consultants for technology information, 442
Contention-based line control systems, 259–260
Contingency management theory, 75–84
Control:
  in communications, 256–257, 263–269
  in computer capacity planning, 416, 420–423,
      430–433
  in distributed data processing, 282–283
  quality, in computer operations, 467
  in systems implementation, 391
Cooper, J. C., 422, 427
Cost in computer operations performance,
    460
Couger, J. Daniel, 7, 9, 94–95
CPE (computer performance evaluation), 414,
    415
Critical success factors (CSFs), 131–132, 140,
    149, 150, 174–175

Data:
  normalization of, 213–217
  transmission of, 241–243, 245–252
  views of, 206–208
  (*See also* Information; *entries beginning with
      the terms:* Communication; Information)
Data centers, 281–286
Data collection:
  in computer capacity planning, 416–419, 423,
      427–428
  in systems hierarchy, 32
Data communications hardware, 252–257
  (*See also* Computer equipment; *entries
      beginning with the term:* Software)
Data communications software, 266–268
  (*See also* Programs, synthetic; *entries
      beginning with the terms:* Hardware;
      Program; Programming)
Data communications systems, 237–271
  history of, 239–242

Data communications systems (*Cont.*):
  networks in (*see* Network view of data;
      Networks)
  technology of, 242–269
  (*See also* Computer systems; Information
      systems)
Data element dictionaries, 209, 340–341
Data flow diagrams, 338, 339
Data function matrixes, 365–366
Data integrity, 213–217
Data processing:
  distributed (DDP), 49, 274–287
  positions in: applicants for, 63–70
    employees in, 63–71
    (*See also* Programmers; Systems analysts)
  and word processing, 278–279
  (*See also* Computers; Information; *entries
      beginning with the terms:* Computer;
      Information)
Data processing systems (*see* Information
    systems)
Data projection and simulation systems, 227–228
Data redundancy, 192–193, 196–197, 203–204
Data subsystems of decision support systems, 225
Data systems, organizational, 294, 295
Data transmission, 245–252
Data transmission services, 241–243
Database administration, 209
Database management systems (DBMSs), 189,
    205–217, 227
Database technology, 198, 203–208
Davis, Charles K., 414
Davis, G. B., 133, 136
Davis, Rod, 349
DBMSs (database management systems), 189,
    205–217, 227
DDA (demand deposit accounting), 190–192
DDP (*see* Distributed data processing)
Debugging in software testing, 373–374
Decentralization of MIS development, 49–53
Decision centers, 332–333
Decision support models, 294, 295
Decision support systems (DSSs):
  applications of, 230–234
  concept of, 222–226
  history of, 220–222
  implementation of, 384
  in systems hierarchy, 32
  technology for, 226–230
Decision tables, 339, 340
Decision trees, 339–340
Decisions, unstructured, 223–224
Dedicated communication services, 240,
    244–246

Dedicated lines, 258, 259
Dedicated minicomputers, 228
Delphi technique, 136
Demand deposit accounting (DDA), 190–192
Design (*see specific entries, for example:* Job redesign; Systems design)
Design overviews in quality assurance, 371
Design specifications, 341–343
Desirable specifications, 446, 447
Detail reviews in quality assurance, 371–372
Development (*see specific entries, for example:* Heuristic development; Systems development)
Development activities, 75–76, 82–83
Development resources, 123
Development support libraries (DSLs), 368
Devol, George, Jr., 306
Dickson, Gary W., 26, 31–32, 58
Digital computers, 239
Digital transmissions, 247, 248
Direct-access technique, 199–201
Disaster recovery in computer operations, 467–469
Distributed data processing (DDP), 49
    defined, 274–275
    history of, 275–277
    managing, 279–287
    predictions about, 277–278
    problems with, 278–279
Document processing systems, 292
DSLs (development support libraries), 368
DSSs (*see* Decision support systems)
Dual-factor theory (Herzberg), 88–89
Dunlavey, Richard F., 430

E/M (ends/means) analysis, 133–135, 140, 149, 150
Eastes, Sue, 11, 349
Effectiveness in MIS evaluations, 167–169
Effectiveness formulas, 453
Effectiveness information, 134, 135
Efficiency:
    managerial, 55–58
    in MIS evaluations, 167–169
Efficiency information, 134
Electronic filing systems, 294, 295
Electronic mail systems, 292
Emergency procedures, 465
Employees:
    data processing, 63–71
        (*See also* Programmers; Systems analysts)
    decision support systems for, 233–234
    motivating (*see* Motivational factors; Motivational theories)

Employees (*Cont.*):
    needs of, 94–100
        (*See also* entries beginning with the term: Job)
End-users, 281–286
Ends/means (E/M) analysis, 133–135, 140, 149, 150
Engelberger, Joseph, 306, 313
Entry phase of systems implementation, 403–404
Environments:
    defined, 78
    organizational, 78–80, 299–300
    processing, 284–285
EPIC Realty Services Inc., 144–153
Equipment, computer (*see* Computer equipment)
Executive support systems, 293
Executives [*see* MIS executives (managers)]
Expectancies in systems implementation, 392–393
Expectancy theory (Vroom), 91–92
Expectations, managerial, about computers, 35
Expectations gap in computer-based information systems, 4–5
Expenditure standards, 165–166
Expert systems, 229
Expertise:
    in distributed data processing, 281–286
    in technology information, 441–442
Extinction in reinforcement theory, 90, 91, 102, 103

Factor studies, 388, 394
Factors in systems implementation, 387–395
Fiber optics, 250–252, 271
Field, John C., 11
File access techniques, 198–203
Files:
    elements of, 198–199
    relationships of, 210–213
Filing systems, electronic, 294, 295
Financial analysis in hardware and software acquisition, 451–453
Financial controllers in MIS assessment, 176–177
Financial planning, 231–232
Flowcharts, systems, 333–335, 338
Forecasting of growth, 419, 423, 425, 428–429
Four-stage MIS planning model, 121, 124–128, 139–144
Fourth generation languages, 206, 207
Frames of reference in systems implementation, 391–392
Fraser, Douglas, 313
Frohman, Alan L., 398, 399, 401

Front-end processors, 257
Full-duplex communications lines, 246
Fully connected structure of networks, 263
Functional organization structure, 57–58

Gantt charts, 139, 140, 155, 156
Gelle, Ken E., 11
Gerrity, Thomas P., Jr., 221
Ginzberg, Michael J., 394, 395
Goal-centered view of MIS effectiveness, 168
Goal-setting theory (Locke), 89
Goals versus policies, 463
Goodling, R. A., 97–98
Gray, Richard C., 95
Gross, Gene D., 11
Group analysis techniques, 68–71
Group structure in advanced office systems,
    295–296
Groups, advisory, 42–43, 62
Guidelines, operating, in computer operations
    management, 457, 462–470

Half-duplex communication lines, 246
Hamilton, Scott, 167–169
Hard-dollar evaluations, 446, 451–452
Hardware, data communications, 252–257
    (See also Computer equipment; entries
        beginning with the term: Software)
Hardware and software acquisition:
    technology choice in, 451–455
    technology design in, 444–451
    technology information in, 440–444
Hardware monitors, 423, 424, 427, 428
Heider, F., 92–93
Herzberg, F., 88–89
Heuristic development, 345–351
Hierarchical view of data, 207, 208
Hierarchies:
    administrative, of guidelines and procedures,
        462–463
    of needs (Maslow), 87–88
    as network structure, 262
    systems, in computer use (Dickson), 26,
        31–32
Hierarchy plus input process output (HIPO)
    technique, 361–362
Housekeeping in computer operations, 467
Human resources (see Employees)

Imbedded pointers, 207
Imitation in reinforcement, 103

Implementation, systems (see Systems
    implementation)
Indexed-access technique, 201–203
Indexes, inverted, 207
Industrial relations information system (IRIS),
    234
Information:
    integration of, 189–198
        (See also Business information analysis and
            integration technique)
    requirements for: management, 343–344
        organizational subsystem, 146–152
    types of: effectiveness, 134, 135
        efficiency, 134
        organizational, 189–198
        quality, 457
        technology, 440–444
    (See also Data; entries beginning with the
        term: Data)
Information centers, 59–60
Information revolution, 314–315
Information-subsystem matrixes, 150–152
Information systems:
    analysis of (see Systems analysis; Systems
        analysts)
    architecture of, 122–123
    deficiencies in, 336
    development of (see Systems development;
        Systems development life cycle)
    in distributed data processing, 281–286
    implementation of (see Systems
        implementation)
    installing, 405
    projects in, managers of, 157–158
    in systems hierarchy, 31–32
    types of: computer-based (see Computer-based
        information systems)
        industrial relations (IRIS), 234
        management (see Management Information
            Systems; entries beginning with the term:
            MIS)
        user-developed, 375–378
    value of, measuring, 170–172
    (See also Computer systems; Data
        communications systems)
Innovation-process approach to change, 399–400
Input/output (IPO) charts, 362
Intelligence (see Artificial intelligence;
    Information)
Interactive computing, 228–229
Interactive decision support systems, 224
Intercept-type monitors, 427
Inventory management, 465
Inverted indexes, 207

Investment, return on (ROI), 135, 140, 173–174
IPO (input/output) charts, 362
IRIS (industrial relations information system), 234
Ives, Blake, 7, 10

Jacopini, G., 356
Job accounting procedures, 423, 425, 428
Job descriptions, 65–66
Job enrichment, 312–313
Job processing, 466
Job productivity and satisfaction, 86–115
   employee needs in, 94–100
   motivational theories in, 87–94
   and organizational requirements, 100–107
Job redesign, 296–297
Job replacement, 313
Job scheduling, 466
Johnson, David A., 11, 348

Kapek, Karel, 304
Kast, Fremont E., 80
Keen, Peter G. W., 221
Kernel evaluation, 453–454
Key volume indicators (KVIs), 423, 425, 428–429
King, W. R., 128, 129
Klenk, Harold, 158
Kolb, David, 398, 399, 401
KVIs (key volume indicators), 423, 425, 428–429

Languages, computer, 206, 207, 231–232, 375–376
Learning, organizational, 39
Leased communication services, 240, 244–246
Leased lines, 258, 259
Leavitt, Don, 421
Leavitt, Harold J., 220–221
Lewin, Kurt, 398, 399
Libraries:
   computer center, 467
   development support (DSLs), 368
   program, 369
Line configurations, 257–259
Line control procedures, 257–261
Line-sharing devices, 255–256
Line switching, 246
Linear projections, 423, 425, 429
Linear structure of networks, 262
Lipner, Leonard, 414, 416–417, 422

Literature for technology information, 442–443
Local area networks, 269–271
Locke, E. A., 89
Logical views of data, 206–207
Loop lines, 258–259
Lucas, Henry C., Jr., 386–387
Lusa, John M., 165

MAGs (management advisory groups), 42–43
Mail systems, electronic, 292
Management:
   styles of, 296
   theories of, 75–84
   (See also Managers; specific entries, for example: Computer capacity management; Project management techniques)
Management advisory groups (MAGs), 42–43
Management Information Systems (MIS):
   in advanced office systems, 293–294
   advisory groups for, 42–43, 62
   assessments of, 174–177, 180–184
      (See also evaluations of, below)
   case studies of, 42–47, 180–184
   computer-based (see Computer-based information systems)
   databases for, 203–205
      (See also Database management systems)
   development of, 42–44, 47, 49–53, 55–58
   evaluations of, 162–184
      case study of, 180–184
      conducting, 177–184
      formal, 169–177
      problem of, 163–169
   image of, 53–54
   information centers within, 59–60
   maintenance of, 59
   management of, robotics in, 315
      [See also MIS executives (managers)]
   management support for, 53–54
   managerial efficiency versus user service in, 55–58
   organizing, 41–54
   positions in, 64–71
      (See also staffing of, below)
   reporting relationships in, 48–49, 54
   staffing of, 41–47, 62–71
   steering committees for, 60–62, 281–286
   structuring, 54–62
   systems builders of, 36–37
   users of (see Users; entries beginning with the term: User)
   (See also entries beginning with the term: MIS)

Management reports, 476, 478–480
Management support facilities (MSFs), 229–230
Manager-subsystem matrixes, 145–147
Managers:
  attitudes of, in quality assurance, 370–371
  computer expectations of, 35
  efficiency of, 55–58
  inexperience of, 5–6
  information requirements of, 343–344
  of information systems projects, 157–158
  MIS [see MIS executives (managers)]
  (See also Management)
Mandatory specifications, 446, 447
Marketing, decision support systems in, 231
Martin, James, 349
Maslow, A. H., 87–88
Mathematical formulas in proposal validation, 454
Matlin, Gerald L., 174
Matrix organization, 56–57
Means specification, 134
  (See also Ends/means analysis)
Medtronic Inc., 377–378
Merten, Alan, 164
Message-switched communications, 241, 245
Microcomputers, 21–23, 60, 208, 228–229
Microwave transmission systems, 248
Milestone planning techniques, 137, 140, 155, 156
Minicomputers, 21–23, 208, 228, 229
MIS (see Management Information Systems)
MIS executives (managers), 3–15
  capabilities (skills) of, 7, 8, 10, 12
  career paths of, 13
  education of, 12
  evolution of, 7–10
  future trends for, 10
  management inexperience of, 5–6
  in MIS assessment, 174–176
  organizational expectations of, 4–5
  professional background of, 12
  successful, 10–13
  time schedules of, 7–10
  turnover rates for, 3, 5, 34
MIS function, 75–84
MIS organizations, factors of, 394, 395
MIS planning:
  evolution of, 119–121
  guidelines for, 141–144
  problems of, 121–123
  strategic, 125–130, 139
MIS planning methodologies:
  four-stage MIS planning model related to, 139–140, 143–144

MIS planning methodologies (Cont.):
  selecting, 123, 143–144
  types of, 128–140, 149, 150, 155, 156
MIS planning model, four-stage, 121, 124–128, 139–144
MIS professionals (see Data processing, positions in; Programmers; Systems analysts)
Modeling procedures, 227–228
Modeling subsystems, 225
Modems (modulator-demodulators), 253–255
Morin, Tom, 377–378
Morse, Samuel F. B., 239
Motivational factors:
  assessing, with Q-sort, 95–101
  and organizational requirements, 100–107
Motivational theories, 87–94
MSFs (management support facilities), 229–230
Multiplexers in data communication, 256
Multipoint (multidrop) lines, 258, 259

Narasimhan, Ram, 397
Natural forecast units, 423, 425, 428–429
Need hierarchy (Maslow), 87–88
Needs:
  employee, 94–100
  perceived, in systems implementation, 389–391
Negative reinforcement, 90, 91, 101–103
Nermyr, James D., 11
Nestle Company, 231
Network view of data, 207, 208
Networks:
  communication, as change approach, 400–401
  in data communication: configurations of, 261–263
    control of, 263–269
    types of, 246, 257–261
Nolan, Richard L., 3, 26–31, 45, 61, 119, 120
Normalization of data, 213–217

Office automation, 290–300
OIRA (organizational information requirements analysis), 124–127, 140, 144–153
Olson, Margrethe H., 7, 10
Open/adaptive/organic organization model, 75–84
Operating guidelines and procedures in computer operations management, 457, 462–470
Oppermann, E. B., 7, 9
Optimizing models, 228
Organization models, 75–84
Organizational data systems, 294, 295

Organizational information, integration of, 189–198
(*See also* Information; *entries beginning with the term:* Information)
Organizational information requirements analysis (OIRA), 124–127, 140, 144–153
Organizational learning, 39
Organizational strategy set, 128–130, 139
Organizations:
  activities of, 75–76, 82–84
  change in (*see* Change; *entries beginning with the term:* Change)
  climates of, 298, 396
  complexity of, 79
  computer use by (*see* Computers; *entries beginning with the term:* Computer)
  environments of, 78–80, 299–300
  Management Information Systems fitted into, 48–49
  (*See also* Management Information Systems; *entries beginning with the term:* MIS)
  MIS function of, 78–84
  outside, technology information from, 443
  plans of, 122
  (*See also* Planning)
  power structure of, 38–39
  (*See also* Power)
  requirements of, and motivational factors, 100–107
  reward systems of, 38
  robotics affecting, 312–315
  sizes of, 298
  structures of, 54–62, 297
  (*See also* power structure of, *above*)
  subsystems of, 144–152
  technology of, functions of, 78–80
  (*See also* Technology; Technology information)

Packet-switched communications, 241–242, 245, 246
Partacz, 421
PBX (private branch exchange), 270
PCM (pulse code modulation), 248
Performance criteria for computer operations, 459–460
Performance evaluation, computer (CPE), 414, 415
Perry, George M., 11
Personal computers (microcomputers), 21–23, 60, 208, 228–229
Personnel (*see* Employees)
PERT (program evaluation and review technique), 137–138, 140, 155, 156

Physical view of data, 207
Planned-change approach, 398–399
Planning:
  in distributed data processing, 282–283
  types of: capacity (*see* Computer capacity planning)
    financial, 231–232
    MIS (*see* MIS planning; *entries beginning with the term:* MIS planning)
    organizational, 122
    project, 124–127, 140, 153–158
PMF (problem management function), 470–474
Point-to-point lines, 258, 259
Policies versus goals, 463
Polling in line control, 260–261
Positive reinforcement, 90, 91, 101–103
Postal source data system (PSDS), 382–383
Power:
  in advanced office systems, 298–299
  in organizations, 38–39
  in systems implementation, 393–394
Powers, R., 58
Predictor variables, 423, 425, 429
Present value evaluation of information systems, 172, 173
PRIDE systems development methodology, 324, 350–351
Private branch exchange (PBX), 270
Problem identification in computer capacity planning, 416–417, 422–423, 426
Problem management in computer operations management, 457, 470–474
Problem management function (PMF), 470–474
Problem reports, 479
Procedures, operating, in computer operations management, 457, 462–470
Processing environment, 284–285
Production activities, 75–76, 82
Production processing, 465–467
Productivity, job (*see* Job productivity and satisfaction)
Program development (*see* Software development)
Program evaluation and review technique (PERT), 137–138, 140, 155, 156
Program librarians, 369
Program measurement in computer capacity planning, 418
Program stubs, 359
Programmed systems in systems hierarchy, 32
Programmers:
  backup, 369
  career paths of, 58
  chief, 369

Programmers (*Cont.*):
  in distributed data processing, 281–286
  in MIS structures, 56–58
  selecting, 64
  (*See also* Systems analysts)
Programming, types of, 355–360
Programming languages, 206, 207, 231–232,
  375–376
Programs, synthetic, 423, 425, 428
Project management techniques, 137–140,
  155–158
Project monitoring systems, 294, 295
Project planning, 124–127, 140, 153–158
Project proposals, 336
Project-related factors in systems implementation,
  394, 395
Project teams:
  chief-programmer, 369
  membership of, 157–158
  for MIS development, 42–44, 47, 58
  staffing, 62–63
Projections, linear, 423, 425, 429
Projects, commitment to, 394–395
Proposal validation, 453–455
Proposals:
  project, 336
  requests for (RFPs), 445–451
Protocols for networks, 265–266, 269
Prototyping, 345–351
PSDS (postal source data system), 382–383
Publications for technology information, 442–443
Pulse code modulation (PCM), 248
Punishment in reinforcement theory, 90, 91, 102,
  103
Pyhrr, Peter A., 136

Q-sort technique, 95–101, 110–115
QA (quality assurance) function, 470–478
Quality assurance in software development,
  370–372
Quality assurance (QA) function, 470–478
Quality circles, 371
Quality control in computer operations, 467
Quality information, 457
Query languages, 206, 207
Queuing theory, 423, 426, 429, 454
Quotations, requests for (RFQs), 445, 446

Rate of return (ROI), 135, 140, 173–174
RCA Corporation, 233–234
Redundancy of data, 192–193, 196–197,
  203–204
Regressions in forecasting, 423, 425, 429

Reinforcement schedules, 104–107
Reinforcement theory, 89–91, 101–103
Relational view of data, 207
Reporting relationships in MIS, 48–49, 54
Reports:
  in computer capacity planning, 421
  in computer operations management, 476,
  478–480
Requests for proposals (RFPs), 445–451
Requests for quotations (RFQs), 445, 446
Requirements analysis, 284
Resource allocation, 123–127, 140
Resource utilization, 418, 460
Resources, human (*see* Employees)
Return on investment (ROI), 135, 140, 173–174
Review in computer capacity planning, 416,
  420–423, 430–433
Reward systems, organizational, 38
RFPs (requests for proposals), 445–451
RFQs (requests for quotations), 445, 446
Ring structure of networks, 262
Risk analysis, 397
Robotics, 303–315
  in MIS management, 315
  technology of, 309–312
Robotics industry, trends in, 307–309
Robots:
  costs of, 304–305, 308
  defined, 304
  impact of, 312–315
  markets for, 307–309
  sight in, 310
  touch in, 310–311
  types of, 304–306
  versatility of, 308–309
Rockart, John F., 131–132, 344
ROI (rate of return; return on investment), 135,
  140, 173–174
Rosenzweig, James D., 80

Sabotage of computers, 33–34, 469
SADT (structured analysis and design
  techniques), 362–365
SAGE (semiautomatic ground environment)
  system, 239–240
Salaries for MIS positions, 64–65
Sampling-type monitors, 427
Sandez, Lou, 414
Schein, Edgar, 398, 399
Scott Morton, Michael S., 221
Scouting phase of systems implementation,
  401–403
Scripting technique, 464

SDD (structured decomposition diagram) technique, 365–367

SDLC (*see* Systems development life cycle)

SDM/70 systems development methodology, 324–325, 350–351

Security, computer, 469–470

Selection in line control, 261

Semiautomatic ground environment (SAGE) system, 239–240

Sequential-access technique, 199, 200

Service agreements, 458–459, 480

Service objectives (levels) in computer capacity planning, 419, 420

Severance, Dennis, 164

Shaping in reinforcement, 103

Sight in robots, 310

Simplex communications lines, 246

Simulation:

in proposal validation, 454

in work-load modeling, 423, 430

(*See also* Data projection and simulation systems)

Skinner, B. F., 89–91

Social change in systems implementation, 393–394

(*See also* Change; *entries beginning with the term:* Change)

Social impact of robots, 312–315

Sociotechnical-systems approach to change, 400

Soft-dollar evaluations, 446–447, 451–452

Software, data communications, 266–268

(*See also* Programs, synthetic; *entries beginning with the terms:* Hardware; Program; Programming)

Software acquisition (*see* Hardware and software acquisition)

Software design techniques, structured, 359–367

Software development, 355–378

managing, 355–370

problems in, 355–356

quality assurance in, 370–372

testing in, 372–374

types of, 358–360

by users, 375–378

(*See also entries beginning with the term:* Programming)

Software monitors, 423–425, 427–428

Software physics, 422–424, 427

Specifications:

design, 341–343

for proposal and quotation requests, 446, 447

Spectrum systems development methodology, 326–328, 350–351

Staffing of Management Information Systems, 41–47, 62–71

Stage hypothesis framework for computer use (Nolan), 26–31

Stamp, Sir Josiah Charles, 315

Standards:

for computers, 37–38

for database management systems, 208

expenditure, 165–166

for networks, 264

Star structure of networks, 261

Steering committees, 60–62, 281–286

Strategic MIS planning, 125–130, 139

Strategy set transformation, 128–130, 139

Structured analysis and design techniques (SADT), 362–365

Structured decomposition diagram (SDD) technique, 365–367

Structured English, 338–339

Structured programming, 356–360

Structured software design techniques, 359–367

Structured systems design techniques, 337–343

Structured walk-throughs in quality assurance, 371–372

Subsystem mapping, 147–150

Subsystems:

of decision support systems, 225

organizational, 144–152

Success factors, 92–93

critical (CSFs), 131–132, 140, 149, 150, 174–175

Switched communications, 240–242, 244–246

Switched lines, 258, 259

Synchronous modems, 254

Synchronous transmissions, 246

Synthetic programs, 423, 425, 428

Systems (*see specific entries, for example:* Decision support systems; Management Information Systems)

Systems administration in database environment, 208, 209

Systems analysis, 208–217, 328–336

Systems analysts:

career paths of, 58

in distributed data processing, 281–286

in MIS structures, 56–58

Systems availability, 457–461

Systems builders of Management Information Systems, 36–37

Systems design, 336–343, 395

Systems development, 284–285, 321–322, 343–351

Systems development life cycle (SDLC), 322–328, 349–351, 370, 372–374

Systems development methodologies, 323–328, 349–351, 370
Systems flowcharts, 333–335, 338
Systems hierarchy framework for computer use (Dickson), 26, 31–32
Systems implementation:
  defined, 380
  in distributed data processing, 285–286
  problems of, 380–408
    awareness of, 381–386
    diagnosis of, 386–397
    treatment for, 397–408
    success studies in, 406–408
Systems measurement in computer capacity planning, 417–418
Systems resources view of MIS effectiveness, 168
Systems tuning in computer operations, 466

Technical advisory groups (TAGs), 42–43, 62
Technical services activities, 75–76, 83–84
Technology:
  computer: acquisition of (see Hardware and software acquisition)
    rigidity of, 37–38
  of data communications systems, 242–269
  database, 198, 203–208
  for decision support systems, 226–230
  defined, 78
  of organizations, functions of, 78–80
  of robotics, 309–312
Technology information, 440–444
Telecommunications (see Data communications systems)
Telephone line communications channels, 247
Telephone wire, twisted-pair, 270
Terminals in data communications, 252–253
Testing:
  aptitude, 67
  in software development, 372–374
3M Company, 158
Throckmorton, James L., 11, 349
Top-down program development, 358–360
Touch in robots, 310–311
Training programs, 66–67
Transmission of data, 245–252
  services for, 241–243
Transportation, decision support systems in, 233
Twisted-pair telephone wire, 270

Understanding your system and application growth environment (USAGE) methodology, 422–424
Union reactions to robots, 313–314
Unstructured decisions, 223–224
USAGE (understanding your system and application growth environment) methodology, 422–424
User liaisons, 56
User service in Management Information Systems, 55–58
User service agreements, 458–459, 480
User-service-level reports, 480
Users:
  end-, 281–286
  software development by, 375–378

Validation:
  proposal, 453–455
  in software testing, 372–373
Value-added networks, 246
Vendors:
  computers pushed by, 38
  for technology information, 442
Vitalari, N., 58
Vroom, V., 91–92

Warnier/Orr (W/O) technique, 364–366
Wetherbe, J. C., 133, 136, 414
Whisler, Thomas L., 220–221
Winkler, Raymond S., 165
W/O (Warnier/Orr) technique, 364–366
Word processing, 278–279, 292
Work groups, structure of, 295–296
Work loads:
  in computer capacity planning, 416, 418–420, 423, 428–430
  in computer operations performance, 459–460
Work plans in computer capacity planning, 416, 417, 422–423
Work stations, 291

Zawacki, Robert A., 7, 9, 94–95
Zero-based budgeting (ZBB), 136–137, 140